Cloud Native Python

Build and deploy resilent applications on the cloud using microservices, AWS, Azure and more

Manish Sethi

Packt>

BIRMINGHAM - MUMBAI

Cloud Native Python

First published: July 2017

Production reference: 1190717

Published by Packt Publishing Ltd.
Livery Place
35 Livery Street
Birmingham
B3 2PB, UK.

ISBN 978-1-78712-931-3

www.packtpub.com

Credits

Author
Manish Sethi

Reviewers
Sanjeev Kumar Jaiswal
Mohit Sethi

Commissioning Editor
Aaron Lazar

Acquisition Editor
Alok Dhuri

Content Development Editor
Lawrence Veigas

Technical Editor
Supriya Thabe

Copy Editor
Sonia Mathur

Project Coordinator
Prajakta Naik

Proofreader
Safis Editing

Indexer
Rekha Nair

Graphics
Abhinash Sahu

Production Coordinator
Nilesh Mohite

Foreword

In 2000, during the peak of the dotcom boom, I developed web applications in C++ and Perl. One had to personally go to the ISP data center and install the machine along with a RAID setup. From 2003-2006, the world moved to shared hosting powered by virtual machines. Today, the world is a different place, one where cloud computing providers, such as AWS, Azure, Google Cloud, and programming languages such as Python, Ruby, and Scala make it child's play to launch and scale websites.

While cloud computing makes it easy to get started, its offerings are ever expanding with new tools, deployment methodologies, and changing workflows. Take, for instance, what compute offerings should a developer build on? Software as a Service, or Platform as a Service, or Infrastructure as a Service Platform? Should the developer choose Docker, or a normal virtual machine setup for deployment? Should the entire software architecture follow an MVC or a microservices model?

Manish has a done a good job in the book, equipping a Python developer with skills to thrive in a cloud computing world. The book starts off with laying the foundation of what cloud computing is all about and its offerings. It's beneficial that most chapters in the book are self-contained, allowing the reader to pick up and learn/refresh their knowledge of what's needed for the current sprint/task. The workings of technologies such as CI and Docker are precisely explained in clear prose that does away with the underlying complexity. The Agile model of software development keeps us developers on toes, requiring developers to learn new tools in days and not weeks. The book's hands-on approach to teaching with screenshots on installation, configuration, and compact code snippets equips developers with the knowledge they need, thus making them productive.

A preference for full-stack developers, the implicit requirement of knowing cloud computing 101, and CIOs wanting to achieve a lot more with small teams are the norms today. *Cloud Native Python* is the book a freshman, beginner, or intermediate Python developer should read to get themselves up to speed on the tools and technology that power today's software development.

The complexity of cloud computing is in the details, be it the deployment workflow, managing infrastructure, security, or the tooling ecosystem. These choices have lasting implications for the software that's being built and the team developing and maintaining it.

Ankur Gupta
Founder of NumerateLabs LLP
Curator of newsletters: ImportPython & DjangoWeekly

About the Author

Manish Sethi works as an engineer in Bangalore, India. Over the course of his career, he has worked for startups and Fortune 10 companies, helping organizations adopt a cloud native approach to architecting massively scalable products.

He regularly spends time learning and implementing new technology paradigms and actively finds himself solving practical problems using serverless architecture, machine and deep learning, and so on. He contributes to Bangalore DevOps and the Docker community by writing blog posts, giving talks in meetups, and so on.

I would like to thank my brother, Mohit Sethi, and my mother, Neelam Sethi, who have been very supportive and encouraged me throughout my career and when writing this book.

About the Reviewers

Sanjeev Kumar Jaiswal is a computer graduate with 8 years of industrial experience. He uses Perl, Python, and GNU/Linux for his day-to-day activities. He is currently working on projects involving Penetration testing, Source Code Review, Security Design and implementations, and Web and Cloud Security projects.

Currently, Sanjeev is learning NodeJS and React Native as well. He loves teaching engineering students and IT professionals, and he has been teaching for the last 8 years in his leisure time.

He founded Alien Coders (`http://www.aliencoders.org`) based on the learning through sharing principle, for computer science students and IT professionals in 2010, which became a huge hit in India among engineering students. You can follow him on Facebook at `http://www.facebook.com/aliencoders`, on Twitter at `@aliencoders`, and on GitHub at `https://github.com/jassics`.

He has authored *Instant PageSpeed Optimization*, and co-authored *Learning Django Web Development*, both by Packt. He has reviewed more than seven books for Packt and looks forward to authoring or reviewing more books for Packt and other publishers.

Mohit Sethi is a solutions architect with 10+ years of experience in building and managing products across the IaaS, PaaS, and SaaS space in the areas of cloud, storage, distributed systems, data analytics, and machine learning. Previously, he worked for a Silicon Valley startup, a Fortune 10 company, and a National Defense Organization. He has been an open source contributor for 12+ years and has been running the DevOps meetup group in Bangalore for more than 3 years.

You can contact him on Twitter at `https://twitter.com/mohitsethi`, LinkedIn (`https://in.linkedin.com/in/mohitsethi7`), and GitHub (`https://github.com/mohitsethi`).

Customer Feedback

Thanks for purchasing this Packt book. At Packt, quality is at the heart of our editorial process. To help us improve, please leave us an honest review on this book's Amazon page at `https://www.amazon.com/dp/1787129314`.

If you'd like to join our team of regular reviewers, you can e-mail us at `customerreviews@packtpub.com`. We award our regular reviewers with free eBooks and videos in exchange for their valuable feedback. Help us be relentless in improving our products!

Table of Contents

Preface

Businesses today are evolving so rapidly that having their own infrastructure to support their expansion is not feasible. As a result, they have been resorting to the elasticity of the cloud to provide a platform to build and deploy their highly scalable applications.

This book will be the one stop for you to learn all about building cloud-native architectures in Python. It will begin by introducing you to cloud-native architecture and will help break it down for you. Then you'll learn how to build microservices in Python using REST API's in an event-driven approach and you will build the web layer. Next, you'll learn about interacting with data services and building web views with React, after which we will take a detailed look at application security and performance. Then, you'll also learn how to Dockerize your services. And finally, you'll learn how to deploy the application on the AWS and Azure platforms. We will end the book by discussing some concepts and techniques around troubleshooting problems that might occur with your applications after you've deployed them.

This book will teach you how to craft applications that are built as small standard units, using all the proven best practices and avoiding the usual traps. It's a practical book; we're going to build everything using Python 3 and its amazing tooling ecosystem. The book will take you on a journey, the destination of which is the creation of a complete Python application based on microservices over the cloud platform.

What this book covers

`Chapter 1`, *Introducing Cloud Native Architecture and Microservices*, discusses basic cloud native architecture and gets you ready to build applications.

`Chapter 2`, *Building Microservices in Python*, gives you complete knowledge of building microservices and extending them as per your use cases.

`Chapter 3`, *Building a Web Application in Python*, builds an initial web application with integration with microservices.

`Chapter 4`, *Interacting Data Services*, gives you hands-on knowledge of how to migrate your application to different database services.

`Chapter 5`, *Building WebViews with React*, discusses how to build a user interface using React.

`Chapter 6`, *Creating UIs to Scale with Flux*, gives you an understanding about Flux for scaling applications.

`Chapter 7`, *Learning Event Sourcing and CQRS*, discusses how to store transactions in the form of events to improve application performance.

`Chapter 8`, *Securing the Web Application*, helps you secure your application from outside threats.

`Chapter 9`, *Continuous Delivery*, gives you knowledge towards frequently application release.

`Chapter 10`, *Dockerizing Your Services*, talks about container services and running applications in Docker.

`Chapter 11`, *Deploying on the AWS Platform*, teaches you how to build an infrastructure and set up a production environment for your application on AWS.

`Chapter 12`, *Implementing on the Azure Platform*, discusses how to build infrastructures and set up a production environment for your application on Azure.

`Chapter 13`, *Monitoring the Cloud Application*, makes you aware of the different infrastructure and application monitoring tools.

What you need for this book

You will need to have Python installed on your system. A text editor, preferably Vim/Sublime/Notepad++, would be great. For one of the chapters, you may be required to download POSTMAN, which is a powerful API testing suite available as a Chrome extension. You can download this at `https://chrome.google.com/webstore/detail/postman/fhbjgbiflinjbdggehcddcbncdddomop?hl=en`.

Other than these, it would be great if you have an account on the following web applications:

- Jenkins
- Docker
- Amazon Web Services
- Terraform

In case you do not have an account, this book will guide you, or at least direct you with regards to creating an account on the previously mentioned web applications.

Who this book is for

This book is for developers with a basic knowledge of Python, the command line, and HTTP-based application principles. It is ideal for those who want to learn to build, test, and scale their Python-based applications. No prior experience of writing microservices in Python is required.

Conventions

In this book, you will find a number of text styles that distinguish between different kinds of information. Here are some examples of these styles and an explanation of their meaning.

Code words in text, database table names, folder names, filenames, file extensions, pathnames, dummy URLs, user input, and Twitter handles are shown as follows: "Create a `signup` route, which will take the `GET` and `POST` methods to read the page, and submit the data to the backend database."

A block of code is set as follows:

```
sendTweet(event){
  event.preventDefault();
  this.props.sendTweet(this.refs.tweetTextArea.value);
  this.refs.tweetTextArea.value = '';
}
```

Any command-line input or output is written as follows:

```
$ apt-get install nodejs
```

New terms and **important words** are shown in bold. Words that you see on the screen, for example, in menus or dialog boxes, appear in the text like this: "Click on the **Create user** button, the user will be created, and the policy will be attached to it."

Warnings or important notes appear like this.

Tips and tricks appear like this.

Reader feedback

Feedback from our readers is always welcome. Let us know what you think about this book-what you liked or disliked. Reader feedback is important for us as it helps us develop titles that you will really get the most out of.
To send us general feedback, simply e-mail `feedback@packtpub.com`, and mention the book's title in the subject of your message.
If there is a topic that you have expertise in and you are interested in either writing or contributing to a book, see our author guide at `www.packtpub.com/authors`.

Customer support

Now that you are the proud owner of a Packt book, we have a number of things to help you to get the most from your purchase.

Downloading the example code

You can download the example code files for this book from your account at `http://www.packtpub.com`. If you purchased this book elsewhere, you can visit `http://www.packtpub.com/support`and register to have the files e-mailed directly to you.

You can download the code files by following these steps:

1. Log in or register to our website using your e-mail address and password.
2. Hover the mouse pointer on the **SUPPORT** tab at the top.
3. Click on **Code Downloads & Errata**.
4. Enter the name of the book in the **Search** box.
5. Select the book for which you're looking to download the code files.
6. Choose from the drop-down menu where you purchased this book from.
7. Click on **Code Download**.

Once the file is downloaded, please make sure that you unzip or extract the folder using the latest version of:

- WinRAR / 7-Zip for Windows
- Zipeg / iZip / UnRarX for Mac
- 7-Zip / PeaZip for Linux

The code bundle for the book is also hosted on GitHub at https://github.com/PacktPublishing/Cloud-Native-Python. We also have other code bundles from our rich catalog of books and videos available at https://github.com/PacktPublishing/. Check them out!

Errata

Although we have taken every care to ensure the accuracy of our content, mistakes do happen. If you find a mistake in one of our books-maybe a mistake in the text or the code-we would be grateful if you could report this to us. By doing so, you can save other readers from frustration and help us improve subsequent versions of this book. If you find any errata, please report them by visiting http://www.packtpub.com/submit-errata, selecting your book, clicking on the **Errata Submission Form** link, and entering the details of your errata. Once your errata are verified, your submission will be accepted and the errata will be uploaded to our website or added to any list of existing errata under the Errata section of that title.

To view the previously submitted errata, go to https://www.packtpub.com/books/content/support and enter the name of the book in the search field. The required information will appear under the **Errata** section.

Piracy

Piracy of copyrighted material on the Internet is an ongoing problem across all media. At Packt, we take the protection of our copyright and licenses very seriously. If you come across any illegal copies of our works in any form on the Internet, please provide us with the location address or website name immediately so that we can pursue a remedy.

Please contact us at copyright@packtpub.com with a link to the suspected pirated material.

We appreciate your help in protecting our authors and our ability to bring you valuable content.

Questions

If you have a problem with any aspect of this book, you can contact us at questions@packtpub.com, and we will do our best to address the problem.

1

Introducing Cloud Native Architecture and Microservices

Here we go! Before we begin to build our application, we need to find answers to some of the following queries:

- What is cloud computing? What are its different types?
- What is microservices and its concept?
- What are the basic requirements for good to go?

In this chapter, we will focus on the different concepts that a developer or application programmer should understand before they start writing an application.

Let's first understand a bit about system building and how it evolves.

For a long time now, we have been discovering better approaches to constructing frameworks. With advances in new technologies and adoption of better approaches, the IT framework becomes more reliable and effective for clients (or customers), and makes engineers happy.

Continuous delivery helps us move our software development cycle into production, and lets us identify different error-prone perspectives of software, insisting on us the idea of considering every check-in to code as a suitable candidate to release it to production.

Our comprehension of how the web functions has driven us to grow better methods for having machines converse with other machines. The virtualization platform has permitted us to make arrangements and resize our machines freely, with foundation computerization giving us an approach to deal with these machines at scale. Some huge, effective cloud platforms, such as Amazon, Azure, and Google have embraced the perspective of little groups owning the full life cycle of their services. Concepts such as **Domain-Driven Design** (**DDD**), **continuous delivery** (**CD**), on-request virtualization, infrastructure robotization, small self-governing groups, and systems at scale are different traits, which effectively, and efficiently, get our software into production. And now, microservices has risen up out of this world. It wasn't developed or portrayed before the reality; it rose as a pattern, or, for example, from true utilization. All through this book, I will haul strands out of this earlier work to help illustrate how to fabricate, oversee, and advance microservices.

Numerous associations have found that by grasping fine-grained microservice structures, they can convey programming speedily, and grasp more up-to-date advancements. Microservices gives us, fundamentally, more flexibility to respond and settle on various choices, permitting us to react quickly to the unavoidable changes that affect every one of us.

Introduction to cloud computing

Before we begin with microservices and cloud native concepts, let's first understand what cloud computing is all about.

Cloud computing is a wide term that portrays a wide scope of administrations. Similarly, as with other huge advancements in innovation, numerous merchants have grabbed the expression *cloud* and are utilizing it for items that sit outside of the basic definition. Since the cloud is an expansive accumulation of administrations, associations can pick where, when, and how they utilize cloud computing.

The cloud computing services can be categorized as follows:

- **SaaS**: These are baked applications that are ready to be grasped by end users
- **PaaS**: These are a collection of tools and services that are useful for users/developers who want to either build their application or quickly host them directly to production without caring about the underlying hardware
- **IaaS**: This is for customers who want to build their own business model and customize it

Cloud computing, as a stack, can be explained as follows:

- Cloud computing is often referred to as stack, which is basically a wide range of services in which each service is built on top of another under a common term, such as **cloud**
- The cloud computing model is considered as a collection of different configurable computing resources (such as servers, databases, and storage), which communicate with each other, and can be provisioned with minimal supervision

The following diagram showcases the cloud computing stack components:

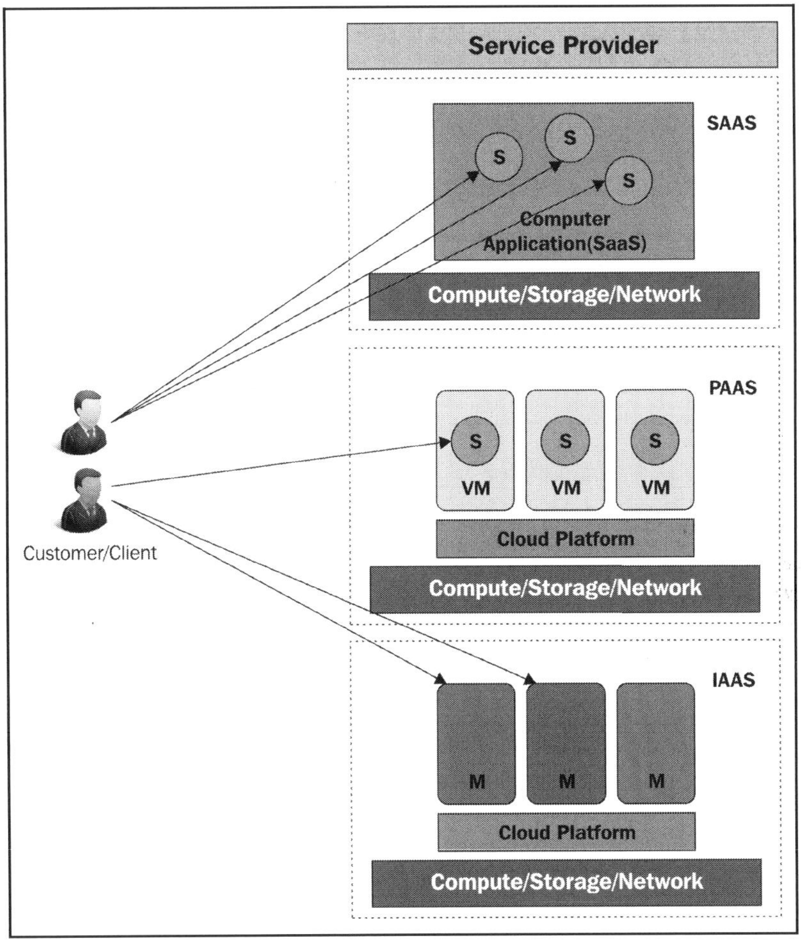

Let's understand cloud computing components in detail, along with their use cases.

Software as a Service

The following are the key points that describe SaaS:

- **Software as a Service** (**SaaS**) offers users the ability to access software hosted on service provider premises, which is provided as a service over the internet through a web browser by a provider. These services are based on subscriptions, and are also referred to as on-demand software.
- SaaS-offering companies include the Google Docs productivity suite, Oracle **CRM** (**Customer Relationships Management**), Microsoft and their Office 365 offering, and Salesforce CRM and QuickBooks.
- SaaS can be further categorized as a vertical SaaS that focuses on the needs of specific industries, such as healthcare and agriculture, or a horizontal SaaS that focuses on the software industry, such as human resources and sales.
- SaaS offerings are, basically, for organizations that quickly want to grasp existing applications that are easy to use and understand, even for a non-technical person. Based on the organization's usage and budget, enterprises to select support plans. Additionally, you can access these SaaS applications from anywhere around the globe, and from any device with the internet enabled.

Platform as a Service

The following are the key points that describe PaaS:

- In PaaS offerings, the organization/enterprise need not worry about hardware and software infrastructure management for their in-house applications
- The biggest benefits of PaaS are for the development teams (local or remote), which can efficiently build, test, and deploy their applications on a common framework, wherein, the underlying hardware and software is managed by the PaaS service provider
- The PaaS service provider delivers the platform, and also provides different services around the platform
- The examples of PaaS providers include Amazon Web Services (AWS Elastic Beanstalk), Microsoft Azure (Azure Websites), Google App Engine, and Oracle (Big Data Cloud Service)

Infrastructure as a Service

The following are the key points that describe IaaS:

- Unlike SaaS offerings, in IaaS, the customer is provided with IT resources, such as bare metal machines to run applications, hard disk for storage, and network cable for network capability, which they can customize based on their business model.
- In IaaS offerings, since the customer has full access to their infrastructure, they can scale their IT resources based on their application requirement. Also, in IaaS offerings, the customer has to manage the security of the application/resources, and needs to build disaster recovery models in case of sudden failures/crashes.
- In IaaS, services are on an on-demand basis, where the customer is charged on usage. So, it's the customer's responsibility to do cost analysis against their resources, which will help restrict them from exceeding their budget.
- It allows customers/consumers to customize their infrastructure based on the requirements of the application, then tear down the infrastructure and recreate it again very quickly and efficiently.
- The pricing model for IaaS-based services is basically on-demand, which means you pay as you go. You are charged as per your usage of resources and the duration of the usage.
- Amazon Web Services (offering **Amazon Elastic Compute Cloud** (**Amazon EC2**) and **Amazon Simple Storage Service** (**Amazon S3**)) was the first out of the gate in this cloud offering; however, players such as Microsoft Azure (virtual machine), Rackspace (virtual cloud servers) and Oracle (bare metal cloud services) have also made a name for themselves.

The cloud native concepts

Cloud native is structuring teams, culture, and technology to utilize automation and architectures to manage complexity and unlock velocity.

The cloud native concept goes beyond the technologies with which it is associated. We need to understand how companies, teams, and people are successful in order to understand where our industry is going.

Currently, companies such as Facebook and Netflix have dedicated a large amount of resources working towards cloud native techniques. Even now, small and more flexible companies have realized the value of these techniques.
With feedback from the proven practices of cloud native, the following are some of the advantages that come to light:

- **Result-oriented and team satisfaction**: The cloud native approach shows the way to break a large problem into smaller ones, which allows each team to focus on the individual part.
- **Grunt work**: Automation reduces the repetitive manual tasks that cause operations pain, and reduces the downtime. This makes your system more productive, and it gives more efficient outcomes.
- **Reliable and efficient application infrastructure**: Automation brings more control over deployment in different environments--whether it is development, stage, or production--and also handles unexpected events or failures. Building automation not only helps normal deployment, but it also makes deployment easy when it comes to a disaster recovery situation.
- **Insights over application**: The tools built around cloud native applications provide more insights into applications, which make them easy to debug, troubleshoot, and audit.
- **Efficient and reliable security**: In every application, the main concern is toward its security, and making sure that it is accessible via required channels with authentication. The cloud native approach provides different ways for the developer to ensure the security of the application.
- **Cost-effective system**: The cloud approach to managing and deploying your application enables efficient usage of resources, which also includes application release and, hence, makes the system cost effective by reducing the wastage of resources.

Cloud native - what it means and why it matters?

Cloud native is a broad term which makes use of different techniques, such as infrastructure automation, developing middleware, and backing services, which are basically a part of your application delivery cycle. The cloud native approach includes frequent software releases that are bug-free and stable, and can scale the application as per the business requirement.

Using the cloud native approach, you will be able to achieve your goal toward application building in a systematic manner.

The cloud native approach is much better than the legacy virtualization-oriented orchestration, which needs a lot of effort to build an environment suitable for development, and then, a far more different one for the software delivery process. An ideal cloud native architecture should have automation and composition functionalities, which work on your behalf. These automation techniques should also be able to manage and deploy your application across different platforms and provide you with results.

There are a couple of other operation factors that your cloud native architecture should be able to identify, such as steady logging, monitoring application and infrastructure in order to make sure the application is up and running.

The cloud native approach really helps developers build their application across different platforms using tools such as Docker, which is lightweight and easy to create and destroy.

The cloud native runtimes

Containers are the best solutions for how to get software to run reliably when moved from one computing environment to another. This could be from one developer machine to the stage environment into production, and perhaps from a physical machine to a virtual machine in a private or public cloud. **Kubernetes** has become synonymous with container services, and is getting popular nowadays.

With the rise of cloud native frameworks and an increase in the applications built around it, the attributes of container orchestration have received more attention and usage. Here is what you need from a container runtime:

- **Managing container state and high availability**: Be sure to maintain the state (such as create and destroy) of containers, specifically in production, as they are very important from a business perspective, and should be able to scale as well, based on business needs
- **Cost analysis and realization**: Containers give you control over resource management as per your business budget, and can reduce costs to a large extent
- **Isolated environment**: Each process that runs within a container should remain isolated within that container
- **Load balancing across clusters**: Application traffic, which is basically handled by a cluster of containers, should be redirected equally within the containers, which will increase the applications response and maintain high availability
- **Debugging and disaster recovery**: Since we are dealing with the production system here, we need to make sure we have the right tools to monitor the health of the application, and to take the necessary action to avoid downtime and provide high availability

Cloud native architecture

The cloud native architecture is similar to any application architecture that we create for a legacy system, but in the cloud native application architecture, we should consider a few characteristics, such as a twelve-factor application (collection of patterns for app development), microservices (decomposition of a monolithic business system into independent deployable services), self-service agile infrastructure (self-service platform), API-based collaboration (interaction between services via API), and antifragility (self-realizing and strengthening the application).

First, let's discuss w*hat is microservices all about?*

Microservices is a broader term that breaks large applications into smaller modules to get them developed and make them mature enough for release. This approach not only helps to manage each module efficiently, but it also identifies the issue at the lower level itself. The following are some of the key aspects of microservices:

- **User-friendly interfaces**: Microservices enable a clear separation between microservices. Versioning of microservices enables more control over APIs, and it also provides more freedom for both the consumers and producers of these services.
- **Deployment and management of APIs across the platform**: Since each microservice is a separate entity, it is possible to update a single microservice without making changes to the others. Also, it is easier to roll back changes for a microservice. This means the artifacts that are deployed for microservices should be compatible in terms of API and data schemas. These APIs must be tested across different platforms, and the test results should be shared across different teams, that is, operation, developers, and so on, to maintain a centralized control system.
- **Flexibility in application**: Microservices that are developed should be capable of handling the request and must respond back, irrespective of the kind of request, which could be a bad input or an invalid request. Also, your microservice should be able to deal with an unexpected load request and respond appropriately. All of these microservices should be tested independently, as well as with integration.
- **Distribution of microservices**: It's better to split the services into small chunks of services so that they can be tracked and developed individually and combined to form a microservice. This technique makes microservices development more efficient and stable in manner.

The following diagram shows a cloud native application's high-level architecture:

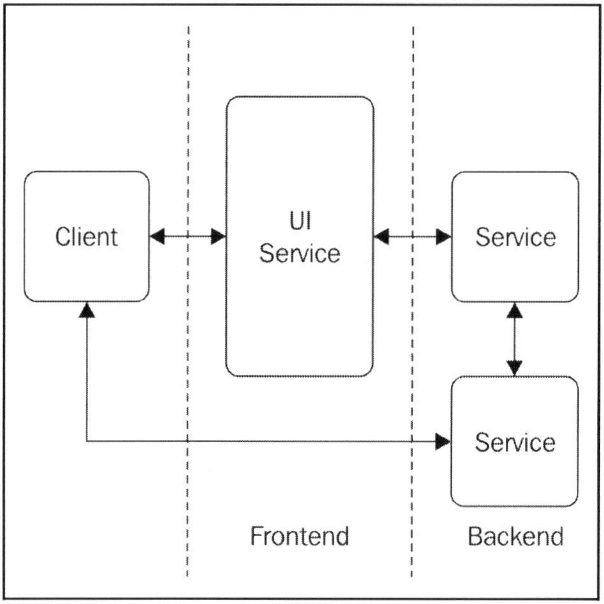

The application architecture should ideally start with two or three service, try to expand it with further versions. It is very important to understand application architecture, as it may need to integrate with different components of the system, and it is possible that a separate team manages those components when it comes to large organizations. Versioning in microservices is vital, as it identifies the supported method during the specified phase of development.

Are microservices a new concept?

Microservices has been in the industry for a very long time now. It is another way of creating a distinction between the different components of a large system. Microservices work in a similar fashion, where they act as a link between the different services, and handle the flow of data for a particular transaction based on the type of requests.

The following diagram depicts the architecture of microservices:

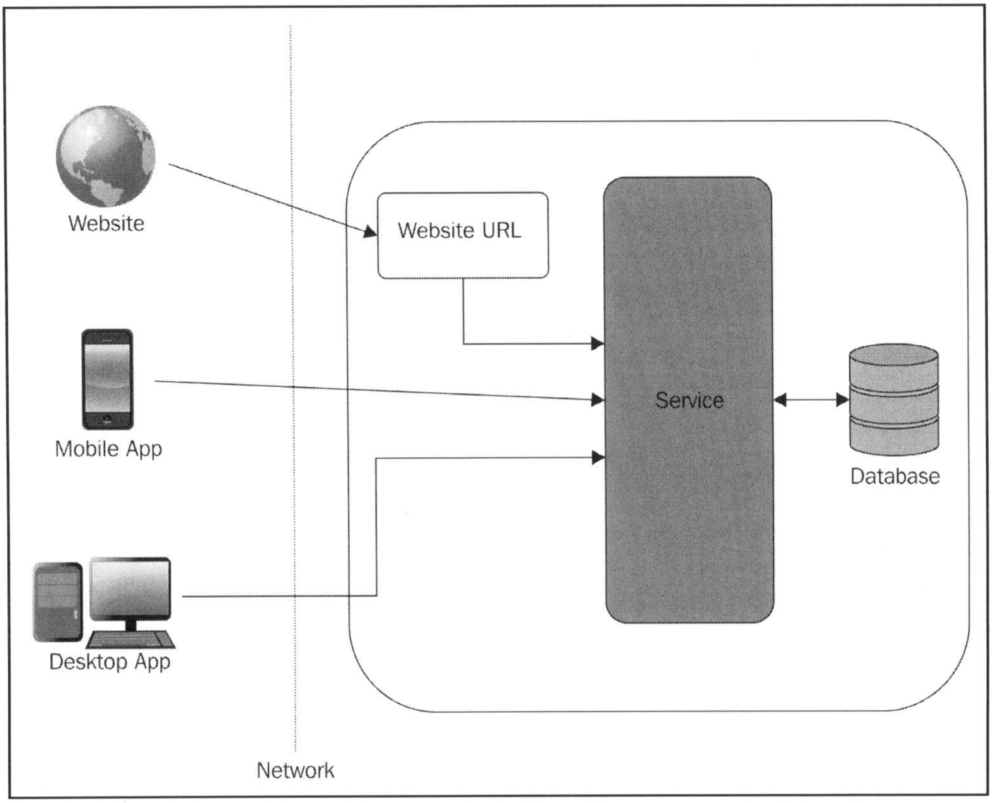

Why is Python the best choice for cloud native microservices development?

Why do I choose Python, and recommend it to as many people as possible? Well, it comes down to the reasons explained in the upcoming subsections.

Readability

Python is highly expressive and an easy-to-learn programming language. Even an amateur can easily discover the different functionalities and scope of Python. Unlike other programming languages, such as Java, which focus more on parenthesis, brackets, commas, and colons, Python let's you spend more time on programming and less time on debugging the syntax.

Libraries and community

Python's broad range of libraries is very portable over different platforms, such as Unix, Windows, or OS X. These libraries can be easily extended based on your application/program requirement. There is a huge community that works on building these libraries and this makes it the best fit for business use cases.

As far as the Python community is concerned, the **Python User Group** (**PUG**) is a community that works on the community-based development model to increase the popularity of Python around the globe. These group members give talks on Python-based frameworks, which help us build large systems.

Interactive mode

The Python interactive mode helps you debug and test a snippet of code, which can later be added as a part of the main program.

Scalable

Python provides better structure and concept, such as modules, to maintain large programs in a more systematic manner than any other scripting language, such as shell scripting.

Understanding the twelve-factor app

Cloud native applications fit in with an agreement intended to augment versatility through predictable practices. This application maintains a manifesto of sorts called the **twelve-factor** app. It outlines a methodology for developers to follow when building modern web-based applications. Developers must change how they code, creating a new contract between the developers and the infrastructure that their applications run on.

The following are a few points to consider when developing a cloud native application:

- Use an informative design to increase application usage with minimal time and cost to customers using automation
- Use application portability across different environments (such as stage and production) and different platforms (such as Unix or Windows)
- Use application suitability over cloud platforms and understand the resource allocation and management
- Use identical environments to reduce bugs with continuous delivery/deployment for maximum agility of software release
- Enable high availability by scaling the application with minimal supervision and designing disaster-recovery architectures

Many of the twelve-factors interact with each other. They focus on speed, safety, and scale by emphasizing on declarative configuration. A twelve-factor app can be described as follows:

- **Centralized code base**: Every code that is deployed is tracked in revision control, and should have multiple instances deployed on multiple platforms.
- **Dependencies management**: An app should be able to declare the dependencies, and isolate them using tools such as Bundler, pip, and Maven.
- **Defining configuration**: Configurations (that is, environment variables) that are likely to be different in different deployment environments (such as development, stage, and production) should be defined at the operating-system level.
- **Backing services**: Every resource is treated as a part of the application itself. Backing services such as databases and message queues should be considered as an attached resource, and consumed equally in all environments.
- **Isolation in build, release, and run cycle**: This involves strict separation between build artifacts, then combining with configuration, and then starting one or more instances from the artifact and configuration combination.

- **Stateless processes**: The app should execute one or more instances/processes (for example, master/workers) that share nothing.
- **Services port binding**: The application should be self-contained, and if any/all services need to be exposed, then it should be done via port binding (preferably HTTP).
- **Scaling stateless processes**: The architecture should emphasize stateless process management in the underlying platform instead of implementing more complexity to the application.
- **Process state management**: Processes should scale up very quickly and shut down gracefully within a small time period. These aspects enable rapid scalability, deployment of changes, and disaster recovery.
- **Continuous delivery/deployment to production**: Always try to keep your different environments similar, whether it is development, stage, or production. This will ensure that you get similar results across multiple environments, and enable continuous delivery from development to production.
- **Logs as event streams**: Logging is very important, whether it is platform level or application level, as this helps understand the activity of the application. Enable different deployable environments (preferably production) to collect, aggregate, index, and analyze the events via centralized services.
- **Ad hoc tasks as on-off processes**: In the cloud native approach, management tasks (for example, database migration) that run as a part of a release should be run as one-off processes into the environment as opposed to the regular app with long-running processes.

Cloud application platforms such as Cloud Foundry, Heroku, and Amazon Beanstalk are optimized for deploying twelve-factor apps.

Considering all these standards and integrating applications with steady engineering interfaces, that is, handling stateless outline design, makes disseminated applications that are cloud prepared. Python revolutionized application systems with its obstinate, tradition-over-setup way to deal with web improvements.

Setting up the Python environment

As we will demonstrate throughout this book, having the right environment (local or for your automated builds) is crucial to the success of any development project. If a workstation has the right tools, and is set up properly, developing on that workstation can feel like a breath of fresh air. Conversely, a poorly set up environment can suffocate any developer trying to use it.

The following are the prerequisite accounts that we require in the later part of the book:

- A GitHub account needs to be created for source code management. Use the article on the following link to do so:

  `https://medium.com/appliedcode/setup-github-account-9a5ec918bcc1`

- AWS and Azure accounts are required for application deployment. Use the articles given on the following links to create these:
  - AWS: `https://medium.com/appliedcode/setup-aws-account-1727ce89353e`
  - Azure: `https://medium.com/appliedcode/setup-microsoft-azure-account-cbd635ebf14b`

Now, let's set up some of the tools that we will need during our development project.

Installing Git

Git (`https://git-scm.com`) is a free and open source distributed, version control system designed to handle everything, ranging from small to very large projects, with speed and efficiency.

Installing Git on Debian-based distribution Linux (such as Ubuntu)

There are a couple of ways by which you can install Git on a Debian system:

1. Using the **Advanced Package Tool** (**APT**) package management tools:

   You can use the APT package management tools to update your local package index. Then, you can download and install the latest Git using the following commands as the root user:

   ```
   $ apt-get update -y
   $ apt-get install git -y
   ```

   The preceding commands will download and install Git on your system.

2. Using the source code, you can do the following:
   1. Download the source from the GitHub repository, and compile the software from the source.

      Before you begin, let's first install the dependencies of Git; execute the following commands as the root user to do so:

      ```
      $ apt-get update -y
      $ apt-get install build-essential libssl-dev
      libcurl4-gnutls-dev libexpat1-dev gettext unzip -y
      ```

      2. After we have installed the necessary dependencies, let's go to the Git project repository (`https://github.com/git/git`) to download the source code, as follows:

      ```
      $ wget https://github.com/git/git/archive/v1.9.1.zip -
      Ogit.zip
      ```

      3. Now, unzip the downloaded ZIP file using the following commands:

      ```
      $ unzip git.zip
      $ cd git-*
      ```

      4. Now you have to make the package and install it as a sudo user. For this, use the commands given next:

      ```
      $ make prefix=/usr/local all
      $ make prefix=/usr/local install
      ```

The preceding commands will install Git on your system at `/usr/local`.

Seting up Git on a Debian-based distribution

Now that we have installed Git on our system, we need to set some configuration so that the commit messages that will be generated for you contain your correct information.

Basically, we need to provide the name and email in the config. Let's add these values using the following commands:

```
$ git config --global user.name "Manish Sethi"
$ git config --global user.email manish@sethis.in
```

Installing Git on Windows

Let's install Git on Windows; you can download the latest version of Git from the official website (`https://git-scm.com/download/win`). Follow the steps listed next to install Git on a Windows system:

1. Once the `.exe` file is downloaded, double-click on it to run it. First of all, you will be provided with a GNU license, as seen in this screenshot:

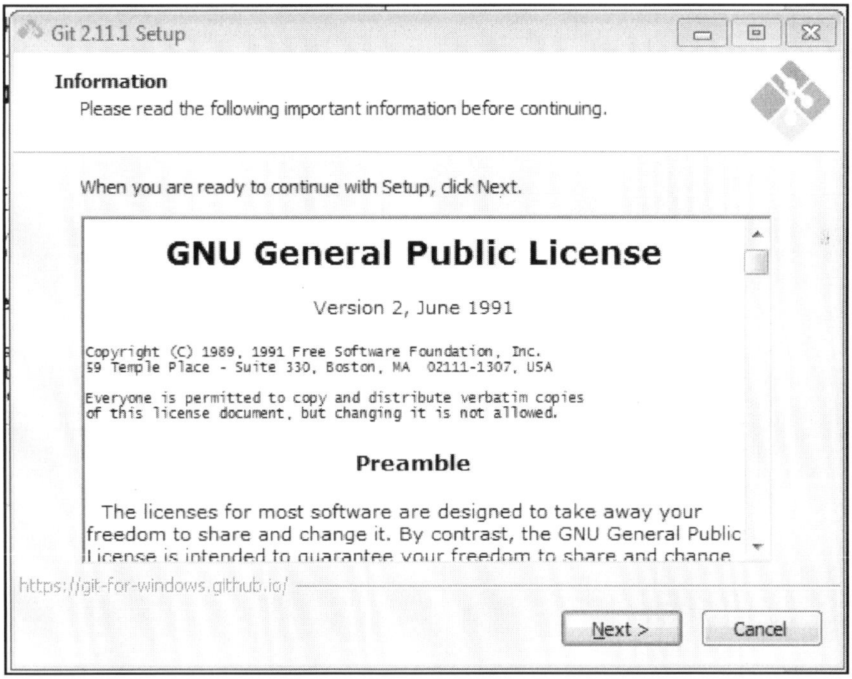

Click on **Next**:

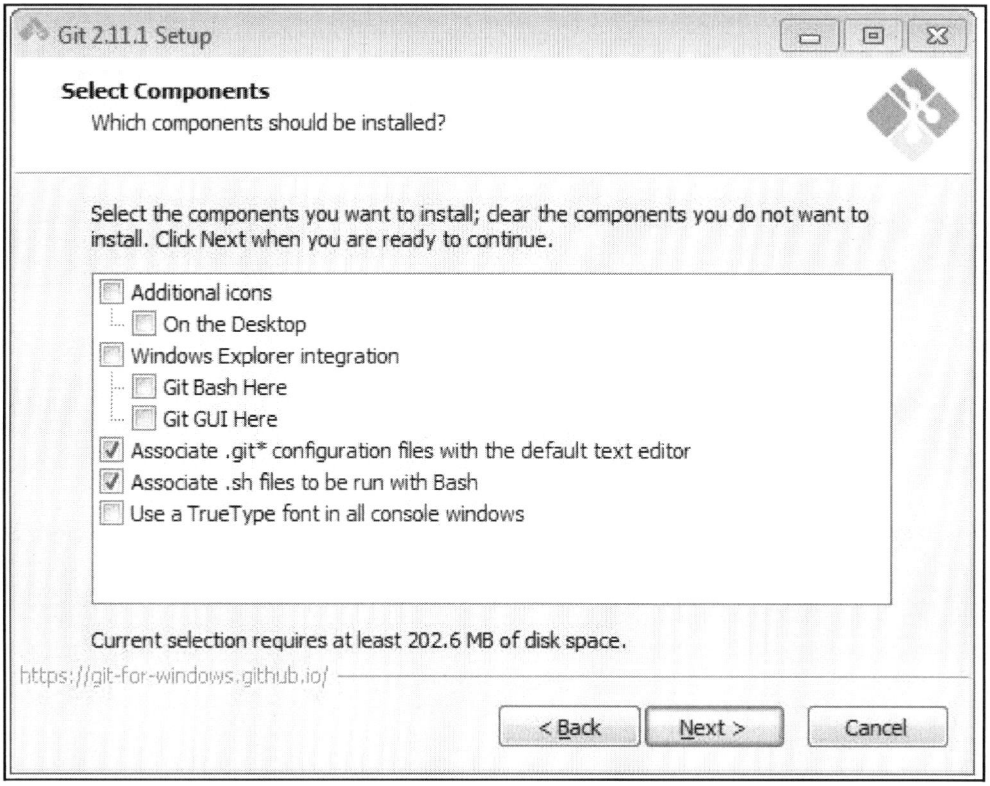

In the section shown in the preceding screenshot, you will customize your setup based on tools that are needed, or you can keep it default, which is okay from the book's perspective.

2. Additionally, you can install Git Bash along with Git; click on **Next**:

3. In the section seen in the next screenshot, you can enable other features that come along with Git packages. Then, click on **Next**:

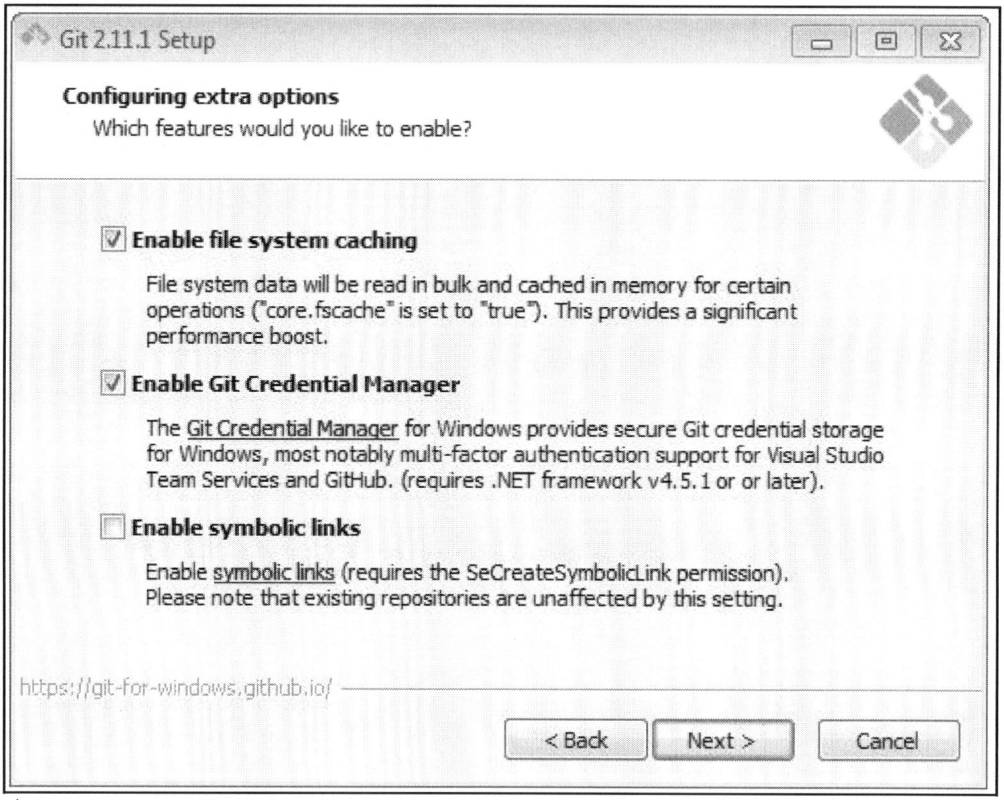

4. You can skip the rest of the steps by clicking on **Next**, and go for the installation part.

Once you complete the installation, you will be able to see a screen like this:

Great!! We have successfully installed Git on Windows!!

Using Chocolatey

This is my preferred way to install Git for Windows on Windows 10. It installs the same package as before, but in one line. If you have not heard of Chocolatey, stop everything, and go learn a bit more. It can install the software with a single command; you don't have to use click-through installers anymore!

Chocolatey is very powerful, and I use it in combination with **Boxstarter** to set up my dev machines. If you are in charge of setting up machines for developers on Windows, it is definitely worth a look.

Let's see how you would install Git using Chocolatey. I assume you have Chocolatey installed (`https://chocolatey.org/install`) already (it's a one-liner in Command Prompt). Then, simply open the `Administrator Command` window, and type this command:

```
$ choco install git -params '"/GitAndUnixToolsOnPath"'
```

This will install Git and the `BASH` tools, and add them to your path.

Installing Git on Mac

Before we begin with the Git installation, we need to install command-line tools for OS X.

Installing the command-line tools for OS X

In order to install any developer, you will need to install Xcode (`https://developer.apple.com/xcode/`), which is a nearly 4 GB developer suite. Apple offers this for free from the Mac App Store. In order to install Git and the GitHub setup, you will need certain command-line tools, which are part of the Xcode development tools.

If you have enough space, download and install Xcode, which is basically a complete package of development tools.

You will need to create an Apple developer account at `developer.apple.com` in order to download command-line tools. Once you have set up your account, you can select the command-line tools or Xcode based on the version, as follows:

- If you are on OS X 10.7.x, download the 10.7 command-line tools. If you are on OS X 10.8.x, download the 10.8 command-line tools.
- Once it is downloaded, open the `DMG` file, and follow the instructions to install it.

Installing Git for OS X

Installing Git on Mac is pretty much similar to how you install it on Windows. Instead of using the `.exe` file, we have the `dmg` file, which you can download from the Git website (`https://git-scm.com/download/mac`) for installation as follows:

1. Double-click on the `dmg` file that got downloaded. It will open a finder with the following files:

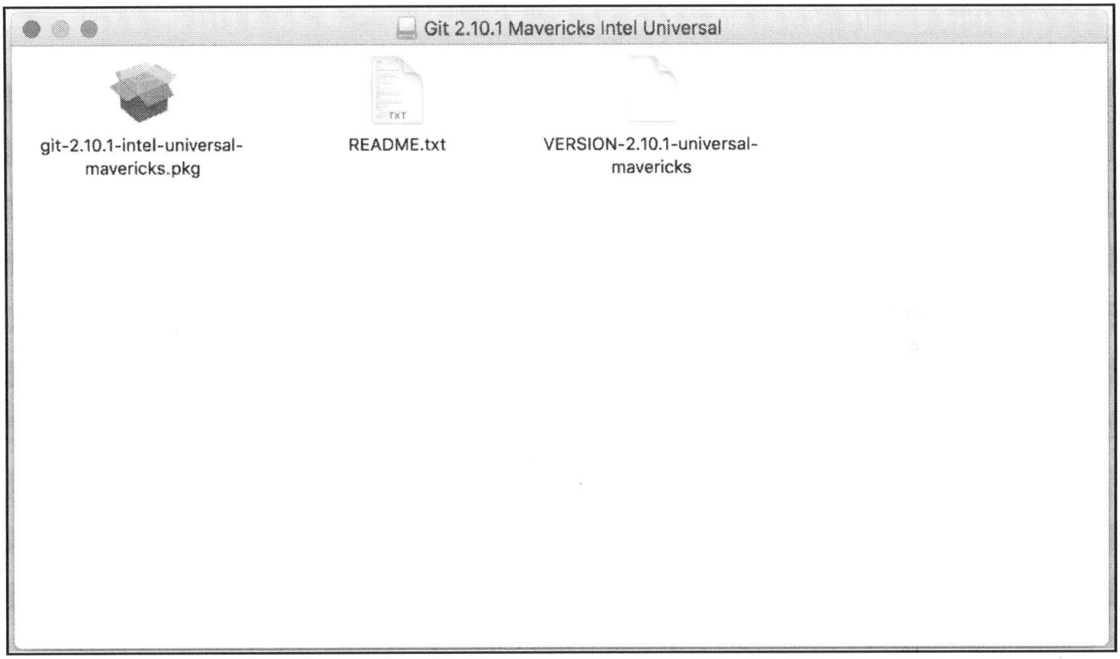

2. Double-click on the package (that is, `git-2.10.1-intel-universal-mavericks.dmg`) file; it will open the installation wizard to install, as seen in the following screenshot:

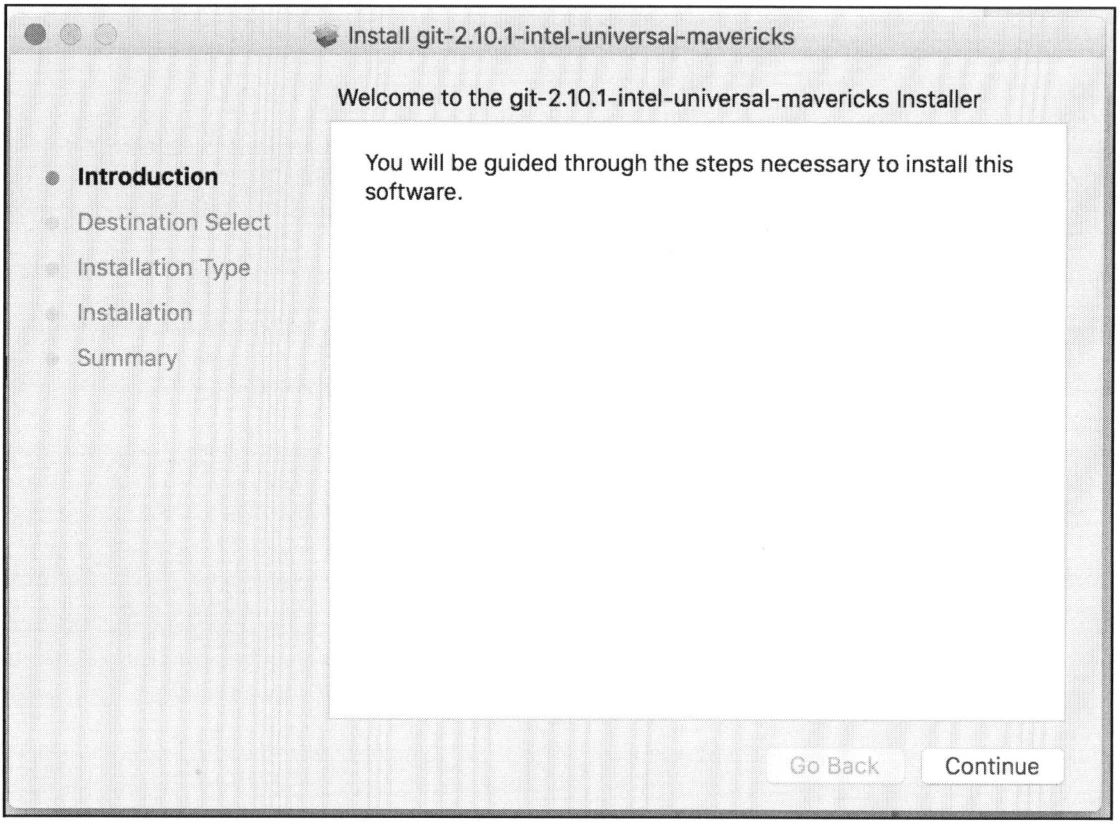

3. Click on **Install** to begin the installation:

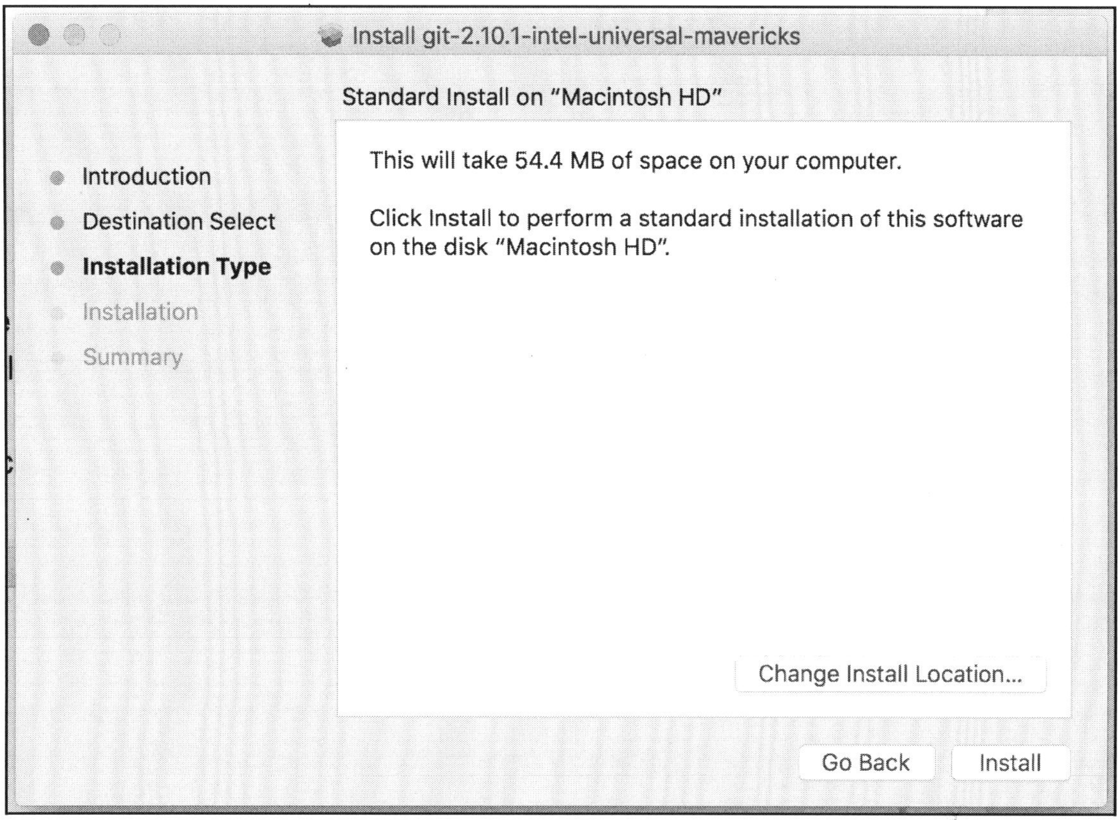

4. Once the installation is complete, you will see something like this:

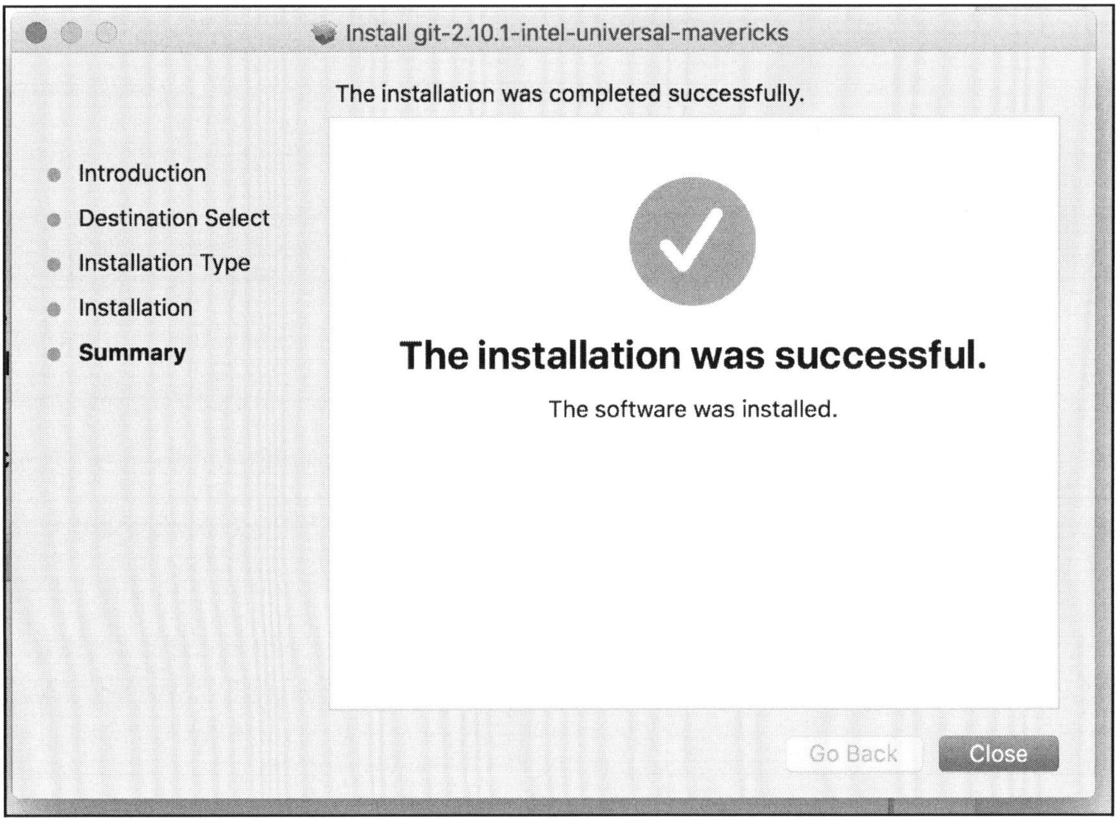

TIP

If you are using OS X 10.8 and haven't already modified your security settings to allow the installation of third-party applications, you'll need to make that adjustment before OS X lets you install these tools.

Installing and configuring Python

Now, let's install Python, which we will use to build our microservices. We will be using the Python 3.x version throughout the book.

Installing Python on a Debian-based distribution (such as Ubuntu)

There are different ways to install Python on a Debian-based distribution.

Using the APT package management tools

You can use the APT package management tools to update your local package index. Then, you can download and install the latest Python using the following commands as a root user:

```
$ apt-get update -y
$ apt-get install python3 -y
```

The following packages will automatically be downloaded and installed, as these are the prerequisites for Python 3 installation:

```
libpython3-dev libpython3.4 libpython3.4-dev python3-chardet

python3-colorama python3-dev python3-distlib python3-html5lib

python3-requests python3-six python3-urllib3 python3-wheel python3.4-de
```

Once the prerequisites are installed, it will download and install Python on your system.

Using source code

You can download the source code from the GitHub repository and compile the software from the source, as follows:

1. Before you begin, let's first install the dependencies of Git; execute the following commands as the root user to do so:

```
$ apt-get update -y
$ apt-get install build-essential checkinstall libreadline-gplv2-
   dev libncursesw5-dev libssl-dev libsqlite3-dev tk-dev libgdbm-
   dev libc6-dev libbz2-dev -y
```

2. Now, let's download Python (`https://www.python.org`) using the following command from Python's official website. You can also download the latest version in place, as specified:

```
$ cd /usr/local
$ wget https://www.python.org/ftp/python/3.4.6/Python-3.4.6.tgz
```

3. Now, let's extract the downloaded package with this command:

```
$ tar xzf Python-3.4.6.tgz
```

4. Now we have to compile the source code. Use the following set of commands to do so:

```
$ cd python-3.4.6
$ sudo ./configure
$ sudo make altinstall
```

5. The preceding commands will install Python on your system at `/usr/local`. Use the following command to check the Python version:

```
$ python3 -V
  Python 3.4.6
```

Installing Python on Windows

Now, let's see how we can install Python on Windows 7 or later systems. Installation of Python on Windows is pretty simple and quick; we will be using Python 3 and above, which you can download from Python's download page (`https://www.python.org/downloads/windows/`). Now perform the following steps:

1. Download the **Windows x86-64 executable installer** based on your system configuration, and open it to begin the installation, as shown in the following screenshot:

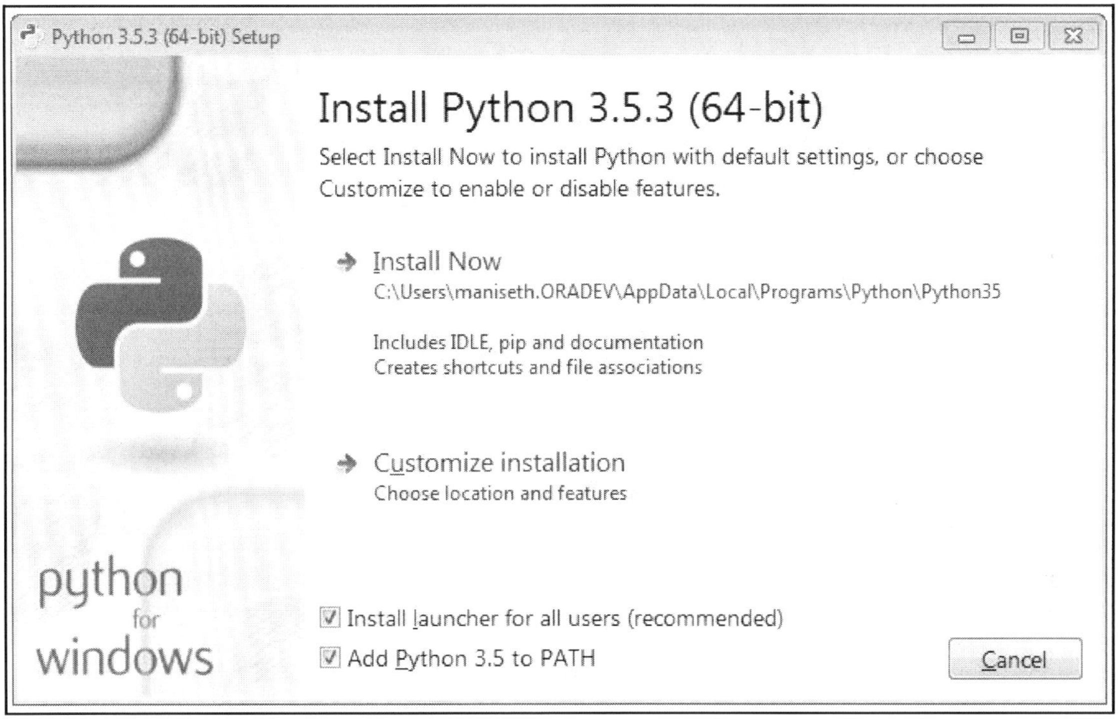

2. Next, select the type of installation you want to go with. We will click on **Install Now** to go for the default installation, as seen in this screenshot:

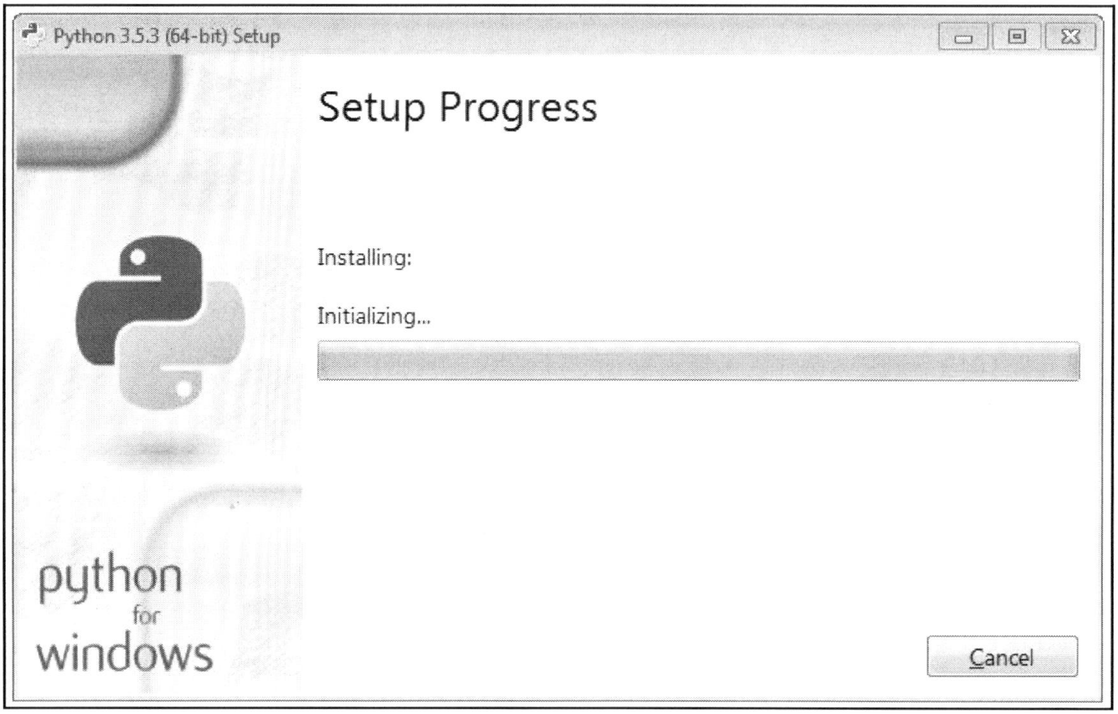

3. Once the installation is complete, you will see the following screen:

Great! We have successfully installed Python on Windows.

Installing Python on Mac

Before we begin with the Python installation, we need to install the command-line tools for OS X. If you have already installed the command-line tools at the time of Git installation, you can ignore this step.

Installing the command-line tools for OS X

In order to install any developer, you need to install Xcode (`https://developer.apple.com/xcode/`); you will need to set up an account on `connect.apple.com` to download the respective Xcode version tools.

However, there is another way you can install command-line tools using a utility, which comes along with an Xcode called `xcode-select`, which is shown here:

```
% xcode-select --install
```

The preceding command should trigger an installation wizard for the command-line tools. Follow the installation wizard, and you will be able to install it successfully.

Installing Python for OS X

Installing Python on Mac is quite similar to how you install Git on Windows. You can download the Python package from the official website (`https://www.python.org/downloads/`). Proceed with the following steps:

1. Once the Python package is downloaded, double-click on it to begin the **installation**; it will show the following pop-up window:

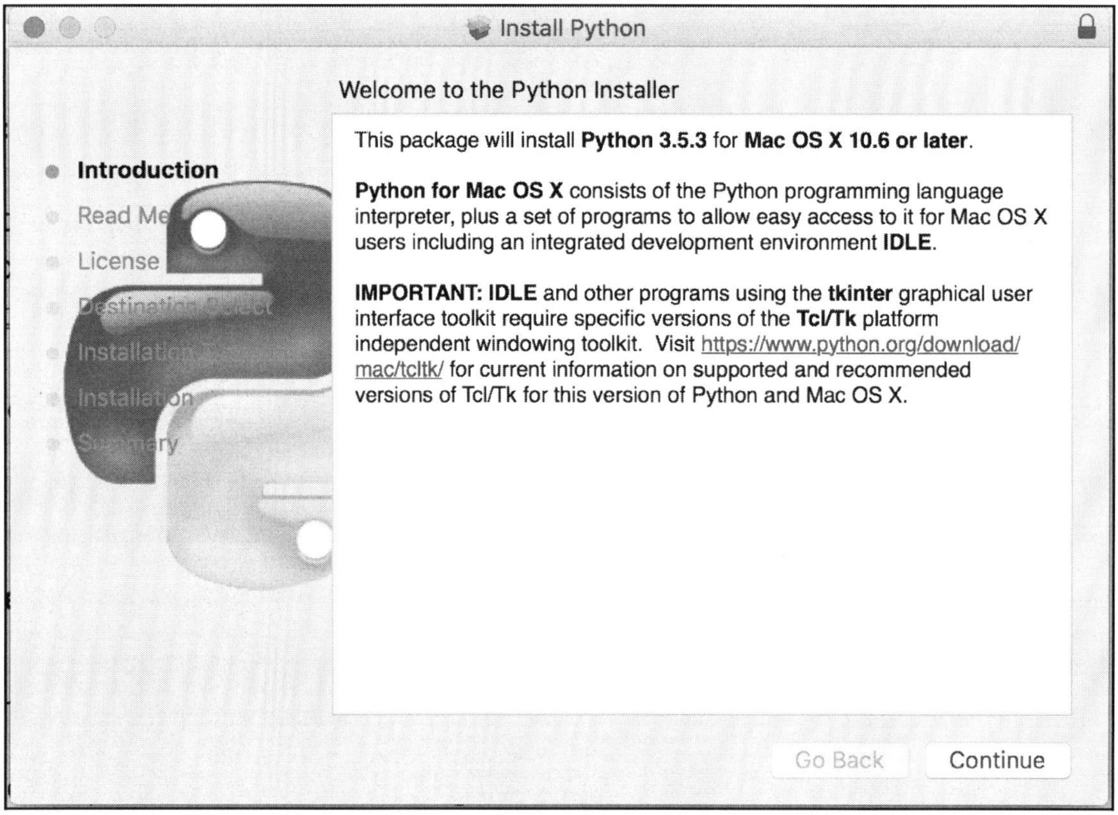

2. The next step will be about the release note and the respective Python version information:

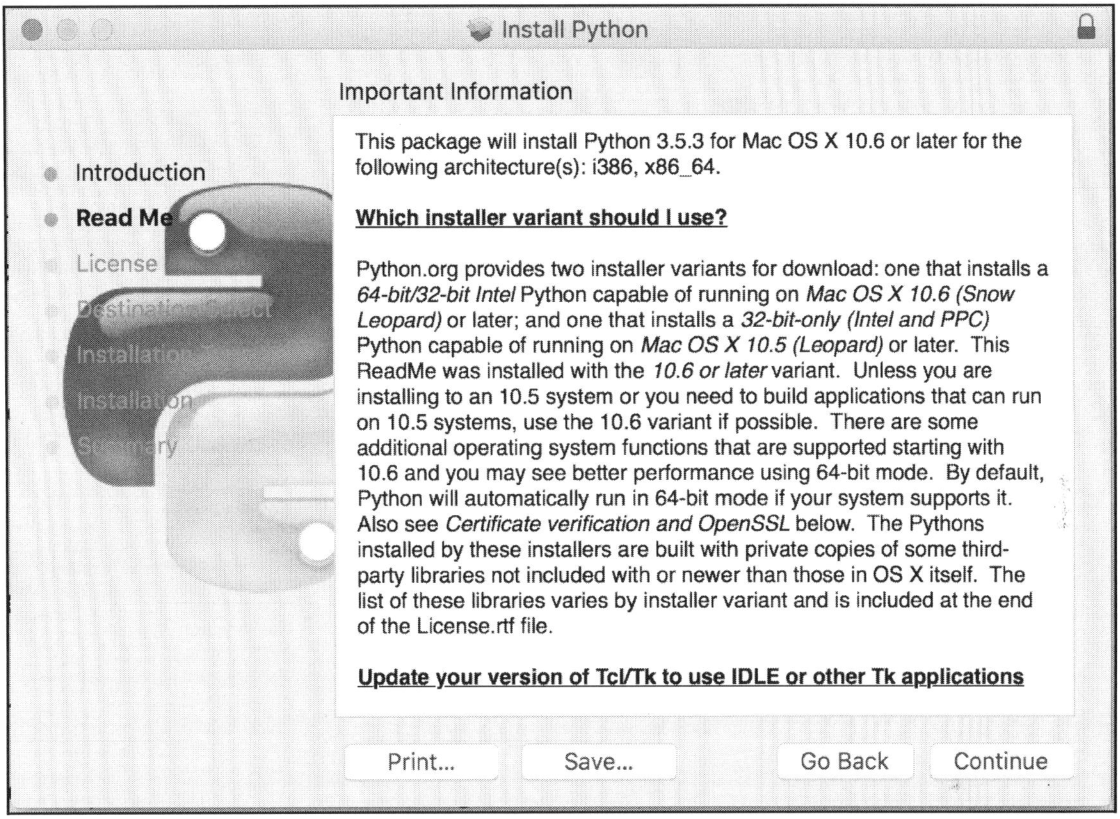

3. Next, you will need to **Agree** with the license, which is mandatory for installation:

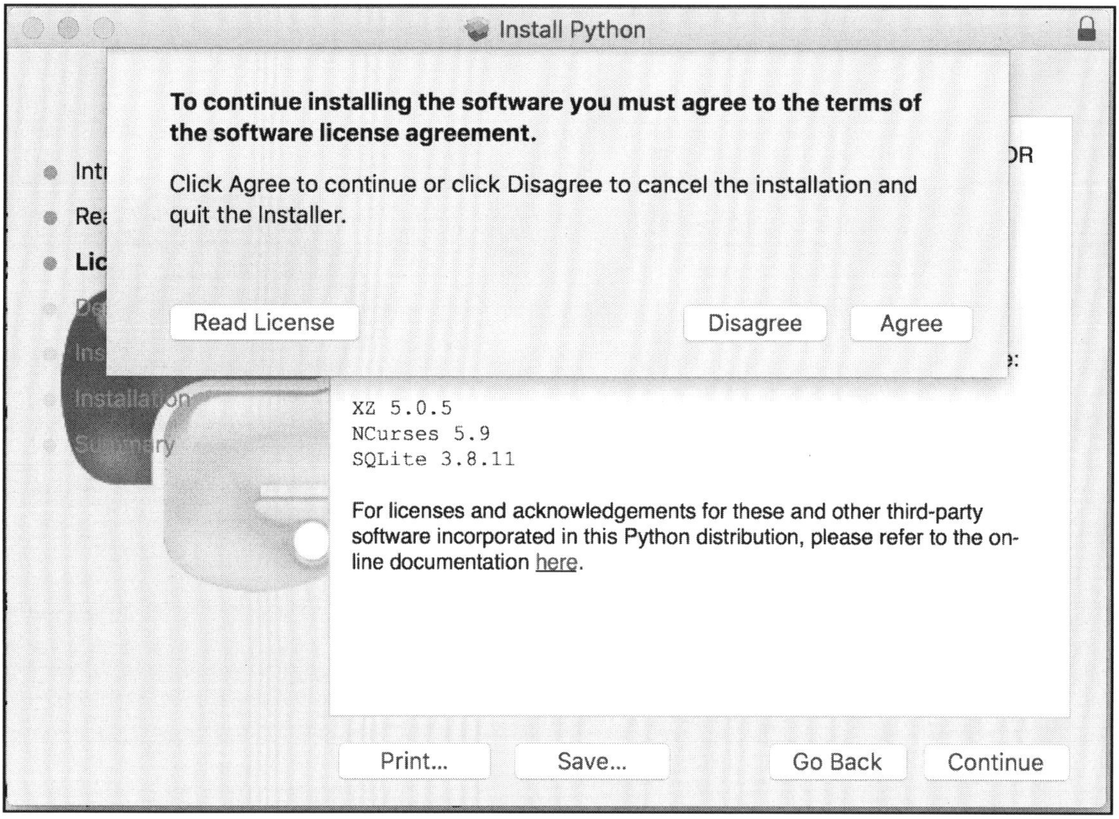

4. Next, it will show you the installation-related information, such as the disk occupied and the path. Click on **Install** to begin:

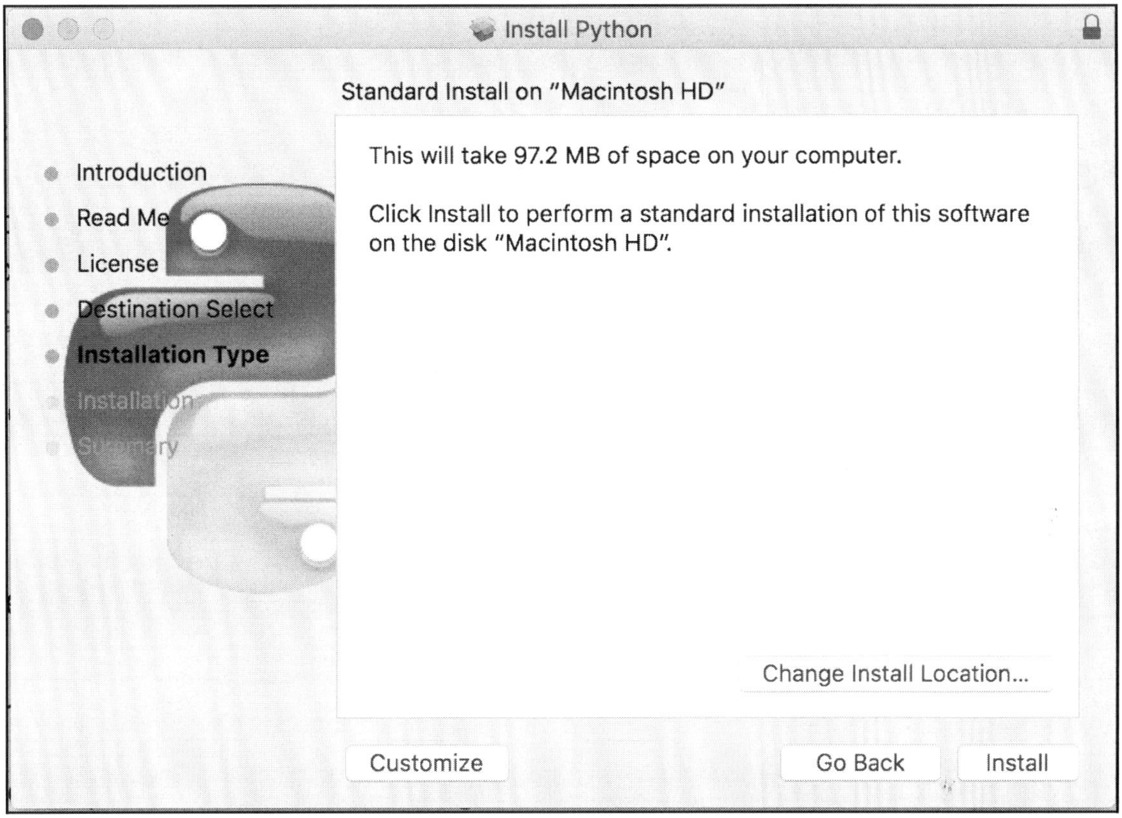

5. Once the installation is complete, you will see the following screen:

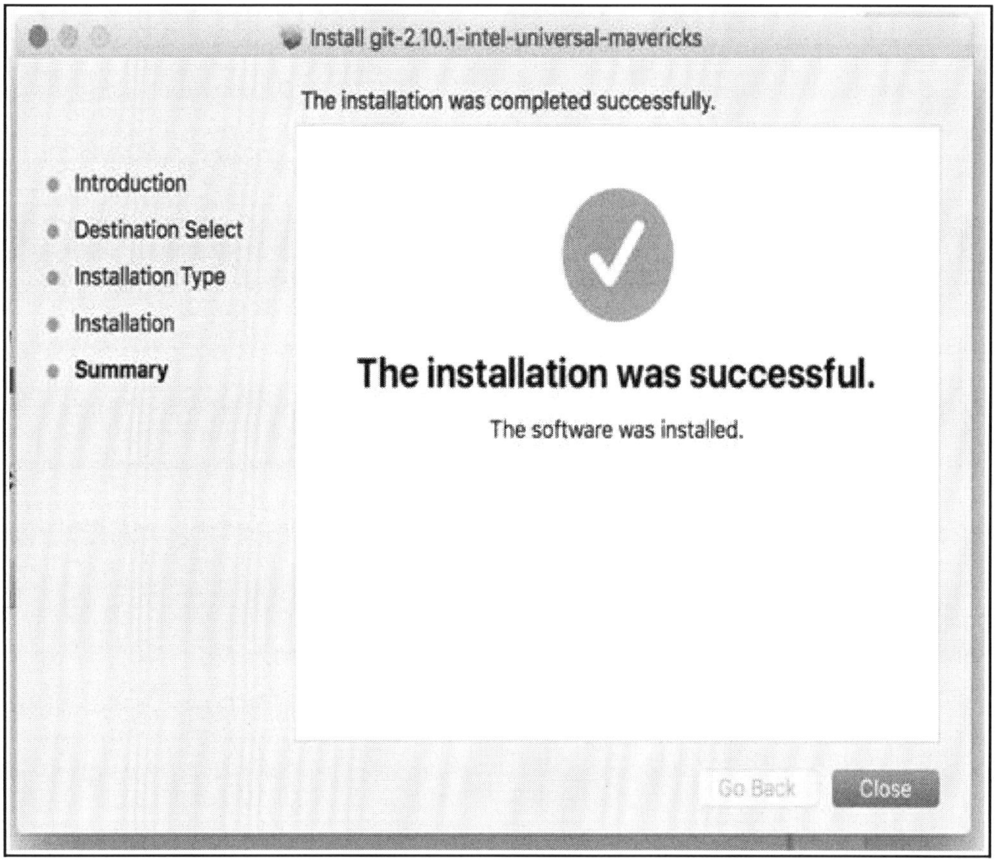

6. Use the following command to see whether the Python version is installed:

```
% python3 -V
  Python 3.5.3
```

Great!! Python is successfully installed.

Getting familiar with the GitHub and Git commands

In this section, we will go through a list of Git commands, which we will be using frequently throughout the book:

- **git init**: This command initializes your local repository once when you are setting it up for the first time
- **git remote add origin <server>**: This command links your local <indexentry content="Git command:git remote add origin " dbid="164250" state="mod">directory to the remote server repository so that all the changes pushed are saved in the remote repository
- **git status**: This command lists the files/directories that are yet to be added, or are modified and need to be committed
- **git add * or git add <filename>**: This command adds files/directories so that `<indexentry content="Git command:git add * or git add " dbid="164250" state="mod">`they can be tracked, and makes them ready to be committed
- **git commit -m "Commit message"**: This command helps you commit your track changes in the local machine and generate the commit ID by which the updated code can be identified
- **git commit -am "Commit message"**: The only difference between the previous command and this command is that this opens a default editor to add the commit message based on an operating system such as Ubuntu (Vim) or Windows (Notepad++) after adding all the files to stage
- **git push origin master**: This command pushes the last committed code from the local directory to the remote repository

Test everything to make sure our environment works.

Here we go. We have installed both Git and Python in the last section, which are needed to begin with building microservices. In this section, we will focus on testing the installed packages and try to get familiar with them.

The first thing we can do is to exercise the Git command, which fetches an external Python code from a repository (usually GitHub) over HTTPs, and copies it into our current workspace in the appropriate directory:

```
$ git clone https://github.com/PacktPublishing/Cloud-Native-
  Python.git
```

The preceding command will create a directory named `Cloud-Native-Python` on your local machine; switch to the `Cloud-Native-Python/chapter1` path from the current location.

We will need to install the requirements of the apps that are needed to run it. In this case, we just need the Flask module to be available:

```
$ cd hello.py
$ pip install requirements.txt
```

Here, Flask works as the web server; we will understand more about it in detail in the next chapter.

Once it is installed successfully, you can run the app using the following command:

```
$ python hello.py
* Running on http://0.0.0.0:5000/ (Press CTRL+C to quit)
```

I think we are good to see the output, which is as follows:

```
$ curl http://0.0.0.0:5000/
Hello World!
```

If you see this output, then our Python development environment is correctly set up.

Now it's time to write some Python code!

Summary

In this chapter, we began with exploring the cloud platform and the cloud computing stack. During this chapter, you learned what the different twelve-factor apps methodologies are, and how they can help develop microservices. Lastly, you got to know about what kind of ideal setup environment a developer machine should have to create or get started with application creation.

In the next chapter, we will start building our microservices by creating backend REST APIs, and testing with the API call or using the Python framework as well.

2
Building Microservices in Python

Now, since you understand what microservices are and, hopefully, have a sense of their key benefits, I'm sure you are eager to begin building them. In this chapter, we will immediately start writing REST APIs, which collectively work as microservices.

The topics we will cover in this chapter are as follows:

- Building a REST API
- Testing an API

Python concepts

Let's first understand a few concepts of Python, which we will use in this book.

Modules

A module basically allows you to logically organize your programming code. It is similar to any other Python program. They are needed in scenarios where we need only a bit of code to be imported instead of the entire program. A **module** can be a combination of one or multiple functions classes, and many more. We will use a couple of inbuilt functions, which are a part of the Python library. Also, wherever needed, we will create our own modules.

The following example code showcases the structure of modules:

```
#myprogram.py
### EXAMPLE PYTHON MODULE
# Define some variables:
numberone = 1
age = 78

# define some functions
def printhello():
 print "hello"

def timesfour(input):
 print input * 4

# define a class
class house:
 def __init__(self):
     self.type = raw_input("What type of house? ")
     self.height = raw_input("What height (in feet)? ")
     self.price = raw_input("How much did it cost? ")
     self.age = raw_input("How old is it (in years)? ")

 def print_details(self):
     print "This house is a/an " + self.height + " foot",
     print self.type, "house, " + self.age, "years old and costing\
     " + self.price + " dollars."
```

You can import the preceding module using the following command:

```
# import myprogram
```

Functions

A function is a block of organized, self-contained programs that perform a specific task, which you can incorporate into your own larger programs. They are defined as follows:

```
# function
def  functionname():
  do something
  return
```

These are a few points to remember:

- Indentation is very important in Python programs
- By default, parameters have a positional behavior, and you need to inform them in the same order that they were defined in

Please see the following code snippet example, which showcases functions:

```
def display ( name ):
#This prints a passed string into this function
  print ("Hello" + name)
  return;
```

You can call the preceding function as follows:

```
display("Manish")
display("Mohit")
```

The following screenshot shows the execution of the preceding `display` function:

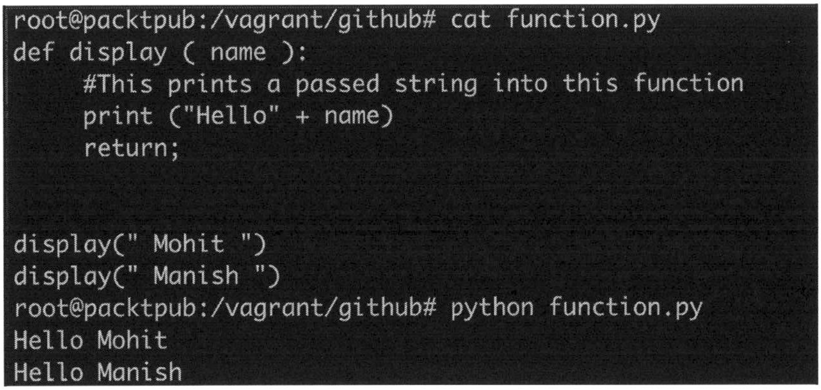

root@packtpub:/vagrant/github# cat function.py
def display (name):
#This prints a passed string into this function
print ("Hello" + name)
return;
display(" Mohit ")
display(" Manish ")
root@packtpub:/vagrant/github# python function.py
Hello Mohit
Hello Manish

TIP

Note that if you have more than one Python version installed on your system, you need to use Python 3 instead of Python, which uses the default version of Python (generally, 2.7.x).

Modeling microservices

In this book, we will develop a full-fledged working web app that works independently.

Now, since we have a basic understanding of Python, let's get started with modeling our microservices and understanding the application workflow.

The following diagram shows the microservices architecture and application workflow:

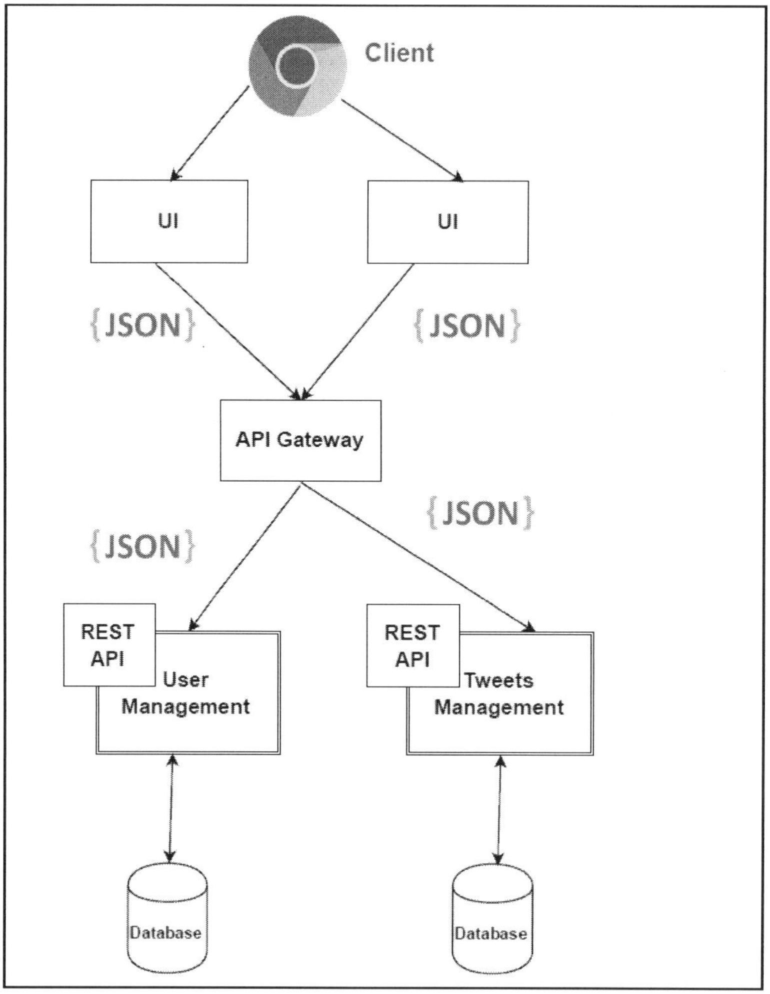

Building microservices

In this book, we will use Flask as a web framework to build our microservices. **Flask** is a powerful web framework, which is easy to learn and simple to use. Additionally, in Flask, we need a little boilerplate code to get a simple app up and running.

Since we will create our application using the twelve-factor app concept, we will begin by ensuring that we have a centralized code base. By now, you should know how to create a GitHub repository. If not, make sure you create it as per the blogpost link provided in `Chapter 1`, *Introducing Cloud Native Architecture and Microservices*. We will be pushing the code regularly to the repository.

Assuming you have created the repository during the course of this book, we will use the GitHub repository (`https://github.com/PacktPublishing/Cloud-Native-Python.git`).

So, let's set up our local directory in sync with the remote repository. To ensure that we are in the app directory, use the following commands:

```
$ mkdir Cloud-Native-Python  # Creating the directory
$ cd Cloud-Native-Python  # Changing the path to working directory
$ git init . # Initialising the local directory
$ echo "Cloud-Native-Python" > README.md  # Adding description of
repository
$ git add README.md  # Adding README.md
$ git commit -am "Initial commit"  # Committing the changes
$ git remote add origin
https://github.com/PacktPublishing/Cloud-Native-Python.git  # Adding to
local repository
$ git push -u origin master  # Pushing changes to remote repository.
```

You will see the following output:

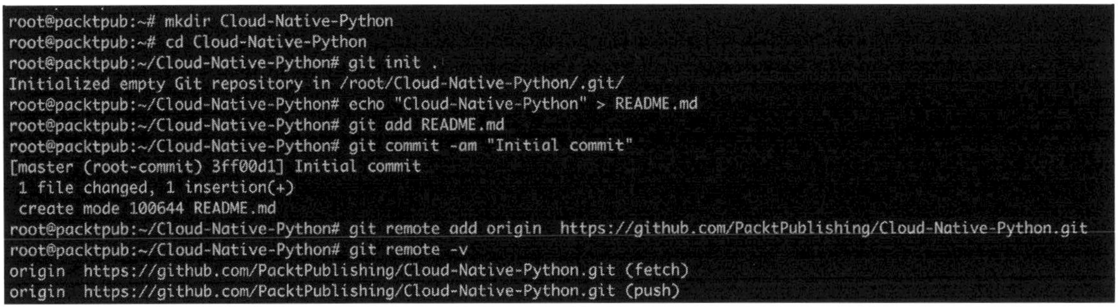

```
root@packtpub:~# mkdir Cloud-Native-Python
root@packtpub:~# cd Cloud-Native-Python
root@packtpub:~/Cloud-Native-Python# git init .
Initialized empty Git repository in /root/Cloud-Native-Python/.git/
root@packtpub:~/Cloud-Native-Python# echo "Cloud-Native-Python" > README.md
root@packtpub:~/Cloud-Native-Python# git add README.md
root@packtpub:~/Cloud-Native-Python# git commit -am "Initial commit"
[master (root-commit) 3ff00d1] Initial commit
 1 file changed, 1 insertion(+)
 create mode 100644 README.md
root@packtpub:~/Cloud-Native-Python# git remote add origin  https://github.com/PacktPublishing/Cloud-Native-Python.git
root@packtpub:~/Cloud-Native-Python# git remote -v
origin  https://github.com/PacktPublishing/Cloud-Native-Python.git (fetch)
origin  https://github.com/PacktPublishing/Cloud-Native-Python.git (push)
```

We have successfully pushed our first commit to the remote repository; we will keep doing so in a similar fashion till we reach a certain milestone in building microservices, as well as the application.

Now, we need to install a file-based database, such as SQLite version 3, which will work as the datastore for our microservices.

To install SQLite 3, use the following command:

```
$ apt-get install sqlite3 libsqlite3-dev -y
```

We can now create and use (source) a `virtualenv` environment, which will isolate the local app's environment from the global `site-packages` installations. If `virtualenv` is not installed, you can install it using the following command:

```
$ pip install virtualenv
```

Now create `virtualenv` as follows:

```
$ virtualenv env --no-site-packages --python=python3
$ source env/bin/activate
```

We should see the output of the preceding command as shown in the following screenshot:

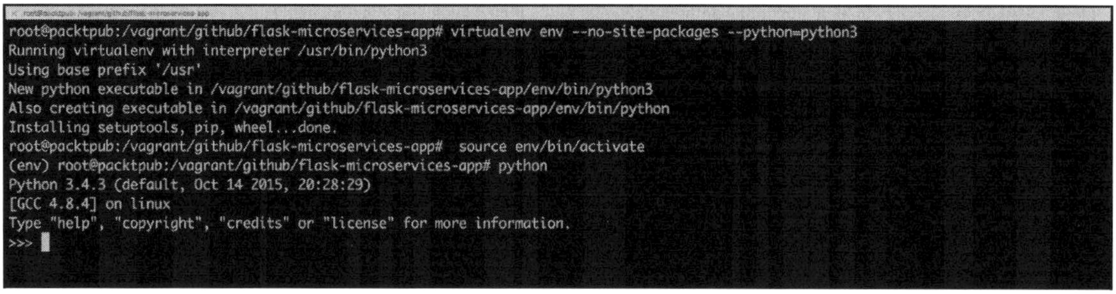

After the `virtualenv` setup, currently, we need one dependency in our virtualenv environment that needs to be installed. Use the following command to add one package dependency into `requirements.txt`:

```
$ echo "Flask==0.10.1" >>  requirements.txt
```

In the future, if any more dependencies are needed as part of the application, they will go inside the `requirements.txt` file.

Let's use the requirements file to install the dependencies into the `virtualenv` environment as follows:

```
$ pip install -r requirements.txt
```

Now that we have the dependencies installed, let's create a file, `app.py`, with the following contents:

```
from flask import Flask

app = Flask(__name__)

if __name__ == "__main__":
 app.run(host='0.0.0.0', port=5000, debug=True)
```

The preceding code is the basic structure to run an application using Flask. It basically initializes the `Flask` variable and runs on port `5000`, which is accessible from anywhere (`0.0.0.0`).

Now, let's test the preceding code and see if everything is working fine.

Execute the following command to run the application:

```
$ python app.py
```

We should see the output of the preceding command as shown in the following screenshot:

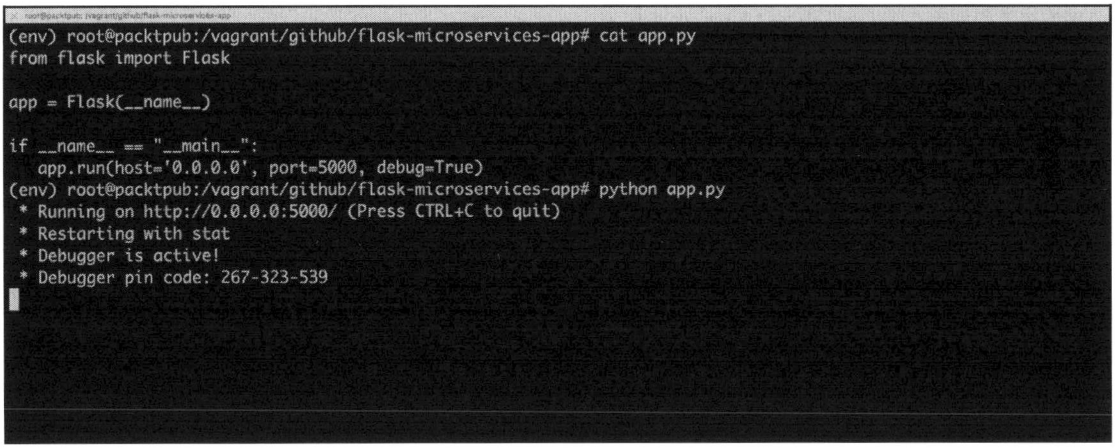
(env) root@packtpub:/vagrant/github/flask-microservices-app# cat app.py
from flask import Flask
app = Flask(__name__)
if __name__ == "__main__":
app.run(host='0.0.0.0', port=5000, debug=True)
(env) root@packtpub:/vagrant/github/flask-microservices-app# python app.py
* Running on http://0.0.0.0:5000/ (Press CTRL+C to quit)
* Restarting with stat
* Debugger is active!
* Debugger pin code: 267-323-539

At this point in time, before we start building RESTful APIs, we need to decide what will be our root URL to access the service, which will further decide the sub URI for the different methods. Consider the following example:

`http://[hostname]/api/v1/.`

Since, in our case, we will be using a local machine, `hostname` can be `localhost` with port, which is, by default, `5000` for a Flask application. So, our root URL will be as follows:

`http://localhost:5000/api/v1/.`

Now, let's decide the resources on which different actions will be performed, and which will be exposed by this service. In this case, we will create two resources: users and tweets.

Our users and info resource will use the HTTP methods as follows:

HTTP Method	**URI**	**Actions**
`GET`	`http://localhost:5000/api/v1/info`	This responds back with the version
`GET`	`http://localhost:5000/api/v1/users`	This responds with the user list
`GET`	`http://localhost:5000/api/v1/users/[user_id]`	The response will be the user details of the specified `user_id`
`POST`	`http://localhost:5000/api/v1/users`	This resource will create new users in the backend server with values from the object passed
`DELETE`	`http://localhost:5000/api/v1/users`	This resource will delete the user with the specified username passed in JSON format

PUT	http://localhost:5000/api/v1/users/[user_id]	This resource updates the user information of the specific user_id based on the JSON object passed as part of the API call.

Using the client, we will perform actions against resources such as add, remove, modify, and many more.

For the scope of this chapter, we will take a file-based database, such as SQLite 3, which we already installed earlier.

Let's go and create our first resource, which is /api/v1/info, and show the available versions and their release details.

Before that, we need to create an apirelease table schema, as defined in SQLite 3, which will contain information about the API version release. This can be done as follows:

```
CREATE TABLE apirelease(
buildtime date,
version varchar(30) primary key,
links varchar2(30), methods varchar2(30));
```

Once it is created, you can add records into SQLite 3 for our first version (v1) using the following command:

```
Insert into apirelease values ('2017-01-01 10:00:00', "v1",
"/api/v1/users", "get, post, put, delete");
```

Let's define the route /api/v1/info and function in app.py, which will basically handle the RESTful call on the /api/v1/info route. This is done as follows:

```
from flask import jsonify
import json
import sqlite3
@app.route("/api/v1/info")
def home_index():
  conn = sqlite3.connect('mydb.db')
  print ("Opened database successfully");
  api_list=[]
  cursor = conn.execute("SELECT buildtime, version,
  methods, links   from apirelease")
for row in cursor:
```

```
            a_dict = {}
            a_dict['version'] = row[0]
            a_dict['buildtime'] = row[1]
            a_dict['methods'] = row[2]
            a_dict['links'] = row[3]
            api_list.append(a_dict)
        conn.close()
        return jsonify({'api_version': api_list}), 200
```

Now that we have added a route and the handle for it, let's make a RESTful call on `http://localhost:5000/api/v1/info`, as shown in this screenshot:

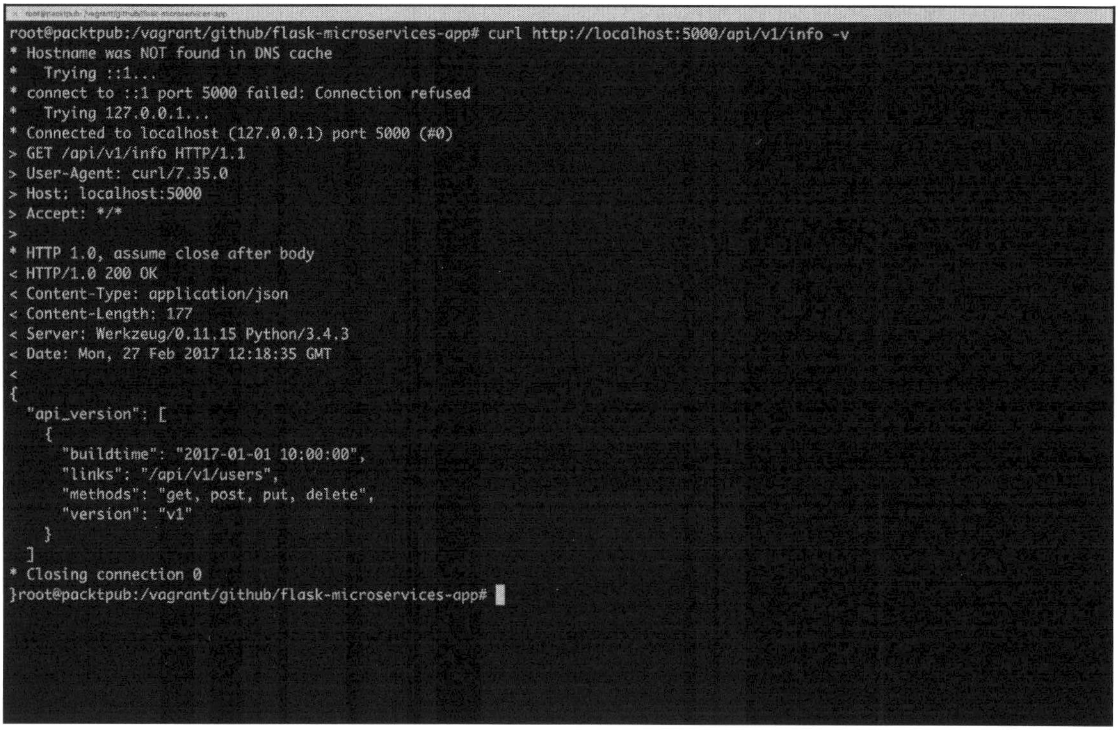

root@packtpub:/vagrant/github/flask-microservices-app# curl http://localhost:5000/api/v1/info -v
* Hostname was NOT found in DNS cache
*   Trying ::1...
* connect to ::1 port 5000 failed: Connection refused
*   Trying 127.0.0.1...
* Connected to localhost (127.0.0.1) port 5000 (#0)
> GET /api/v1/info HTTP/1.1
> User-Agent: curl/7.35.0
> Host: localhost:5000
> Accept: */*
>
* HTTP 1.0, assume close after body
< HTTP/1.0 200 OK
< Content-Type: application/json
< Content-Length: 177
< Server: Werkzeug/0.11.15 Python/3.4.3
< Date: Mon, 27 Feb 2017 12:18:35 GMT
<
{
"api_version": [
{
"buildtime": "2017-01-01 10:00:00",
"links": "/api/v1/users",
"methods": "get, post, put, delete",
"version": "v1"
}
]
* Closing connection 0
}root@packtpub:/vagrant/github/flask-microservices-app#

Awesome! It works!!

Let's move on to the /api/v1/users resource, which will help us perform various actions on the user's records.

We can define a user as having the following fields:

- id: This is a unique identifier for users (Numeric type)
- username: This is a unique identifier or handler for users for authentication (String type)
- emailid: This is the user's email (String type)
- password: This is the user's password (String type)
- full_name: This is the full name of the user (String type)

In order to create the user's table schema in SQLite, use the following command:

```
CREATE TABLE users(
username varchar2(30),
emailid varchar2(30),
password varchar2(30), full_name varchar(30),
id integer primary key autoincrement);
```

Building resource user methods

Let's define our GET methods for user resources.

GET /api/v1/users

The GET/api/v1/users method shows the list of all users.

Let's create an /api/v1/users route by adding the following code snippet to app.py:

```
@app.route('/api/v1/users', methods=['GET'])
def get_users():
  return list_users()
```

Now that we have added the route, we need to define the list_users() function, which will connect with the database to get you the complete list of users. Add the following code to app.py:

```
def list_users():
conn = sqlite3.connect('mydb.db')
print ("Opened database successfully");
api_list=[]
```

```
cursor = conn.execute("SELECT username, full_name,
email, password, id from users")
for row in cursor:
a_dict = {}
a_dict['username'] = row[0]
a_dict['name'] = row[1]
a_dict['email'] = row[2]
a_dict['password'] = row[3]
a_dict['id'] = row[4]
api_list.append(a_dict)
conn.close()
  return jsonify({'user_list': api_list})
```

Now that we have added the route and the handle for it, let's test check the `http://localhost:5000/api/v1/users` URL as follows:

root@packtpub:/vagrant/github/flask-microservices-app# curl http://localhost:5000/api/v1/users
{
"user_list": [
{
"email": "manishest@gmail.com",
"id": 1,
"name": "Manish",
"password": "manish123",
"username": "manish123"
}
]
}root@packtpub:/vagrant/github/flask-microservices-app#

GET /api/v1/users/[user_id]

The `GET/api/v1/users/[user_id]` method shows the user details defined by `user_id`.

Let's create the route for preceding a `GET` request into the `app.py` file as follows:

```
@app.route('/api/v1/users/<int:user_id>', methods=['GET'])
def get_user(user_id):
  return list_user(user_id)
```

As you can see in the preceding code, we call the `list_user(user_id)` route into the `list_user(user)` function, which is not yet defined in `app.py`. Let's define it to get the details of the specified user, as follows, in the `app.py` file:

```
def list_user(user_id):
  conn = sqlite3.connect('mydb.db')
  print ("Opened database successfully");
  api_list=[]
  cursor=conn.cursor()
  cursor.execute("SELECT * from users where id=?",(user_id,))
  data = cursor.fetchall()
  if len(data) != 0:
     user = {}
           user['username'] = data[0][0]
     user['name'] = data[0][1]
     user['email'] = data[0][2]
     user['password'] = data[0][3]
     user['id'] = data[0][4]
        conn.close()
        return jsonify(a_dict)
```

Now that we've added the `list_user(user_id)` function, let's test it out and see if everything is working fine:

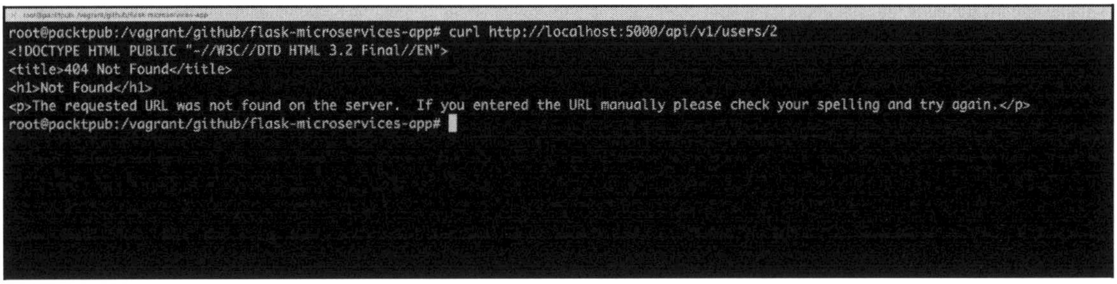
root@packtpub:/vagrant/github/flask-microservices-app# curl http://localhost:5000/api/v1/users/2
<!DOCTYPE HTML PUBLIC "-//W3C//DTD HTML 3.2 Final//EN">
<title>404 Not Found</title>
<h1>Not Found</h1>
<p>The requested URL was not found on the server. If you entered the URL manually please check your spelling and try again.</p>
root@packtpub:/vagrant/github/flask-microservices-app#

Oops! It seems the ID is not present; usually, Flask applications respond with an HTML message with a `404` error if the ID is not present. Since this is a web service application, and we are getting a response in JSON for other APIs, we need to write `handler` for the `404` error so that, instead of the HTML response, it should respond back in JSON, even for errors. For example, see the following code for `404` error handling. Now, the server will respond with proper messages which are part of the code, as follows:

```
from flask import make_response

@app.errorhandler(404)
def resource_not_found(error):
  return make_response(jsonify({'error':
  'Resource not found!'}),  404)
```

root@packtpub:/vagrant/github/flask-microservices-app# curl http://localhost:5000/api/v1/users/2
{
"error": "Resource not found!"
}root@packtpub:/vagrant/github/flask-microservices-app#

Additionally, you can add the `abort` library from Flask, which is basically for calling exceptions. Similarly, you can create multiple error handlers for different HTTP error codes.

Now that our `GET` methods are working fine, we will go forward and write the `POST` method, which is similar to adding new users to the users list.

There are two methods to pass the data into the `POST` method, which are as follows:

- **JSON**: In this approach, we pass the JSON record in the form of an object as part of the request. The RESTful API call would look like this:

```
curl -i -H "Content-Type: application/json" -X POST -d
{"field1":"value"} resource_url
```

- **Parameterized**: In this approach, we pass the values of the record as parameters, as follows:

```
curl -i -H "Content-Type: application/json" -X POST
resource_url?field1=val1&field2=val2
```

In the JSON method, we provide the input data in the form of `json`, and we read it in the same way. On the other hand, in the parameterized method, we provide the input data (that is, `username`, and so on) in the form of URL parameters, and read data in the same way.

Also note that the API creation at the backend will vary with the type of API call being made.

POST /api/v1/users

In this book, we go with the first approach to the `POST` method. So, let's define our route for the `post` method in `app.py`, and call the function to update the user record to the database file, as follows:

```
@app.route('/api/v1/users', methods=['POST'])
def create_user():
  if not request.json or not 'username' in request.json or not
  'email' in request.json or not 'password' in request.json:
    abort(400)
 user = {
    'username': request.json['username'],
    'email': request.json['email'],
    'name': request.json.get('name',""),
    'password': request.json['password']
 }
  return jsonify({'status': add_user(user)}), 201
```

As you can see, in the preceding method, we called the exception with error code `400`; let's write its handler now:

```
@app.errorhandler(400)
def invalid_request(error):
   return make_response(jsonify({'error': 'Bad Request'}), 400)
```

We still need to define the `add_user(user)` function, which will update the new user record. Let's define it in `app.py`, as follows:

```
def add_user(new_user):
 conn = sqlite3.connect('mydb.db')
 print ("Opened database successfully");
 api_list=[]
 cursor=conn.cursor()
 cursor.execute("SELECT * from users where username=? or
  emailid=?",(new_user['username'],new_user['email']))
data = cursor.fetchall()
if len(data) != 0:
```

```
            abort(409)
        else:
            cursor.execute("insert into users (username, emailid, password,
      full_name) values(?,?,?,?)",(new_user['username'],new_user['email'],
       new_user['password'], new_user['name']))
            conn.commit()
            return "Success"
        conn.close()
        return jsonify(a_dict)
```

Now that we have added `handler`, as well as the route for the `POST` method of the user, let's test it by adding a new user using the following API call:

```
curl -i -H "Content-Type: application/json" -X POST -d '{
"username":"mahesh@rocks", "email": "mahesh99@gmail.com",
"password": "mahesh123", "name":"Mahesh" }'
http://localhost:5000/api/v1/users
```

Then, validate the user's list curl, `http://localhost:5000/api/v1/users`, as shown in the following screenshot:

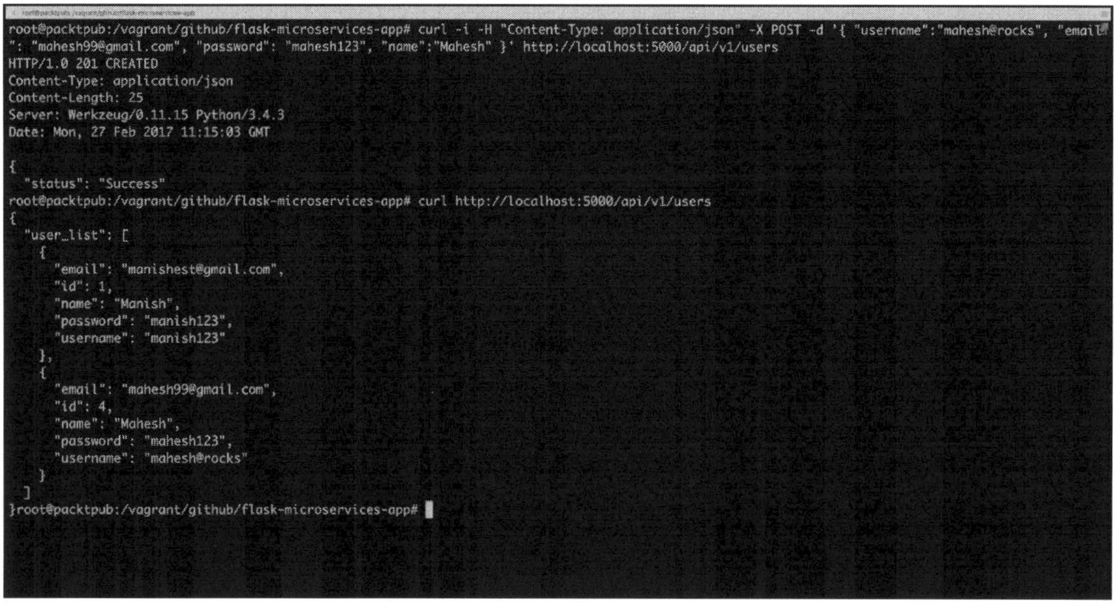
root@packtpub:/vagrant/github/flask-microservices-app# curl -i -H "Content-Type: application/json" -X POST -d '{ "username":"mahesh@rocks", "email": "mahesh99@gmail.com", "password": "mahesh123", "name":"Mahesh" }' http://localhost:5000/api/v1/users
HTTP/1.0 201 CREATED
Content-Type: application/json
Content-Length: 25
Server: Werkzeug/0.11.15 Python/3.4.3
Date: Mon, 27 Feb 2017 11:15:03 GMT
{
"status": "Success"
root@packtpub:/vagrant/github/flask-microservices-app# curl http://localhost:5000/api/v1/users
{
"user_list": [
{
"email": "manishest@gmail.com",
"id": 1,
"name": "Manish",
"password": "manish123",
"username": "manish123"
},
{
"email": "mahesh99@gmail.com",
"id": 4,
"name": "Mahesh",
"password": "mahesh123",
"username": "mahesh@rocks"
}
]
}root@packtpub:/vagrant/github/flask-microservices-app#

DELETE /api/v1/users

The `delete` method helps remove a specific record, which is defined by a username. We will pass `username` as the JSON object that needs to be deleted from the database.

The following code snippet will create a new route in `app.py` for the `DELETE` method for users:

```
@app.route('/api/v1/users', methods=['DELETE'])
def delete_user():
 if not request.json or not 'username' in request.json:
    abort(400)
 user=request.json['username']
  return jsonify({'status': del_user(user)}), 200
```

In the next code snippet, we will call `del_user`, which deletes the user record specified by `username` after validating whether it exists or not:

```
def del_user(del_user):
  conn = sqlite3.connect('mydb.db')
  print ("Opened database successfully");
  cursor=conn.cursor()
  cursor.execute("SELECT * from users where username=? ",
  (del_user,))
  data = cursor.fetchall()
  print ("Data" ,data)
  if len(data) == 0:
    abort(404)
  else:
   cursor.execute("delete from users where username==?",
   (del_user,))
   conn.commit()
     return "Success"
```

Great! We have added the route `/handler` for the `DELETE` method for the user resource; let's test it using the following `test` API call:

```
    curl -i -H "Content-Type: application/json" -X delete -d '{
"username":"manish123" }' http://localhost:5000/api/v1/users
```

Then, hit the user list API (`curl http://localhost:5000/api/v1/users`) to see if the changes have been made:

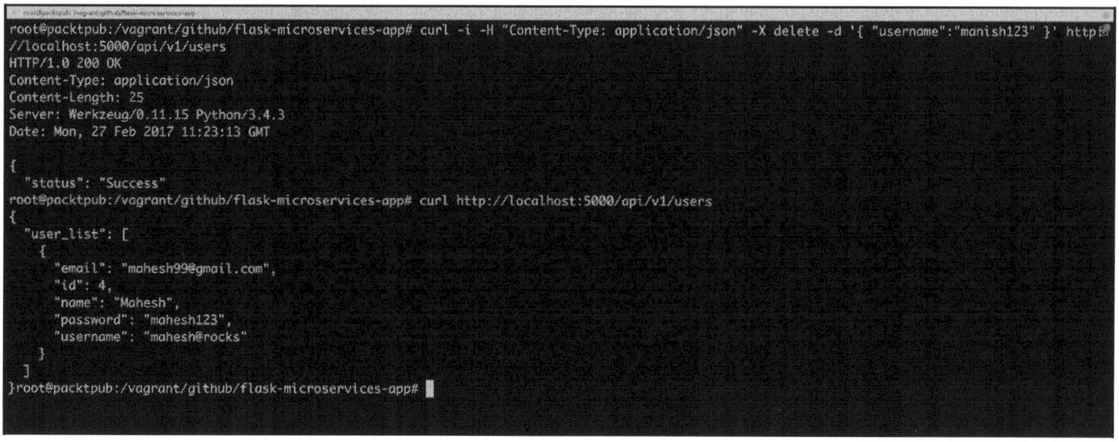
root@packtpub:/vagrant/github/flask-microservices-app# curl -i -H "Content-Type: application/json" -X delete -d '{ "username":"manish123" }' http://localhost:5000/api/v1/users
HTTP/1.0 200 OK
Content-Type: application/json
Content-Length: 25
Server: Werkzeug/0.11.15 Python/3.4.3
Date: Mon, 27 Feb 2017 11:23:13 GMT
{
"status": "Success"
root@packtpub:/vagrant/github/flask-microservices-app# curl http://localhost:5000/api/v1/users
{
"user_list": [
{
"email": "mahesh99@gmail.com",
"id": 4,
"name": "Mahesh",
"password": "mahesh123",
"username": "mahesh@rocks"
}
]
}root@packtpub:/vagrant/github/flask-microservices-app#

Awesome! User deletion is successful.

PUT /api/v1/users

The PUT API basically helps us update a user's record specified by `user_id`.

Go ahead and create a route with the `PUT` method to update the `user` records defined in the `app.py` file, as follows:

```
@app.route('/api/v1/users/<int:user_id>', methods=['PUT'])
def update_user(user_id):
 user = {}
 if not request.json:
     abort(400)
 user['id']=user_id
 key_list = request.json.keys()
 for i in key_list:
    user[i] = request.json[i]
 print (user)
 return jsonify({'status': upd_user(user)}), 200
```

Let's specify the definition of the `upd_user(user)` function, which basically updates the information in the database with the check that the user `id` exists:

```
def upd_user(user):
  conn = sqlite3.connect('mydb.db')
  print ("Opened database successfully");
  cursor=conn.cursor()
  cursor.execute("SELECT * from users where id=? ",(user['id'],))
  data = cursor.fetchall()
  print (data)
  if len(data) == 0:
    abort(404)
  else:
    key_list=user.keys()
    for i in key_list:
        if i != "id":
            print (user, i)
            # cursor.execute("UPDATE users set {0}=? where id=? ",
             (i, user[i], user['id']))
            cursor.execute("""UPDATE users SET {0} = ? WHERE id =
            ?""".format(i), (user[i], user['id']))
            conn.commit()
    return "Success"
```

Now that we have added the API handle for the `PUT` method for the user resource, let's test it out as follows:

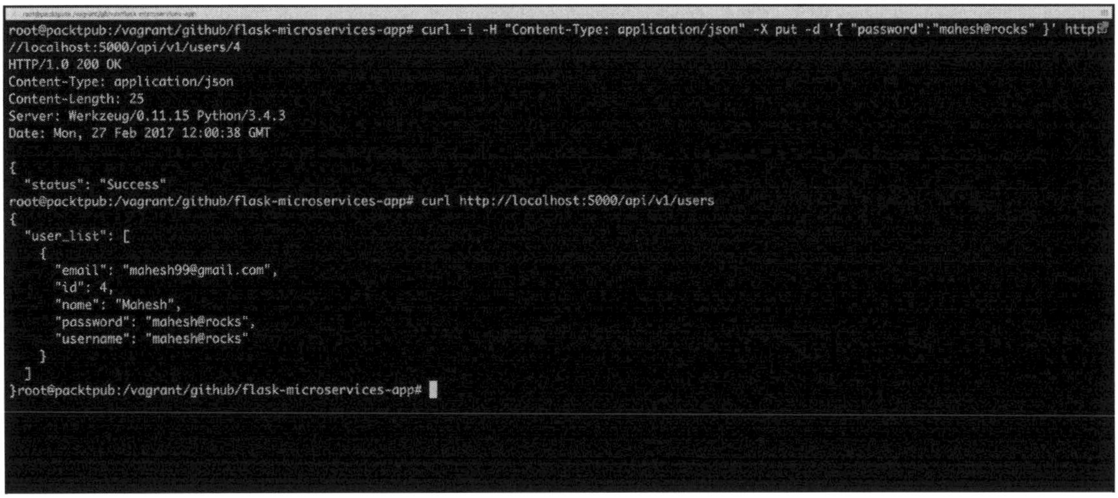
root@packtpub:/vagrant/github/flask-microservices-app# curl -i -H "Content-Type: application/json" -X put -d '{ "password":"mahesh@rocks" }' http:
//localhost:5000/api/v1/users/4
HTTP/1.0 200 OK
Content-Type: application/json
Content-Length: 25
Server: Werkzeug/0.11.15 Python/3.4.3
Date: Mon, 27 Feb 2017 12:00:38 GMT
{
"status": "Success"
root@packtpub:/vagrant/github/flask-microservices-app# curl http://localhost:5000/api/v1/users
{
"user_list": [
{
"email": "mahesh99@gmail.com",
"id": 4,
"name": "Mahesh",
"password": "mahesh@rocks",
"username": "mahesh@rocks"
}
]
}root@packtpub:/vagrant/github/flask-microservices-app#

We have defined our resources that are a part of version `v1`. Now, let's define our next version release, `v2`, which will add a tweet resource to our microservices. Users who are defined in users resources are allowed to perform actions on their tweets. Now, `/api/info` will be shown, as follows:

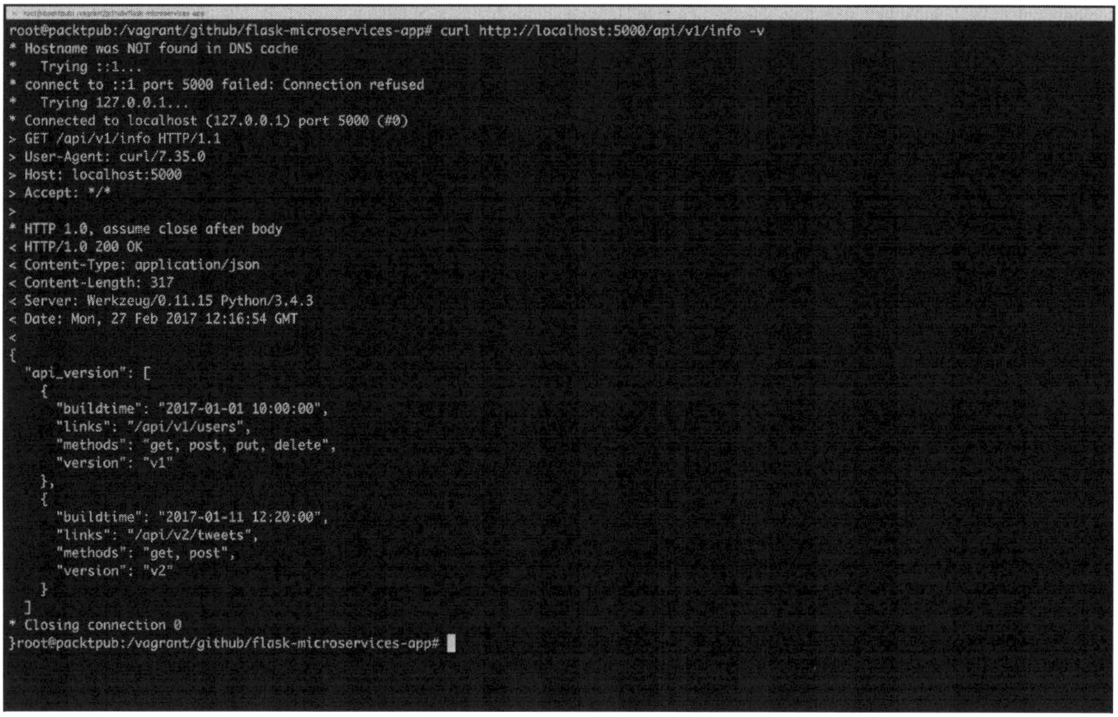

root@packtpub:/vagrant/github/flask-microservices-app# curl http://localhost:5000/api/v1/info -v
* Hostname was NOT found in DNS cache
*   Trying ::1...
* connect to ::1 port 5000 failed: Connection refused
*   Trying 127.0.0.1...
* Connected to localhost (127.0.0.1) port 5000 (#0)
> GET /api/v1/info HTTP/1.1
> User-Agent: curl/7.35.0
> Host: localhost:5000
> Accept: */*
>
* HTTP 1.0, assume close after body
< HTTP/1.0 200 OK
< Content-Type: application/json
< Content-Length: 317
< Server: Werkzeug/0.11.15 Python/3.4.3
< Date: Mon, 27 Feb 2017 12:16:54 GMT
<
{
"api_version": [
{
"buildtime": "2017-01-01 10:00:00",
"links": "/api/v1/users",
"methods": "get, post, put, delete",
"version": "v1"
},
{
"buildtime": "2017-01-11 12:20:00",
"links": "/api/v2/tweets",
"methods": "get, post",
"version": "v2"
}
]
* Closing connection 0
}root@packtpub:/vagrant/github/flask-microservices-app#

Our tweets resource will use the `HTTP` methods as follows:

HTTP Method	**URI**	**Actions**
`GET`	`http://localhost:5000/api/v2/tweets`	This retrieves the tweets list
`GET`	`http://localhost:5000/api/v2/users/[user_id]`	This retrieves a tweet that is given a specific ID

POST	`http://localhost:5000/api/v2/tweets`	This resource will register new tweets with the JSON data passed as part of the API call into the backend database

We can define a tweet as having the following fields:

- `id`: This is the unique identifier for each tweet (Numeric type)
- `username`: This should exist as a user in the users resources (String type)
- `body`: This is the content of the tweet (String type)
- `Tweet_time`: (Specify type)

You can define the preceding tweets resource schema in SQLite 3 as follows:

```
CREATE TABLE tweets(
id integer primary key autoincrement,
username varchar2(30),
body varchar2(30),
tweet_time date);
```

Great! The tweets resource schema is ready; let's create our `GET` methods for the tweets resource.

Building resource tweets methods

In this section, we will be creating APIs for the tweet resource with a different method which will help us perform different operations on the backend database for tweets.

GET /api/v2/tweets

This method lists all the tweets from all the users.

Add the following code to `app.py` to add the route for the `GET` method:

```
@app.route('/api/v2/tweets', methods=['GET'])
def get_tweets():
  return list_tweets()
Let's define list_tweets() function which connects to database and
get us all the tweets and respond back with tweets list
```

```
def list_tweets():
  conn = sqlite3.connect('mydb.db')
  print ("Opened database successfully");
  api_list=[]
  cursor = conn.execute("SELECT username, body, tweet_time, id from
  tweets")
 data = cursor.fetchall()
 if data != 0:
     for row in cursor:
         tweets = {}
         tweets['Tweet By'] = row[0]
         tweets['Body'] = row[1]
         tweets['Timestamp'] = row[2]
 tweets['id'] = row[3]
         api_list.append(tweets)
 else:
     return api_list
 conn.close()
 return jsonify({'tweets_list': api_list})
```

So, now that we've added a function to get the complete tweets list, let's test out the preceding code by making a RESTful API call as follows:

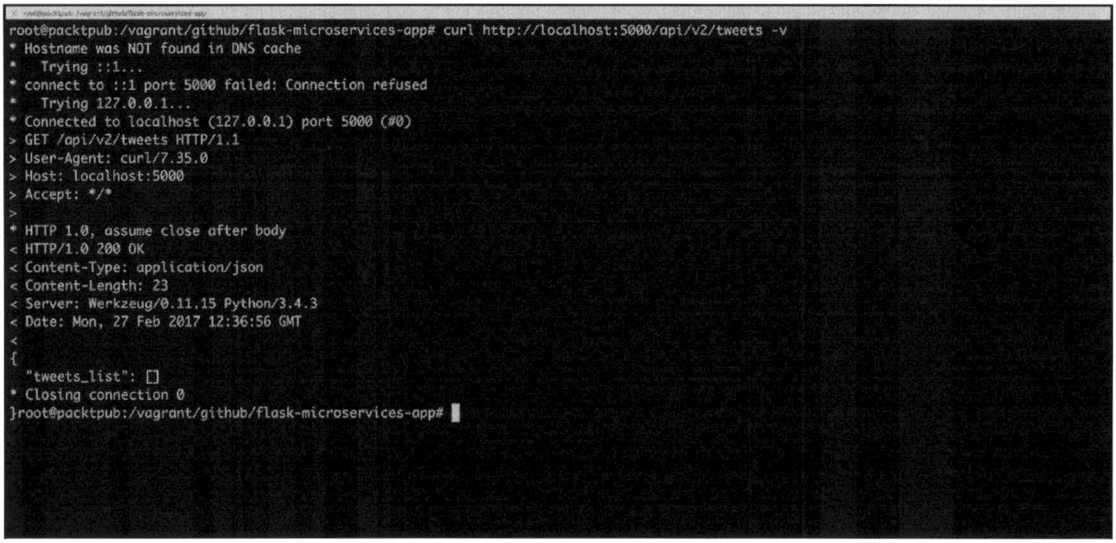

root@packtpub:/vagrant/github/flask-microservices-app# curl http://localhost:5000/api/v2/tweets -v
* Hostname was NOT found in DNS cache
*   Trying ::1...
* connect to ::1 port 5000 failed: Connection refused
*   Trying 127.0.0.1...
* Connected to localhost (127.0.0.1) port 5000 (#0)
> GET /api/v2/tweets HTTP/1.1
> User-Agent: curl/7.35.0
> Host: localhost:5000
> Accept: */*
>
* HTTP 1.0, assume close after body
< HTTP/1.0 200 OK
< Content-Type: application/json
< Content-Length: 23
< Server: Werkzeug/0.11.15 Python/3.4.3
< Date: Mon, 27 Feb 2017 12:36:56 GMT
<
{
"tweets_list": []
* Closing connection 0
}root@packtpub:/vagrant/github/flask-microservices-app#

Currently, we haven't added any tweet, that's why it returned the empty set. Let's add a few tweets.

POST /api/v2/tweets

The POST method adds new tweets by a specified user.

Add the following code to `app.py` to add the route for the `POST` method for the tweets resource:

```
@app.route('/api/v2/tweets', methods=['POST'])
def add_tweets():
  user_tweet = {}
  if not request.json or not 'username' in request.json or not
 'body' in request.json:
    abort(400)
user_tweet['username'] = request.json['username']
user_tweet['body'] = request.json['body']
user_tweet['created_at']=strftime("%Y-%m-%dT%H:%M:%SZ", gmtime())
print (user_tweet)
return  jsonify({'status': add_tweet(user_tweet)}), 200
```

Let's add the definition of `add_tweet(user_tweet)` to add tweets by a specified user, as follows:

```
def add_tweet(new_tweets):
  conn = sqlite3.connect('mydb.db')
  print ("Opened database successfully");
  cursor=conn.cursor()
  cursor.execute("SELECT * from users where username=? ",
(new_tweets['username'],))
data = cursor.fetchall()

if len(data) == 0:
    abort(404)
else:
   cursor.execute("INSERT into tweets (username, body, tweet_time)
values(?,?,?)",(new_tweets['username'],new_tweets['body'],
new_tweets['created_at']))
   conn.commit()
   return "Success"
```

So, now that we've added the function to add the tweets list to the database, let's test out the preceding code by making a RESTful API call as follows:

```
curl -i -H "Content-Type: application/json" -X POST -d '{
"username":"mahesh@rocks","body": "It works" }'
http://localhost:5000/api/v2/tweets
```

We should see the output of the preceding API call similar to the following screenshot:

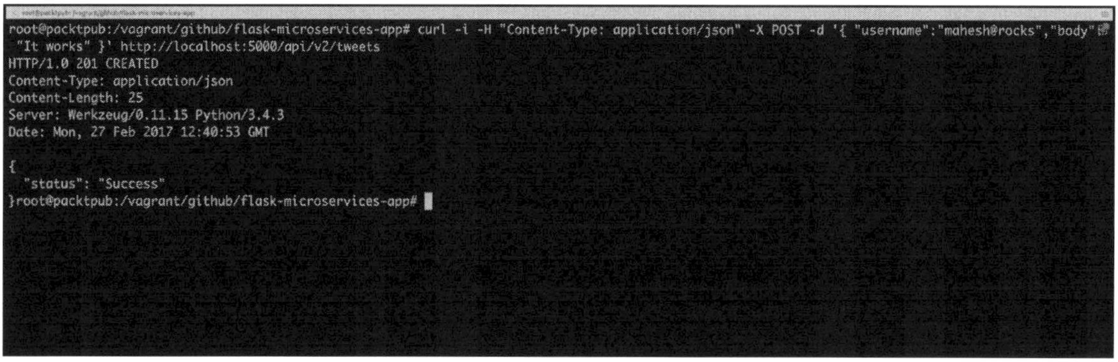

```
root@packtpub:/vagrant/github/flask-microservices-app# curl -i -H "Content-Type: application/json" -X POST -d '{ "username":"mahesh@rocks","body":
 "It works" }' http://localhost:5000/api/v2/tweets
HTTP/1.0 201 CREATED
Content-Type: application/json
Content-Length: 25
Server: Werkzeug/0.11.15 Python/3.4.3
Date: Mon, 27 Feb 2017 12:40:53 GMT

{
  "status": "Success"
}root@packtpub:/vagrant/github/flask-microservices-app#
```

Let's check whether the tweet was added successfully or not by checking the tweets status using:

```
curl http://localhost:5000/api/v2/tweets -v
```

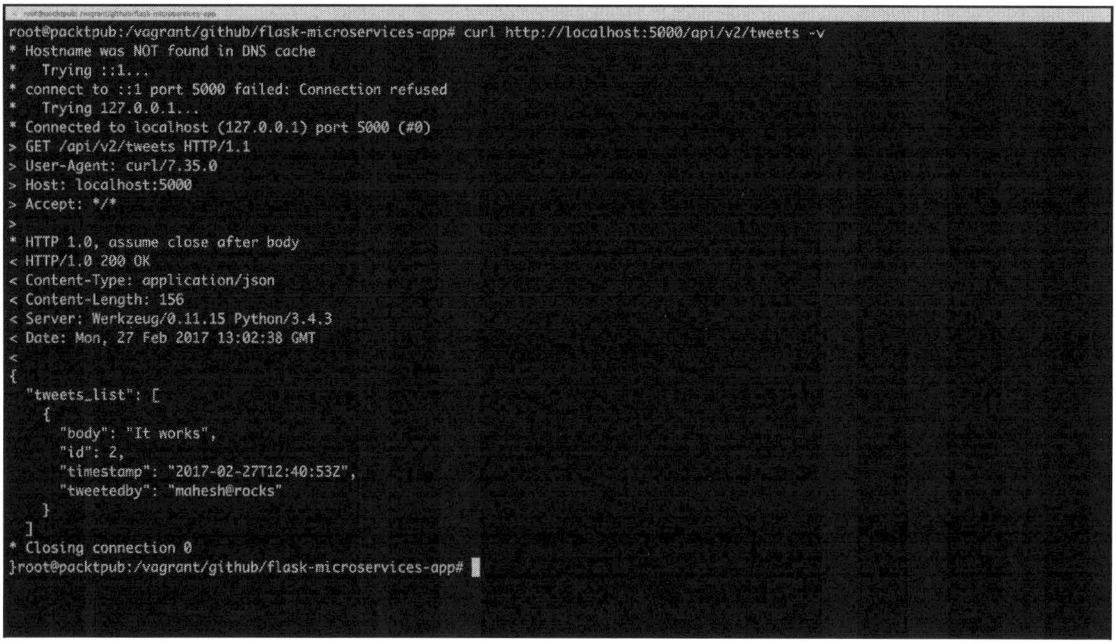

```
root@packtpub:/vagrant/github/flask-microservices-app# curl http://localhost:5000/api/v2/tweets -v
* Hostname was NOT found in DNS cache
*   Trying ::1...
* connect to ::1 port 5000 failed: Connection refused
*   Trying 127.0.0.1...
* Connected to localhost (127.0.0.1) port 5000 (#0)
> GET /api/v2/tweets HTTP/1.1
> User-Agent: curl/7.35.0
> Host: localhost:5000
> Accept: */*
>
* HTTP 1.0, assume close after body
< HTTP/1.0 200 OK
< Content-Type: application/json
< Content-Length: 156
< Server: Werkzeug/0.11.15 Python/3.4.3
< Date: Mon, 27 Feb 2017 13:02:38 GMT
<
{
  "tweets_list": [
    {
      "body": "It works",
      "id": 2,
      "timestamp": "2017-02-27T12:40:53Z",
      "tweetedby": "mahesh@rocks"
    }
  ]
* Closing connection 0
}root@packtpub:/vagrant/github/flask-microservices-app#
```

Now that we have added our first tweet, what if we need to see only a tweet with a certain ID? In that case, we go for the `GET` method with `user_id`.

GET /api/v2/tweets/[id]

The `GET` method lists the tweets made by the specified ID.

Add the following code to `app.py` to add a route for the `GET` method with a specified ID:

```
@app.route('/api/v2/tweets/<int:id>', methods=['GET'])
def get_tweet(id):
  return list_tweet(id)
```

Let's define the `list_tweet()` function, which connects to the database, gets us the tweets with the specified ID, and responds with the JSON data. This is done as follows:

```
def list_tweet(user_id):
  print (user_id)
  conn = sqlite3.connect('mydb.db')
  print ("Opened database successfully");
  api_list=[]
 cursor=conn.cursor()
 cursor.execute("SELECT * from tweets  where id=?",(user_id,))
 data = cursor.fetchall()
 print (data)
 if len(data) == 0:
   abort(404)
else:

   user = {}
   user['id'] = data[0][0]
   user['username'] = data[0][1]
   user['body'] = data[0][2]
   user['tweet_time'] = data[0][3]

conn.close()
return jsonify(user)
```

Now that we've added the function to get a tweet with the specified ID, let's test out the preceding code by making a RESTful API call at:

```
curl http://localhost:5000/api/v2/tweets/2
```

root@packtpub:/vagrant/github/flask-microservices-app# curl http://localhost:5000/api/v2/tweets/2
{
"body": "It works",
"id": 2,
"tweet_time": "2017-02-27T12:40:53Z",
"username": "mahesh@rocks"
}root@packtpub:/vagrant/github/flask-microservices-app#

With this addition of tweets, we have successfully built the RESTful API that collectively works as the microservices needed to access data and perform various actions around it.

Testing the RESTful API

So far, we have been building the RESTful API and hitting the URL for the root URL to see the response and to understand whether the different methods are working properly in the backend or not. Since it's new code, everything should be tested 100% to make sure it works fine in the production environment. In this section, we will write the test cases, which should work individually, and also as a system, to make sure that the complete backend service is good to go for production.

There are different types of testing, which are defined as follows:

- **Functional testing**: This is basically used to test the functionality of a component or a system. We do this test against the functional specification of a component.
- **Non-function testing**: This kind of testing is done against the quality characteristics of a component, which includes efficiency testing, reliability testing, and so on.
- **Structural testing**: This type of testing is used to test the structure of the system. To write test cases, testers are required to have a knowledge of the internal implementations of the code.

In this section, we will write the test cases, specifically, unit test cases, against our application. We will write Python code which will run automatically, test out all the API calls, and respond back with the test results.

Unit testing

A unit test is a piece of code that tests a unit of work or the logical unit in the tested system. The following are the characteristics of unit test cases:

- **Automated**: They should be executed automatically
- **Independent**: They shouldn't have any dependencies
- **Consistent and repeatable**: They should maintain idempotency
- **Maintainable**: They should be easy enough to understand and update

We will use a unit testing framework called **nose**. As an alternative, we can use docstest (`https://docs.python.org/2/library/doctest.html`) for testing.

So, let's install nose using `pip` with the following command:

```
$ pip install nose
```

Or, you can put it in `requirement.txt`, and use the following command to install it:

```
$ pip install -r requirements.txt
```

Now that we have installed the nose test framework, let's begin writing the initial test cases on a separate file, say, `flask_test.py`, as follows:

```
 from app import app
 import unittest

class FlaskappTests(unittest.TestCase):
  def setUp(self):
      # creates a test client
      self.app = app.test_client()
      # propagate the exceptions to the test client
      self.app.testing = True
```

The preceding code will test the app and initialize `self.app` with our app.

Let's write our test case to get the response code for `GET /api/v1/users` and add it to our FlaskappTest class as follows:

```
def test_users_status_code(self):
    # sends HTTP GET request to the application
    result = self.app.get('/api/v1/users')
    # assert the status code of the response
    self.assertEqual(result.status_code, 200)
```

The preceding code will test whether we get the response on `/api/v1/users` as `200`; if not, it will throw an error and our test will fail. As you can see, as this code doesn't have any dependency from any other code, we will call it as a unit test case.

Now, how to run this code? Since we have installed the nose testing framework, simply execute the following command from the current working directory of the test case file (in this case, `flask_test.py`):

```
$ nosetests
```

Great! Similarly, let's write more test cases for the RESTful API for the different methods of the resources that we created earlier in this chapter.

- The GET `/api/v2/tweets` test case is given as follows:

```
def test_tweets_status_code(self):
    # sends HTTP GET request to the application
    result = self.app.get('/api/v2/tweets')
    # assert the status code of the response
    self.assertEqual(result.status_code, 200)
```

- The GET `/api/v1/info` test case is as follows:

```
def test_tweets_status_code(self):
    # sends HTTP GET request to the application
    result = self.app.get('/api/v1/info')
    # assert the status code of the response
    self.assertEqual(result.status_code, 200)
```

- The POST `/api/v1/users` test case is written like this:

```
def test_addusers_status_code(self):
    # sends HTTP POST request to the application
    result = self.app.post('/api/v1/users', data='{"username":
"manish21", "email":"manishtest@gmail.com", "password": "test123"}',
content_type='application/json')
    print (result)
    # assert the status code of the response
    self.assertEquals(result.status_code, 201)
```

- The PUT `/api/v1/users` test case is as follows:

```
def test_updusers_status_code(self):
    # sends HTTP PUT request to the application
    # on the specified path
    result = self.app.put('/api/v1/users/4', data='{"password":
"testing123"}', content_type='application/json')
    # assert the status code of the response
    self.assertEquals(result.status_code, 200)
```

- The POST `/api/v1/tweets` test case is as follows:

```
def test_addtweets_status_code(self):
    # sends HTTP GET request to the application
    # on the specified path
    result = self.app.post('/api/v2/tweets', data='{"username":
"mahesh@rocks", "body":"Wow! Is it working #testing"}',
content_type='application/json')

    # assert the status code of the response
    self.assertEqual(result.status_code, 201)
```

- The DELETE `/api/v1/users` test case is given as follows:

```
def test_delusers_status_code(self):
    # sends HTTP Delete request to the application
    result = self.app.delete('/api/v1/users', data='{"username":
"manish21"}', content_type='application/json')
    # assert the status code of the response
    self.assertEquals(result.status_code, 200)
```

Similarly, you can write more test cases based on your thinking to make these RESTful APIs more reliable and bug-free.

Let's execute all of them together and check whether all the tests have passed. The following screenshot shows the test result to the `flask_test.py` script:

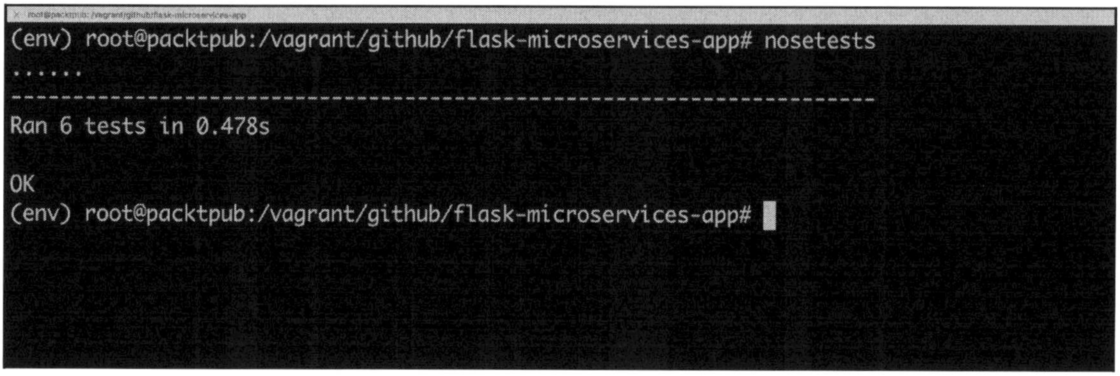

(env) root@packtpub:/vagrant/github/flask-microservices-app# nosetests
......
Ran 6 tests in 0.478s
OK
(env) root@packtpub:/vagrant/github/flask-microservices-app#

Awesome! Now that all our tests have passed, we are good to go for the next level of creating web pages around these RESTful API's.

Summary

In this chapter, we focused on writing lots of code to build our microservices. We basically got an understanding of how the RESTful APIs work. We also saw how we can extend these APIs and make sure that we understand the `HTTP` response by the response given by these APIs. Moreover, you learned how to write test cases, which are most important to ensure that our code works well and is good to go for the production environment.

3
Building a Web Application in Python

In the previous chapter, we focused on building our microservices, which is, basically, backend RESTful APIs, and testing it to make sure the response will be as expected. So far, we have been testing these RESTful APIs using curl, or maybe, using a testing framework, that is, nose, unittest2, and so on. In this chapter, we will create some HTML pages and write a JavaScript REST client, which will interact with microservices.

The topics that we will cover in this chapter are as follows:

- Building HTML pages and data binding
- JavaScript REST client using knockout.js

In this chapter, we will create a client application which will need to create dynamic content that is gathered from an HTML web page and, based on the actions of the user, will update the content as a response on the backend service.

As a developer, you must have come across many application frameworks that adopt the MVC pattern. It is a large category, which is a combination of **MVC** (**Model View Controller**), **MVP** (**Model View Presenter**), and **MVVM** (**Model View ViewModel**).

In our case, we will use **knockout.js**, which is a library in JavaScript based on the MVVM pattern that helps developers build rich and responsive websites. It can work as a standalone or used along with other JavaScript libraries, such as jQuery. Knockout.js binds the UI with the underlying JavaScript model. The models are updated based on the changes in the UI and vice versa, which is basically two-way data binding.

In knockout.js, we will be dealing with two important concepts: Binding and Observables.

> Knockout.js is a JavaScript library that is generally used to develop desktop-like web applications. It is useful, as it provides a responsive mechanism that syncs with your data sources. It provides a two-way binding mechanism between your data model and user interface. Read more about knockout.js at `http://knockoutjs.com/documentation/introduction.html`.

In this chapter, we will create web applications to add a user and tweets to the database, and validate them.

Getting started with applications

Let's get started with creating a basic HTML template. Create a directory named `template` in your app root location; we will create all our future templates inside this directory.

Now, let's create the basic skeleton for the `adduser.html` file as follows:

```
<!DOCTYPE html>
<html>
  <head>
    <title>Tweet Application</title>
  </head>
  <body>
    <div class="navbar">
     <div class="navbar-inner">
       <a class="brand" href="#">Tweet App Demo</a>
     </div>
    </div>
   <div id="main" class="container">

     Main content here!

   </div>
  <meta name="viewport" content="width=device-width, initial-
   scale=1.0">
  <link href="http://netdna.bootstrapcdn.com/twitter-
```

```
    bootstrap/2.3.2/css/bootstrap-combined.min.css"
    rel="stylesheet">
   <script src="http://ajax.aspnetcdn.com/ajax/jquery/jquery-
    1.9.0.js"></script>
   <script src="http://netdna.bootstrapcdn.com/twitter-
     bootstrap/2.3.2/js/bootstrap.min.js"></script>
   <script src="http://ajax.aspnetcdn.com/ajax/knockout/knockout-
     2.2.1.js"></script>
   </body>
</html>
```

As you can see in the preceding code, we have specified a couple of `.js` scripts that are needed to make our HTML responsive. This is similar to twitter-bootstrap, which has a `<meta name="viewport">` attribute to help scale the page based on the browser dimensions.

Creating application users

Before we start writing our web page, we need to create a route to create a user, as follows:

```
from flask import render_template

@app.route('/adduser')
def adduser():
 return render_template('adduser.html')
```

Now that we have created the route, let's create a form in `adduser.html`, which will ask for the required information related to the user and help them submit the information:

```
<html>
  <head>
    <title>Twitter Application</title>
  </head>
  <body>
   <form >
     <div class="navbar">
      <div class="navbar-inner">
        <a class="brand" href="#">Tweet App Demo</a>
      </div>
    </div>
    <div id="main" class="container">

     <table class="table table-striped">
       Name: <input placeholder="Full Name of user" type "text"/>
       </div>
```

```
          <div>
            Username: <input placeholder="Username" type="username">
            </input>
          </div>
          <div>
            email: <input placeholder="Email id" type="email"></input>
          </div>
          <div>
            password: <input type="password" placeholder="Password">
            </input>
          </div>
           <button type="submit">Add User</button>
         </table>
       </form>
      <script src="http://cdnjs.cloudflare.com/ajax/libs/
       jquery/1.8.3/jquery.min.js"></script>
     <script src="http://cdnjs.cloudflare.com/ajax/libs/knockout
       /2.2.0/knockout-min.js"></script>
     <link href="http://netdna.bootstrapcdn.com/twitter-
      bootstrap/2.3.2/css/bootstrap-combined.min.css"
      rel="stylesheet">
     <!-- <script src="http://ajax.aspnetcdn.com/ajax/jquery/jquery-
      1.9.0.js"></script> -->
    <script src="http://netdna.bootstrapcdn.com/twitter-
      bootstrap/2.3.2/js/bootstrap.min.js"></script>
  </body>
</html>
```

Currently, the preceding HTML page shows only empty fields, and if you try to submit it with data, it won't work, since no data binding is done with the backend service as yet.

Now we are ready to create JavaScript, which will make a REST call to the backend service, and add the user content provided from the HTML page.

Working with Observables and AJAX

In order to get the data from the RESTful API, we will use AJAX. Observables keep a track of the changes made on the data and reflect them, automatically, on all the locations where it is used and defined by `ViewModel`.

By using Observables, it becomes very easy to make the UI and `ViewModel` communicate dynamically.

Let's create a file named `app.js`, which has Observables declared, inside the static directory with the following code--if the directory does not exist, create it:

```
function User(data) {
  this.id = ko.observable(data.id);
  this.name = ko.observable(data.name);
  this.username = ko.observable(data.username);
  this.email = ko.observable(data.email);
  this.password = ko.observable(data.password);
}

function UserListViewModel() {
 var self = this;
 self.user_list = ko.observableArray([]);
 self.name = ko.observable();
 self.username= ko.observable();
 self.email= ko.observable();
 self.password= ko.observable();
 self.addUser = function() {
  self.save();
  self.name("");
  self.username("");
  self.email("");
  self.password("");
 };
self.save = function() {
  return $.ajax({
  url: '/api/v1/users',
  contentType: 'application/json',
  type: 'POST',
  data: JSON.stringify({
     'name': self.name(),
     'username': self.username(),
     'email': self.email(),
     'password': self.password()
  }),
  success: function(data) {
     alert("success")
          console.log("Pushing to users array");
          self.push(new User({ name: data.name, username:
          data.username,email: data.email ,password:
           data.password}));
          return;
  },
  error: function() {
     return console.log("Failed");
   }
 });
```

```
    };
    }

ko.applyBindings(new UserListViewModel());
```

I understand it's a lot of code; let's understand the usage of each part of the preceding code.

When you submit your content on the HTML page, a request will be received at `app.js`, and the following code will handle the request:

```
ko.applyBindings(new UserListViewModel());
```

It creates the model and sends the content to the following function:

```
self.addUser = function() {
  self.save();
  self.name("");
  self.username("");
  self.email("");
  self.password("");
};
```

The preceding `addUser` function calls the `self.save` function with a passing data object. The `save` function makes an AJAX RESTful call to the backend services and performs the `POST` operation with the data gathered from the HTML pages. It then clears the content of the HTML pages as well.

Our work is not yet done. As we mentioned earlier, it is two-way data binding, so we need to send the data from the HTML side as well, so that it can be processed further in the database.

In the script section, add the following line, which will identify the `.js` file path:

```
<script src="{{ url_for('static', filename='app.js') }}"></script>
```

Binding data for the adduser template

Data binding is useful to bind your data with the UI. The property from the UI will be processed only for the first time if we do not use Observables. In this case, it cannot update automatically based on the underlying data update. To achieve this, bindings must be referred to the Observable properties.

Now we need to bind our data with the form and its field, as shown in the following code:

```
<form data-bind="submit: addUser">
 <div class="navbar">
   <div class="navbar-inner">
       <a class="brand" href="#">Tweet App Demo</a>
   </div>
 </div>
 <div id="main" class="container">
  <table class="table table-striped">
   Name: <input data-bind="value: name" placeholder="Full Name of
   user" type "text"/>
 </div>
 <div>
   Username: <input data-bind="value: username"
   placeholder="Username" type="username"></input>
 </div>
<div>
  email: <input data-bind="value: email" placeholder="Email id"
  type="email"></input>
</div>
<div>
   password: <input data-bind="value: password" type="password"
   placeholder="Password"></input>
</div>
   <button type="submit">Add User</button>
 </table>
</form>
```

Now we are ready to add our users through the template. However, how will we validate whether the user is added successfully to our database or not? One way would be to manually log in to the database. However, since we are working on a web application, let's show our data (present in the database) on the web page itself--even the newly added entries.

In order to read the database and get the user list, add the following code to `app.js`:

```
$.getJSON('/api/v1/users', function(userModels) {
  var t = $.map(userModels.user_list, function(item) {
    return new User(item);
  });
 self.user_list(t);
});
```

Now we need to make changes in `adduser.html` to show our user list. For that, let's add the following code:

```
<ul data-bind="foreach: user_list, visible: user_list().length >
0">
  <li>
    <p data-bind="text: name"></p>
    <p data-bind="text: username"></p>
    <p data-bind="text: email"></p>
   <p data-bind="text: password"></p>
 </li>
</ul>
```

Awesome! We are done with adding the web page which will create new users for our application. It will look something like this:

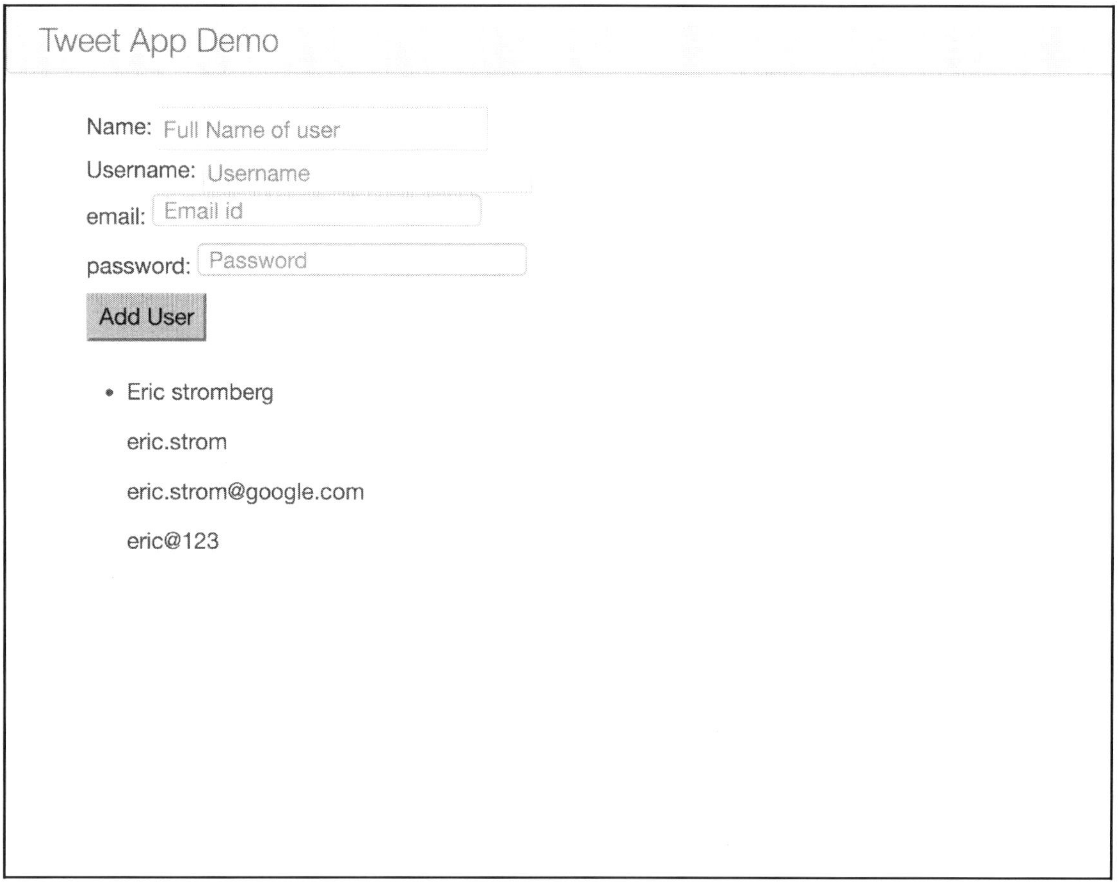

Creating tweets from users

Before we start writing our web page, we need to create a route to create tweets. This can be done as follows:

```
from flask import render_template

@app.route('/addtweets')
def addtweetjs():
 return render_template('addtweets.html')
```

Now that, we have created the route, let's create another form in `addtweets.html`, which will ask the user for the required information related to tweets, and help them submit the information:

```
<html>
 <head>
  <title>Twitter Application</title>
 </head>
<body>
<form >
 <div class="navbar">
   <div class="navbar-inner">
       <a class="brand" href="#">Tweet App Demo</a>
   </div>
  </div>
  <div id="main" class="container">
   <table class="table table-striped">
     Username: <input placeholder="Username" type="username">
      </input>
  </div>
  <div>
    body: <textarea placeholder="Content of tweet" type="text">
    </textarea>
  </div>
  <div>
  </div>
   <button type="submit">Add Tweet</button>
  </table>

 </form>
  <script src="http://cdnjs.cloudflare.com/ajax/libs/
   jquery/1.8.3/jquery.min.js"></script>
  <script src="http://cdnjs.cloudflare.com/ajax/libs/
    knockout/2.2.0/knockout-min.js"></script>
   <link href="http://netdna.bootstrapcdn.com/twitter-
     bootstrap/2.3.2/css/bootstrap-combined.min.css"
```

```
    rel="stylesheet">
  <!-- <script src="http://ajax.aspnetcdn.com/ajax/jquery/jquery-
    1.9.0.js"></script> -->
  <script src="http://netdna.bootstrapcdn.com/twitter-
    bootstrap/2.3.2/js/bootstrap.min.js"></script>
 </body>
</html>
```

Note that currently, this form doesn't have data binding to communicate with the RESTful services.

Working on Observables with AJAX for the addtweet template

Let's develop a JavaScript that will make a REST call to the backend service and add the tweet content provided from the HTML page.

Let's create a file with the name `tweet.js` inside the static directory that we created earlier with the following code:

```
function Tweet(data) {
  this.id = ko.observable(data.id);
  this.username = ko.observable(data.tweetedby);
  this.body = ko.observable(data.body);
  this.timestamp = ko.observable(data.timestamp);
}

function TweetListViewModel() {
  var self = this;
  self.tweets_list = ko.observableArray([]);
  self.username= ko.observable();
  self.body= ko.observable();

  self.addTweet = function() {
  self.save();
  self.username("");
  self.body("");
   };

  $.getJSON('/api/v2/tweets', function(tweetModels) {
  var t = $.map(tweetModels.tweets_list, function(item) {
    return new Tweet(item);
  });
  self.tweets_list(t);
  });
```

```
self.save = function() {
 return $.ajax({
 url: '/api/v2/tweets',
 contentType: 'application/json',
 type: 'POST',
 data: JSON.stringify({
    'username': self.username(),
    'body': self.body(),
 }),
 success: function(data) {
    alert("success")
         console.log("Pushing to users array");
         self.push(new Tweet({ username: data.username,body:
         data.body}));
         return;
 },
 error: function() {
    return console.log("Failed");
 }
});
 };
}

ko.applyBindings(new TweetListViewModel());
```

Let's understand the usage of each part of this last code.

When you submit your content on the HTML page, a request will come to `tweet.js`, and the following part of the code will handle the request:

```
ko.applyBindings(new TweetListViewModel());
```

The preceding code snippet creates the model and sends the content to the following function:

```
self.addTweet = function() {
  self.save();
  self.username("");
  self.body("");
  };
```

The preceding `addTweet` function calls the `self.save` function with a passing data object. The save function makes an AJAX RESTful call to the backend services, and performs the `POST` operation with the data gathered from the HTML pages. It then clears the content of the HTML pages as well.

In order to show data on the web page, and to keep the data on it in sync with the data in the backend service, the following code is needed:

```
function Tweet(data) {
  this.id = ko.observable(data.id);
  this.username = ko.observable(data.tweetedby);
  this.body = ko.observable(data.body);
  this.timestamp = ko.observable(data.timestamp);
}
```

Our work is not yet done. As we mentioned earlier, it is two-way data binding, so, we will need to send the data from the HTML side as well, so that it can be processed further in the database.

In the script section, add the following line, which will identify the `.js` file with the path:

```
<script src="{{ url_for('static', filename='tweet.js') }}"></script>
```

Data binding for the addtweet template

Once this is done, we need to now bind our data with the form and its field, as shown in the following code:

```
<form data-bind="submit: addTweet">
  <div class="navbar">
    <div class="navbar-inner">
       <a class="brand" href="#">Tweet App Demo</a>
    </div>
   </div>
   <div id="main" class="container">

    <table class="table table-striped">
      Username: <input data-bind="value: username"
      placeholder="Username" type="username"></input>
   </div>
   <div>
     body: <textarea data-bind="value: body" placeholder="Content
     of tweet" type="text"></textarea>
   </div>
   <div>
```

```
    </div>
    <button type="submit">Add Tweet</button>
    </table>
</form>
```

Now we are ready to add our tweet through the template. We perform validation for tweets just as we performed validation for users.

In order to read the database and get the tweet list, add the following code to `tweet.js`:

```
$.getJSON('/api/v2/tweets', function(tweetModels) {
  var t = $.map(tweetModels.tweets_list, function(item) {
  return new Tweet(item);
 });
  self.tweets_list(t);
 });
```

Now, we need to make changes in `addtweets.html` to show our tweet list. For that, let's add the following code:

```
<ul data-bind="foreach: tweets_list, visible: tweets_list().length
> 0">
 <li>
   <p data-bind="text: username"></p>
   <p data-bind="text: body"></p>
   <p data-bind="text: timestamp"></p>

 </li>
</ul>
```

Awesome! Let's test it out. It will look something like this:

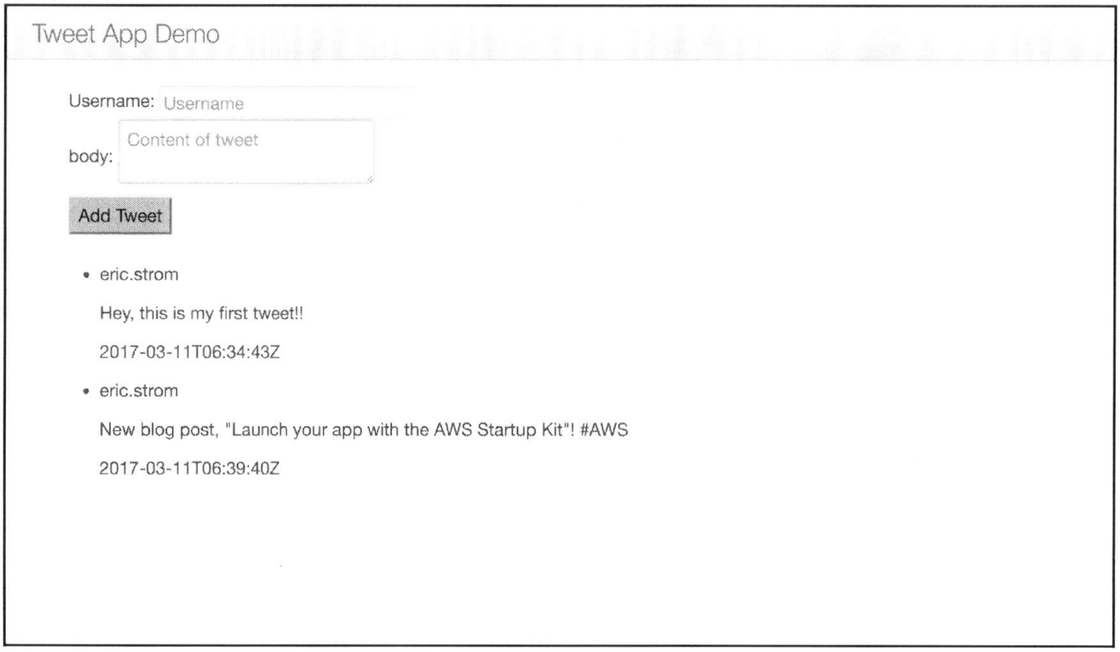

In a similar fashion, you can extend this use case by deleting users from the web page application, or can update user information in the backend services.

Also, to know more about the knockout.js library, go through the live examples at `http://knockoutjs.com/examples/helloWorld.html`, which will help you gain a better understanding, and help you with implementing it in your application.

We created these web pages to make sure our microservices work and to give you an understanding about how a web application is developed generally; and, as developers, we can create these web applications based on our own use case as well.

CORS - Cross-Origin Resource Sharing

CORS helps maintain data integrity between the API server and the client for the API request.

The idea behind using CORS is that the server and client should have enough information about each other so that they can authenticate each other, and transfer data over a secure channel using the HTTP header.

When a client makes an API call, it is either a GET or POST request, where the body is usually text/plain with headers called **Origin**--this includes protocol, domain name, and port with respect to the requesting page. When the server acknowledges the request, and sends the response along with the `Access-Control-Allow-Origin` header to the same Origin, it makes sure the response is received at the correct Origin.

In this way, resource sharing happens between Origins.

Almost all browsers now support CORS, which includes IE 8+, Firefox 3.5+, and Chrome.

Now, since we have the web application ready, but it is not CORS-enabled yet, let's enable it.

Firstly, you need to install the module for CORS in Flask using the following command:

```
$pip install flask-cors
```

The preceding package exposes a Flask extension which, by default, enables CORS support on all the routes for all Origins and methods. Once the package is installed, let's include it in `app.py` as follows:

```
from flask_cors import CORS, cross_origin
```

To enable CORS, you need to add the following line:

```
CORS(app)
```

That's it. Now this CORS is enabled for all the resources in your Flask application.

In case you want to enable CORS on specific resources, then add the following code with your specific resource:

```
cors = CORS(app, resources={r"/api/*": {"origins": "*"}})
```

Currently, we don't have a domain setup, but we are working at the localhost level. You can test CORS by adding a custom domain in the domain name server as follows:

```
127.0.0.1    <your-domain-name>
```

Now, if you try to access this `<your-domain-name>`, it should be able to work properly with this domain name, and you will be able to access the resource.

Session management

Sessions are a sequence of request and response transactions associated with a single user. The sessions are usually maintained on the server level by authenticating the user and keeping track of his/her activity over the web page.

Session with each client is assigned a session ID. Sessions are generally stored on top of cookies and the server signs them cryptographically--they are decrypted by the Flask application using the secret key for a temporary duration.

Currently, we haven't set up authentication--we will be defining it in `Chapter 8`, *Securing the Web Application*. So, at this point in time, we will create the session by asking about the username accessing the web page and making sure that the user is identified using the sessions.

Now let's create a web page, say, `main.html`, which will have a URL to create the session if it is needed to be set up, and routes to perform operations on the backend services. You could clear the session if it already exists. See the following code:

```
<html>
  <head>
    <title>Twitter App Demo</title>
    <link rel=stylesheet type=text/css href="{{ url_for('static',
    filename='style.css') }}">
</head>
<body>
    <div id="container">
      <div class="title">
        <h1></h1>
      </div>
      <div id="content">
        {% if session['name'] %}
        Your name seems to be <strong>{{session['name']}}</strong>.
       <br/>
        {% else %}
        Please set username by clicking it <a href="{{
        url_for('addname') }}">here</a>.<br/>
        {% endif %}
       Visit <a href="{{ url_for('adduser') }}">this for adding new
       application user </a> or <a href="{{ url_for('addtweetjs')
       }}">this to add new tweets</a> page to interact with RESTFUL
       API.

       <br /><br />
       <strong><a href="{{ url_for('clearsession') }}">Clear
       session</a></strong>
```

```
            </div>
            </div>
        </div>
      </body>
    </html>
```

Currently in this web page, a few URLs, such as `clearsession` and `addname` won't work, since we haven't set up the web page and route for them.

Also, we haven't set up the route for the `main.html` web page; let's first add it in `app.py`, as follows:

```
@app.route('/')

def main():
  return render_template('main.html')
```

Since we have added the route for `main.html`, let's add the route for `addname` in `app.py`, as follows:

```
@app.route('/addname')

def addname():
if request.args.get('yourname'):
 session['name'] = request.args.get('yourname')
 # And then redirect the user to the main page
   return redirect(url_for('main'))

 else:
   return render_template('addname.html', session=session)
```

As you can see in the preceding route, it calls `addname.html`, which we haven't created yet. Let's create the `addname` template with the following code:

```
 <html>
  <head>
    <title>Twitter App Demo</title>
    <link rel=stylesheet type=text/css href="{{ url_for('static',
     filename='style.css') }}">
  </head>
<body>
    <div id="container">
        <div class="title">
            <h1>Enter your name</h1>
        </div>
     <div id="content">
       <form method="get" action="{{ url_for('addname') }}">
         <label for="yourname">Please enter your name:</label>
```

```
            <input type="text" name="yourname" /><br />
            <input type="submit" />
          </form>
        </div>
        <div class="title">
               <h1></h1>
        </div>
        <code><pre>
        </pre></code>
        </div>
      </div>
    </body>
  </html>
```

Great! Now we can set the session using the preceding code; you will see a web page that looks something like this:

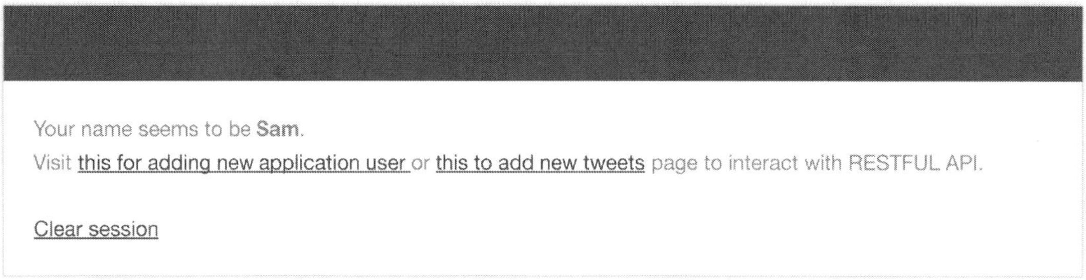

Now, what if we need to clear sessions? Since we are already calling the `clearsession` function from the main web page, we need to create a route in `app.py`, which further calls the session's `Clear` inbuilt function as follows:

```
@app.route('/clear')

 def clearsession():
  # Clear the session
  session.clear()
  # Redirect the user to the main page
  return redirect(url_for('main'))
```

This is how we can set the session, maintain it for users, and clear the session, as per the requirement.

Cookies

Cookies are similar to sessions, other than the fact that they are maintained on the client computer in the form of a text file; whereas, sessions are maintained on the server side.

Their main purpose is to keep track of the client's usage and, based on their activity, improve the experience by understanding the cookies.

The cookies attribute is stored in the response object, which is a collection of key-value pairs that have cookies, variables, and their respective values.

We can set the cookies using the `set_cookie()` function of the response object to store a cookie as follows:

```
@app.route('/set_cookie')
def cookie_insertion():
  redirect_to_main = redirect('/')
  response = current_app.make_response(redirect_to_main )
  response.set_cookie('cookie_name',value='values')
  return response
```

Similarly, reading cookies is pretty easy; the `get()` function will help you get the cookies if it is already set, as shown here:

```
import flask
cookie = flask.request.cookies.get('my_cookie')
```

If the cookie exists, it will get assigned to the cookie, and if not, then the cookie will return `None`.

Summary

In this chapter, you learned how to integrate your microservices with the web application using a JavaScript library such as knockout.js. You learned about the MVVM pattern, and how these can be helpful to create fully developed web applications. You also learned user management concepts, such as cookies and sessions, and how to make use of them.

In the next chapter, we will try to make our database side stronger and secure by moving it from SQLite to other NoSQL database services, such as MongoDB.

4
Interacting Data Services

In the previous chapter, we built up our application using JavaScript/HTML and integrated it with RESTful APIs with AJAX. You also learned how to set cookies on the client and sessions on the server for a better experience for users. In this chapter, we will focus on improving our backend database by using a NoSQL database, such as MongoDB instead of an SQLite database, which we are currently using, or a MySQL database, and integrate our application with it.

The topics that we will cover in this chapter are as follows:

- Setting up MongoDB service
- Integrating an application with MongoDB

MongoDB - How it is advantageous, and why are we using it?

Before we begin with the MongoDB installation, let's understand why we have chosen the MongoDB database and what it is needed for.

Let's take a look at the advantages of MongoDB over RDBMS:

- **Flexible schema**: MongoDB is a document database in which one collection holds multiple documents. We don't need to define the schema of the documents prior to inserting the data, which means MongoDB defines the document's schema based on the data inserted into the documents; whereas, in an RDBMS, we need to define the schema of the tables before inserting data into it.
- **Less complexity**: There are no complex joins in MongoDB, as we have in the case of RDBMS (for example: MySQL) databases.
- **Easier scalability**: It is very easy to scale out MongoDB as compared to an RDBMS.
- **Fast accessibility**: There is faster retrieval of data in MongoDB as compared to an RDBMS, that is, the MySQL database.
- **Dynamic querying**: MongoDB supports dynamic queries on documents, being a document-based query language, which makes it advantageous over other RDBMS, which could be MySQL.

The following are the reasons why we should use MongoDB:

- MongoDB stores data in JSON-style documents, which makes it easy to integrate with the application
- We can set an index on any file and property
- MongoDB does auto-sharding, which makes it easy to manage and enables it to be faster
- MongoDB provides replication and high availability when used in a cluster

There are different use cases in which to use MongoDB. Let's check them here:

- Big data
- User data management
- Content delivery and management

The following image shows the architecture diagram of MongoDB integration with your web application:

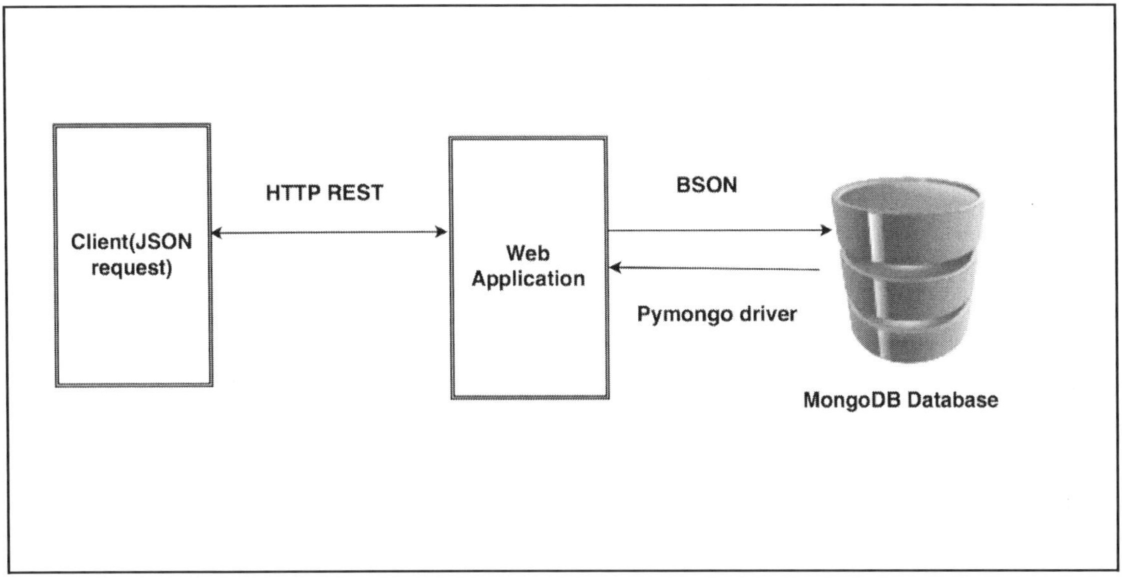

MongoDB terminology

Let's look at the different terminologies of MongoDB, which are listed next:

- **Database**: This is similar to the database that we have in **RDBMS (Relational Database Management System),** but, instead of tables, in MongoDB a database is a physical container of collections. MongoDB can have multiple databases.
- **Collections**: This is basically a combination of documents that has its own schema. Collections don't contribute toward the schema of documents. It's quite equivalent to the tables in RDBMS.
- **Document**: This is similar to a tuple/row in an RDBMS. It's a set of key-value pairs. They have a dynamic schema, where each document may or may not have the same schema within a single collection. They may have different fields as well.

The following code is a sample collection for your understanding:

```
{
    _id : ObjectId(58ccdd1a19b08311417b14ee),
    body : 'New blog post,Launch your app with the AWS Startup Kit!
    #AWS',
    timestamp : "2017-03-11T06:39:40Z",
    id : 18,
    tweetedby : "eric.strom"
}
```

MongoDB represents JSON documents in a binary-encoded format called **BSON**.

Setting up MongoDB

In the current scenario, we are working on the Ubuntu workstation, so let's install MongoDB on Ubuntu as follows.

We will use the Ubuntu package management tool, such as `apt`, to install the MongoDB packages by authenticating the distributor-signed packages with the GPG keys.

To import the GPG keys, use the following command:

```
$ sudo apt-key adv --keyserver hkp://keyserver.ubuntu.com:80 --recv
EA312927
```

Next, we need to set the MongoDB repository path to our operating system, as follows:

```
$ echo "deb http://repo.mongodb.org/apt/ubuntu trusty/mongodb-org/3.2
multiverse" | sudo tee /etc/apt/sources.list.d/mongodb-org-3.2.list
```

Once this is added, we need to update our Ubuntu repository as follows:

```
$ sudo apt-get update
```

Now that the repository is updated, let's install the latest stable MongoDB release using the following command:

```
$ sudo apt-get install -y mongodb-org
```

Once it is installed, the MongoDB service should run on port `27017`. We can check the service status using the following command:

```
$ sudo service mongodb status
```

If it does not run, you can start the service by executing the following command:

```
$ sudo service mongodb start
```

Great! Now we have installed MongoDB on our local machine. At this point in time, we only need a standalone MongoDB instance, but if you want to create a shared MongoDB cluster, then you can follow the steps defined on the following link:

`https://docs.mongodb.com/manual/tutorial/deploy-shard-cluster/`

So, now that we have enabled the MongoDB service on our machine, we are good to go to create a database on top of it.

Initializing the MongoDB database

Previously, when we were creating a database in SQLite3, we needed to create a database and define the schema of tables manually. Since MongoDB is schemaless, we will directly add new documents, and collections will get created automatically. Also, in this case, we will initialize the database using Python only.

Before we add new documents into MongoDB, we need to install the Python driver for it, that is, `pymongo`.

Add the `pymongo` driver to `requirements.txt`, and then install it using the `pip` package manager as follows:

```
$echo "pymongo==3.4.0" >> requirements.txt
$ pip install -r requirements.txt
```

Once it is installed, we will import it by adding the following line to `app.py`:

```
from pymongo import MongoClient
```

Now that we have imported the MongoDB driver for Python, we will create a connection to MongoDB and define a function in `app.py`, which will initialize the database with initial **data documents**, as follows:

```
connection = MongoClient("mongodb://localhost:27017/")
def create_mongodatabase():
try:
   dbnames = connection.database_names()
   if 'cloud_native' not in dbnames:
       db = connection.cloud_native.users
       db_tweets = connection.cloud_native.tweets
       db_api = connection.cloud_native.apirelease
```

```
        db.insert({
        "email": "eric.strom@google.com",
        "id": 33,
        "name": "Eric stromberg",
        "password": "eric@123",
        "username": "eric.strom"
        })

        db_tweets.insert({
        "body": "New blog post,Launch your app with the AWS Startup
        Kit! #AWS",
        "id": 18,
        "timestamp": "2017-03-11T06:39:40Z",
        "tweetedby": "eric.strom"
        })

        db_api.insert( {
          "buildtime": "2017-01-01 10:00:00",
          "links": "/api/v1/users",
          "methods": "get, post, put, delete",
          "version": "v1"
        })
        db_api.insert( {
          "buildtime": "2017-02-11 10:00:00",
          "links": "api/v2/tweets",
          "methods": "get, post",
          "version": "2017-01-10 10:00:00"
        })
        print ("Database Initialize completed!")
    else:
        print ("Database already Initialized!")
    except:
        print ("Database creation failed!!")
```

It is recommended that you initialize your resource collections with some documents in the collection so that we get some response data when we begin testing the APIs, otherwise, you can go ahead without initializing the collections.

The preceding function should be called before starting the application; our main function will be something like this:

```
if __name__ == '__main__':
  create_mongodatabase()
  app.run(host='0.0.0.0', port=5000, debug=True)
```

Integrating microservices with MongoDB

Since we have initialized our MongoDB database, it's time to rewrite our microservices functions to store and retrieve data from MongoDB instead of SQLite 3.

Previously, we used the `curl` command to get a response from the API; instead of that, we will use a new tool called **POSTMAN** (`https://www.getpostman.com`), which is an application that will help you build, test, and document your APIs faster.

> For more information on the workings of POSTMAN, read the documentation at the following link:
> `https://www.getpostman.com/docs/`

POSTMAN is supported by both Chrome and Firefox, as it can be integrated very easily as an add-on.

First, we will modify the `api_version` info API to collect the information from MongoDB instead of SQLite3, as follows:

```
@app.route("/api/v1/info")
def home_index():
 api_list=[]
 db = connection.cloud_native.apirelease
 for row in db.find():
   api_list.append(str(row))
 return jsonify({'api_version': api_list}), 200
```

Now, if you test it using POSTMAN, it should give an output that looks somewhat like this:

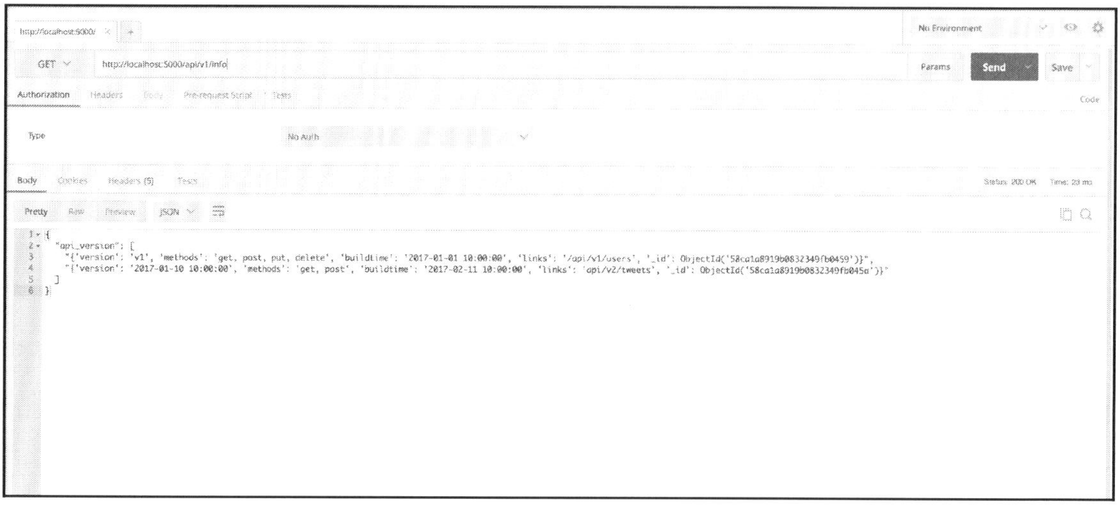

Great! It works. Now, let's update the other resources of microservices.

Working with user resources

We will modify our user resources' API functions for different methods in `app.py` as follows.

GET api/v1/users

The GET API function gets a complete list of users.

In order to get the complete user list from the MongoDB database, we will rewrite the `list_users()` function as follows:

```
def list_users():
 api_list=[]
 db = connection.cloud_native.users
 for row in db.find():
   api_list.append(str(row))
 return jsonify({'user_list': api_list})
```

Let's test it on POSTMAN and see if the API responds as expected:

Since we currently have only one document in the user's collection of the MongoDB database, you can see only one user in the users list in the preceding screenshot.

GET api/v1/users/[user_id]

This API function gets the details of a specific user.

In order to list the details of a specific user from the MongoDB database, use the `modify list_user(user_id)` function as follows:

```
def list_user(user_id):
 api_list=[]
 db = connection.cloud_native.users
 for i in db.find({'id':user_id}):
   api_list.append(str(i))

 if api_list == []:
   abort(404)
 return jsonify({'user_details':api_list}
```

Let's test it on POSTMAN to see if it works as expected:

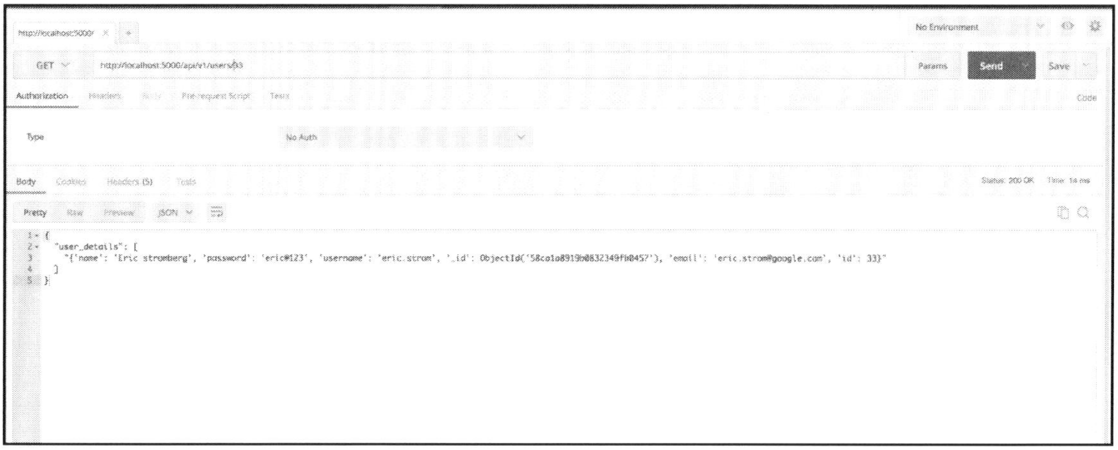

Also, we need to test the scenario where a user entry is not present; try this out, as shown in the following code:

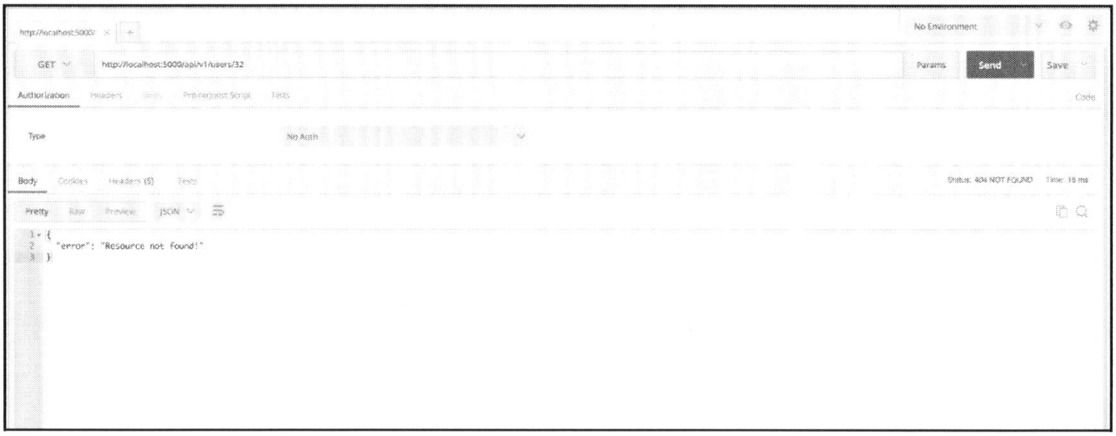

POST api/v1/users

This API function adds new users to the users list.

In this code, we will rewrite the `add_user(new_user)` function to interact with MongoDB to add a user to the users collection:

```
def add_user(new_user):
 api_list=[]
 print (new_user)
 db = connection.cloud_native.users
 user = db.find({'$or':[{"username":new_user['username']}     ,
{"email":new_user['email']}]})
 for i in user:
   print (str(i))
   api_list.append(str(i))

 if api_list == []:
   db.insert(new_user)
   return "Success"
 else :
   abort(409)
```

Now that we have modified our function, one more thing needs to be done--earlier, IDs were generated by SQLite 3, but now, we need to generate them with a random module by adding it to its route function, as follows:

```
def create_user():
 if not request.json or not 'username' in request.json or not
'email' in request.json or not 'password' in request.json:
   abort(400)
 user = {
   'username': request.json['username'],
   'email': request.json['email'],
   'name': request.json.get('name',""),
   'password': request.json['password'],
   'id': random.randint(1,1000)
 }
```

Let's add one record to the users list to test whether it works as expected.

The following screenshot shows the output status of adding a new record using POSTMAN in MongoDB:

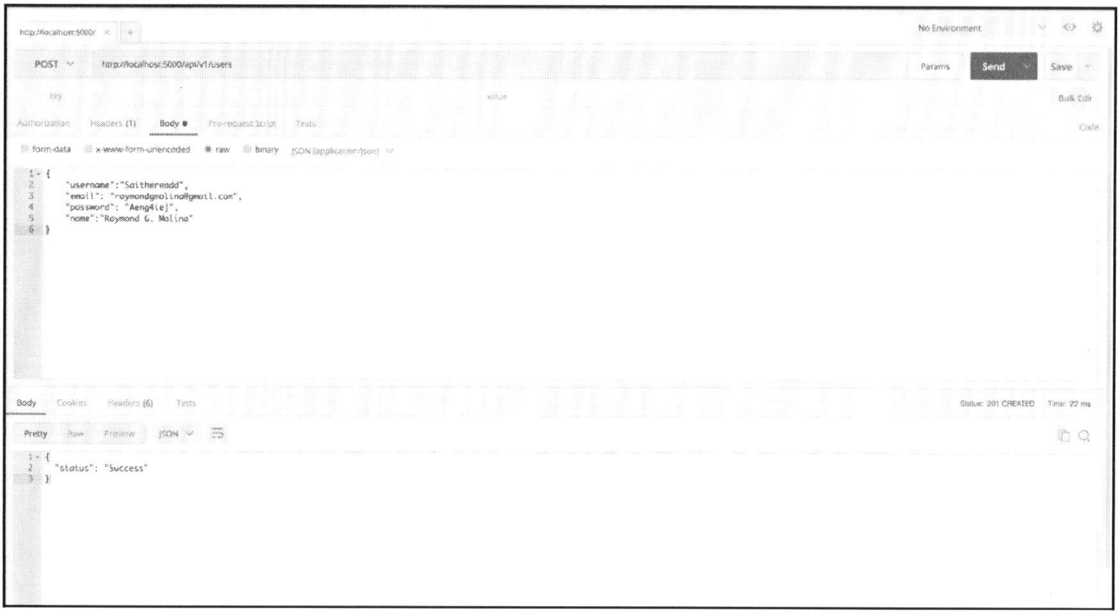

Let's validate whether it has updated the properties in the MongoDB collection as well.

The following screenshot validates that our new record has been added successfully:

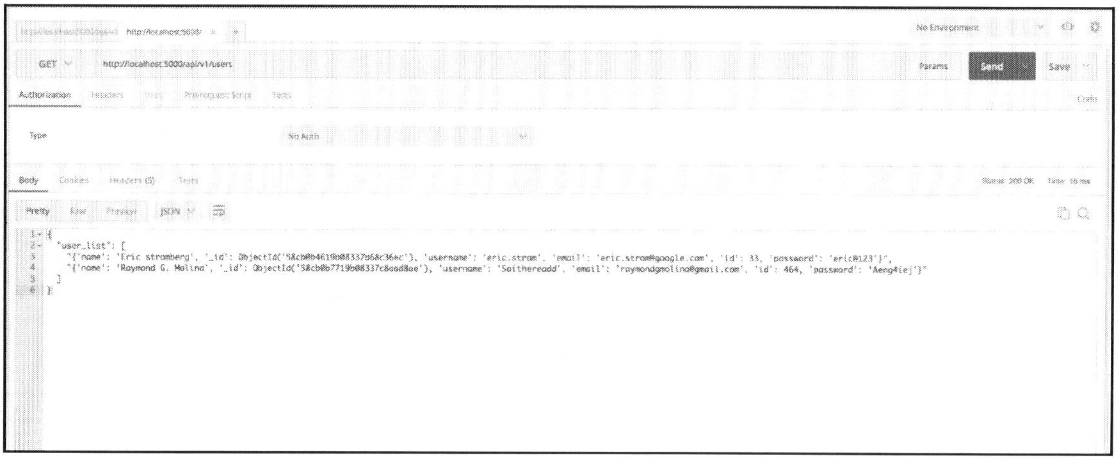

PUT api/v1/users/[user_id]

This API function is used to update the attributes of the users in the MongoDB users collection.

In order to update the documents in the MongoDB user collection for a specific user, we will need to rewrite the `upd_user(user)` method as follows:

```
def upd_user(user):
 api_list=[]
 print (user)
 db_user = connection.cloud_native.users
 users = db_user.find_one({"id":user['id']})
 for i in users:
   api_list.append(str(i))
  if api_list == []:
   abort(409)
  else:
   db_user.update({'id':user['id']},{'$set': user}, upsert=False )
   return "Success"
```

Now that we have updated the method, let's test it on POSTMAN and check the response.

The following screenshot shows the response of the update API request using POSTMAN:

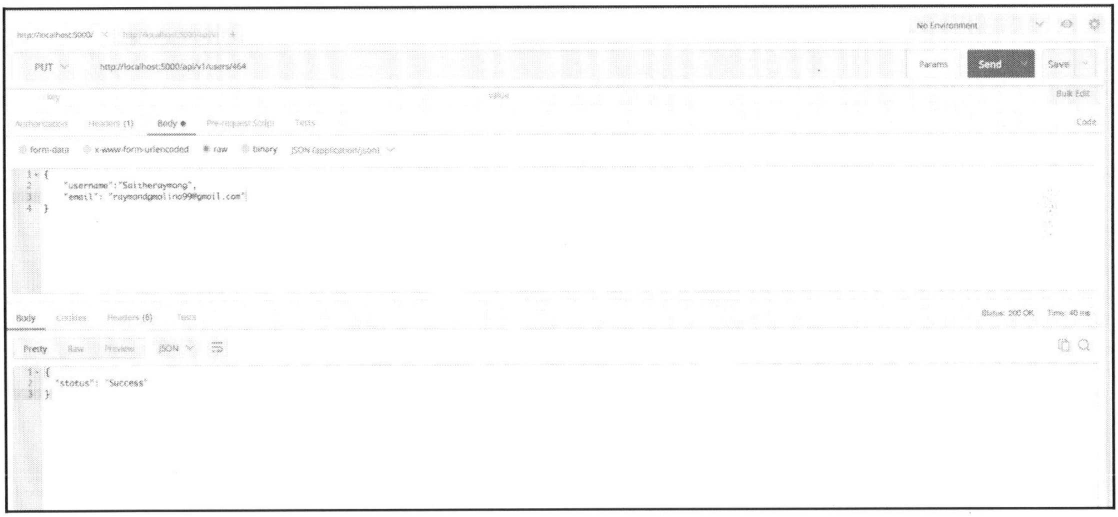

Let's validate the user document to check whether the fields were modified or not:

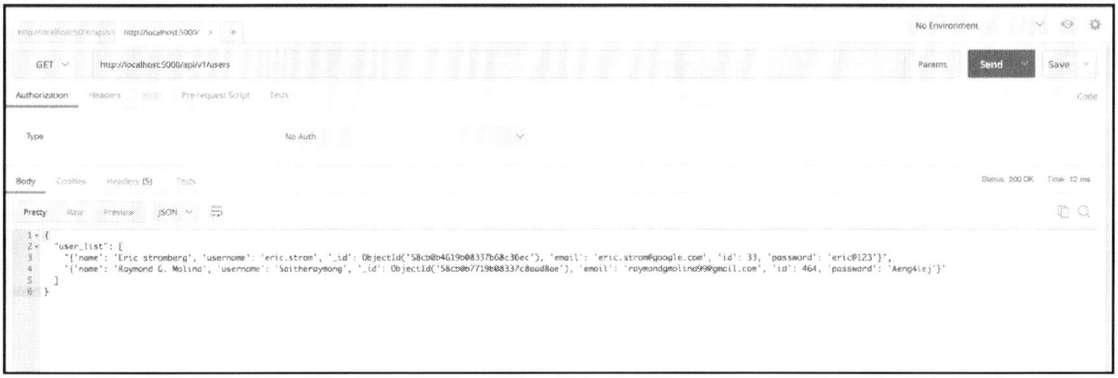

DELETE api/v1/users

This API deletes a specific user from the users list.

In this case, we will modify the `del_user(del_user)` method to delete a user from the MongoDB users collection as follows:

```
def del_user(del_user):
 db = connection.cloud_native.users
api_list = []
for i in db.find({'username':del_user}):
   api_list.append(str(i))

 if api_list == []:
   abort(404)
else:
  db.remove({"username":del_user})
  return "Success"
```

Let's test it out over POSTMAN and see if the response is as expected:

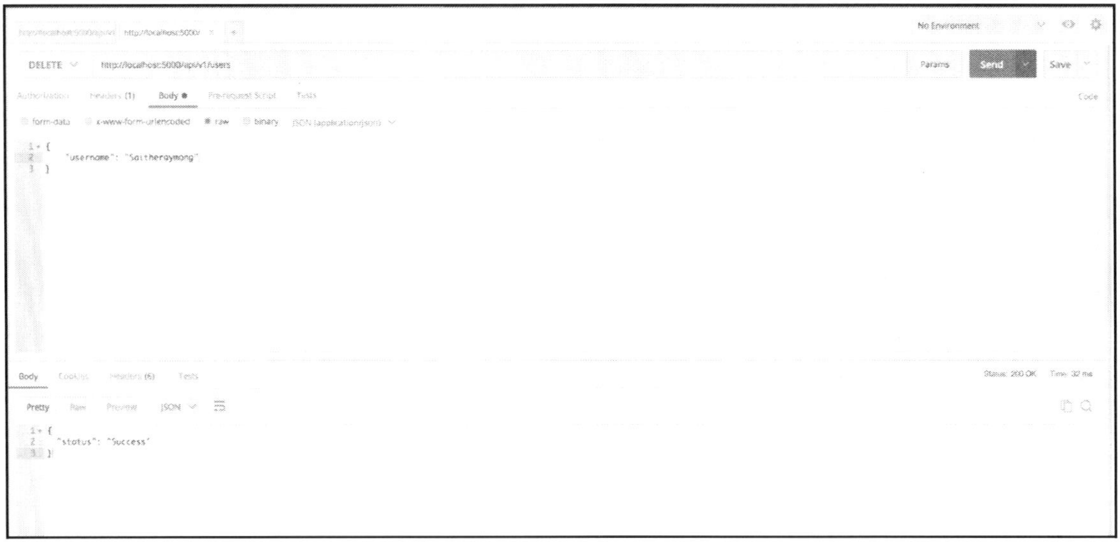

Now that we've deleted one user, let's see if it made any changes in the overall users list:

Great! We have made changes in all the RESTful API URLs for the user resources, and validated them as well.

Working with the tweets resources

Now that our user resources APIs are working fine with MongoDB as the database service, we will do the same for the tweets resources as well.

GET api/v2/tweets

This function gets the complete list of tweets from all the users.

Let's update our `list_tweets()` method to begin getting the list of tweets from the tweets collection of MongoDB using the following code snippet:

```
def list_tweets():
    api_list=[]
    db = connection.cloud_native.tweet
    for row in db.find():
        api_list.append(str(row))
    return jsonify({'tweets_list': api_list})
```

Now that we have updated the code, let's test it out on POSTMAN. The following screenshot lists all the tweets by making an API request using POSTMAN:

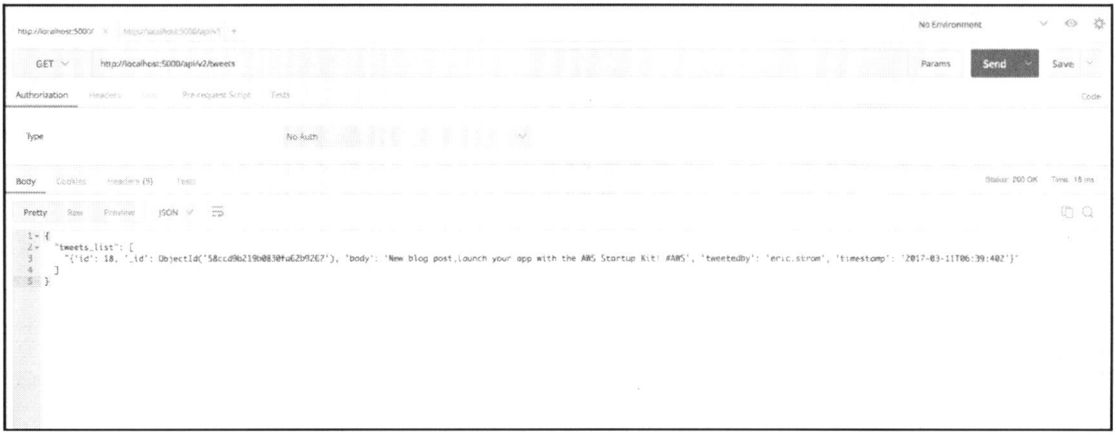

GET api/v2/tweets/[user_id]

This function gets the tweets from a specific user.

In order to get tweets from a specific user from the tweets collection, we need to modify our current `list_tweet(user_id)` function as follows:

```
def list_tweet(user_id):
 db = connection.cloud_native.tweets
 api_list=[]
 tweet = db.find({'id':user_id})
 for i in tweet:
   api_list.append(str(i))
if api_list == []:
   abort(404)
return jsonify({'tweet': api_list})
```

Let's test out our API and validate whether it is working as expected or not:

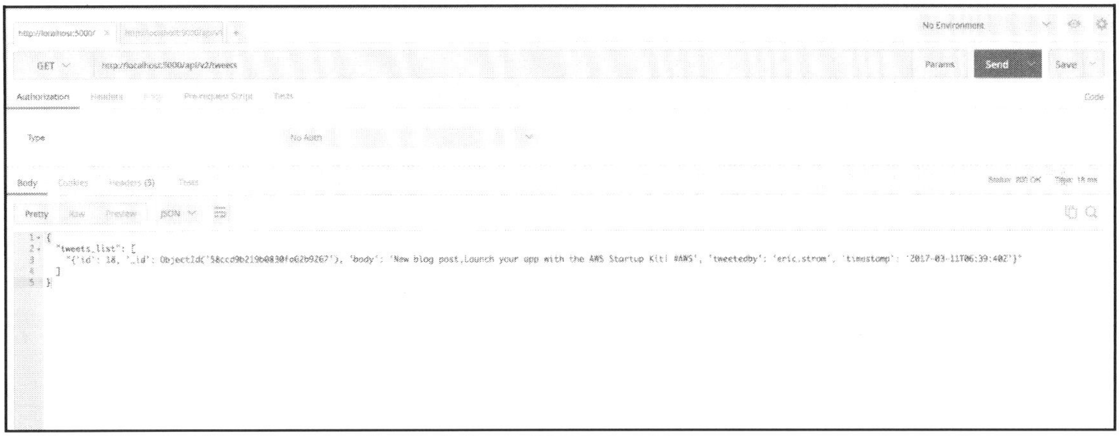

POST api/v2/tweets

This function adds new tweets from an existing user.

In this case, we need to modify our `add_tweet(new_tweet)` method to interact with users, and the tweets collection in MongoDB to add new tweets, as follows:

```
def add_tweet(new_tweet):
 api_list=[]
 print (new_tweet)
 db_user = connection.cloud_native.users
 db_tweet = connection.cloud_native.tweets
 user = db_user.find({"username":new_tweet['tweetedby']})
 for i in user:
   api_list.append(str(i))
```

```
        if api_list == []:
         abort(404)
        else:
          db_tweet.insert(new_tweet)
          return "Success"
```

Now that we have modified the record, let's test it out. The following screenshot shows the success status of the `POST` request to add new tweets using POSTMAN:

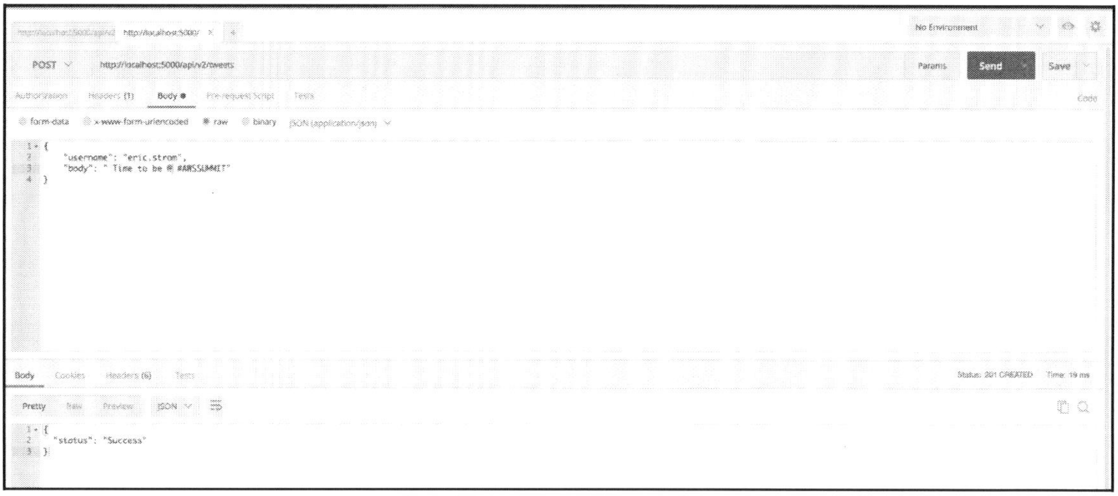

Let's now validate whether the newly added tweets were updated in the tweet list, as shown in the following screenshot:

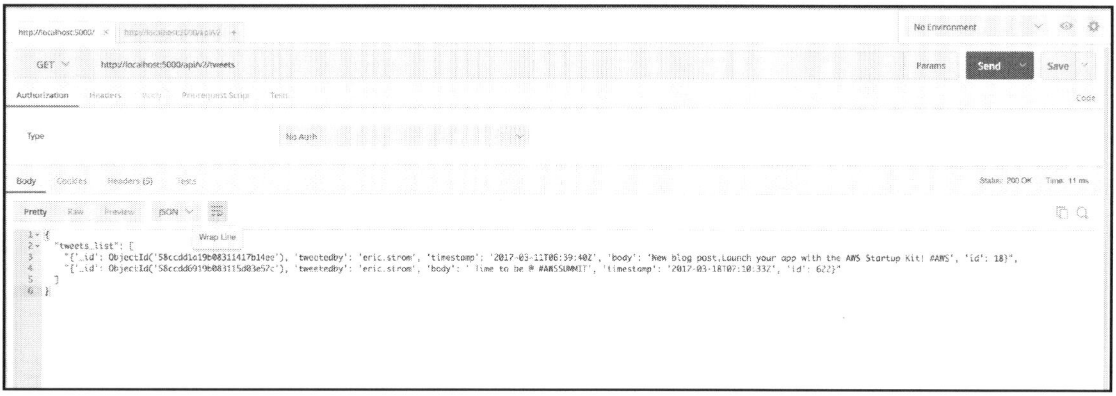

Summary

In this chapter, we migrated our file-based database service (SQLite) to a NoSQL-document-based database service (MongoDB). You learned how to integrate MongoDB with your RESTful APIs to respond to hold data, and respond based on the request from the client. The next chapter will be more interesting, as we will build our frontend web views using React.

5

Building WebViews with React

So far, we have been building our microservices and making our backend services more responsive and efficient. Also, we have been trying out different database services which can secure and increase the performance of the storage and retrieval of data, which is of essence here.

In this chapter, we will focus on building our frontend page using React and integrating these pages with the backend to form a complete application.

The topics that we will cover in this chapter are as follows:

- Setting up a React environment
- Creating a user authentication panel
- Integrating react with backend APIs

Understanding React

In simpler terms, React is the UI layer of your application. It is a Javascript library to build fast and quick user interfaces. React, basically, helps you to create awesome webViews for each state of your application. So, we are going to use React for this purpose. But before we do that, let's understand a few concepts/key points of React, which are listed next:

- **Components**: All your collections of HTML and JavaScript are called **components**. React, basically, provides hooks to render HTML pages with JavaScript enabled. The important thing here is that React works as a controller to render different web pages for each state of your application.

- **Props for static version in React**: Usually, in HTML, you need a lot of code for showing all the data on the frontend and, moreover, it's repetitive. React props help you solve this problem. Props, basically, keep the state of data and pass values from the parent to the child.
- **Identifying the minimal state**: To build your app correctly, you first need to think of the minimal set of the mutable state that your app needs. Like, in our case, we need to keep the state of users always available during the different states of the application.
- **Identifying active state**: React is all about one-way data flow down the component hierarchy. We need to understand every component that renders something based on that state. Also, we need to understand how states change at the level of component hierarchy.
- **React-DOM**: The react-dom is a combination of React and DOM. React contains the functionality utilized in web and mobile apps. The react-dom functionality is utilized only in web apps.

Setting up the React environment

In order to run React, we need to set up an initial environment, which includes installing a couple of libraries of `node.js`.

Installing node

Before we start installing React and the package list, we need to have `node.js` installed on our system.

In Linux (Debian-based system), the process of installation is pretty simple.

First, we need to add PPA from the `node.js` official website by using the following commands:

```
$ sudo apt-get install python-software-properties
$ curl -sL https://deb.nodesource.com/setup_7.x | sudo -E bash -
```

Once it is set up, we can install `node.js` with the following command:

```
$ apt-get install nodejs
```

Now let's check the `node` and `npm` versions, as follows:

```
$ npm -v
  4.1.2
$ node -v
  V7.7.4
```

In our setup, we use the aforementioned version, but the node version around v7.x should be fine, and for npm, v4.x should work fine.

Creating package.json

This file is, basically, metadata for your application, which contains the complete libraries /dependencies that need to be installed for your application. Another real-world advantage is that it makes your build reproducible, which means that it's way easier to share it with other developers. There are different ways in which you can create your customized `package.json`.

The following is the minimum information that needs to be provided in `packages.json`:

```
"Name" - lowercase.
"version"  - in the form of x.x.x
For example:
{
  "name": "my-twitter-package",
  "version": "1.0.0"
}
```

In order to create the `package.json` template, you can use the following command:

```
$ npm init                  # in your workspace
```

It will ask for values such as name, version, description, author, license, and so on; fill in the values, and it will generate `package.json`.

If you don't want to fill the information in now, you can use the `--yes` or `-y` attribute to use the default values as follows:

```
$npm init --yes
```

For our application, I have generated `package.json`, which looks something like this:

```
{
  "name": "twitter",
  "version": "1.0.0",
```

```
    "description": "Twitter App",
    "main": "index.js",
    "dependencies": {
      "babel-loader": "^6.4.1",
      "fbjs": "^0.8.11",
      "object-assign": "^4.1.1",
      "react": "^15.4.2",
      "react-dev": "0.0.1",
      "react-dom": "^0.14.7",
      "requirejs": "^2.3.3"
    },
   "devDependencies": {
     "babel-core": "^6.4.5",
     "babel-loader": "^6.2.1",
     "babel-preset-es2015": "^6.3.13",
     "babel-preset-react": "^6.3.13",
     "webpack": "^1.12.12"
    },
  "scripts": {
    "test": "echo \"Error: no test specified\" && exit 1"
   },
  "author": "Manish Sethi",
  "license": "ISC"
}
```

Now, that we have generated `package.json`, we need to install these dependencies on our workstation using the following command:

```
$ npm install
```

Please make sure that, when you execute the preceding command, `package.json` should be in the current working directory.

Building webViews with React

First of all, we will create a home view from which React will be called. So, let's create `index.html`, which has the following contents, in the template directory:

```
<!DOCTYPE html>
<html>
 <head lang="en">
  <meta charset="UTF-8">
  <title>Flask react</title>
</head>
<body>
 <div class="container">
```

```
        <h1></h1>
        <br>
        <div id="react"></div>

     </div>

    <!-- scripts -->
     <script src="https://code.jquery.com/jquery-2.1.1.min.js"></script>
     <script src="https://cdnjs.cloudflare.com/ajax/libs/
       react/15.1.0/react.min.js"></script>
     <script src="https://npmcdn.com/react-
       router@2.8.1/umd/ReactRouter.min.js"></script>
     <script src="https://cdnjs.cloudflare.com/ajax/
       libs/react/15.1.0/react-dom.min.js"></script>
     <script src="http://cdnjs.cloudflare.com/ajax/libs/
       react/0.13.3/JSXTransformer.js"></script>


     </body>
    </html>
```

As you can see in the preceding HTML page, we have defined `id ="react"`, which we will use to call the React main function based on the ID, and perform a certain operation.

So, let's create our `main.js`, which will send a response, with the following code:

```
     import Tweet from "./components/Tweet";
     class Main extends React.Component{
     render(){
       return (
       <div>
         <h1>Welcome to cloud-native-app!</h1>
       </div>
       );
     }
    }


    let documentReady =() =>{
     ReactDOM.render(
     <Main />,
      document.getElementById('react')
     );
   };
   $(documentReady);
```

Now we have defined our basic structure of the React response. Since we are building an application with multiple views, we need a build tool which will help us put all our assets, including JavaScript, images, fonts, and CSS, under one package, and generate it into a single file.

Webpack is the tool which will help us solve this problem.

Webpack should already be available, as we defined the Webpack package as part of `package.json`, which we installed earlier.

Webpack, basically, reads a single entry file, which could be the `.js` file, reads its child components, and then converts them into a single `.js` file.

Since we have already defined it in `package.json`, it is already installed.

In Webpack, we need to define a configuration which will help it to identify the entry file and the loader that is to be used to generate a single `.js` file. Also, you need to define the filename for the generated code.

Our Webpack configuration would be something like this:

```
module.exports = {
  entry: "./static/main.js",
  output: {
    path: __dirname + "/static/build/",
    filename: "bundle.js"
  },
 resolve: {
   extensions: ['', '.js', '.jsx']
 },
 module: {
    loaders: [
        { test: /\.js$/, exclude: /node_modules/, loader: "babel-
    loader", query:{presets:['react','es2015']} }
    ]
 }
};
```

You can extend the preceding configuration based on your use cases. Sometimes, developers try *.html as the entry point. In that case, you need to make appropriate changes.

Let's move on to build our first webView using the following command:

```
$ webpack -d
```

The `-d` attribute in the last command is used for debugging; it generates another file, `bundle.js.map`, which shows the activity of Webpack.

Since we are going to build the application repeatedly, we can use another flag, `--watch` or `-w`, which will keep track of the changes in the `main.js` file.

So, now our Webpack command should be something like the following:

```
$ webpack -d -w
```

Now we have built our application. Remember to change your routes in `app.py` so that home should be navigated as follows:

```
@app.route('/index')
def index():
 return render_template('index.html')
```

Let's check what our home page looks like now.

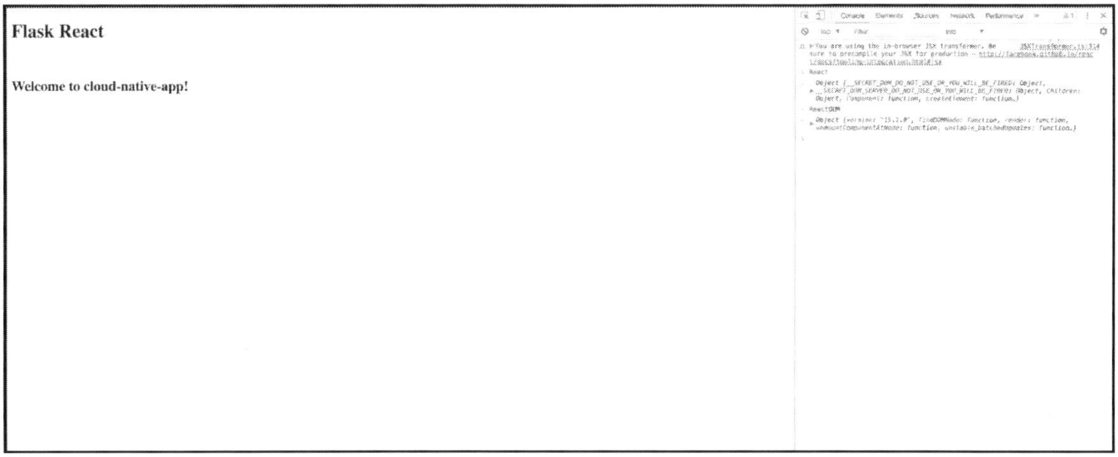

You can also check whether we have React and react-dom running in the background in the inspect mode.

This is a very basic structure to understand the workings of React. Let's move on to our use case, where we have created tweet webViews, and the user can view the old tweets as well.

So, let's create `Tweet.js`, which will have the basic structure of tweets, such as a textbox for contents, and a button to post tweets. Add the following code to `Tweet.js`:

```
export default class Tweet extends React.Component {

render(){
 return(
    <div className="row">
            </nav>
    <form >
      <div >
        <textarea ref="tweetTextArea" />
        <label>How you doing?</label>
          <button >Tweet now</button>
      </div>
     </form>
    </div>
    );
  }
}
```

Let's call this function from `main.js`, so that it is loaded on the home page, by updating the `render` function as follows:

```
import Tweet from "./components/Tweet";
render(){
  return (
  <div>
    <Tweet />
  </div>
 );
}
```

If you load the page now, it will be pretty simple. Since we want to create a web application, which should be attractive, we will use a couple of CSS here to do so. In our case, we are using Materialize CSS (`http://materializecss.com/getting-started.html`).

Add the following block of code in `index.html`:

```
<link rel="stylesheet"
  href="https://cdnjs.cloudflare.com/ajax/libs/
  materialize/0.98.1/css/materialize.min.css">
<script src="https://cdnjs.cloudflare.com/ajax/libs/
  materialize/0.98.1/js/materialize.min.js"></script>

Also, we need to update Tweet.js as follows
```

```
render(){
 return(
     <div className="row">
      <form >
       <div className="input-field">
         <textarea ref="tweetTextArea" className="materialize-
          textarea" />
         <label>How you doing?</label>
           <button className="btn waves-effect waves-light
            right">Tweet now <i className="material-icons
            right">send</i></button>
       </div>
      </form>
    </div>
   );
 }
```

Let's try to add tweets, and send them across with state so that some tweets should be shown.

In the `Main` class of `main.js`, add the following constructor function to initialize the state:

```
constructor(props){
 super(props);
 this.state =  { userId: cookie.load('session') };
 this.state={tweets:[{'id': 1, 'name': 'guest', 'body': '"Listen to
 your heart. It knows all things." - Paulo Coelho #Motivation' }]}
}
```

Now update the `render` function as follows:

```
render(){
  return (
  <div>
     <TweetList tweets={this.state.tweets}/>
  </div>
  );
 }
}
```

Let's create another file, `TweetList.js`, which will show the tweets, with the following code:

```
export default class TweetList extends React.Component {
 render(){
    return(
    <div>
      <ul className="collection">
```

```
            <li className="collection-item avatar">
            <i className="material-icons circle red">play_arrow</i>
            <span className="title">{this.props.tweetedby}</span>
           <p>{this.props.body}</p>
           <p>{this.props.timestamp}</p>
           </li>
          </ul>
         </div>
        );
      }
    }
```

Great! Now we have added this template. Let's check out our home page and see how the CSS works there. But before that, since we are using Webpack for building, make sure you add the following line to load `bundle.js` every time--this will run the webViews in the `index.html` file.

```
<script type="text/javascript" src="./static/build/bundle.js">
 </script>
```

Awesome! The home page should look something like this:

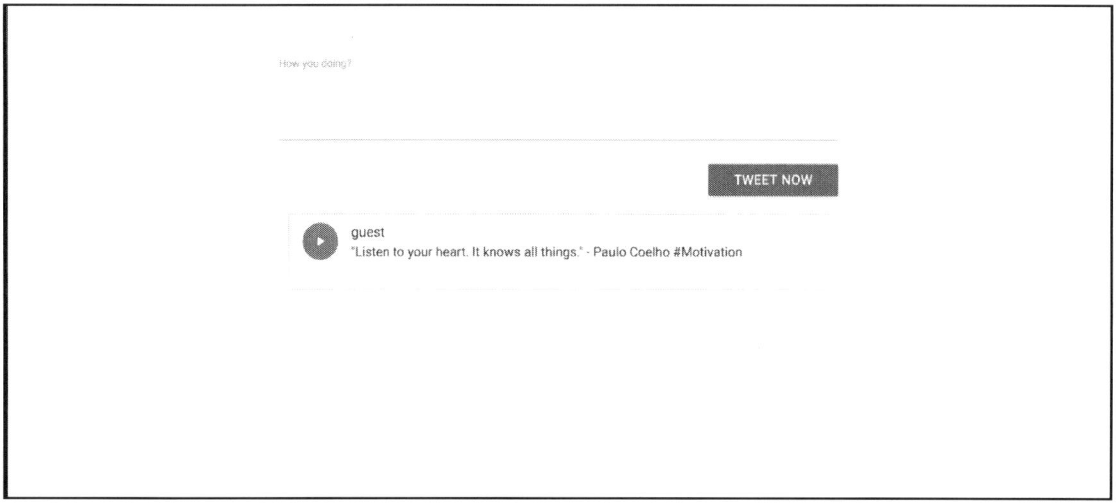

Let's move forward to post tweets--we should be able to add new tweets, and they should be updated in `TweetList.js` as well.

Let's update our Tweet.js code so that it sends the tweets to main.js to process them. Now, we need to send our tweets to main.js, in order to do so , we need to update our Tweet.js file with the following code:

```
sendTweet(event){
  event.preventDefault();
  this.props.sendTweet(this.refs.tweetTextArea.value);
  this.refs.tweetTextArea.value = '';
 }
```

Also, be sure to update the render function with the form onSubmit attribute as follows:

```
<form onSubmit={this.sendTweet.bind(this)}>
```

So, after adding content into the text area, it should submit the tweet as well.

Now, let's update the render function of main.js to add new tweets, as follows:

```
<Tweet sendTweet={this.addTweet.bind(this)}/>
```

We also need to add the addTweet function in the Main class, defined in the following:

```
addTweet(tweet):
 let newTweet = this.state.tweets;
 newTweet.unshift({{'id': Date.now(), 'name': 'guest','body':
  tweet})
 this.setState({tweets: newTweet})
```

Your page, after adding the new tweet, should look something like this:

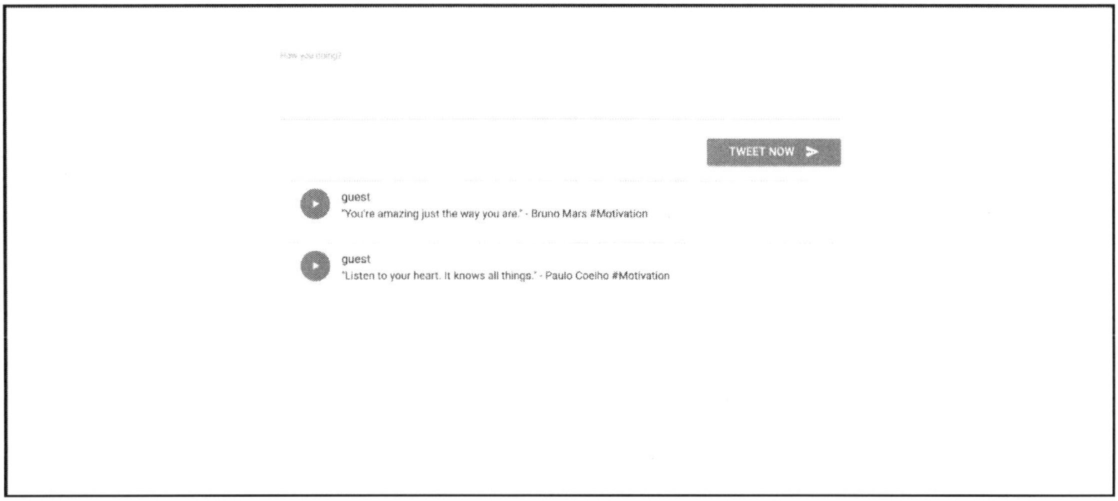

Currently, we are using React to hold the data in an array. Since we have built our microservices to hold this kind of data, we should integrate our webView with the backend services.

Integrating webView with microservices

In order to integrate our microservices with webViews, we will use AJAX to make API calls.

We need to add the following code snippet in `main.js` to pull our entire tweet list:

```
componentDidMount() {
  var self=this;
  $.ajax({url: `/api/v2/tweets/`,
  success: function(data) {
    self.setState({tweets: data['tweets_list']});
    alert(self.state.tweets);
    return console.log("success");
   },
 error: function() {
  return console.log("Failed");
  }
});
```

Similarly, we need to modify our `addTweet` function in our `main.js` as follows:

```
addTweet(tweet){
  var self = this;
  $.ajax({
    url: '/api/v2/tweets/',
    contentType: 'application/json',
    type: 'POST',
    data: JSON.stringify({
      'username': "Agnsur",
   'body': tweet,
    }),
    success: function(data) {
         return console.log("success");
    },
    error: function() {
      return console.log("Failed");
    }
  });
}
```

Since there will be multiple tweets which need to be iterated with a similar template of tweet, let's create another component called `templatetweet.js` with the following code:

```
export default class Tweettemplate extends React.Component {
 render(props){
  return(
  <li className="collection-item avatar">
    <i className="material-icons circle red">play_arrow</i>
    <span className="title">{this.props.tweetedby}</span>
    <p>{this.props.body}</p>
    <p>{this.props.timestamp}</p>
  </li>

  );
 }
}
```

Remember, we have changed the field of props based on our database collection keys.

Also, we need to update our `TweetList.js` to use the preceding template by adding it as follows:

```
import Tweettemplate from './templatetweet'

export default class TweetList extends React.Component {
render(){
 let tweetlist = this.props.tweets.map(tweet => <Tweettemplate key=
 {tweet.id} {...tweet} />);
return(
    <div>
      <ul className="collection">
        {tweetlist}
      </ul>
    </div>
  );
 }
}
```

Great! Your home page should look like this now:

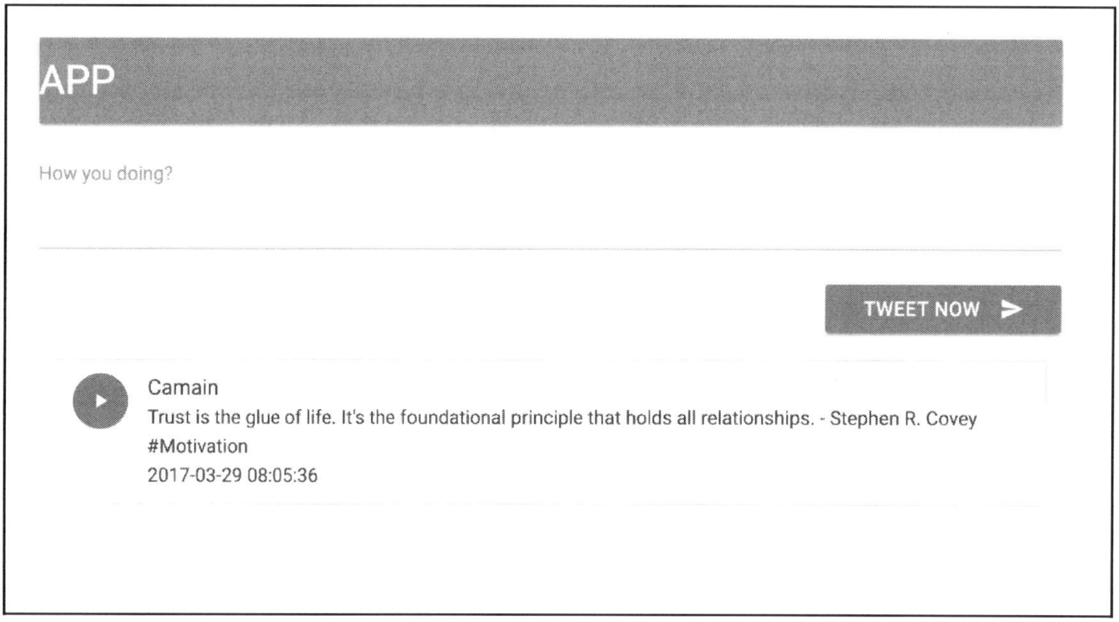

User authentication

All our tweets are protected, and should react only to the audience which we want to showcase them to. Also, anonymous users should not be allowed to tweet. For that, we will create a database and web pages to enable new users to sign in and log in to the tweet webView as well. Remember, we will use Flask to authenticate users, and also to post data to the backend user.

Login user

Let's create our login page template, where the existing users need to fill in their username and password to authenticate. The following is the code snippet:

```
<form action="/login" method="POST">
 <div class="login">
 <div class="login-screen">
 <div class="app-title">
  <h1>Login</h1>
 </div>
```

```
<div class="login-form">
<div class="control-group">

 <input type="text" class="login-field" value=""
  placeholder="username" name="username">
 <label class="login-field-icon fui-user" for="login-name">
 </label>
</div>

<div class="control-group">
  <input type="password" class="login-field" value=""
   placeholder="password" name="password">
  <label class="login-field-icon fui-lock" for="login-pass">
  </label>
</div>
 <input type="submit" value="Log in" class="btn btn-primary btn-
 large btn-block" ><br>
 Don't have an account? <a href="{{ url_for('signup') }}">Sign up
 here</a>.
</div>
```

We will post the data to the login page, which we will define in the `app.py` file.

But first, check if the session is present or not. If not, then you will be redirected to the login page. Add the following code to `app.py`, which will validate session details for the user:

```
@app.route('/')
def home():
  if not session.get('logged_in'):
     return render_template('login.html')
  else:
     return render_template('index.html', session =
  session['username'])
```

Let's create the route for login, and validate the credentials to authenticate users to tweet.

Here is the code snippet:

```
@app.route('/login', methods=['POST'])
def do_admin_login():
  users = mongo.db.users
  api_list=[]
  login_user = users.find({'username': request.form['username']})
  for i in login_user:
    api_list.append(i)
  print (api_list)
  if api_list != []:
     if api_list[0]['password'].decode('utf-8') ==
```

```
            bcrypt.hashpw(request.form['password'].encode('utf-8'),
            api_list[0]['password']).decode('utf-8'):
               session['logged_in'] = api_list[0]['username']
               return redirect(url_for('index'))
           return 'Invalid username/password!'
         else:
           flash("Invalid Authentication")

       return 'Invalid User!'
```

Once you are done with this, your login page will appear at the root URL, and it should look something like this:

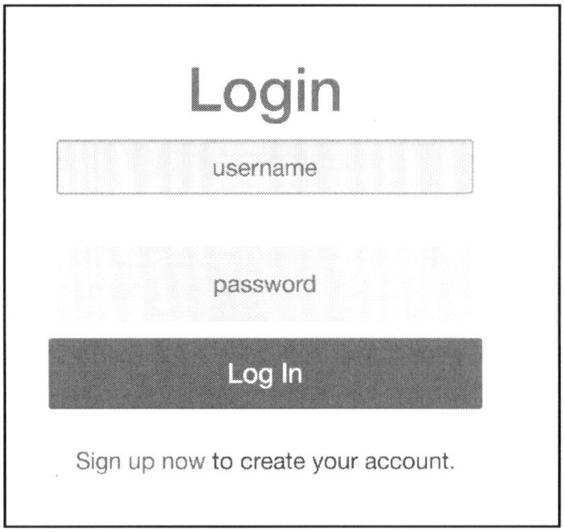

As you can see, we have provided a link, **Sign up now**, to create an account for the new user.

Remember, we are using APIs to authenticate the user from the user collection in our database.

Sign up user

Let's move on to create our sign up page to help register new users so that they can tweet as well.

Let's create `signup.html`, which will ask for user details. Check the following code snippet for this:

```
<div class="container">
 <div class="row">
   <center><h2>Sign up</h2></center>
     <div class="col-md-4 col-md-offset-4">
         <form method=POST action="{{ url_for('signup') }}">
             <div class="form-group">
                 <label >Username</label>
                 <input type="text" class="form-control"
                   name="username" placeholder="Username">
             </div>
             <div class="form-group">
                 <label >Password</label>
                 <input type="password" class="form-control"
                 name="pass" placeholder="Password">
             </div>
             <div class="form-group">
                 <label >Email</label>
                 <input type="email" class="form-control"
                name="email" placeholder="email">
             </div>
             <div class="form-group">
                 <label >Full Name</label>
                 <input type="text" class="form-control"
                 name="name" placeholder="name">
             </div>
             <button type="submit" class="btn btn-primary btn-
                block">Signup</button>
          </form>
          <br>
       </div>
     </div>
 </div>
```

The preceding code is, basically, the template which needs the backend API to submit the data to the user.

Let's create a `signup` route, which will take the `GET` and `POST` methods to read the page, and submit the data to the backend database. The following is the code snippet which needs to be added to `app.py`:

```
@app.route('/signup', methods=['GET', 'POST'])
def signup():
  if request.method=='POST':
    users = mongo.db.users
```

```
            api_list=[]
            existing_user = users.find({'$or':
            [{"username":request.form['username']} ,
             {"email":request.form['email']}]})
                for i in existing_user:
                  api_list.append(str(i))
                if api_list == []:
                  users.insert({
                  "email": request.form['email'],
                  "id": random.randint(1,1000),
                  "name": request.form['name'],
                  "password": bcrypt.hashpw(request.form['pass'].
                    encode('utf-8'), bcrypt.gensalt()),
                  "username": request.form['username']
                })
                session['username'] = request.form['username']
                return redirect(url_for('home'))

              return 'That user already exists'
          else :
            return render_template('signup.html')
```

Once the user has signed up, it will set the session, and redirect it to your home page.

Your **Sign up** page should look something like this:

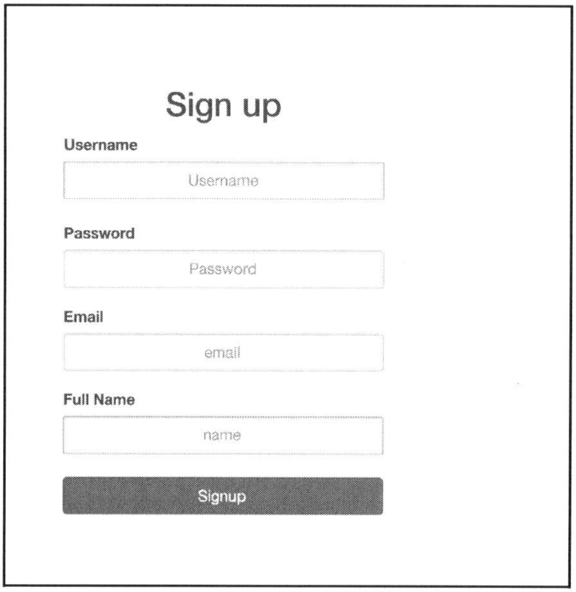

We have authenticated the user, but what if he wants to update his/her personal information? Let's create a profile page, which will help them do so.

User profile

Let's create a profile page (`profile.html`), which will be accessible by the user already logged in at the home page in the navigation panel.

Add the following code to `profile.html`:

```
<div class="container">
 <div class="row">
   <center><h2>Profile</h2></center>
     <div class="col-md-4 col-md-offset-4">
         <form method=POST action="{{ url_for('profile') }}">
             <div class="form-group">
                 <label >Username</label>
                 <input type="text" class="form-control"
                  name="username" value='{{username}}'>
             </div>
             <div class="form-group">
                 <label >Password</label>
                 <input type="password" class="form-control"
                 name="pass" value='{{password}}'>
             </div>
             <div class="form-group">
                 <label >Email</label>
                 <input type="email" class="form-control"
                 name="email" value={{email}}>
             </div>
             <div class="form-group">
                 <label >Full Name</label>
                 <input type="text" class="form-control"
                 name="name" value={{name}}>
             </div>
             <button type="submit" class="btn btn-primary btn-
              block">Update</button>
           </form>
         <br>
      </div>
  </div>
</div>
```

Since we have created the profile, we need to create a route for the profile, which will read the database to get user details and POST back to the database as well.

The following is the code snippet from `app.py`:

```
def profile():
    if request.method=='POST':
      users = mongo.db.users
      api_list=[]
      existing_users = users.find({"username":session['username']})
      for i in existing_users:
         api_list.append(str(i))
      user = {}
      print (api_list)
      if api_list != []:
         print (request.form['email'])
         user['email']=request.form['email']
         user['name']= request.form['name']
         user['password']=request.form['pass']
         users.update({'username':session['username']},{'$set':
       user} )
     else:
         return 'User not found!'
     return redirect(url_for('index'))
   if request.method=='GET':
     users = mongo.db.users
     user=[]
     print (session['username'])
     existing_user = users.find({"username":session['username']})
     for i in existing_user:
         user.append(i)
     return render_template('profile.html', name=user[0]['name'],
     username=user[0]['username'], password=user[0]['password'],
     email=user[0]['email'])
```

Once this last bit of code is added, your profile page should look something like this:

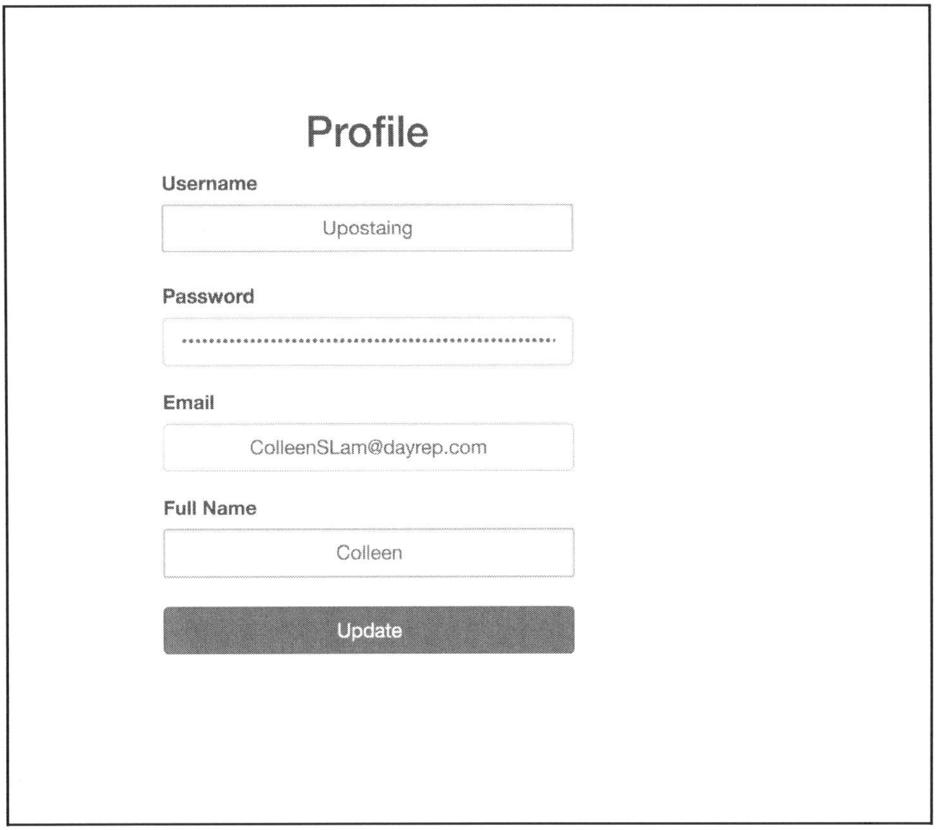

Also, we should add the profile link in `Tweet.js` in the navigation template by adding the following lines:

```
<li><a href="/profile">Profile</a></li>
<li><a href="/logout">Logout</a></li>
```

Now your home page will look something like this:

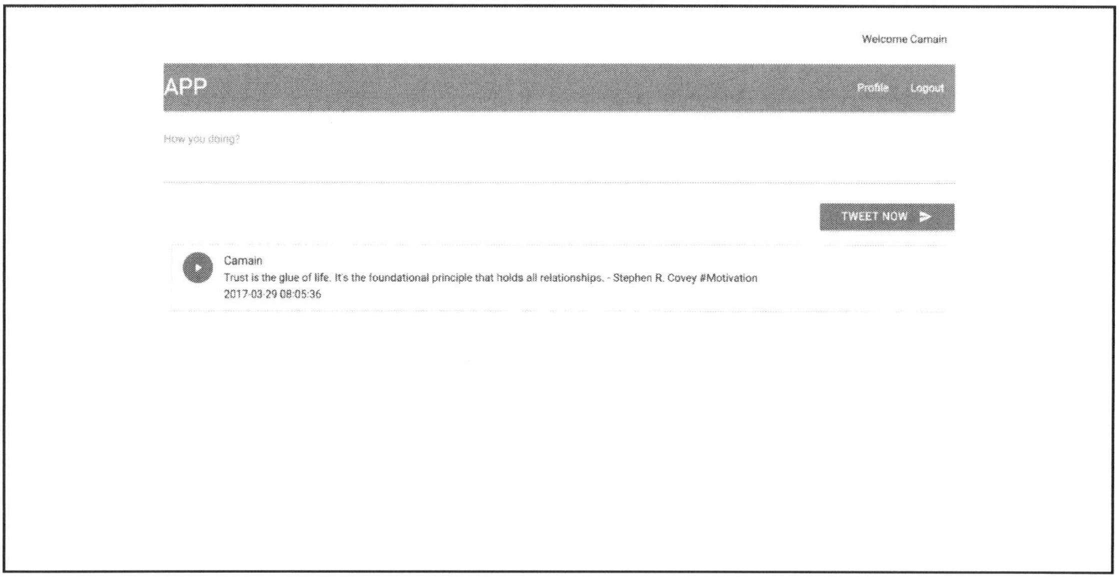

Log out users

As you can see, in the preceding section, we provided the route to log out, which, basically, removes the user session, and redirects the user to the login page. The following is the code snippet from `app.py`:

```
@app.route("/logout")
def logout():
  session['logged_in'] = False
  return redirect(url_for('home'))
```

Now our application is fully built-up, starting from the users logging in, to submitting their tweets, and then logging out.

Testing the React webViews

Since we are building webViews, we need to test them to catch some of the bugs before they happen. Also, testing will help you build better code.

There are a number of UI-testing frameworks which could help you test your web apps. Two of them are discussed in the following section.

Jest

Jest is a unit testing framework, which is provided by Facebook to test JavaScript. It is used to test individual components. It is simple, standard, and standalone.

It tests your components based on fake DOM implementations, and runs different tests to check the functionalities. It automatically resolves dependencies. Also, you can run all the tests in parallel.

You can refer to the following link, which could help you write test cases for your React application:

`https://facebook.github.io/jest/docs/tutorial-react.html`

Selenium

Selenium is an open source and portable automated software testing tool for testing web applications. It provides end-to-end testing, which means that it is a process of executing test scenarios against a real browser to test the entire stack of a multi-tiered application.

It has the following different components:

- **IDE**: This helps you describe the testing workflow.
- **Selenium WebDriver**: This automates browser testing. It sends commands directly to the browser and receives the results.
- **Selenium RC**: This remote control helps you to create test cases.
- **Grid**: This runs test cases across different browsers, and in parallel.

This is one of the best tools you can use to test our web application, which I would recommend.

You can gather more about Selenium at `http://www.seleniumhq.org/docs/`.

Summary

In this chapter, our focus was on creating frontend user webViews and how to improve them to attract consumers. You also learnt how React can help us to build these webViews and implement interactions with backend services. In the upcoming chapter, things will get more interesting, as we will play around with our frontend application, and will explain how we scale it using Flux to handle a large number of incoming requests from the internet.

6

Creating UIs to Scale with Flux

In the last chapter, we created webViews for our application and also saw the integration between our frontend and backend application, which was very important to understand.

In this chapter, we will focus on structuring our frontend. Ideally, each module should be responsible for a single thing. As in our main components, we are running too many operations within single modules. Besides rendering the different views, we have code to make an API request to endpoints and receive, handle, and format the response.

In this chapter, we will cover the following topics:

- Understanding Flux
- Implementing Flux on React

Understanding Flux

Flux is a pattern that Facebook created to build consistent and stable webapps with React. React doesn't give you the ability to manage data; rather, it simply accepts data through props and components, and further, the components process the data.

The React library doesn't really tell you how to get the components, or where to store the data, that's why it's called the **view layer**. In React, we don't have a framework as we have in the case of Angular or Backbone. That's where Flux comes in. Flux is not really a framework, but it's a pattern that will have you building your own views.

What is a Flux pattern? We have your React components, such as a Tweet component and so on, and these components do two things in the Flux pattern--they either perform actions or they listen to stores. In our use case, if a user wants to post a tweet, the components need to perform actions and actions then interact with stores, update the pattern to the API, and give a response to the components. The following diagram will give you more clarity on Flux:

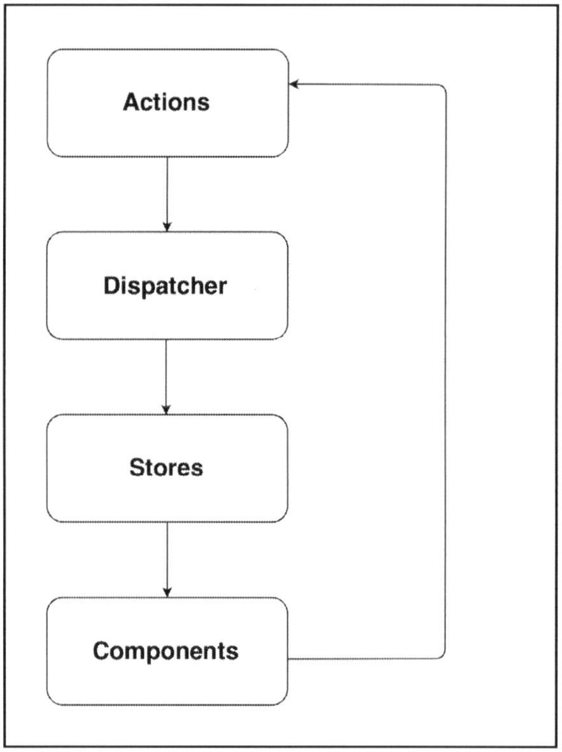

Flux concepts

The following are the Flux concepts that you need to understood before moving ahead:

- **Actions**: This is the way components interact with API endpoints and update them. In our case, we post new tweets using it. Actions pipe the action to the dispatcher. It might create multiple actions.

- **Dispatcher**: This dispatches every single event that comes in and sends it across to every single subscriber, which are basically stores.
- **Stores**: This is an important part of Flux. Components always listen to stores for any changes. Say, if you wrote a new tweet, that's an action, and wherever the tweet is updated in the store, an event is fired and the component is made aware that it has to be updated with the latest data. If you come from the AngularJS world, store is a service, or if you are of Backbone.js, stores are nothing but a collection.
- **Components**: This is used to store the action names.

We will be using the `JSX` file instead of `JS`, as there is not much difference--`JS` is a standard Javascript and `JSX` is an HTML-like syntax that you can use with React to create React components easily and perceptively.

Adding dates to UI

Before we deep dive into Flux, a little thing we need to add to our views is the date feature. Earlier, you were seeing the timing of the tweets that are stored in the database as the **TZ** format; however, ideally, it should be compared with current timings and should be shown in reference to it.

In order to do that, we will need to update our `main.jsx` file so that it will format our tweets. Add the following code to `main.jsx`:

```
updatetweets(tweets){
    let updatelist = tweets.map(tweet => {
     tweet.updatedate = moment(tweet.timestamp).fromNow();
     return tweet;
   });
}
```

Our work is done here. Now, our tweet should look something like this:

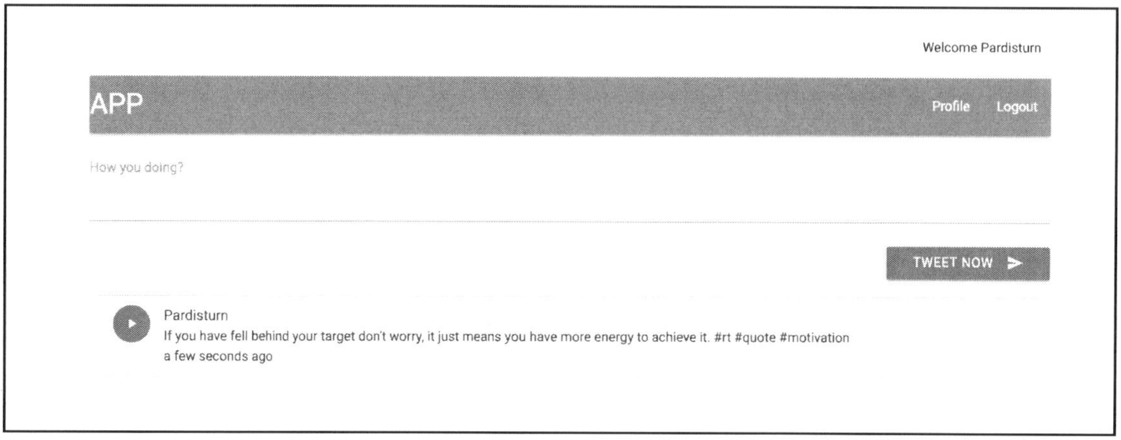

Building user interfaces with Flux

In Flux, we will be defining the responsibility of every module, and it should also be single. The React responsibility is to re-render the view when that data changes, which is good for us. All we need to do is listen to these data events using something like Flux, which will manage our data.

With Flux, you not only separate the responsibility of modules, but also get to do a unidirectional flow within your app, and that's why Flux is so popular.

In the Flux loop, for every module, there's always one direction to go through. This intentional constraint on the flow is what makes the Flux applications easy to design, easy to grow, and easy to manage and maintain.

The following diagram will give you more clarity on the Flux architecture:

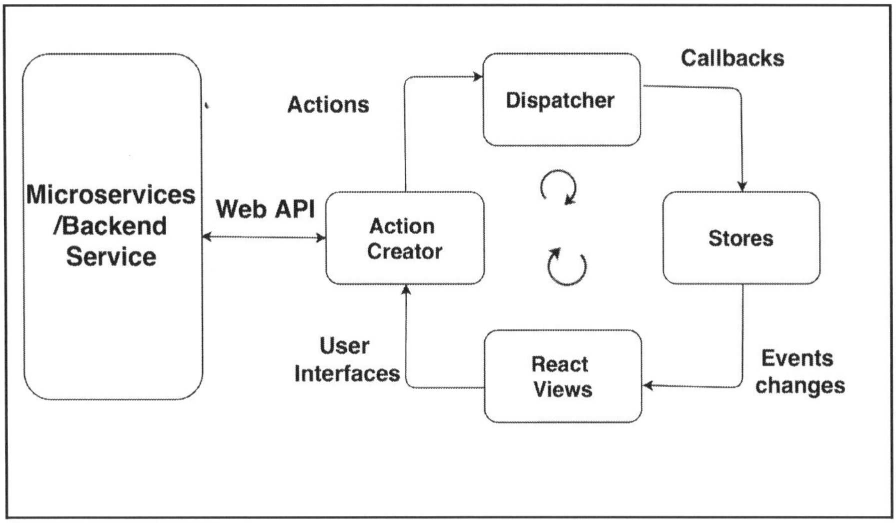

For the diagram, I have taken reference from the Flux repository (`https://github.com/facebook/flux`).

Actions and dispatcher

To begin with Flux, we have to pick a starting point. It could be anything. I find it good to start with the actions. You'll also have to pick a direction of flow. You could go clockwise or counterclockwise. Clockwise is probably good for you as a starting point, so we'll do that.

Don't forget to install the Flux library directly using the following command:

```
$ npm install flux --save
```

Note that the preceding command should be executed from our application directory, or you can add it in `package.json` and execute `npm install` to install the packages.

Now, let's begin with action as our starting point, where we will be following a single responsibility principle. We'll be creating an actions library to communicate with the API, and another action to communicate with the dispatcher.

Let's begin by creating the `actions` folder in the static directory. We will be saving all our actions in this directory.

Since we have two actions that need to be performed--it could be listing the tweets or adding new tweets--we'll start with listing the tweets. Create a `Tactions` file with the `getAllTweets` function, which should be calling REST API's to get all the tweets, as follows:

```
export default{
 getAllTweets(){
 //API calls to get tweets.
 }
}
```

I mentioned that Flux-based applications are easy to design, right? Here's why. Because we know this actions module has a single responsibility with a single flow--either we provide the API call here or it's better to invoke a module that will make all API calls for the application.

Update the `Tactions.jsx` file as follows:

```
import API from "../API"
 export default{
  getAllTweets(){
   console.log(1, "Tactions for tweets");
    API.getAllTweets();
  },
}
```

As you can see, we imported the API module, which will invoke the API's to get the tweets.

So, let's create `API.jsx` in the static directory with the following code snippet to get tweets from the backend server:

```
export default{
  getAllTweets(){
   console.log(2, "API get tweets");
   $.getJSON('/api/v2/tweets', function(tweetModels) {
      var t = tweetModels
    // We need to push the tweets to Server actions to dispatch
    further to stores.
   });
  }
```

Create the `Sactions` file in the actions directory, which will call the dispatcher and define the `actionType`:

```
export default{
  receivedTweets(rawTweets){
   console.log(3, "received tweets");
  //define dispatcher.
 }
}
```

As you can see, we still need to define the dispatcher. Luckily, Facebook created a dispatcher that comes along with the Flux packages.

As mentioned earlier, **Dispatcher** is the central hub for your application, which dispatched the **Actions** and data for registered callbacks. You can refer to the following diagram for a better understanding of the data flow:

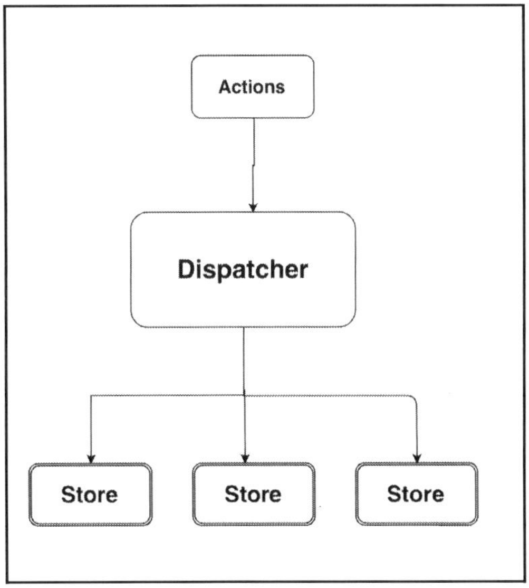

Create a new file named `dispatcher.jsx`, which will create an instance of dispatcher with the following lines of code:

```
import Flux from 'flux';

export default new Flux.Dispatcher();
```

That's it. Now you can import this dispatcher anywhere in your application.

So, let's update our `Sactions.jsx` file, in which you will find the `receivedTweets` function, as shown in the following code snippet:

```
import AppDispatcher from '../dispatcher';
receivedTweets(rawTweets){
  console.log(3, "received tweets");
  AppDispatcher.dispatch({
    actionType: "RECEIVED_TWEETS",
     rawTweets
  })
 }
```

In the `receivedTweets` function , there are three things to be described. Firstly, `rawTweets` will be received from the `getAllTweets` function in `API.jsx`, which we need to update as follows:

```
import SActions from './actions/SActions';

getAllTweets(){
  console.log(2, "API get tweets");
  $.getJSON('/api/v2/tweets', function(tweetModels) {
     var t = tweetModels
     SActions.receivedTweets(t)
 });
```

Stores

Stores manage the application state by taking control of the data within your application, which means stores manage the data, data retrieval methods, dispatcher callbacks, and so on.

For a better understanding, refer to the following diagram:

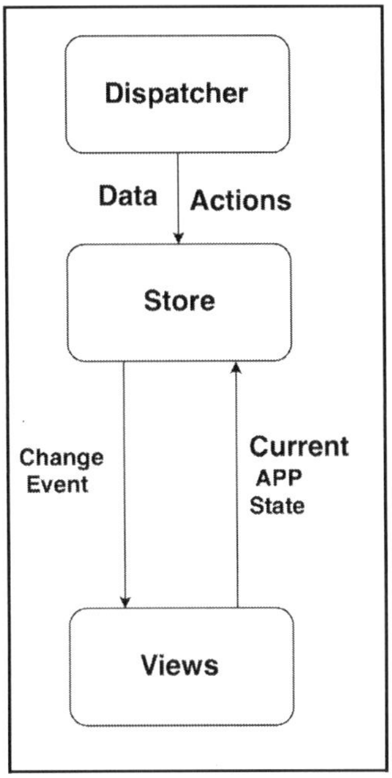

Now that we have defined our dispatcher, next, we need to identify the subscriber's for the change provided by the dispatcher.

Create a separate directory in stores in the static directory, which will contain all the store definitions.

Let's create a `TStore` file that will subscribe to any changes emitted by the dispatcher. Add the following code to the `TStore` file which does so:

```
import AppDispatcher from "../dispatcher";

AppDispatcher.register(action =>{
 switch (action.actionType) {
 Case "RECEIVED_TWEETS" :
console.log(4, "Tstore for tweets");
 break;
  default:
 }
});
```

At this point, we have started the tweet action, which sent the API module a message to get all the tweets. The API did that and then invoked the server actions to pass on the data to the dispatcher. The dispatcher then labeled the data and dispatched it. We also created stores that basically manage the data and request data from the dispatcher.

Currently, your stores are not connected with our app. The stores are supposed to emit changes whenever they occur and, based on that, views will be changed as well.

So, our main component is interested in changes emitted events by the store. For now, let's import our store.

Before we move forward, let's see if our complete flow of application is working fine. It should be something like this:

TIP: It's good practice to keep on checking the user interfaces after you have reached a certain stable state of your application creation.

Let's move on. Currently, we are just dispatching the tweets, next, we need to decide what we need to do with these tweets. So, let's first receive the tweets and then emit changes to the views accordingly. We will be using emitter to do that.

Emitter is a part of the events library that we previously installed using `npm`. So, we can import it from there. Note how it is not the default export, but rather the destructed property on it. Then, our store will be an instance of this tweet `EventEmitter` class.

Let's update our `TStore.jsx` file as follows:

```
import { EventEmitter } from "events";

let _tweets = []
 const CHANGE_EVENT = "CHANGE";

 class TweetEventEmitter extends EventEmitter{
 getAll(){
   let updatelist = _tweets.map(tweet => {
      tweet.updatedate = moment(tweet.timestamp).fromNow();
     return tweet;
    });
 return _tweets;
 }
 emitChange(){
   this.emit(CHANGE_EVENT);
 }

 addChangeListener(callback){
  this.on(CHANGE_EVENT, callback);
 }
 removeChangeListener(callback){
   this.removeListener(CHANGE_EVENT, callback);
 }
}
let TStore = new TweetEventEmitter();

AppDispatcher.register(action =>{
 switch (action.actionType) {
   case ActionTypes.RECEIVED_TWEETS:
     console.log(4, "Tstore for tweets");
     _tweets = action.rawTweets;
     TStore.emitChange();
   break;
  }
  });
 export default TStore;
```

Wow, that's a lot of code to understand at one time! Let's understand it part by part, and the flow of the code as well.

Firstly, we will import the `EventEmitter` library from the events packages by using the following import utility:

```
import { EventEmitter } from "events";
```

Next, we will store the received tweets in `_tweets` and update the tweets in the `getAll()` function so that, in views, it will show the tweet's timing with reference to the current system time:

```
getAll(){
  let updatelist = _tweets.map(tweet => {
      tweet.updatedate = moment(tweet.timestamp).fromNow();
      return tweet;
    });
  return _tweets;
}
```

We have also created functions for the views to add and remove the change event listener. These two functions will also be just a wrap around the `EventEmitter` syntax.

These functions take `callback` arguments that will be sent by views. These functions are basically to add or remove listener for the views to start or stop listening to these changes in the store. Add the following code to `TStore.jsx` to do so:

```
addChangeListener(callback){
  this.on(CHANGE_EVENT, callback);
}
removeChangeListener(callback){
 this.removeListener(CHANGE_EVENT, callback);
}
```

Make sure you have no errors in the console with all the updated code.

Let's move on to views, that is, the main component where we will create a function to pull data from the store and prepare an object for the state of component.

Let's write `getAppState()` function in `main.jsx`, which maintains the state of the app, as shown in the following code:

```
let getAppState = () =>{
  return { tweetslist: TStore.getAll()};
}
```

As mentioned earlier, the file extension doesn't really matter, whether it is `.js` or `.jsx`.

Now, we will be calling this function from the `Main` class, and we will also call the add and remove listener functions that we created in `main.jsx`, using the following code block:

```
import TStore from "./stores/TStore";

class Main extends React.Component{
  constructor(props){
   super(props);
   this.state= getAppState();
   this._onChange = this._onChange.bind(this);
   //defining the state of component.
  }
// function to pull tweets
  componentDidMount() {
  TStore.addChangeListener(this._onChange);
 }
componentWillUnMount() {
  TStore.removeChangeListener(this._onChange);
 }

_onChange(){
 this.setState(getAppState());
 }
```

Also, we have to update the `render` function to get the `Tweetslist` state to show in view, and it is done using the following code snippet:

```
render(){
  return (
   <div>
   <Tweet sendTweet={this.addTweet.bind(this)}/>
      <TweetList tweet={this.state.tweetslist}/>
   </div>
   );
  }
```

Great, we have done pretty much everything now; our tweet should be shown without any problems, as follows:

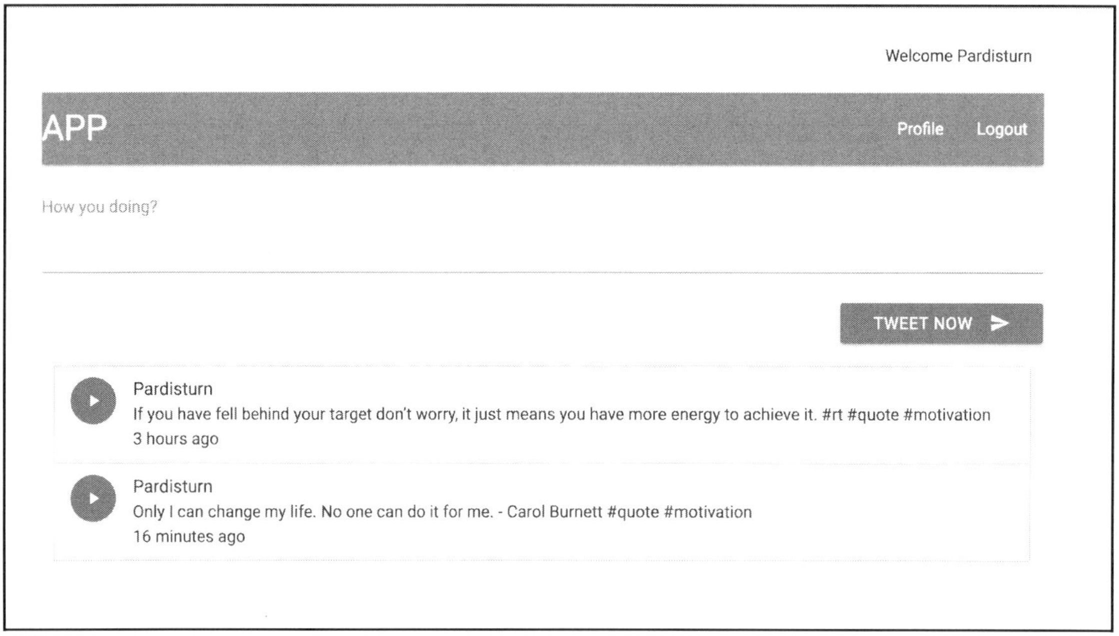

Awesome! Our application is working fine.

If you look at the architecture diagram of Flux, we have completed the flow of Flux once, but we still need to complete the cycle by creating the API's to add new tweets.

Let's implement it by sending a new tweet feature using Flux. We will be making a couple of changes in `main.jsx`. In the `render` function, the `Tweetcall` to `addTweet` function into following line:

```
<Tweet sendTweet={this.addTweet.bind(this)}/>
```

Instead, we will call the `Tweet` component without a parameter, as follows:

```
<Tweet />
```

Moreover, in the `Tweet` component, we will call the `TActions` module to add new tweets. Update the code in the `Tweet` component as follows:

```
import TActions from "../actions/Tactions"
export default class Tweet extends React.Component {
 sendTweet(event){
  event.preventDefault();
  // this.props.sendTweet(this.refs.tweetTextArea.value);
  TActions.sendTweet(this.refs.tweetTextArea.value);
  this.refs.tweetTextArea.value = '';
 }

}
```

The `Render` function in the `Tweet` component remains the same.

Let's add a new `sendTweet` function that will invoke an API call to the endpoint URL of the backend application and add it to the backend database.

Now, our `Taction.jsx` file should look like this:

```
import API from "../API"

export default{
  getAllTweets(){
   console.log(1, "Tactions for tweets");
   API.getAllTweets();
  },
  sendTweet(body){
    API.addTweet(body);
   }
}
```

Now, add the `API.addTweet` function in `API.jsx`, which will make an API call and also update the state of tweetlists as well. Add the following `addTweet` function to the `API.jsx` file:

```
addTweet(body){
   $.ajax({
       url: '/api/v2/tweets',
       contentType: 'application/json',
       type: 'POST',
       data: JSON.stringify({
      'username': "Pardisturn",
      'body': body,
       }),
     success: function() {
```

```
            rawTweet => SActions.receivedTweet({ tweetedby:
            "Pardisturn",body: tweet, timestamp: Date.now})
        },
        error: function() {
              return console.log("Failed");
         }
      });
    }
```

Also, we are passing the newly added tweets to the server actions to get them dispatched and available for stores.

Let's add a new function, `receivedTweet`, which will dispatch them. Use the following code snippet to do so:

```
receivedTweet(rawTweet){
  AppDispatcher.dispatch({
    actionType: ActionTypes.RECEIVED_TWEET,
    rawTweet
   })
 }
```

`ActionTypes` are constantly defined in `constants.jsx` in the static directory.

Now, let's define the `RECEIVED_TWEETactiontype` case in the tweet store to emit changes for the view to take further action. The following is the updated `Appdispatcher.register` function defined in `TStore.jsx`:

```
AppDispatcher.register(action =>{
 switch (action.actionType) {
      case ActionTypes.RECEIVED_TWEETS:
      console.log(4, "Tstore for tweets");
      _tweets = action.rawTweets;
      TStore.emitChange();
       break;
     case ActionTypes.RECEIVED_TWEET:
       _tweets.unshift(action.rawTweet);
       TStore.emitChange();
       break;
    default:

   }
 });
```

Now, we are pretty much done with adding a new tweet module using Flux and it should work totally fine, as shown in the following screenshot:

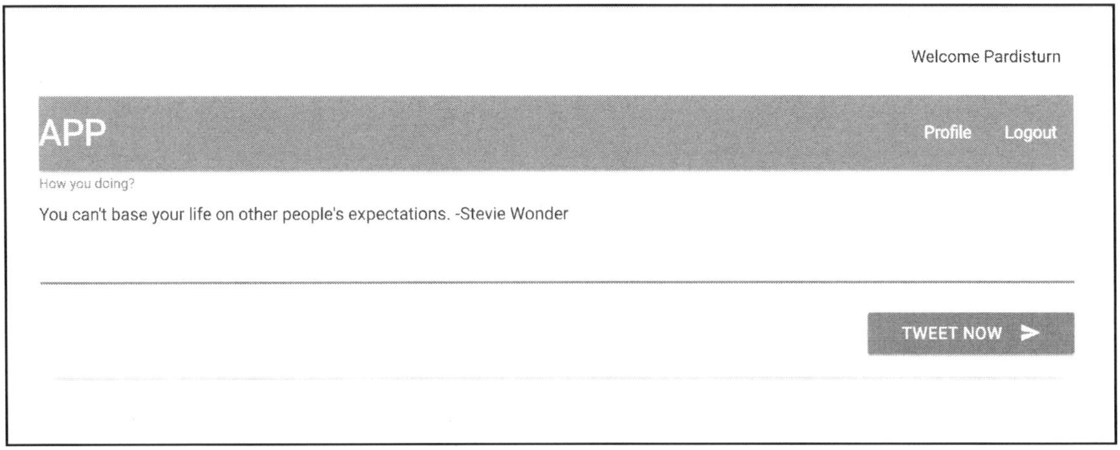

Now, if we click on the **Tweet Now** button, the tweet should be added and it should project in the following panel, as shown here:

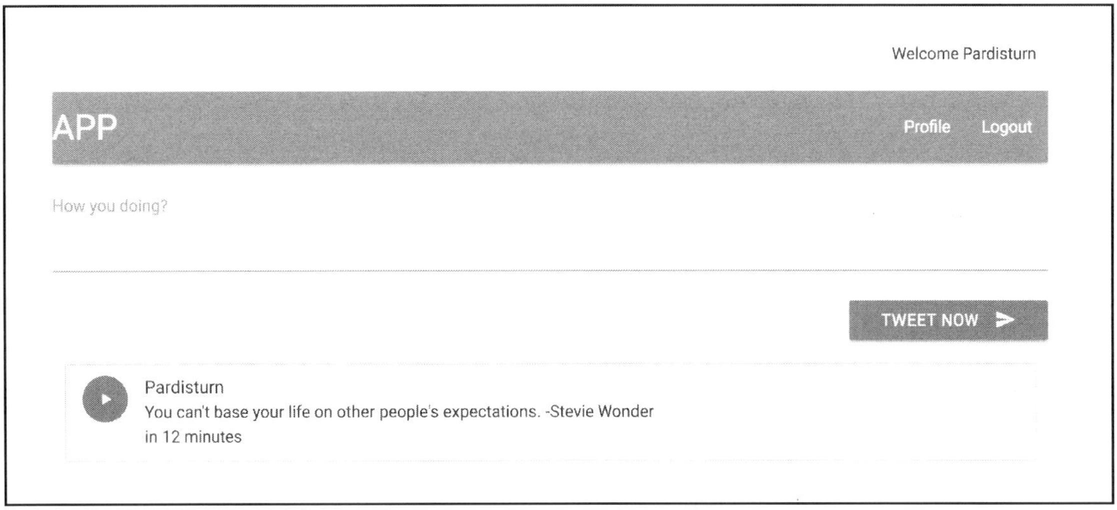

Summary

In this chapter, you learned how to structure our application by using the Flux pattern, and we also got an understanding of the different concepts of Flux, such as dispatcher, stores, and so on. Flux gives you good patterns to distribute responsibility between modules, which really needs to be understood, as we are developing an application for the cloud platform, such as AWS, Azure, and so on, so our application should be highly responsive. That's all we have from the building user interfaces side, but in the coming chapter, we will understand a few important concepts, such as event sourcing, and how we can make the application more secure by using different authentication methods.

7
Learning Event Sourcing and CQRS

In the last chapter, we looked into the drawbacks of our current business model, and now, in this chapter, we'll look at how **Event Sourcing** (**ES**) and **CQRS** (**Command Query Responsibility Segregation**) would be helpful to overcome those.

In this chapter, we will talk about some architectural designs that deal with massive scalability. We will also look at two patterns, Event Sourcing and CQRS, which are all about solving the problem response behavior for such an enormous number of requests.

Many of us think that compliance with twelve-factor apps will make our application a cloud native application with higher scalability, but there are other strategies, such as ES and CQRS, which can make our application more reliable.

Since cloud native applications are internet facing, we expect thousands or millions of requests from different sources. Implementing infrastructure architecture to handle the requests by scaling up or down aren't enough. You need to make your application support such enormous scaling. That's when these patterns come into the picture.

The topics that we will cover in this chapter are listed as follows:

- Introduction to Event Sourcing
- Introduction to Command Query Responsibility Segregation
- Example code to implement ES and CQRS
- Event Sourcing with Apache Kafka

Introduction

Let's start with reviewing the *n*-tier architecture, where we have some clients, a network, a business model, some business logic, some data storage, and so on. This is a basic model, which you will find as part of any architectural design. It looks something like the following diagram:

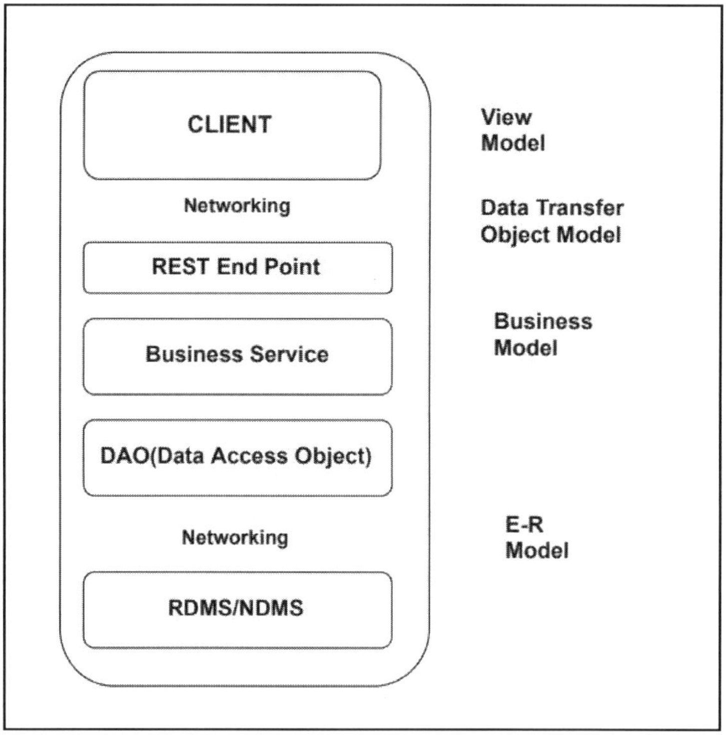

As you can see in this architecture, we have these different models that come into action:

- **View Model**: This is basically for client-side interaction
- **DTO Model**: This is for communication between the client and the REST Endpoints
- **Business Model**: This is a combination of **DAO** (**Data Access Object**) and business service, which interprets the user requests, and communicates with the storage service
- **E-R Model**: This defines the relationship between entities (that is, **DTO** and **RDMS/NDMS**)

Now that you have some idea about the architecture, let's understand its characteristics, which are listed as follows:

- **Identical stack for application**: In this model, we use the same stack of elements for all read and write operations, starting from REST API to business service, and then we access the storage services, and so on, as all the different component codes are deployed together as a single entity.
  The following diagram shows the **Read/Write** operation flow through different models:

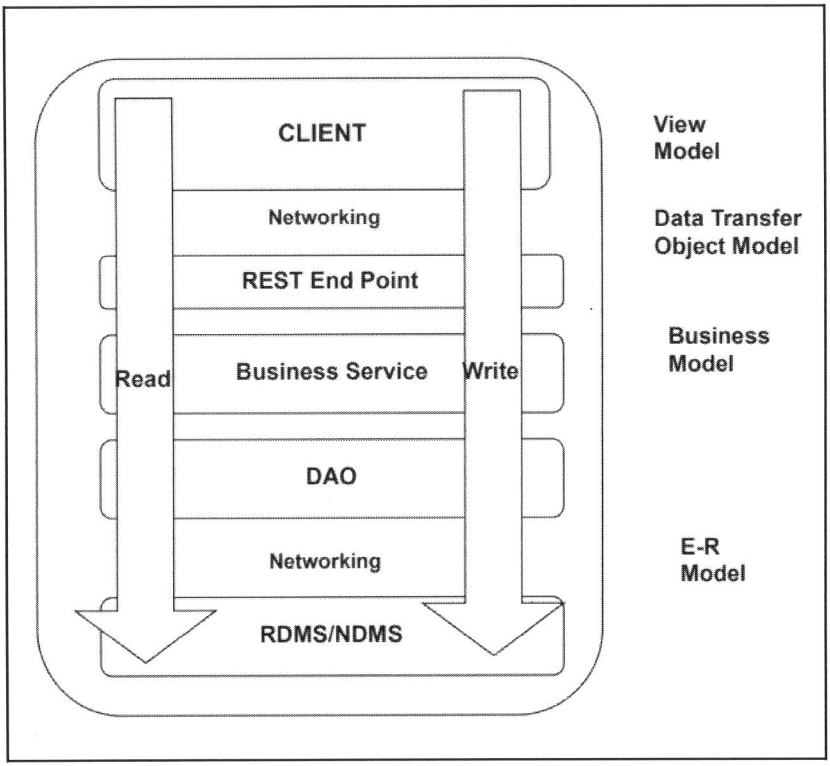

- **Identical Data Model**: In this scenario, you will find that most of the times, we use the same or a similar data model for business logic processing, or for reading and writing data.

- **Deployment Units**: We use coarse-grained deployment units, which consist of the following:
    - A build (an executable collection of components)
    - Documents (end-user support material and release notes)
    - Installation artifacts, which combine both the read and write code together
- **Accessing data directly:** If we want to change data, we usually go ahead. Especially, in the case of RDBMS, we change the data directly, as in the following case--if we want to update the row with **User ID 1** with another dataset, we usually do it directly. Also, once we have updated this value, the old value will be void from the application as well as the storage side, and cannot be retrieved:

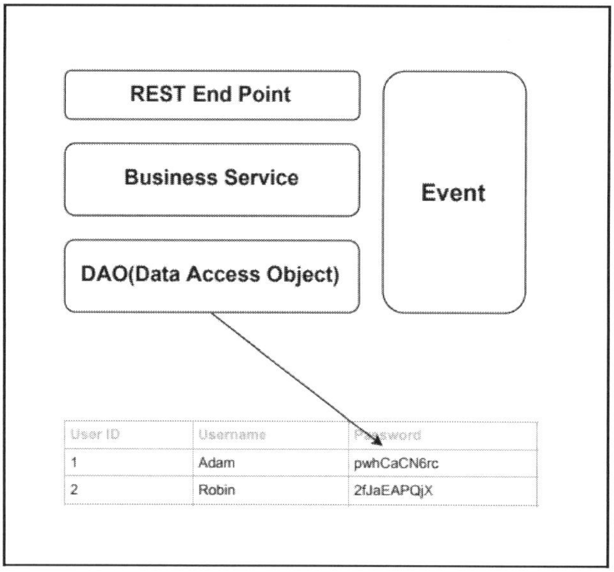

So far, we have been making use of the preceding approach, and I would say that it is pretty much proven and successful in terms of the response from user requests. However, there are other alternate approaches which can perform much better than this when compared.

Let's discuss the drawbacks of the aforementioned business architecture approach, which are as follows:

- **Inability to scale independently**: Since our code for the read and write operations reside at the same location, we cannot scale our read or write for the application independently. Say you have 90% read and 10% write from the application side at a particular point in time, we can't scale our read independently. In order to scale reads, we need to scale out the complete architecture, which is of no use, and increases the waste of resources.
- **No data history**: Since we are dealing with the scenario where we update the data directly, once the data is updated, the application will start showing the latest dataset after some period of time. Also, once the dataset is updated, old data values are not tracked, and hence, are lost. Even if we want to implement such kinds of features, we need to write lots of code to enable it.
- **Monolithic approach**: This approach tends to be a monolithic approach, as we try to merge things together. Moreover, we have coarse-grained deployment units, and we try to keep the code of the different components together. So, this kind of approach will ultimately result in a mess, which will be difficult to resolve.

One kind of approach which addresses these challenges is Event Sourcing.

Understanding Event Sourcing

By simple definition, Event Sourcing is an architectural pattern which determines the state of an application by a sequence of events.

The best way to understand Event Sourcing is by using an analogy. One of the best examples would be **online shopping**, which is an event processing system. Somebody places an order, which gets registered in an order queue for a vendor ordering system. Then, this status is notified to the customer at different stages of the order being delivered.

All these events, which occur one after the other, form a sequence of events called an event stream, which should look something like the following diagram:

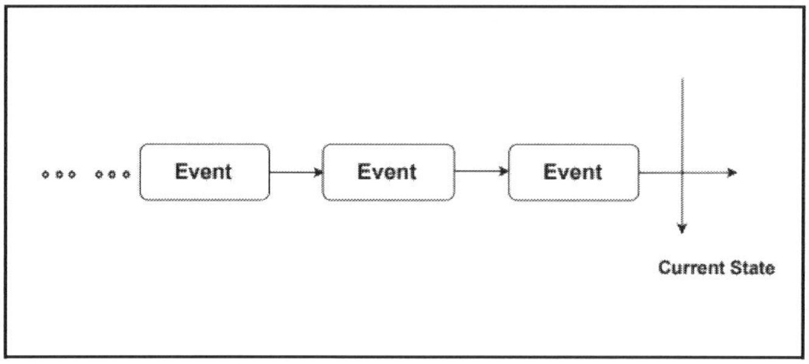

So, Event Sourcing takes consideration of events which happened in the past, and are recorded for processing based on certain transactions.

An ideal Event Sourcing system is based on the building blocks shown in the following diagram:

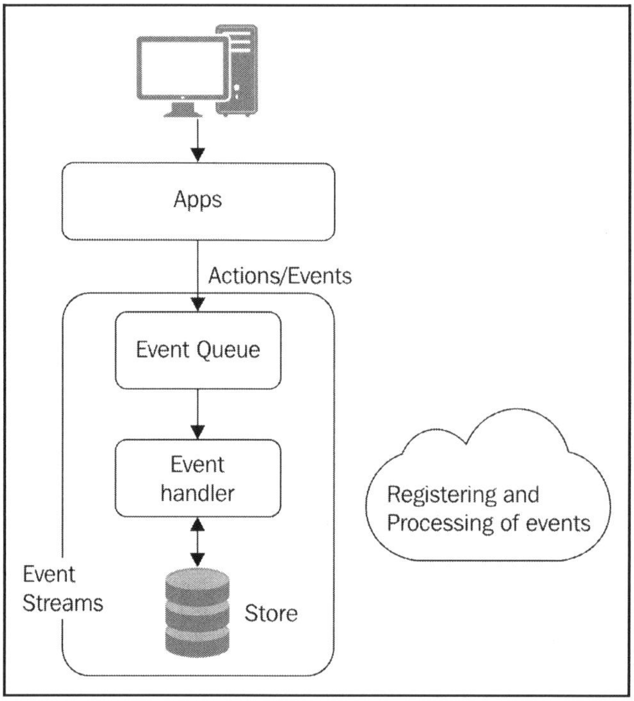

The preceding diagram depicts an ideal event processing system, starting from the application to the creation of **Events** related to a certain incident, and then putting them in an **Event Queue** for further processing, which is performed by an **Event Handler**. Based on the description of the **Events**, the **Event Handler** processes them accordingly, and registers them in the **Store**.

Event Sourcing follows certain laws/tenets, which make application development a structured and disciplined process. Most people usually feel that Event Sourcing is hard or they think it is outright because of these tenets, which must not be broken, as doing so will create a huge chaos in the application.

Laws of Event Sourcing

Listed next are some of the Event Sourcing laws which need to be maintained while implementing ES on any system (that is, application design):

- **Idempotency**: An ideal event-sourced business logic must be idempotent. This means that when you execute a business logic against an input stream of data, the resultant state of the application will always remain the same. Yes, that's true, it will remain the same irrespective of the number of times you execute the business logic.
- **Isolation**: Event Sourcing must not depend on the external event streams. This is one of the most important tenets of Event Sourcing. Generally, business logic is rarely ever executed in a vacuum. Applications usually interact with external entities for reference. Moreover, applications make use of cached information from external sources, even if developers don't consider that point. Now, the question that arises is what happens if your business logic uses the external input to compute results? Let's take the example of a stock exchange, where stock prices keep on changing, which means that the stock price at the time of state computation won't be the same on multiple evaluations, which violates the idempotent rule.

> - As per the developer's understanding, this is a very difficult condition to satisfy. However, the solution to deal with this is to inject notifications into the main event stream from external events. Since these notifications are now part of the main events stream, you will get the expected result every time.

- **Quality assurance**: An event-sourced application, after being developed completely, should be a well-tested application. Writing test cases for the event-sourced application is easy--it usually takes a list of inputs and returns some state, considering that you are writing test cases following the previously defined principles.
- **Recoverable**: Event-sourced applications should support recovery and replay. If you have a cloud native application which adheres to all the guidelines of the twelve-factor apps to create an application suitable for the cloud platform, Event Sourcing plays a vital role in disaster recovery.
  Assuming that the event stream is durable, an event-sourced application's initial advantage is to compute the state of the application. Usually, in a cloud environment, it is possible that the application crashes because of numerous reasons; Event Sourcing can help us identify the last state of the application, and recover it quickly to reduce the downtime. Moreover, Event Sourcing's replay functionality gives you the ability to look at the past state at the time of auditing, as well as troubleshooting.
- **Big Data**: Event Sourcing applications often generate huge amounts of data. Since an event-sourced application keeps track of every event, it is possible that it will generate huge amounts of data. It depends on how many events you have, how often they arrive, and how huge the data payload is for the events.
- **Consistency**: Event-sourced applications often maintain consistency for the registering of events. Think of banking transactions--every event happening during a bank transaction is very crucial. It should be noted that consistency should be maintained while recording it.

It is very important to understand that these events are something that happened in the past, because when we name these events, they should be understandable. Examples of a few valid names for events could be as follows:

- `PackageDeliveredEvent`
- `UserVerifiedEvent`
- `PaymentVerifiedEvent`

Invalid events would be named as follows:

- `CreateUserEvent`
- `AddtoCartEvent`

The following is some example code for an event:

```
class ExampleApplication(ApplicationWithPersistencePolicies):
  def __init__(self, **kwargs):
    super(ExampleApplication, self).__init__(**kwargs)
   self.snapshot_strategy = None
   if self.snapshot_event_store:
       self.snapshot_strategy = EventSourcedStrategy(
           event_store=self.snapshot_event_store,
       )
   assert self.integer_sequenced_event_store is not None
   self.example_repository = ExampleRepository(
       event_store=self.integer_sequenced_event_store,
       snapshot_strategy=self.snapshot_strategy,
   )
```

There are a few points that you should know:

- Every event is immutable, which means that an event, once fired, cannot be reverted.
- You never delete an event. Even if we try to delete an event, we consider deletion also as an event.
- Event streams are driven by message-broker architecture. Some of the message brokers are RabbitMQ, ActiveMQ, and so on.

Now, let's discuss some of the pros of Event Sourcing, which are as follows:

- Event Sourcing gives the capability to rebuild the system very quickly
- Event Sourcing gives you command over the data, which means that the data we require for our processing is easy to acquire by looking at the event stream for your processing purpose, say by audit, analysis, and so it should be audit, analysis, and so on
- By looking at the events, it is easy to understand what went wrong during a period of time, considering a set of data
- Event replay would be advantageous during troubleshooting or bug fixing

Now, the question arises that since we are generating such a huge amount of events, does this affect the performance of the application? I would say, YES!

As our application is generating events for every transaction which needs to be processed by the event handler, the response time of the application is reduced. The solution to this problem is CQRS.

Introduction to CQRS

Command Query Responsibility Segregation is a fancy pattern name, which means decoupling the input and the output of your system. In CQRS, we mainly talk about the read and write characteristics of our application; so, the commands in the context of CQRS are mainly write operations, while the queries are read operations, and responsibility means that we separate our read and write operations.

If we look at the architecture described in the first section, Introduction, and apply CQRS, the architecture will be divided into half, and would look something like this:

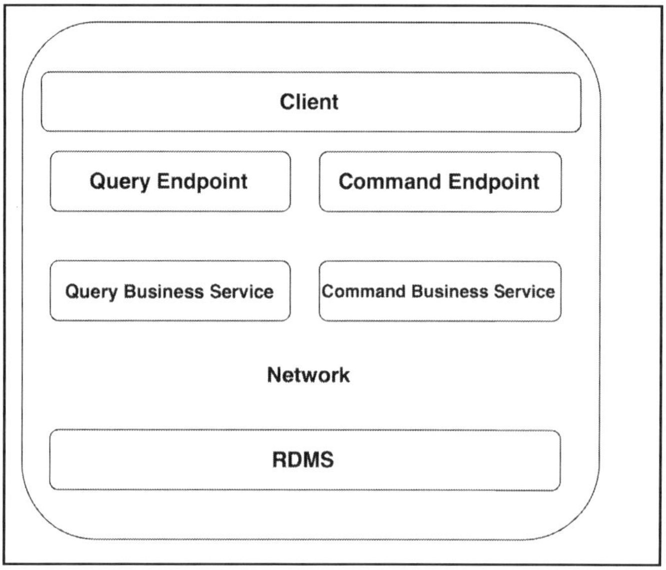

Now we will look at some code examples.

A traditional interface module would look something like this:

```
Class managementservice(interface):
 Saveuser(userdata);
Updateuser(userid);
listuserbyusername(username);
listuserbyid(userid);
```

Split-up, or as I prefer to call them, CQRS-ified interfaces, would look something like this:

```
Class managementcommandservice(interface):
  Saveuser(userdata);
Updateuser(userid);
Class managementqueryservice(interface):
listuserbyusername(username);
listuserbyid(userid);
```

So, the overall architecture, after the implementation of CQRS and Event Sourcing, would be something like the one shown in the following diagram:

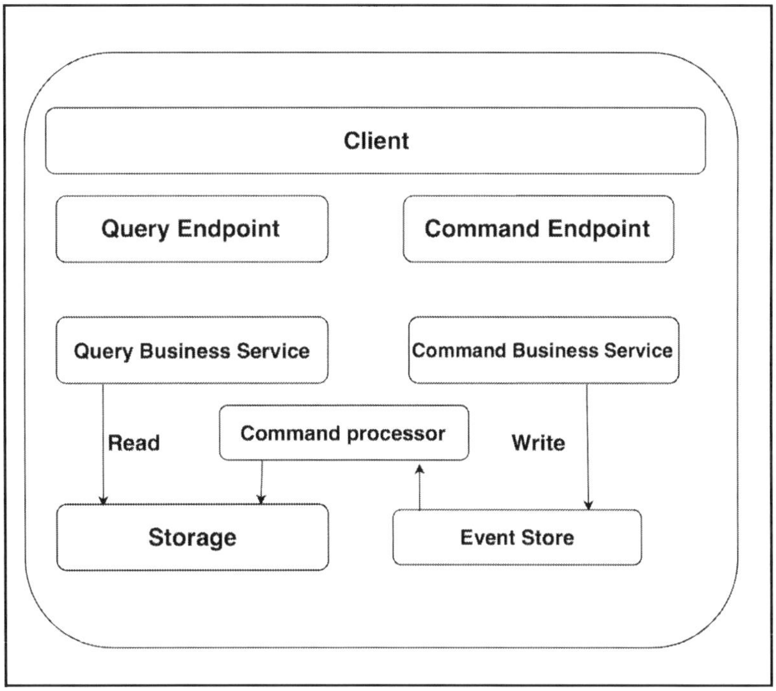

This is the complete architecture after the implementation of Event Sourcing and CQRS.

In a classic monolithic application, you have endpoints that write to a database, and endpoints that read from it. The same database is used for both read and write operations, and you don't reply to the endpoints until an acknowledgement or commit is received from the database.

On a massive scale, with a high inbound event throughput and complex event processing requirements, you can't afford to run slow queries for reads, nor can you afford to sit and wait for processing to take place every time you get a new inbound event.

The flow for both read and write operations works as follows:

- **Write model**: In this case, when a command is fired from the endpoint and received at the **Command Business Service**, it first issues the events for every incident to the **Event Store**. In the **Event Store**, you also have a **Command processor**, or, in other words, event handler, and this **Command processor** is able to derive the application state into a separate **Storage**, which could be a relational storage.
- **Read model**: In the case of the **Read** model, we simply use the **Query Endpoints** to query the data which we want to **Read** or retrieve for the application usage by the client.

The biggest advantage is that we don't need to go through the **Write** model (which is on the right-hand side of the preceding image). When it comes to querying the database, this process makes our query execution faster, and reduces the response time which, in turn, increases the application's performance.

Advantages of the CQRS-ified architecture

This architecture has the following advantages:

- **Independent scalability and deployment**: We can now scale and deploy an individual component based on its usage. As in the case of microservices, we can now have separate microservices for each of the tasks, say a read microservice and a write microservice, in this architecture stack.
- **Choice of technologies**: Freedom with regards to the choice of technologies for the different sections of the business model. For instance, for the command functionality, we could choose Scala or similar (assuming that we have a complex business model, and we have a lot of data to write). In the case of a query, we can choose, for example, ROR (Ruby on Rails) or Python (which we are already using).

This type of architecture is best suited for bounded context from **DDD** (**Domain-Driven design**), because we can define the business context for the microservices.

Challenges related to ES and CQRS

Every architecture design model has its own challenges for implementation. Let's discuss the challenges of ES and CQRS:

- **Inconsistency**: Systems developed using ES and CQRS are mostly consistent. However, as we store the events issued by the **Command Business Service** at the **Event Store**, and store the state of the application in the main **Storage** as well, I would say this kind of system is not fully consistent. If we really want to make our system fully consistent using ES and CQRS, we need to keep our **Event Store** and main **Storage** on a single **Relational Database**, and our **Command processor** should handle all our incoming events, and store them in both storages at the same time, as depicted in the following diagram:

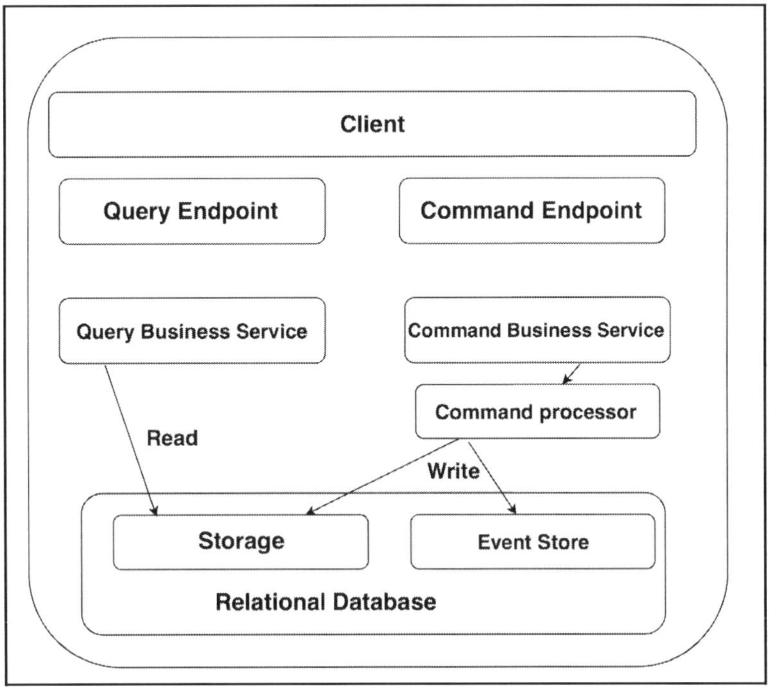

I would say that the consistency level should be defined by understanding the business domain. How much consistency you would need in events, and how much these consistencies would cost, needs to be understood. After inspecting your business domain, you will be able to make these decisions considering the aforementioned factors.

- **Validation**: It is very easy when we talk in terms of validating the customer registration form, where we need to validate the individual field, and so on. But actual validation comes when we have to do validation based on uniqueness--say we have a customer with certain user credentials (username/password). So, to make sure that the username is unique is a crucial validation when we have more than 2 million customers who need to be registered. A few questions that need to be asked in terms of validation are as follows:
    - What is the data requirement for validation?
    - Where to retrieve the data for validation from?
    - What is the probability of validation?
    - What is the impact of validation failure on the business?
- **Parallel data updates**: This is very crucial in terms of data consistency. Say, you have a user who wants to update certain records at the same time, or within a difference of nanoseconds. In this case, the possibility of consistency as well as validation checks is challenging, as there is a possibility that one user might end up overwriting the other user information which could create chaos.

Overcoming challenges

One way to solve such a problem in Event Sourcing is to add versions in events, which will act as a handle for making changes to the data and make sure it is validated fully.

Problem solving

Let's take the use case shown in the following diagram for Event Sourcing and CQRS to understand it in terms of writing code for it:

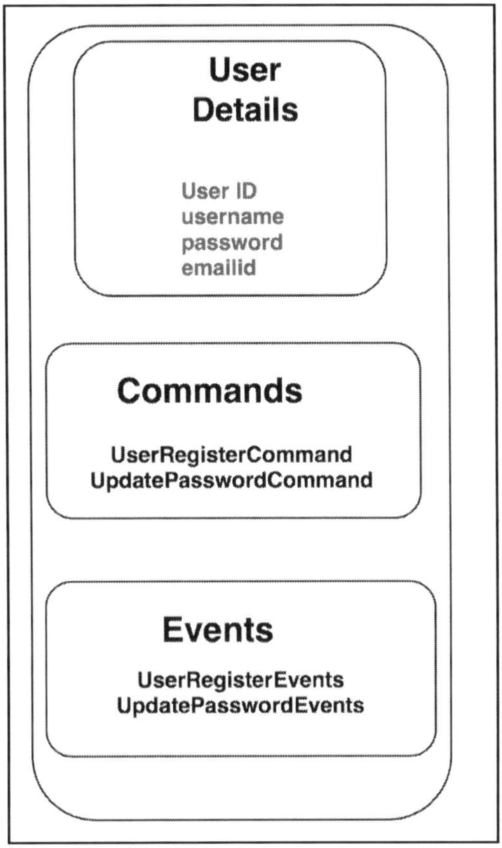

Explanation of the problem

In this case, we are provided with **User Details** such as **User ID** (which should be unique), **username**, **password**, **email ID**, and so on, and we have to create two write **Commands** to be fired--**UserRegistrationCommand** and **UpdatePasswordCommand**, which trigger two **Events: UserRegisterEvents** and **UpdatePasswordEvents**. The idea is that a user, once registered, should be able to reset the password as per their needs.

The solution

In order to solve this problem, we will need to write functions related to write commands to receive the inputs and update the event store.

Now, let's add the following code to the `commands.py` file, which will have code related to the write commands that need to be performed as described:

```
class userregister(object):
  def __init__(self, user_id, user_name, password, emailid):
    self.user_id = user_id
    self.user_name = user_name
    self.password = password
    self.emailid = emaild

class updatepassword(object):
  def __init__(self, user_id, new_password, original_version):
    self.item_id = item_id
    self.new_password = new__password
    self.original_version = original_version
```

So, we have added the functions related to the commands, but it should be called from somewhere with the user details.

Let's add a new file called `main.py` from where the preceding command's function will be called.

In the following code, we call the preceding code by triggering events:

```
 from aggregate import Aggregate
 from errors import InvalidOperationError
 from events import *

class userdetails(Aggregate):
  def __init__(self, id = None, name = '"", password = "", emailid =
  "" ):
    Aggregate.__init__(self)
    self._apply_changes(Userdetails(id, name, password, emailid))

def userRegister(self, userdetails):
    userdetails = {1, "robin99", "xxxxxx", "robinatkevin@gmail.com"
}
    self._apply_changes(UserRegisterevent(userdetails))

def updatePassword(self, count):
   password = ""
    self._apply_changes(UserPasswordEvent(password))
```

Let's understand the preceding code, function by function:

```
def __init__(self, id = None, name = '"", password = "", emailid =
 "" ):
   Aggregate.__init__(self)
   self._apply_changes(Userdetails(id, name, password, emailid))
```

The last code initializes the `self` object with some default values; it is similar to the initialize function in any programming language.

Next, we defined the `userRegister` function, which, basically, collects `userdetails`, and then creates the event (`UserRegisterevent(userdetails))`) as follows:

```
def userRegister(self, userdetails):
   userdetails = {1, "robin99", "xxxxxx", "robinatkevin@gmail.com"
}
   self._apply_changes(UserRegisterevent(userdetails))
```

So, once the user is registered, he/she is authorized to update the profile details, which could be the email ID, password, username, and others--in our case, it is the password. Please refer to the following code:

```
def updatePassword(self, count):
 password = ""
self._apply_changes(UserPasswordEvent(password))
```

You can write similar code for updating the email ID, username, or others.

Moving on, we need to add error handling, as in our `main.py` file, we call a custom module, `errors`, to handle operation-related errors. Let's add the following code to `errors.py` to pass the errors if caught:

```
class InvalidOperationError(RuntimeError):
 pass
```

As you can see in `main.py`, we call the `Aggregate` module, and you must be wondering why it is being used. The `Aggregate` module is very important as it keeps track of the changes that need to be applied. In other words, it forces the event to commit all its uncommented changes to the event store.

In order to do so, let's add the following code to a new file called `aggregate.py`:

```
class Aggregate(object):
  def __init__(self):
    self.uncommitted_changes = []

  @classmethod
  def from_events(cls, events):
    aggregate = cls()
    for event in events: event.apply_changes(aggregate)
    aggregate.uncommitted_changes = []
    return aggregate

 def changes_committed(self):
    self.uncommitted_changes = []

 def _apply_changes(self, event):
    self.uncommitted_changes.append(event)
    event.apply_changes(self)
```

In `aggregate.py`, we initialize the `self` object, which is called in `main.py`, and then keep a track of events which are being triggered. After a period of time, we will make a call to apply the changes from `main.py` to update `eventstore` with the updated values and events.

Let's create a new file, `events.py`, which contains the definition for the command that needs to be registered in the backend. The following code snippet needs to be updated in `events.py`:

```
class UserRegisterEvent(object):
 def apply_changes(self, userdetails):
    id = userdetails.id
    name = userdetails.name
    password = userdetails.password
    emailid = userdetails.emailid

class UserPasswordEvent(object):
 def __init__(self, password):
    self.password = password

 def apply_changes(password):
    user.password = password
```

Now we are left with the command handler, which is very important, as it decides which operation needs to be performed and the respective events that need to be triggered. Let's add the file `command_handler.py` with the following code:

```
from commands import *

class UserCommandsHandler(object):
 def __init__(self, user_repository):
   self.user_repository = user_repository

 def handle(self, command):
   if command.__class__ == UserRegisterEvent:
       self.user_repository.save(commands.userRegister(command.id,
 command.name, command.password, command.emailid))
   if command.__class__ == UpdatePasswordEvent:
       with self._user_(command.password, command.original_version)
  as item:
           user.update(command.password)
@contextmanager
 def _user(self, id, user_version):
   user = self.user_repository.find_by_id(id)
   yield user
   self.user.save(password, user_version)
```

In `command_handler.py`, we have written a handle function which will make the decision of the flow of event execution.

As you can see, we called the `@contextmanager` module, which is very important to understand here.

Let's take a scenario: suppose there are two people, Bob and Alice, and both are using the same user credentials. Let's say they both are trying to update the profile details field, for example, the password, at the same time. Now, we need to understand how these commands get requested. In short, whose request will hit the event store first. Also, if both the users update the password, then it is highly possible that one user's updated password will be overwritten by another.

One way of solving the problem is to use version along with user schema, as we use it in the context manager. We take `user_version` as an argument, which will determine the state of the user data, and once it is modified, we can increment the version to make the data consistent.

So, in our case, if Bob's modified value is updated first (of course, with the new version), and if Alice's request version field doesn't match with the version in the database, then Alice's update request will be rejected.

Once this is updated, we should be able to register and update the password. Though this is an example to show how to implement CQRS, you can extend this to create microservices on top of it.

Kafka as an eventstore

Although we have already seen the CQRS implementation, I still feel that you may have a few queries related to `eventstore`, and how it works. That's why I'll take the use case of Kafka, which can be used as an `eventstore` for your application.

Kafka is, typically, a message broker or message queue (similar to RabbitMQ, JMS, and others).

As per the Kafka documentation, Event Sourcing is a style of application design where the state changes are logged as a time-ordered sequence of records. Kafka's support for very large stored log data makes it an excellent backend for an application built in this style.

For more information related to implementing Kafka, read its documentation at this link: `https://kafka.apache.org/documentation/`.

Kafka has the following basic components:

- **Producers**: This sends messages to Kafka
- **Consumers**: These subscribe to streams of messages in Kafka

Kafka works in the following manner:

- Producers write messages in Kafka topics, which could be users
- Every message that is in a Kafka topic is appended at the end of the partition

Kafka only supports **write** operations.

- Partitions represent streams of events, and topics can be categorized into multiple topics
- Partitions in topics are independent of each other
- To avoid disaster, Kafka partitions are replicated across several machines
- To consume Kafka messages, the client reads the message sequentially, starting from the offset, which is set in Kafka by the consumer

Applying Event Sourcing with Kafka

Let's take a use case where the client tries to perform a certain operation, and we are using Kafka as an eventstore to capture all the messages that are being passed. In this case, we have the user management service, which could be a microservice responsible for managing all user requests. We will start with identifying the topics for Kafka based on user events, which could be one of the following:

- `UserCreatedEvent`
- `UserUpdatedEvent`
- `UserDeletionEvent`
- `UserLoggedinEvent`
- `UserRoleUpdatedEvent`

These events will, ideally, be published by the **User Management Service**, and all microservices will consume these events. The following diagram shows the user request flow:

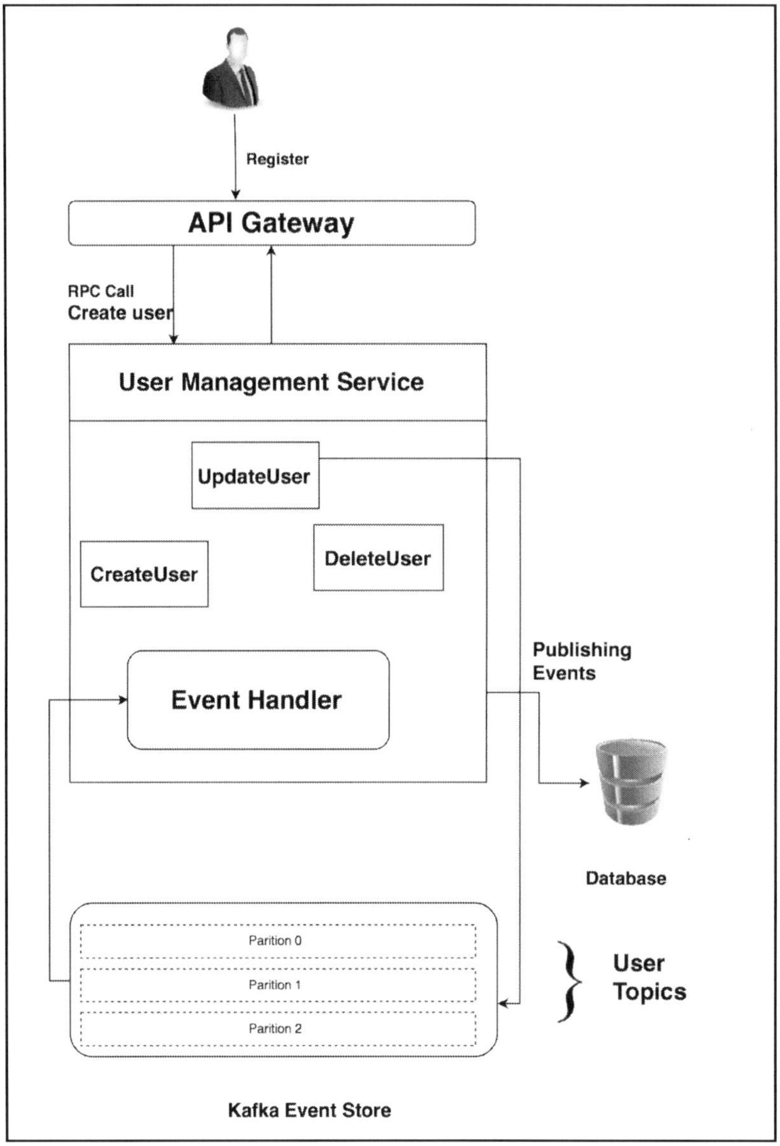

How it works

A user makes a `POST` request to the API gateway, which is an entry point for the user management service to register users. The API gateway, in turn, makes an **RPC** Call (**Remote procedure call**) to the `createUser` method in the management service. The `createUser` endpoint performs a set of validations on the user input. If the input is invalid, it will throw an exception, and return the error to the API gateway. Once the user input is validated, the user is registered, and `UserCreatedEvent` is triggered to get published in Kafka. In Kafka, partitions capture the events. In our example, the users topic has three partitions, so the event will be published to one of the three partitions based on some defined logic; this logic is defined by us, which varies based on the use case.

> All read operations such as listing user, and more, can be retrieved directly from readStore (database such as PostgreSQL).

Summary

This was a complex chapter, but if you understand it fully, it will make your application efficient and high performance.

We kicked off by understanding the drawbacks of the classic architecture, and then moved on to discuss the concept and implementation of ES and CQRS. We also looked at the implementation of a sample problem. We talked about why these patterns are useful, and how they have a particular harmony with massive-scale, cloud native applications.

In the upcoming chapter, we are going to deep dive into the security of the application. Stay tuned!

8

Securing the Web Application

In this chapter, we will mainly discuss how to secure your application from external threats that could cause data loss, which, in turn, affects the overall business.

Web application security is always a concern for any business unit. Therefore, we not only look at the traditional application logic and data-related security issues, but at the protocol and platform concerns as well. Developers have become more responsible for ensuring compliance with the best practices regarding web application security.

Keeping this in mind, this book is intended for application developers, system administrators, as well as DevOps professionals who want to keep their application secure, whether it is at the application level or platform.

We will cover the following topics in this chapter:

- Network security versus application security
- Implementation of application authorization using different methods, such as OAuth, client authentication, and others
- Word on developing security-enabled web applications

Network security versus application security

In today's scenario, web application security depends upon two primary surfaces--the web application itself and the platform on which it is deployed. You can separate these two surfaces, as any web application cannot be deployed with a platform.

The web application stack

It is very important to understand the distinction between a platform and an application because of the impact it has on security. A typical web application would have an architecture similar to the one depicted in the following diagram:

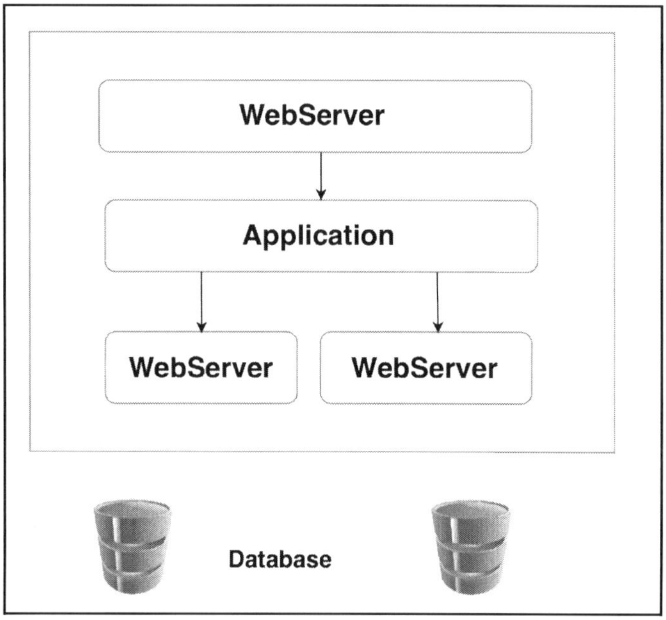

Most web applications depend on web servers, such as Apache/HTTP server, Rails, nginx, and others, which actually handle the incoming request based on the type of application. These web servers keep track of the incoming traffic; they also validate the request and respond to it accordingly, considering all user authentication is validated. In our case, Flask acts as the web server for our application.

Application - security alternatives in the platform

As described earlier, every web application needs to be deployed on some kind of a platform before it can be exposed to the outside world. An application platform provides the protocol support application, which is needed to communicate over a network. TCP, and, to a large extent, HTTP, are all handled at the application level.

In the network stack of software architecture, there are two distinct layers, which include protocols ripe for web application attacks, in the application platform. These layers are as follows:

- Transport
- Application

Let's see these layers in detail.

Transport protocol

In the **Open Systems Interconnection** model (**OSI** model), the transport layer is commonly referred to as layer 4. Web applications use TCP protocols as their transport protocol because of their reliability.

In **TCP** (**Transport Control Protocol**), each packet is closely monitored, and error recovery mechanisms are inbuilt, which is very useful in case of a communication failure. These mechanisms are exploited to attack web applications.

The most common attack is the **SYN flood** attack, which is a TCP request for acknowledgment attack. The SYN flood attack severely affects the application by using an idle session to establish a connection with the application server, and keeps on requesting until the server runs out of resources, and is no longer able to handle more requests.

In order to avoid such kinds of attacks, system administrators (developers have no control here) should set up a configuration related to timeout and idle behaviors after considering the impact on the customers. Another example of such kinds of attacks is the **Smurf attack** (please refer to this link for more details: `https://en.wikipedia.org/wiki/Smurf_attack`).

Secure transport protocols

In the OSI network model, we also have some protocols on layer 5, which can make your network more secure and reliable--SSL/TLS. However, this layer also has some vulnerabilities (for example, Heartbleed, 2014 in SSL and man-in-the-middle renegotiation attack, 2009 in TLS).

Application protocol

In layer 7 (the topmost layer) of the OSI network model, the actual application resides in and uses the HTTP protocol for communication, which is where most of the application attacks occur.

HTTP (**Hypertext Transfer Protocol**) has mainly these two components:

- **Metadata**: HTTP headers contain the metadata, which is important for both, the application as well as the platform. Some examples of headers are cookies, content-type, status, connection, and so on.
- **Behavior**: This defines the behavior between the client and the server. There is a well-defined flow of how messages should be exchanged between an HTTP client (such as a browser) and the server.

The main problem here is that an application, generally, doesn't have an inbuilt capability to identify suspicious behavior.

For example, a client accesses the web application over a network, which may be attacked by consumption-based **denial-of-service** (**DoS**) attacks. In this attack, the client purposefully receives the data at a slower rate than the normal indicates which they are capable of in an attempt to maintain an open connection longer. Due to this, the web server's queue starts filling, and consumes more resources. If all the resources are used up with sufficient open connections, it is highly possible that the server may get unresponsive.

Application - security threats in application logic

In this section, we look at the different methods that authenticate users, and make sure that our application is accessed by a genuine entity.

Web application security alternatives

In order to secure our application from outside threats, there are a couple of alternative methods, which are described here. Usually, our application doesn't have any intelligence to identify suspicious activities. Hence, some of the important security measures are described as follows:

- HTTP-based Auth
- OAuth/OpenID
- Windows authentication

HTTP-based Auth

A simple **username** and **password** are hashed and sent to the web server by the client, like the one we have set up for our web application, as depicted in the following screenshot:

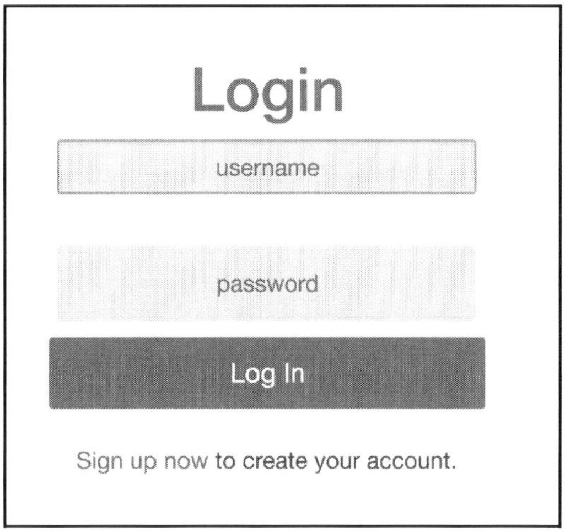

This preceding screenshot image is of the UI that we created in `Chapter 6`, *Creating UIs to Scale with Flux*. It is authenticated by the backend service (microservices) and user database, which is stored in the MongoDB database server. Also, in case of validating the user to log in to the home page, user data is read from the MongoDB collections, and then the user is authenticated to proceed further into the application. The following is the code snippet for the API that is called:

```
@app.route('/login', methods=['POST'])
def do_admin_login():
 users = mongo.db.users
 api_list=[]
 login_user = users.find({'username': request.form['username']})
 for i in login_user:
   api_list.append(i)
  print (api_list)
  if api_list != []:
    #print (api_list[0]['password'].decode('utf-8'),
     bcrypt.hashpw(request.form['password'].encode('utf-8'),
     api_list[0]['password']).decode('utf-8'))
   if api_list[0]['password'].decode('utf-8') ==
     bcrypt.hashpw(request.form['password'].encode('utf-8'),
     api_list[0]['password']).decode('utf-8'):
       session['logged_in'] = api_list[0]['username']
       return redirect(url_for('index'))
       return 'Invalide username/password!'
   else:
     flash("Invalid Authentication")
  return 'Invalid User!'
```

This is one of the ways of setting up security at the application level so that application data can be made secure.

OAuth/OpenID

OAuth is an open standard for authorization, and is very common among websites that allow users to authenticate using third-party credentials, which is, generally, the email ID.

Listed next are the few key features that make OAuth better than other security measures:

- It has nothing related to any **OS** (**operating system**) or installation
- It's simple and easy to use
- It is more reliable and provides high performance
- It is designed, specifically, for distributed systems, which need a centralized authentication method
- It is a free-to-use, open source-based identity provider server software
- It provides support for cloud-based identity providers such as Google, Auth0, LinkedIn, and others
- It is also called **SSO** (**single signed-on** or token-based authentication)

Setting up admin account

OAuth doesn't work without a service to grant a **JWT** (**JSON Web Token**, a URL-safe JSON format for expressing claims that can be transferred between parties). You can learn more about JWT at `https://jwt.io/introduction/`.

An identity provider is responsible for authenticating a user for a web application that depends on authorization provided from a third party.

You can use any identity provider based on your preference, as features would be similar between them, but they will be variant in terms of functionality. For the scope of this chapter, I will show you how to authenticate using Google web apps (which is a developer API from Google) and Auth0 third-party applications.

Setting up using an Auth0 account

In this section, we will set up an account in the Google developer tools for authentication, and in a third-party free application called **Auth0** (`auth0.com`).

Let's kickstart the account setup in Auth0 (`auth0.com`), where the only requirement is an email ID to get registered or to sign up. Refer to the following screenshot:

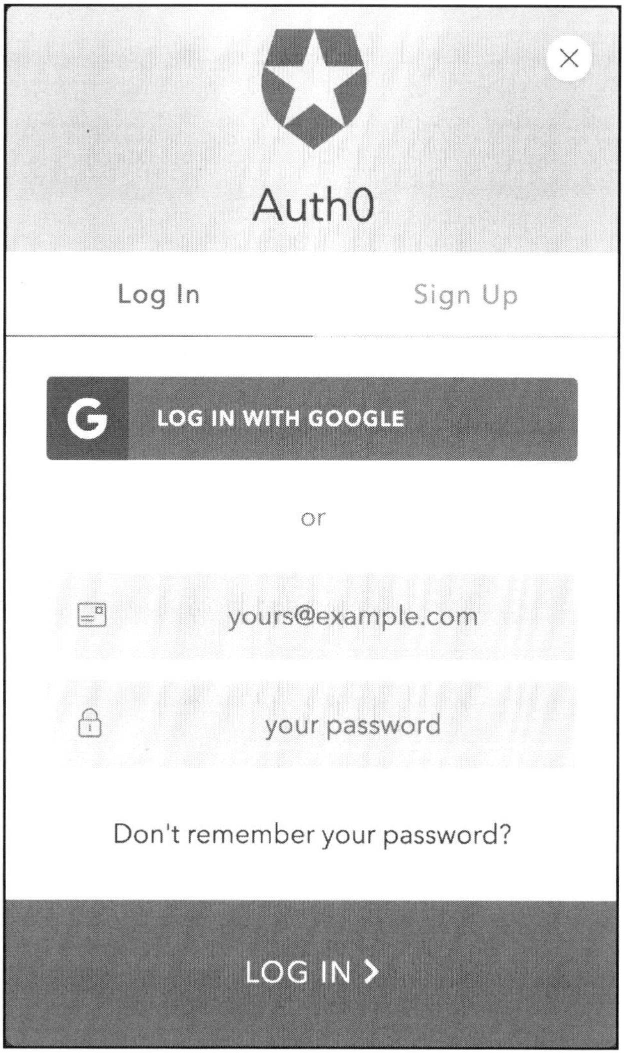

Once you are registered/signed up for the Auth0 account, you will see the following screen:

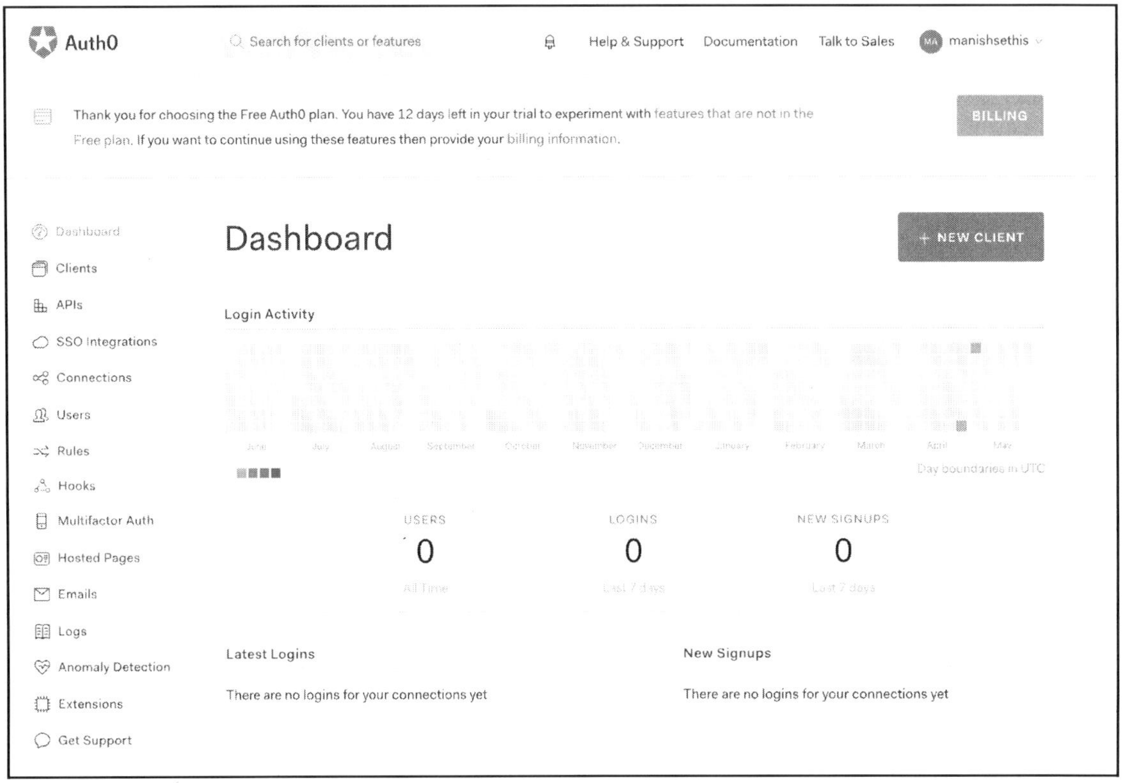

This preceding screen is the dashboard where we can see the login activity as the user who logged in to the application. It also showcases the login attempts by the user, and keeps a log of the user's activity. In short, the dashboard gives you an insight into your application's user activity.

Now we need to add a new client for our application, so click on the **+NEW CLIENT** button to create it. The following screen will appear once you click on the **+NEW CLIENT** button:

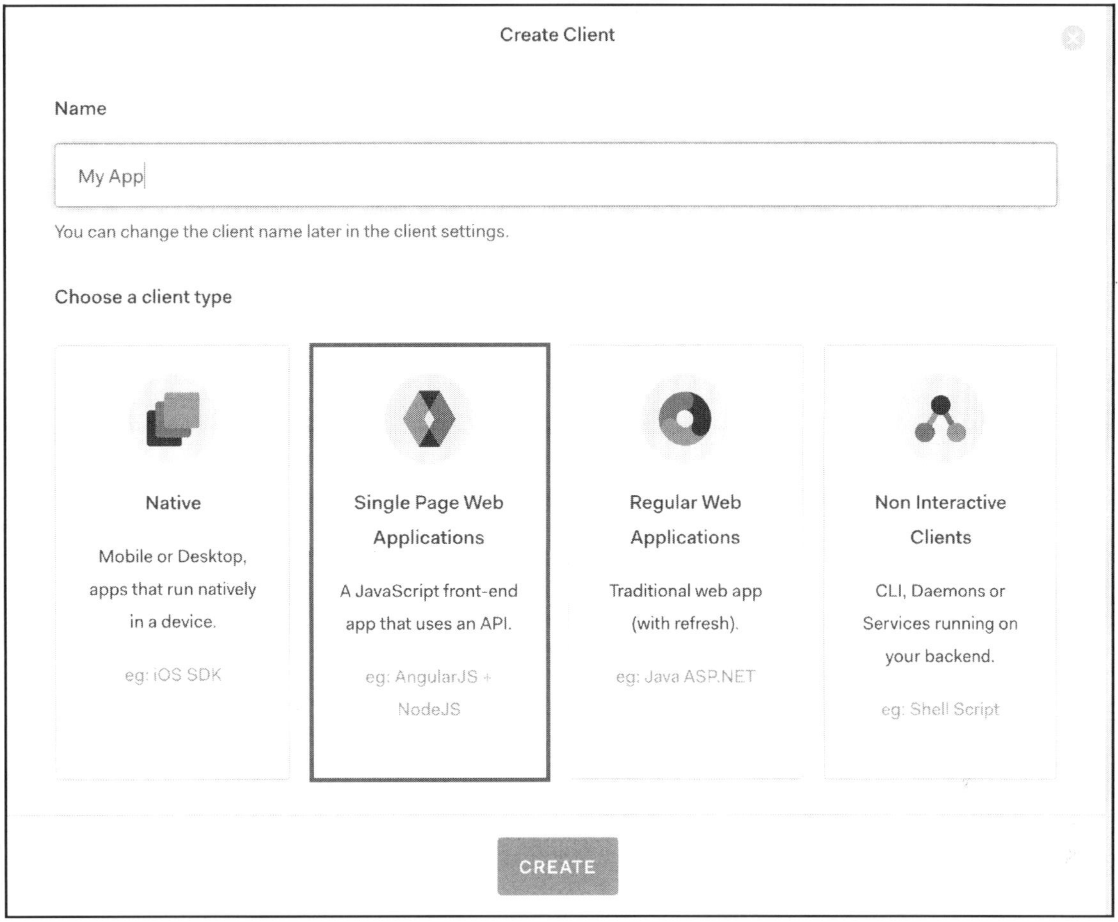

The preceding screenshot is self explanatory--you need to provide a user-defined name for the client (generally, the name should be related to the app). Also, you need to select the category of your application. Coming back to our case, I have given the name as `My App`, and selected the second option, that is, **Single Page Web Applications**, as we are using the technologies mentioned under it. Alternatively, you can also select **Regular Web Applications**--it works just fine. These categories are used for distinction between the kinds of applications we are writing, because it is highly possible we might be developing hundreds of applications under one account.

Click on the **CREATE** button to proceed with the creation of the client. Once it is created, you will see the following screen:

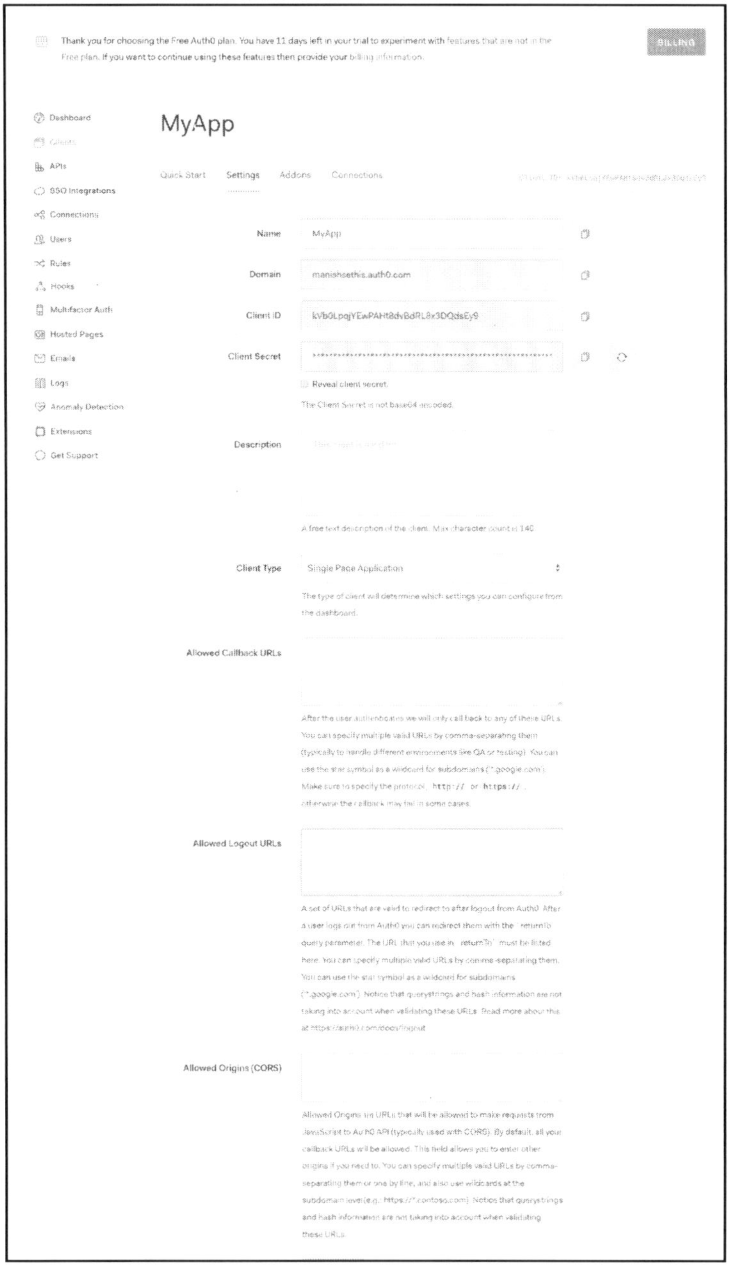

In the section seen in the preceding screenshot, we have a lot of settings that are auto-generated, and we need them to be integrated with our web application. A few of the sections are defined as follows:

- **Client ID**: This is a unique ID assigned to a particular application
- **Domain**: This is similar to the authentication server, which will be called at application login
- **Client Secret**: This is a secret key, which should be kept safe and not be shared with anyone, as it could cause a security breach
- **Client Type**: This defines the type of the application
- **Allowed Callback URLs**: This specifies the allowed callback URLs after user authentication, such as `http://localhost:5000/callback`
- **Allowed Logout URLs**: This defines the URLs that will be allowed to be hit at the time of user logout, such as `http://localhost:5000/logout`
- **Token Endpoint Authentication Method**: This defines the method of authentication, which could be none, or post, or basic

Other features of an Auth0 account that could be useful to manage your application are as follows:

- **SSO Integrations**: In this section, you can set up an SSO login with a couple of other third-party applications such as Slack, Salesforce, Zoom, and so on:

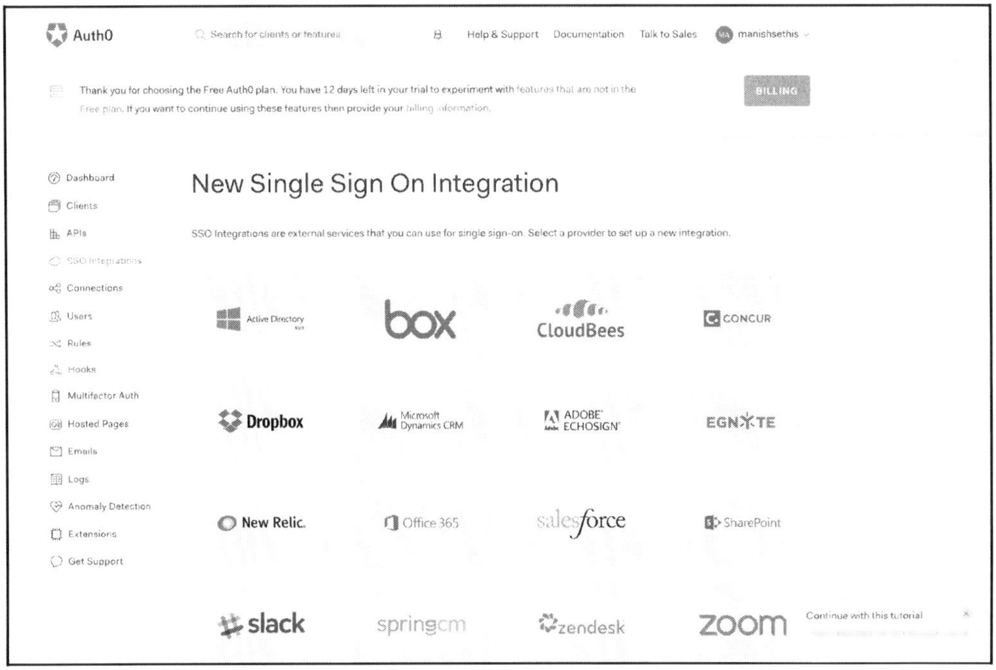

- **Connections**: This defines the type of authentication you want to define for your application, such as Database (username-password database), Social (integration with the existing account from social media websites such as Google, LinkedIn, and so on), Enterprise (for enterprise apps such as AD, Google Apps, and others), or Passwordless (by sms, email, and so on). By default, the username-password authentication is enabled.

- **APIs**: In this section, you can manage the **Auth0 Management API** for your application, and test it, as described in the following screenshot:

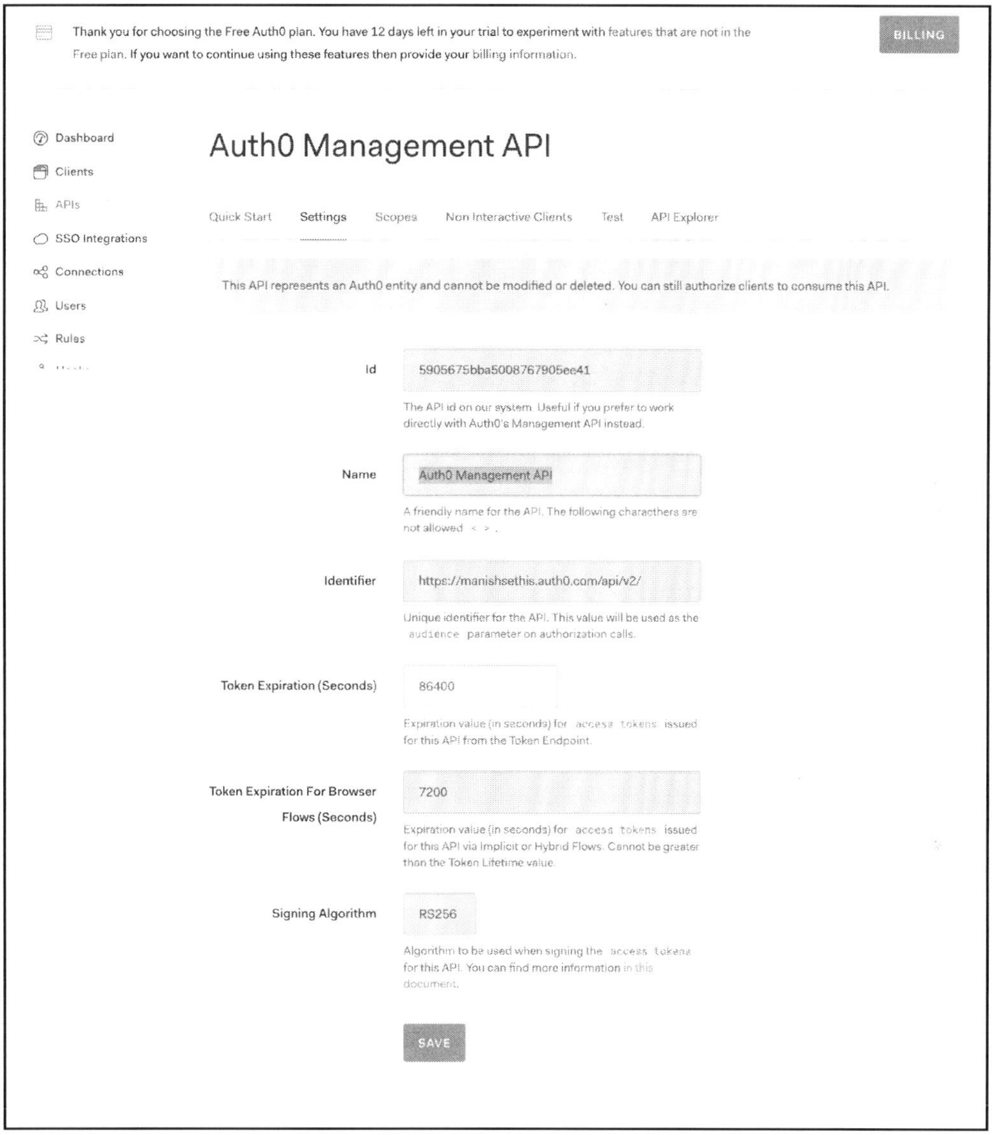

- **Logs**: This section keeps a track of your activity on the Auth0 account, which is very useful to debug as well as to identify suspicious activity at the time of threats. Refer to the following screenshot to find out more about Logs:

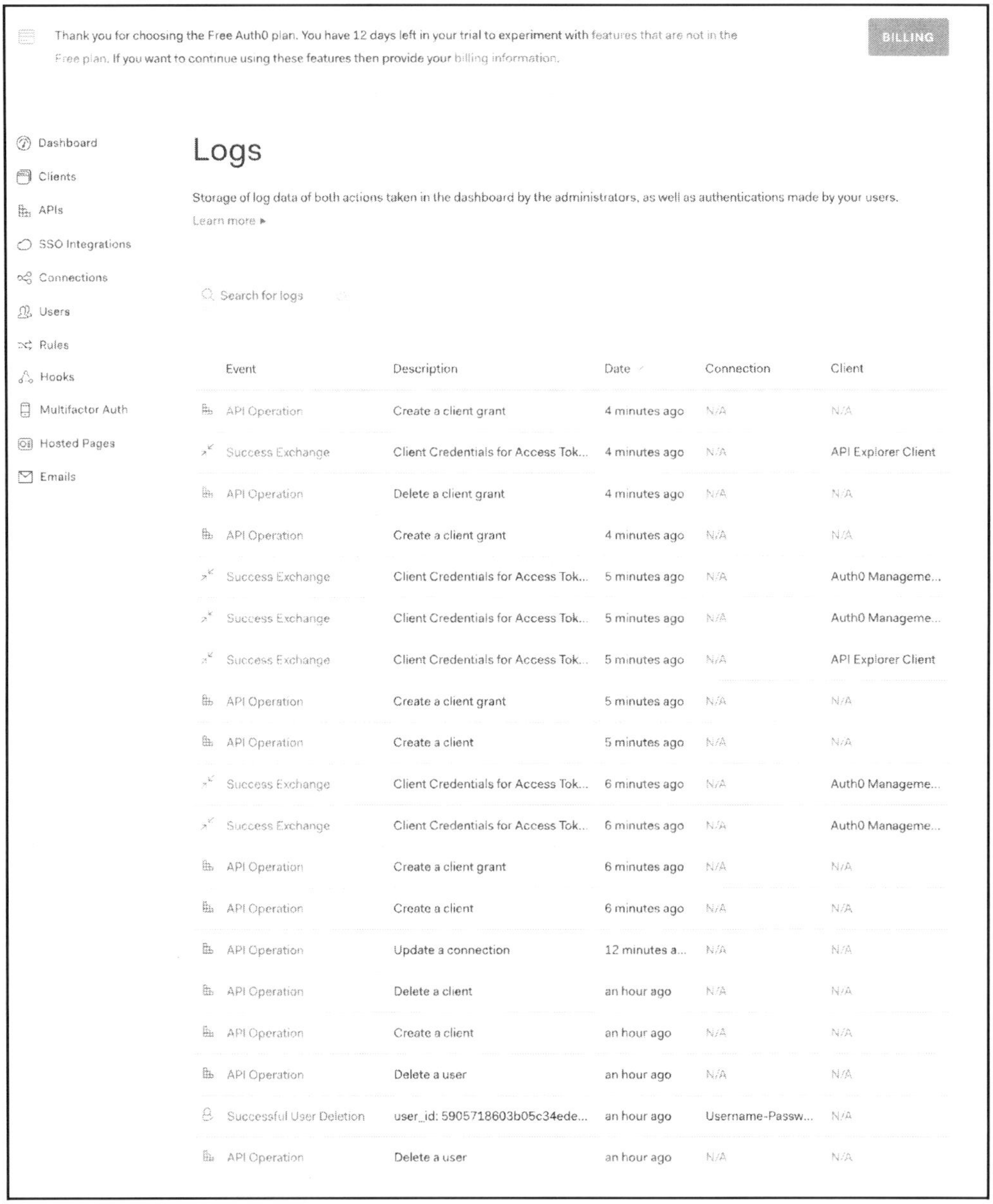

These are the most important features of an Auth0 account that could help you manage your web application security in an efficient way.

Now, our Auth0 admin account is set up, and is ready to get integrated with our web application.

Setting up a Google API account

Google APIs use the OAuth 2.0 protocol for authentication and authorization. Google supports common OAuth 2.0 scenarios, such as those for web server, installed, and client-side applications.

To kickstart, log in to the Google API Console (`https://console.developers.google.com`) with your Google account to get the OAuth client credentials such as **Client ID**, **Client Secret**, and others. You will need these credentials to integrate with your application. You will see the following screen once you have logged in:

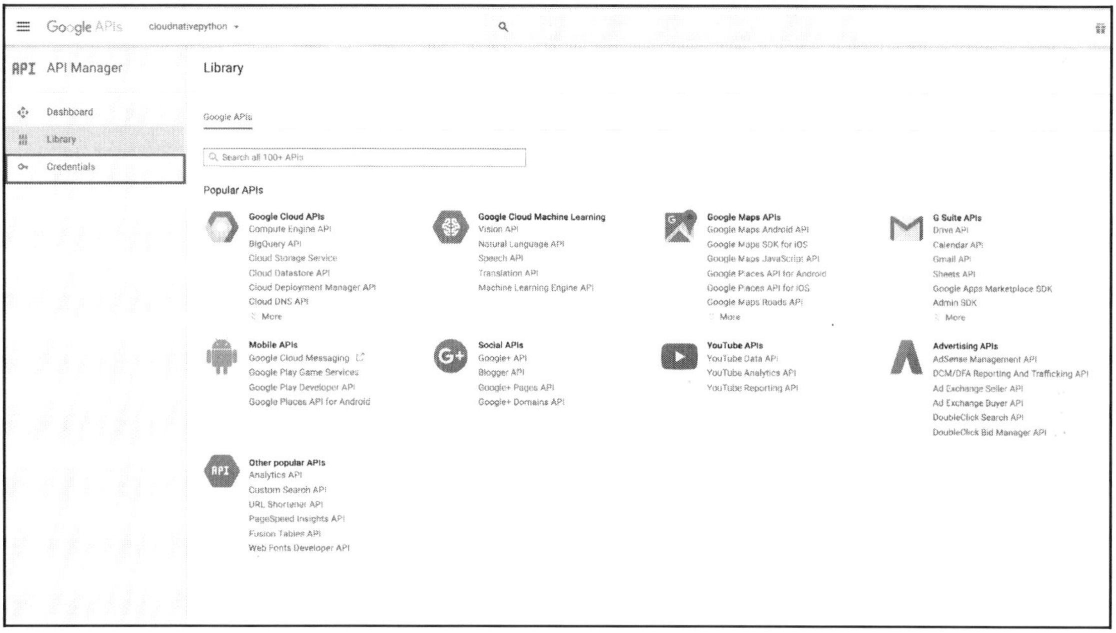

The preceding screen showcases the Google library API offerings for their different Google products. Now, click on **Credentials** in the panel on the left-hand side to navigate to the next screen, as seen in this screenshot:

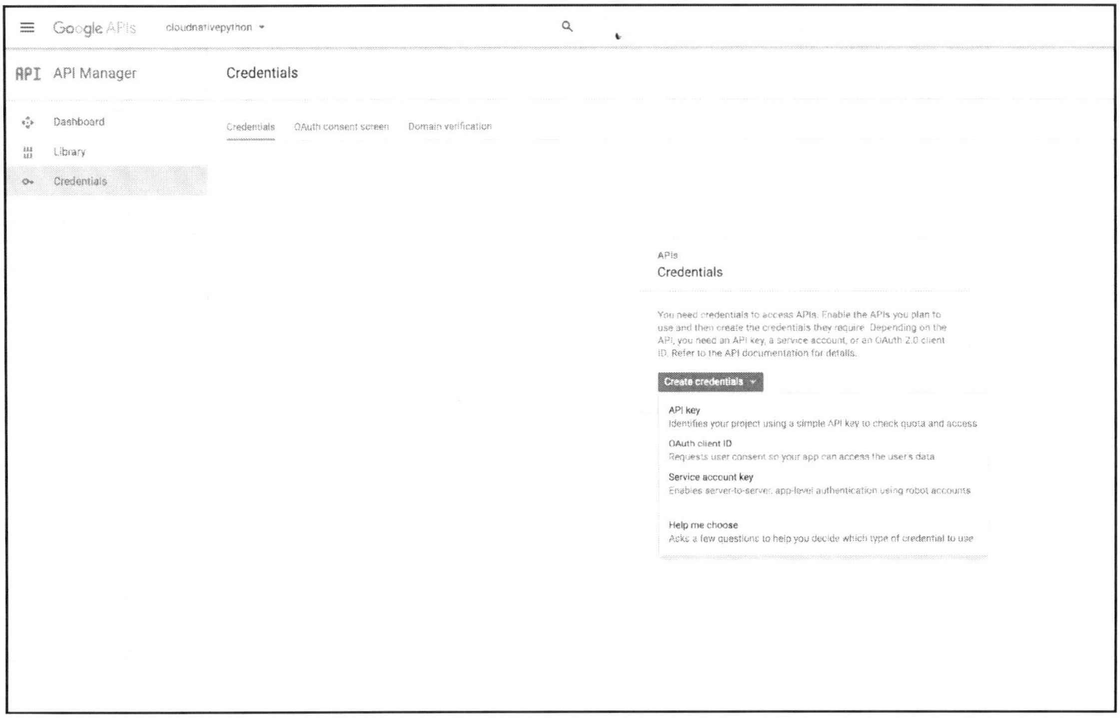

Now, click on **Create credentials**, and then on the **OAuth client ID** option to initiate the generation of client credentials from the API manager.

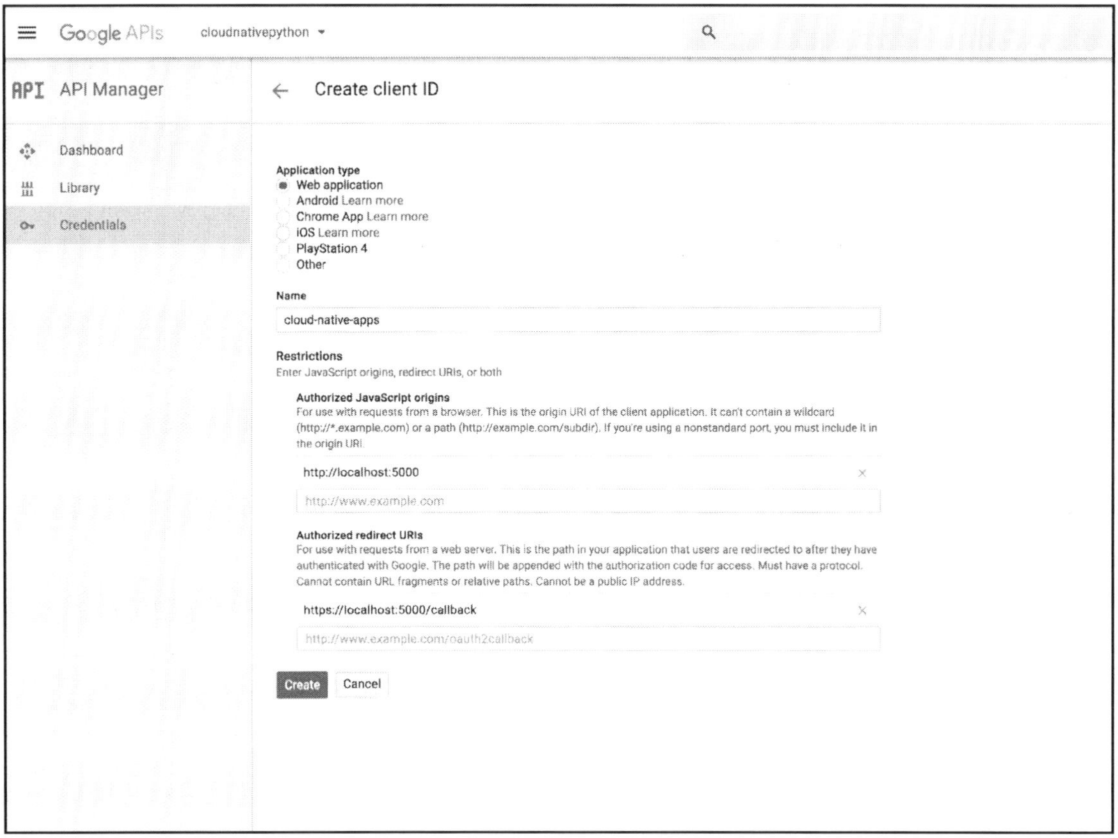

Now we need to feed some information about our application; you must remember these details that we have provided at the time of OAuth account as well. Once you are ready, and have filled the mandatory fields, click on **Create** to generate the credentials.

Once the client ID is created, you will see the following screen, which will have the information related to the client ID (**Credentials**):

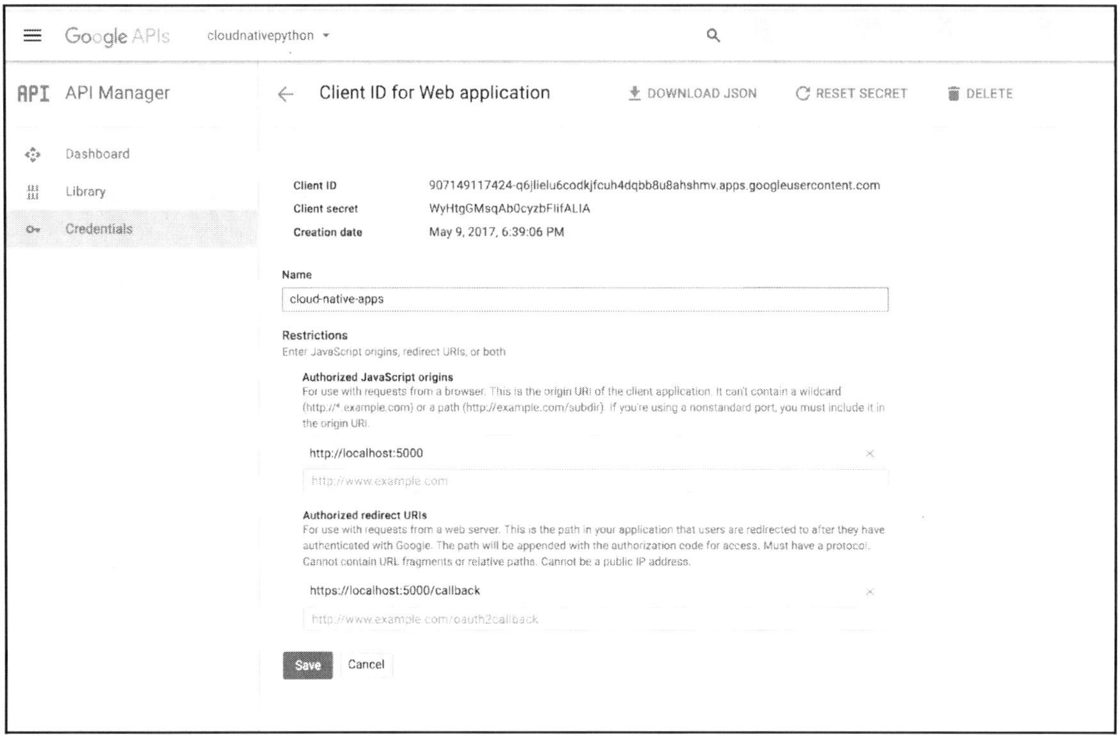

Remember, NEVER share the client ID details with anyone. In case you do, then reset it immediately. Now our Google API account is ready to be integrated with our web application.

Integration of a web application with an Auth0 account

In order to integrate the Auth0 account with our application, we need to create a new route for our callback. This route will set up the session after user authentication from the Auth0 account. So, let's add the following code to the `app.py` file:

```
@app.route('/callback')
def callback_handling():
  code = request.args.get('code')
  get_token = GetToken('manishsethis.auth0.com')
  auth0_users = Users('manishsethis.auth0.com')
  token = get_token.authorization_code(os.environ['CLIENT_ID'],
                                      os.environ['CLIENT_SECRET'],
```

```
      code, 'http://localhost:5000/callback')
      user_info = auth0_users.userinfo(token['access_token'])
      session['profile'] = json.loads(user_info)
    return redirect('/dashboard')
```

As you can see in the preceding code, I have used client credentials that we got from the Auth0 account console. These are the credentials we generated at the time of client creation.

Now let's add the route/dashboard to which the user is redirected after being authenticated:

```
@app.route("/dashboard")
def dashboard():
  return render_template('index.html', user=session['profile'])
```

This preceding route simply calls `index.html`, and passes the session details to `index.html` as parameters.

Now we have to modify our `index.html` to trigger authentication via Auth0. There are two ways of triggering. The first one is to make the Auth0 domain as the landing page, which means that as soon as they hit the URL (`http://localhost:5000`), the users will be redirected to the landing page for the Auth0 account. The other way is to trigger it manually by providing a button to trigger it.

For the scope of this chapter, we will be using a manual trigger, where the Auth0 account can be used as an alternative to log in to the application.

Let's add the following code to `login.html`. This code will make a button appear on the login page, and if you click on that button, it will trigger the Auth0 user signup page:

```
<center><button onclick="lock.show();">Login using Auth0</button>
  </center>
<script src="https://cdn.auth0.com/js/lock/10.14/lock.min.js">
  </script>
<script>
 var lock = new Auth0Lock(os.environ['CLIENT_ID'],
  'manishsethis.auth0.com', {
   auth: {
    redirectUrl: 'http://localhost:5000/callback',
    responseType: 'code',
    params: {
      scope: 'openid email' // Learn about scopes:
      https://auth0.com/docs/scopes
     }
    }
  });
</script>
```

There is one more thing we need to take care of before we test our application--how to make our application aware of the session details.

As our `index.html` takes the session values and showcases them on our home page as well, it is used to manage the tweets from the user.

So, update the body tag of `index.html` as follows:

```
<h1></h1>
<div align="right"> Welcome {{ user['given_name'] }}</div>
<br>
<div id="react"></div>
```

The previous code is needed to show the user's full name on the user interface. Next, you need to update the `localStorage` session details as follows:

```
<script>
  // Check browser support
  if (typeof(Storage) !== "undefined") {
 // Store
  localStorage.setItem("sessionid","{{ user['emailid'] }}" );
 // Retrieve
  document.getElementById("react").innerHTML =
  localStorage.getItem("sessionid");
  } else {
    document.getElementById("react").innerHTML = "Sorry, your
    browser does not support Web Storage...";
  }
</script>
```

We are almost done now. I hope you remember that we have set up authentication checks when you tweet for a particular user in our microservices APIs. We need to remove those checks, because in this case, we are using Auth0 for authentication purposes.

Awesome! Run your application, and see if you can see a screen like the following one at `http://localhost:5000/`:

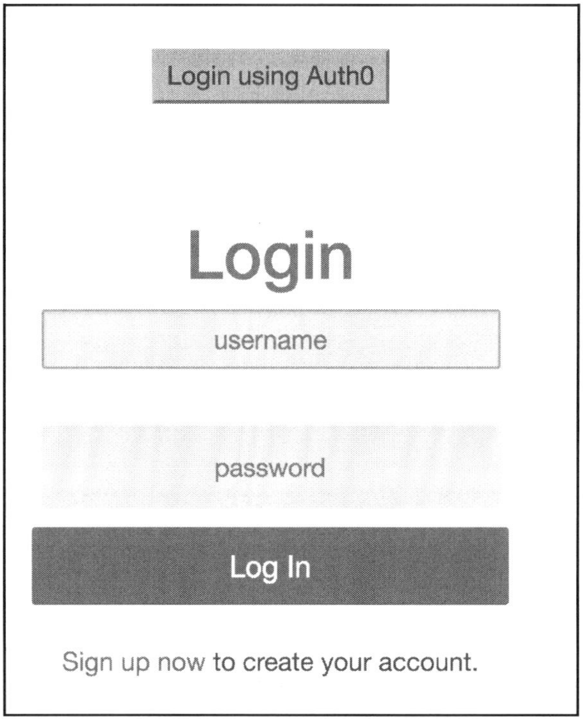

Next, click on the **Login using Auth0** button to get the Auth0 login/signup panel as shown in the next screenshot.

Provide the required details, and click on **Sign up now**, and it will get registered in the Auth0 account. Remember, in this case, you don't see any way to log in via email directly, because we are using username-password authentication. If you want to sign up via email directly, then you need to enable the google-OAuth2 way extension in the social connection section. Once you enable it, you will be able to see your sign up page as follows:

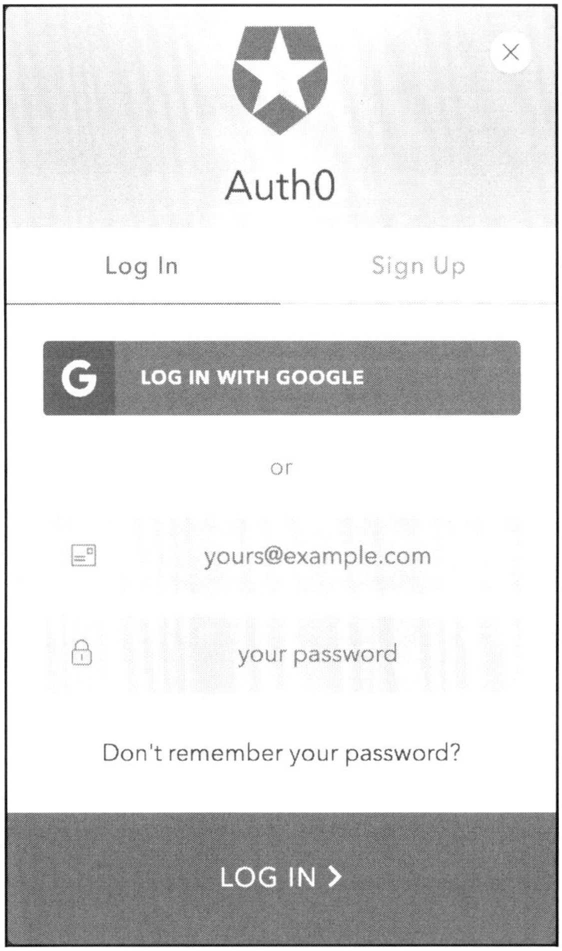

Once you have signed up successfully, you will be redirected to the home page, where you can tweet. If you see the following screen, that means it works:

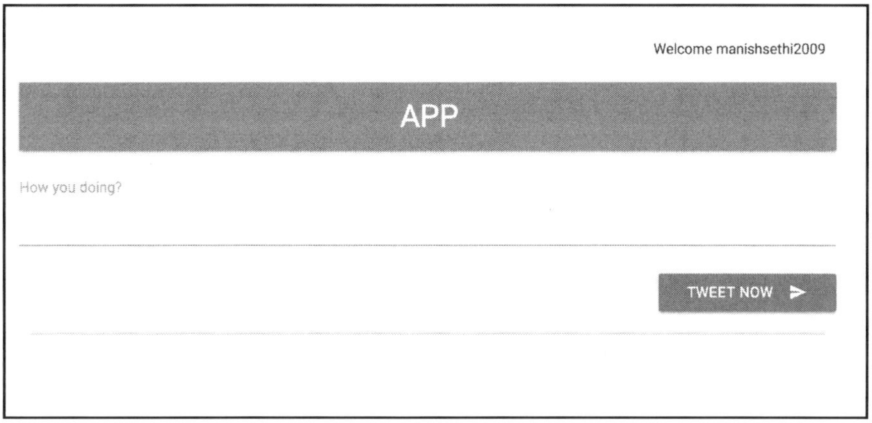

An important thing to notice here is that for each signup, a user is created in your Auth0 account with **User Details**, as shown in this screenshot:

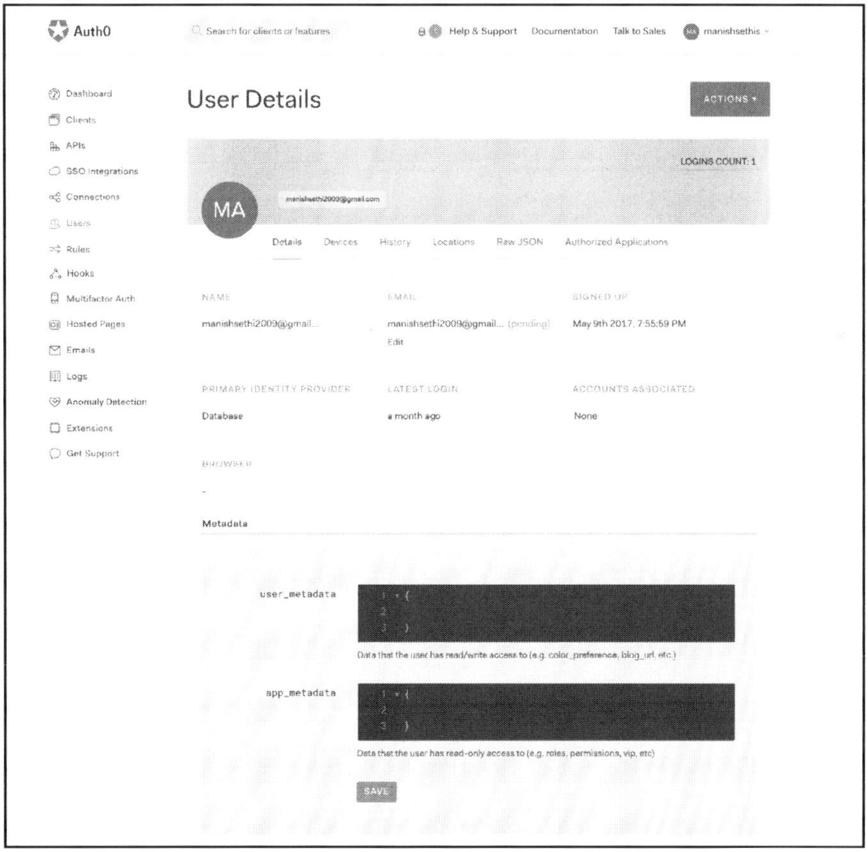

Awesome! Now your application is integrated with the Auth0 account, and you can keep track of a user who makes use of your application.

Integrating your Google API with the web application

Integrating your Google API with your web application is quite similar to what we have seen in Auth0 integration. You need to follow the steps listed next for the integration of the Google API:

1. **Gathering OAuth credentials**: As discussed in the Google API client setup, we have already generated client credentials. We need to capture details such as **Client ID**, **Client Secret**, and others.
2. **Obtaining an access token from the Google authorization server**: Before your application user can log in and access private data, it needs to generate an authentication token provided by Google, which acts as an authenticator for the user. A single access token can grant varying degrees of access to multiple APIs. A scope parameter contains the information about the extent to which the user will have access, that is, from which of the APIs the user can view data. Requesting of token depends on the way your application has been developed.
3. **Saving a token to the API**: Once a token is received by the application, it sends that token across to the Google API HTTP authorization headers. As mentioned earlier, this token is authorized to perform actions on a certain set of APIs based on the scope parameter defined.
4. **Refreshing a token**: It is best practice to refresh a token after a certain period of time to avoid any security breach.
5. **Token Expiration**: It is good practice to write for token expiration after a certain period of time, which makes the application secure; it is highly recommended.

Since we are developing an application based on Python, you can follow the docs URL, which has information about the implementation of Google-API-token-based authentication at the following link:

`https://developers.google.com/api-client-library/python/guide/aaa_oauth`.

Once the user is authenticated, and starts using the application, you can monitor the user login activities on the **API Manager** (`https://console.developers.google.com/apis/`), as shown here:

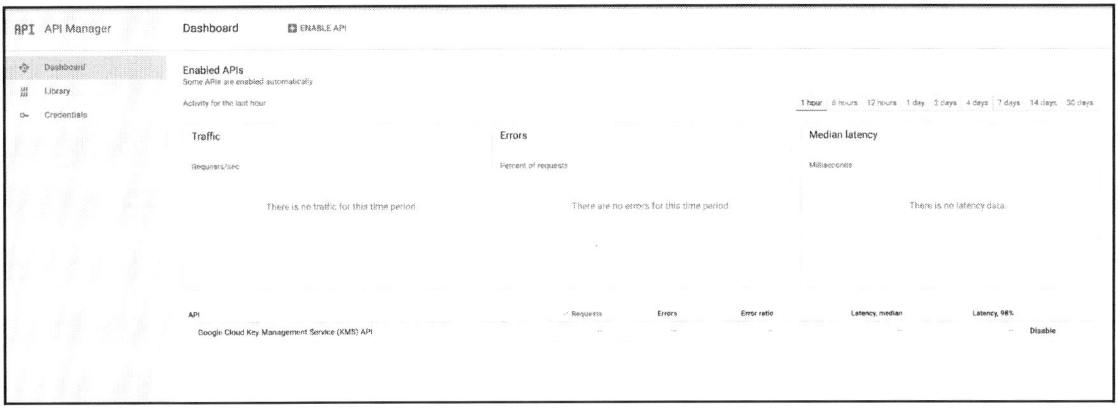

Setting up authentication using Google is slightly difficult, and needs supervision. That's why, developers go with tools like Auth0, which can provide integration with Google directly.

Windows authentication

Historically, this option has been preferred for applications being used for intranet and enterprise sites even if they are deployed on internal or private clouds. However, this is not suitable for the cloud native security option for a number of reasons.

> For more information on Windows authentication, go to the link `https://en.wikipedia.org/wiki/Integrated_Windows_Authentication`. We have showcased these security methods for your understanding, but our authentication method remains the same.

A word on developing security-enabled web applications

With an increase in web applications on the **World Wide Web** (**WWW**), the concerns over application security have increased as well. Now, the first question that arises in our mind is why we need security-enabled applications--the answer to this is quite obvious. But what are its essential principles? Following are the principles that we should keep in mind:

- A hacker can easily exploit your application if he gets familiar with the language in which the application got created. That's why, we enable techniques such as CORS to secure our code.
- Access to the application and its data should be given to very limited people in your organization.
- A way of authentication, authorization secures your application from both, the WWW as well as within your private network.

All these factors, or as I would say, principles, drive us to create security-enabled applications.

Summary

In this chapter, we kickstarted by defining security on different application stacks, and how we can implement or integrate different application security measures with our application, based on your preference and application requirement.

So far we've talked about application building. But from now on, we will focus entirely on building a platform for moving our application from the development stage to production using DevOps tools. So, things are going to get more interesting. Stay tuned for further chapters.

9

Continuous Delivery

In the previous chapters, we worked towards building our application and preparing it for the cloud environment. Since our application is stable now and ready for its first release, we need to start thinking about the platform (that is, the cloud platform) as well as the tools that can help us move our application to production.

This chapter discusses the following topics:

- Introduction to continuous integration and continuous delivery
- Understanding continuous integration with Jenkins

Evolution of continuous integration and continuous delivery

Nowadays, lots of people are talking about **CI** (**continuous integration**) and **CD** (**continuous delivery**), and after examining the perspectives of different technologists, I believe all have different understandings of CI and CD, and there is still some confusion about them. Let's dive deeply into these and understand them.

In order to understand continuous integration, you need to first understand the background to **SDLC** (**system development life cycle**) and the **Agile software development** process, which can help during your build and release processes.

Understanding SDLC

SDLC is the process of planning, developing, testing, and deploying your software. This process consists of a sequence of phases, and each phase takes the outcome from the previous phase to proceed further. The following diagram depicts SDLC:

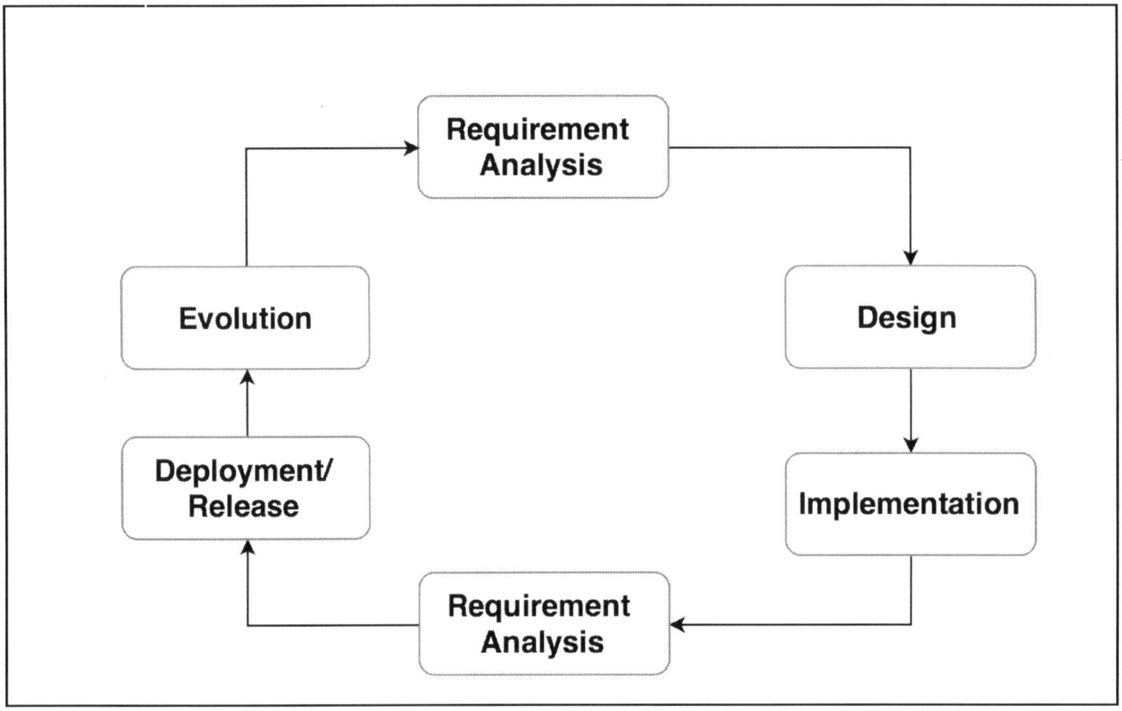

Let's understand each phase in detail:

- **Requirement Analysis**: This is the initial phase for problem analysis, where business analysts perform requirement analysis, and understand the business needs. The requirements can be internal to the organization or external from a customer. Requirements include the scope of the problem, which could either be for improving the system or building a new one, cost analysis, and project goals.

- **Design**: In this phase, the design for the implementation of the features of the software solution is prepared and approved. This includes process diagrams, documentations, layouts, and so on.
- **Implementation**: In this phase, actual implementation, based on the design, is carried out. Usually, developers develop the code depending on the goals defined in the design phase.
- **Testing**: In this phase, the developed code is tested by the **QA** (**quality assurance**) team under different scenarios. Each and every module is tested using unit testing as well as integration testing. In case of test failure, the developers are informed about the bug, and then they are required to fix it.
- **Deployment/Release**: In this phase, the tested feature is moved to production for customer review.
- **Evolution**: This phase gets the customer's review of the developed, tested, and published upgrades.

The Agile software development process

The Agile software development process is an alternative to the traditional software development one. It is more like a process which helps frequent and efficient release of production with minimal bugs.

The Agile process is based on the following principles:

- Continuous delivery of software upgrades and customer feedback at each stage
- Additional improvements are welcome at any stage of the development cycle
- Stable releases should be frequent (in weeks)
- Continuous communication between the business team and the developers
- Continuous improvement towards technical excellence and good design
- Working software is the principal measure of progress
- Continuous adaptation towards changing circumstances

How does the Agile software development process work?

In the Agile software development process, the complete system is divided into different phases, all modules or features are delivered in iterations, and cross-functional teams from various areas such as planning, unit testing, design, requirement analysis, coding, and so on work simultaneously. As a result, every team member is involved in the process, and there is no single person sitting idle, whereas, in the traditional SDLC, when the software is in the development phase, the remaining teams either sit idle or underutilized. All this makes the Agile process more advantageous over the traditional mode. The following diagram shows information about the workflow of the Agile development process:

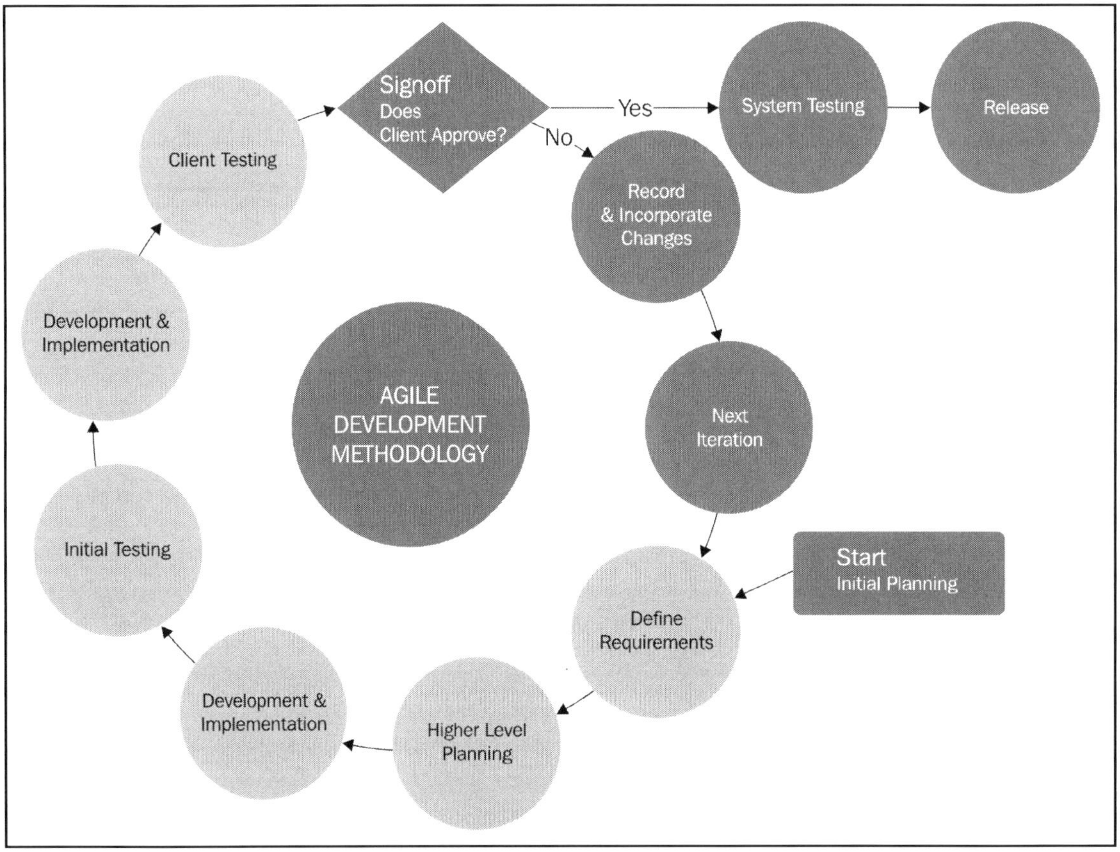

In the preceding diagram, you won't find any requirement analysis or design phases, as those are accumulated in high-level planning.

The following is the sequence of events in an Agile process:

1. We start with initial planning, which gives us the details about the software features, and then, the goals are defined in high-level planning.
2. Once the goals are set, the developer starts coding for the required feature. Once the software upgrade is ready, the testing team (QA) starts executing both unit and integration testing.
3. If any bugs are found, they are fixed immediately, and then the code is delivered for client testing (that is, on stage or the pre-production environment). At this stage, the code is not released yet.
4. If the code passes all client-based testing, which could be UI-based testing, then the code is pushed to production; otherwise, it iterates through the same cycle again.

Now that we have understood the Agile work process, let's get to know its advantages over the traditional SDLC, which are listed as follows:

- In Agile, each functionality can be developed and demonstrated frequently and quickly. The idea here is to develop features without bugs until its deployment in a week or so. This ensures that the customer is happy with the additional features.
- There is no separate team for development, testing, or otherwise. There is a single team, which consists of 8-10 members (based on the requirements), and each member is capable of doing everything.
- Agile promotes teamwork.
- It requires minimal documentation.
- Agile is best suited for parallel features development.

Looking at the preceding advantages, now companies have started adopting the Agile SDLC in their software development.

So far, we have been looking at the methodologies which are adopted as part of software development. Let's now look at a very crucial aspect of the Agile process, that is, continuous integration, which makes our development job easier.

Continuous integration

Continuous integration is a process of collaborating the code into the mainline code base. In simple words, continuous integration helps developers to test their new code at the initial stage by creating frequent builds while they are developing and generating test results, and if everything works, then merging the code to the mainline code.

This can be understood by the following diagram, which depicts the issues that occur during SDLC:

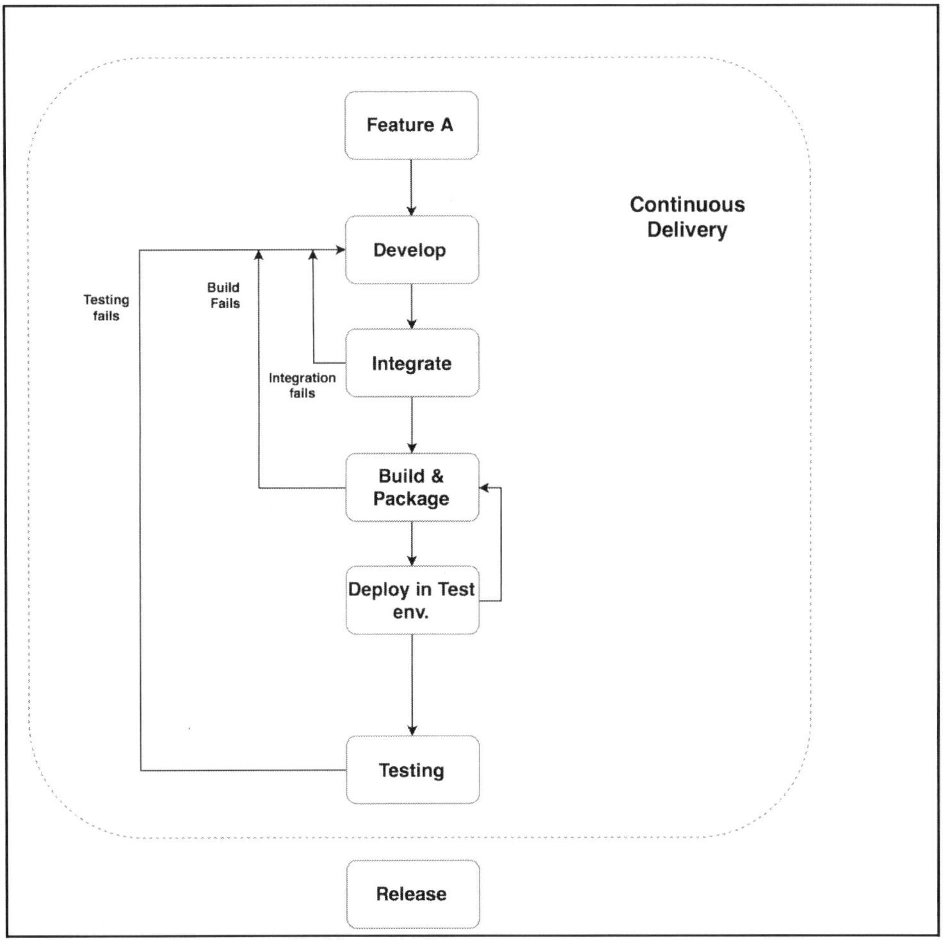

There are, basically, the following types of issues that occur during continuous integration:

- Build failure before integration
- Integration failures
- Build failure (after integration)

In order to solve those issues, the developer needs to modify the code to fix it, and the complete integration process is repeated again until the feature is successfully deployed.

Jenkins - a continuous integration tool

Jenkins is an open-source tool to perform continuous integration and build automation. It has the same purpose as any other continuous integration tool, such as Bamboo (CirclCI), which tests the code as early as possible in the development stage.

In Jenkins, you define the set of instructions to deploy your application over different application environments (development, pre-production stage, and so on).

Before going forward to set up a job (basically, a project) in Jenkins, and learn about the Jenkins plugins, let's first set up Jenkins and configure it as per our requirements.

Installing Jenkins

Installation for Jenkins is straightforward in every environment whether it is Linux (Debian, Red Hat, and the like), Windows, or macOS.

Prerequisite

Make sure you have Java 8 installed on your Ubuntu system. If it is not installed, you can follow the instructions given at the following link:

`https://medium.com/appliedcode/how-to-install-java-8-jdk-8u45-on-ubuntu-linuxmint-via-ppa-1115d64ae325.`

Installation on a Debian (Ubuntu)-based system

Follow the steps listed next to install Jenkins on a Debian-based system:

1. We begin our Jenkins installation by adding the Jenkins key to the APT package list by executing this command:

```
$ wget -q -O - https://pkg.jenkins.io/debian/jenkins-ci.org.key |
sudo apt-key add -
```

2. Next, update the source file with the server that needs to be communicated to validate the key, as follows:

```
$ sudo sh -c 'echo deb http://pkg.jenkins.io/debian-stable binary/ >
/etc/apt/sources.list.d/jenkins.list'
```

3. Once the source list file is updated, update the APT repository by executing the following command at the terminal:

```
$ sudo apt-get update -y
```

4. Now we are ready to install Jenkins over Ubuntu; use the following command to do so:

```
$ sudo apt-get install jenkins  -y
```

5. Now that the installation is completed, remember that Jenkins runs on port `8080` by default. But if you want to run it over a different port, then you need to update the following line in the Jenkins configuration file (`/etc/default/jenkins`):

```
HTTP_PORT=8080
```

6. Next, check the Jenkins GUI by using this URL:

- If the installation is local, then go to `http://localhost:8080/`
- If the installation is on a remote machine, go to `http://ip-address:8080`

Remember, in this case, we have installed the Jenkins version (2.61); the previous as well as upcoming steps are valid for Jenkins version 2.x.x.

If you see the following screen, it means your installation is successful:

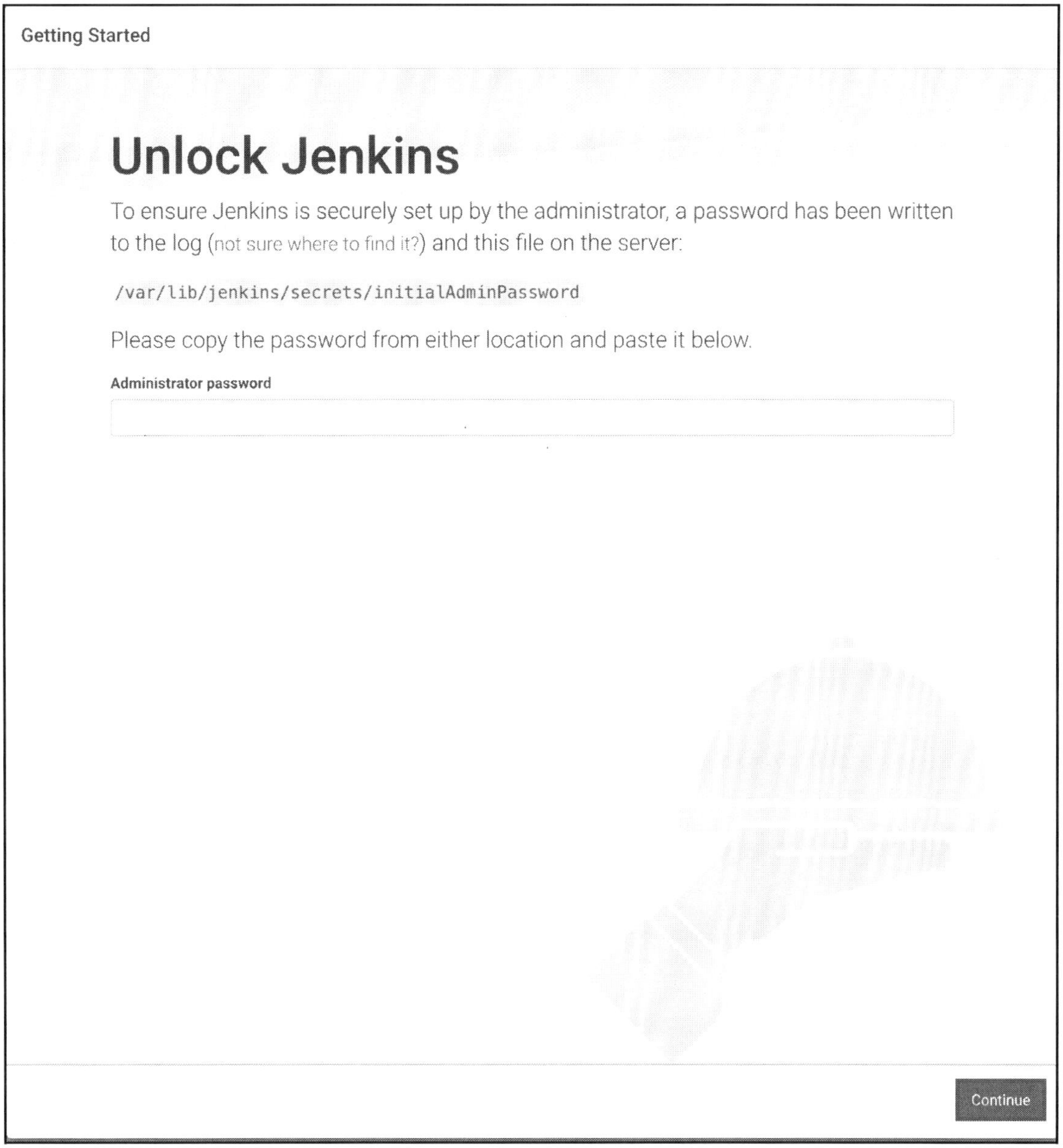

As you can see in the preceding image, there is a path where your default password is stored inside the system where Jenkins is installed.

This proves that Jenkins is installed successfully.

Installation on Windows
Jenkins installation on Windows is pretty simple. Usually, on a Windows machine, Jenkins is not run as a service. But if you want to enable it as a service (which is optional), you can follow the complete installation Jenkins docs for Windows at the following URL: `https://wiki.Jenkins-ci.org/display/JENKINS/Installing+Jenkins+as+a+Windows+service#InstallingJenkinsasaWindowsservice-InstallJenkinsasaWindowsservice`.

Configuring Jenkins

It's time to configure Jenkins, So, let's get the password from the path specified (that is, `/var/lib/Jenkins/secrets/initialAdminPassword`) from your system, paste it into the space provided in the installation wizard, and click on **Continue**. You should see a screen similar to the following one after hitting **Continue**:

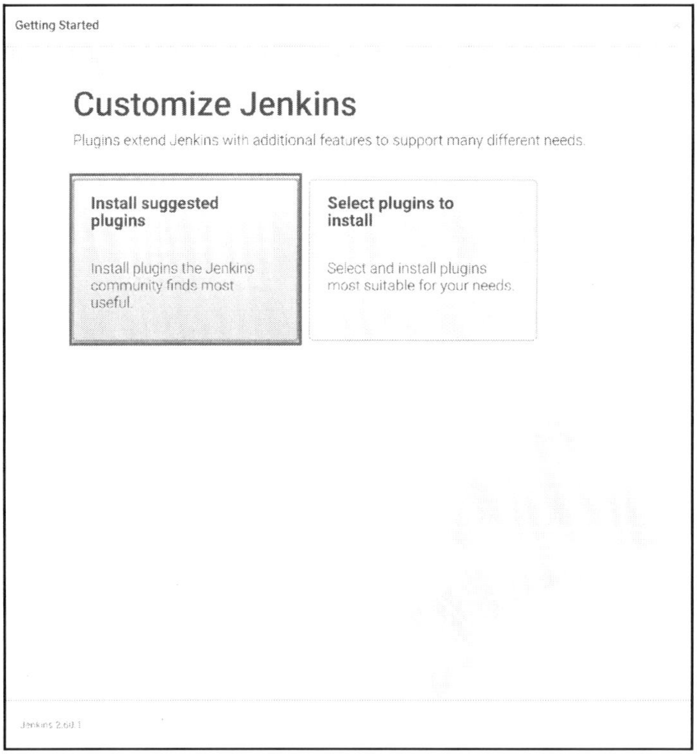

In the next screen, you will see the screen where you can install the plugins which we will need for the integration. We will go with the **Install suggested plugins** option for now. Note that we can install additional plugins after the initial configuration as well. So, no need to worry!

Once you click on **Install suggested plugins**, you will see the following screen, which shows the progress of the plugin installation:

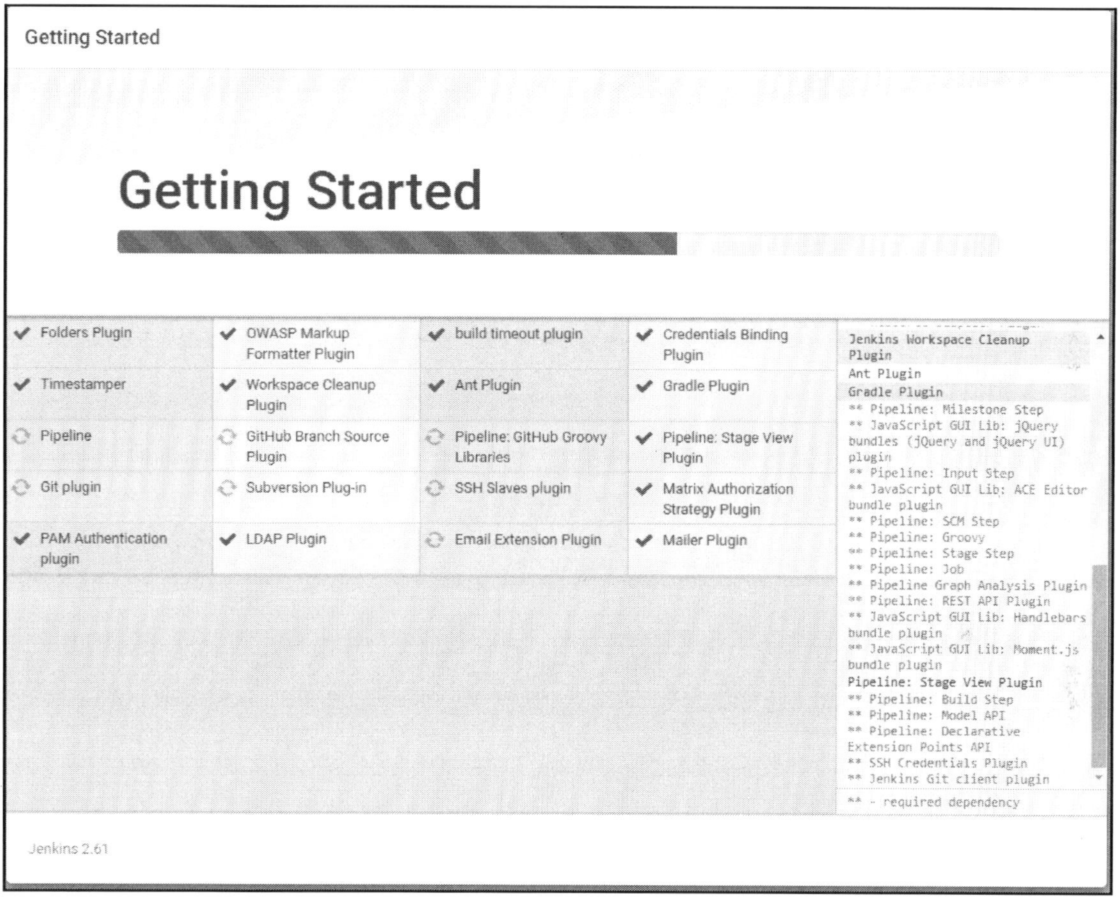

It might take a while for the plugin installation. All these plugins are suggested by Jenkins, as you might require them during your project-related jobs.

Once the plugin installation is complete, it will ask you to create an admin user to access the Jenkins console. Note that for setting up Jenkins, we used temporary credentials.

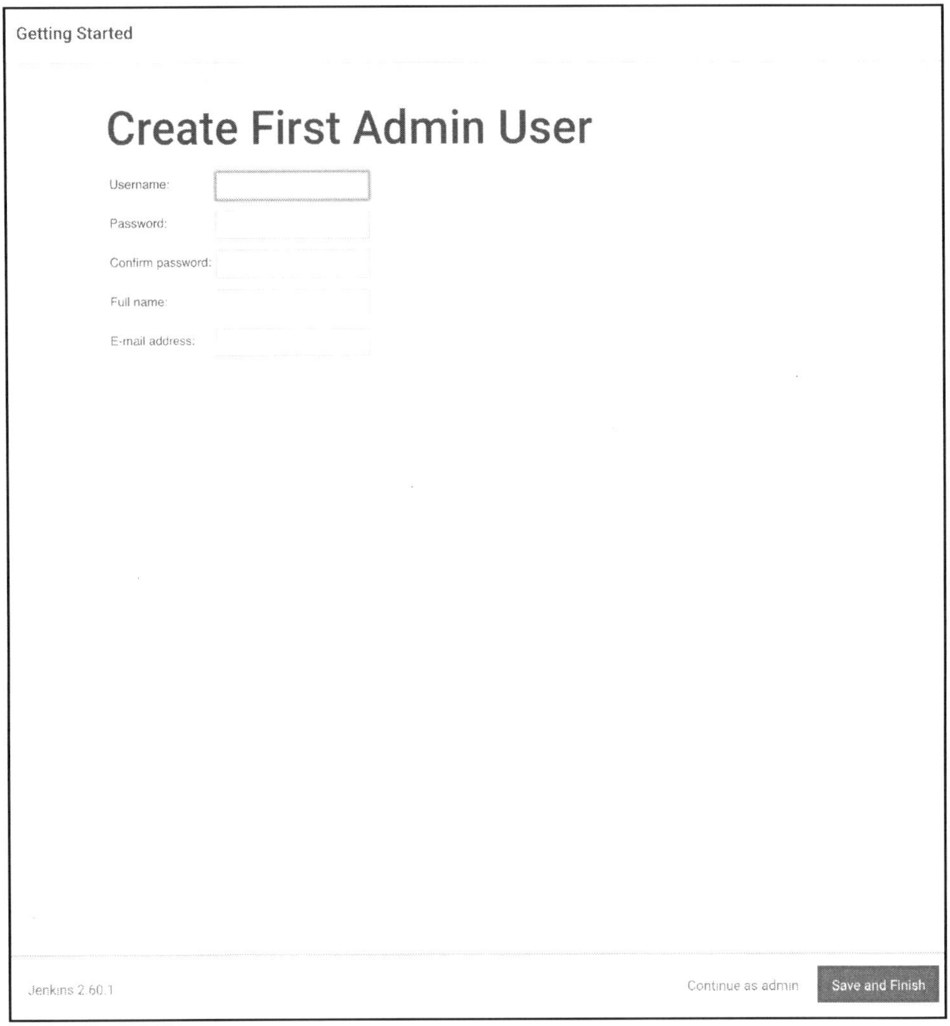

Once you have entered the user details, click on **Save and Finish** to complete the setup.

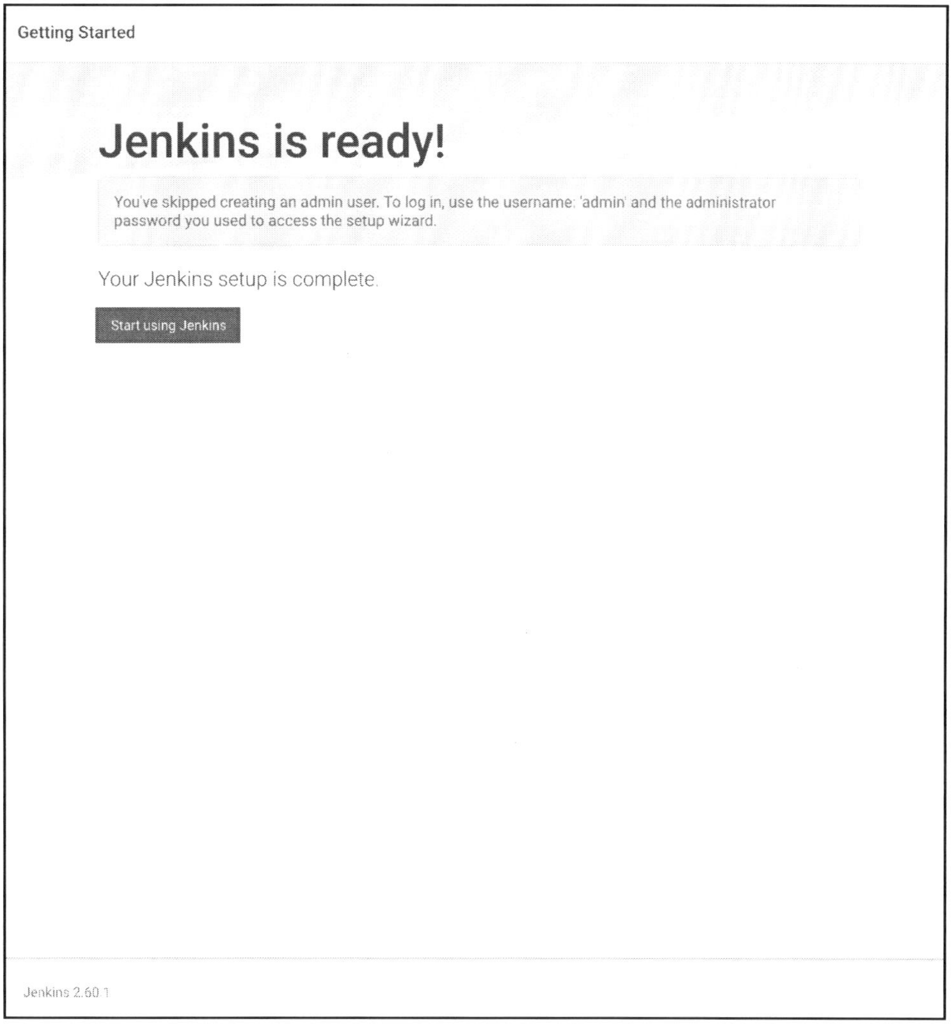

Your Jenkins setup is successfully completed.

Automating Jenkins

In this section, we will cover the different parts of the Jenkins configuration, and will take a look at how we can successfully create our first job and build our application.

Ideally, our Jenkins home page, after successful login, should look something like this:

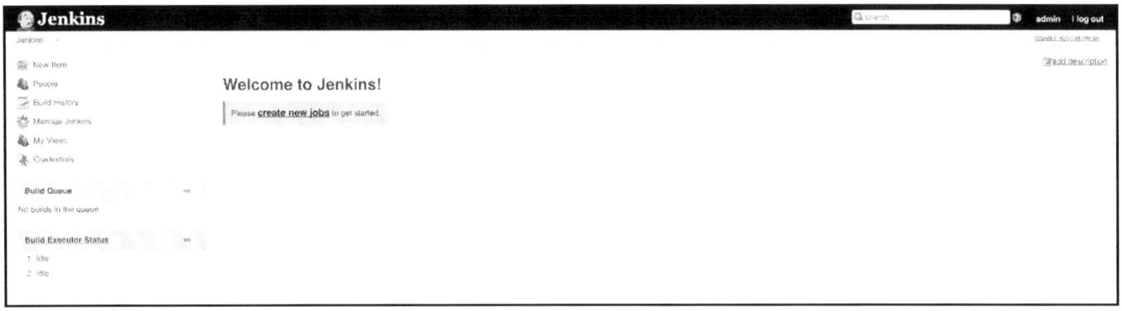

Securing Jenkins

It is highly recommended to set up the Jenkins security to make your console secure, because we are exposing our application to Jenkins.

From the Jenkins home page, click on **Manage Jenkins** to navigate to the settings section of Jenkins, then click on **Configure Global Security** in the right pane to open the security panel.

In the **Configure Global Security** section, we can manage user authorization as shown in the following screenshot:

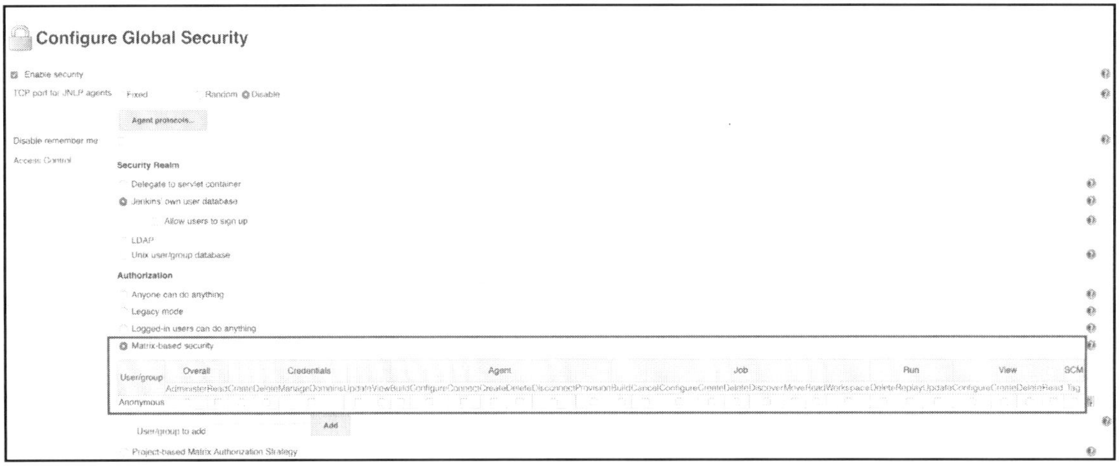

As you can see in the preceding screenshot, here, you can define an access list for the users based on their role. Generally, in large organizations, user access is provided to different people based on their usage so that Jenkins security can be maintained. Usually, we go with either a Unix-based user/group database or Jenkins, own user database.

Plugins management

Plugins management is very important, as these plugins give us the capability to integrate different environments (which could be cloud platform) or on-premises resources with Jenkins, and also give us the capability to manage data on our resources like app servers, database servers, and so on.

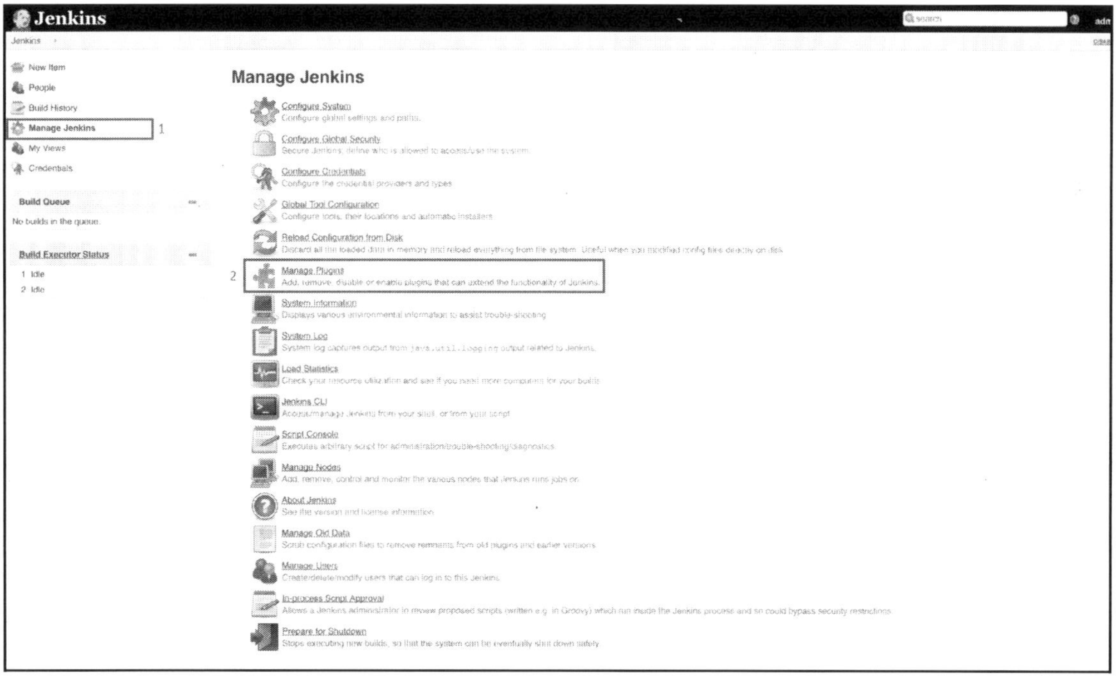

From the **Manage Jenkins** Panel, select the **Manage Plugins** option to open the **Manage Plugins** panel, which would look something like this:

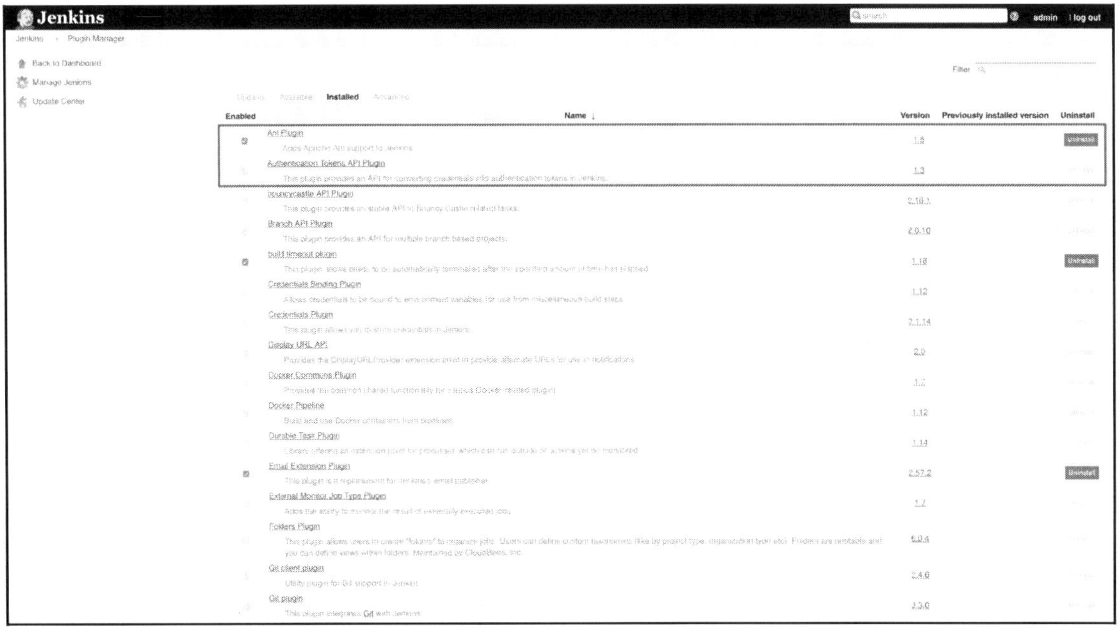

In this panel, you will able to install, uninstall, and upgrade any specific plugins from the system. From the same panel, you can upgrade Jenkins as well.

Version control systems

Jenkins can be used mainly to either build a particular application code, or to deploy code over any infrastructure platform (that is, for continuous deployment).

Nowadays, organizations store their application code over any version control system, such as Git, where the administrator has central control, and can provide the required access based on the user role. Also, since we are talking of continuous integration, then it is recommended to store the application code at a centralized location with version control to maintain the integrity of the code.

So, in order to maintain the version code, make sure you install the Git plugin from the **Manage plugin panel**.

To clone a Git repository via Jenkins, you need to enter the email and username for your Jenkins system. For this, switch to your job directory, and run the Git config command as follows:

```
# Need to configure the Git email and user for the Jenkins job

# switch to the job directory
cd /var/lib/Jenkins/jobs/myjob/workspace

# setup name and email
sudo git config user.name "Jenkins"
sudo git config user.email "test@gmail.com"
```

This needs to be set up in order to download the code from the repository, or at the time of merging the branches in Git, and other cases.

Setting up a Jenkins job

Now we are ready to set up our first Jenkins job. As discussed earlier, each job is created to perform certain specific tasks, which could be individual or could be in a pipeline.

According to Andrew Phillips, ideally, a pipeline breaks down the software delivery process into stages. Each stage is aimed at verifying the quality of the new features from a different angle to validate the new functionality, and to prevent errors from affecting your users. If any error is encountered, a feedback is returned in the form of reports, and it is ensured that the required quality of the software is achieved.

In order to initiate job creation, on the Jenkins home page, click on either **New item** on the left-hand side, or click on the **create new jobs** link in the right-hand side pane:

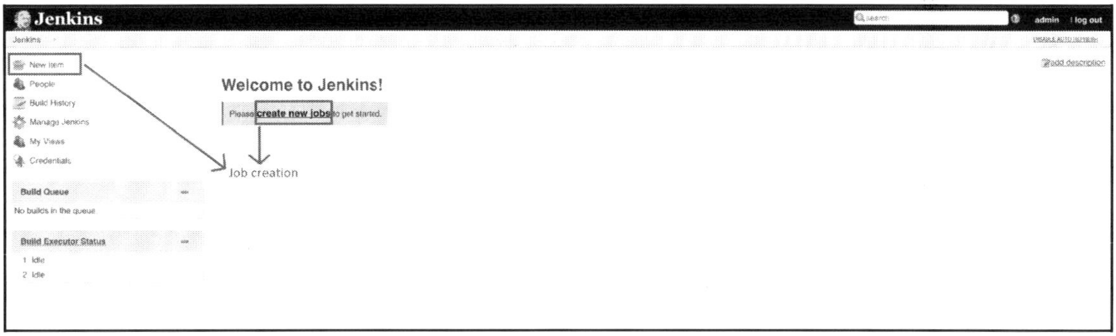

Once you click on it, it will open a wizard which will ask for your project/job name as well as the type of job you want to create, as shown in the following screenshot:

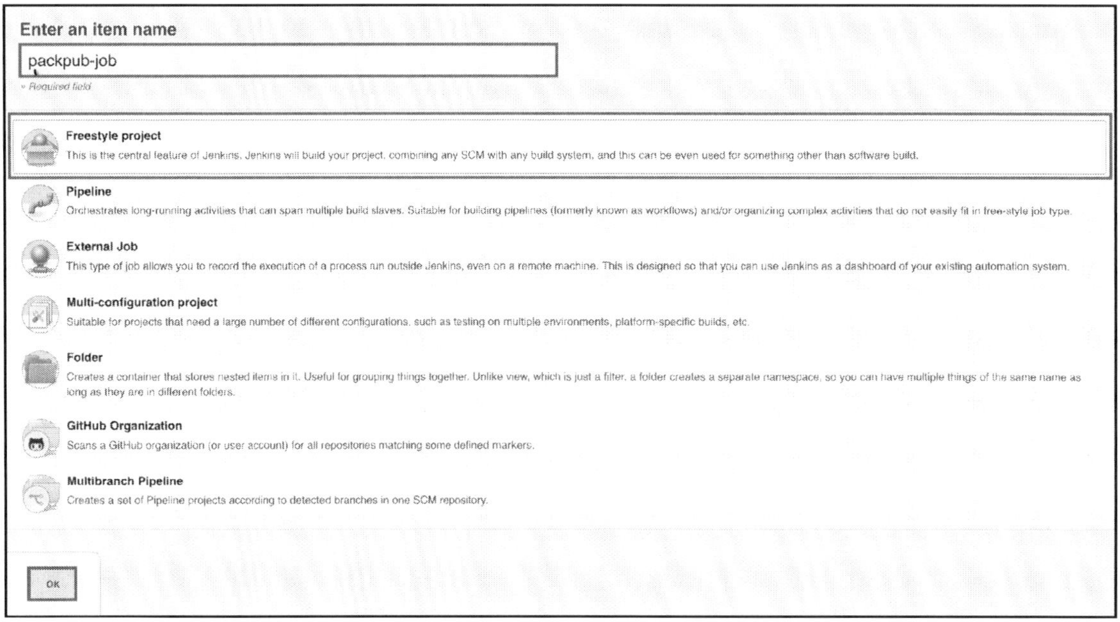

The description is already provided along with the project type to give us an overview of the different options available in Jenkins. These types need to selected, as they have different configurations based on the type.

Note that since we are working on the latest Jenkins version, it is possible that some of the project types might not be there in the older versions, so make sure you have the latest Jenkins installed.

For now, we will select the Freestyle project, specify a unique job name, and then click on **OK** to continue to configure our job. Once you click on **OK**, you will see the following page:

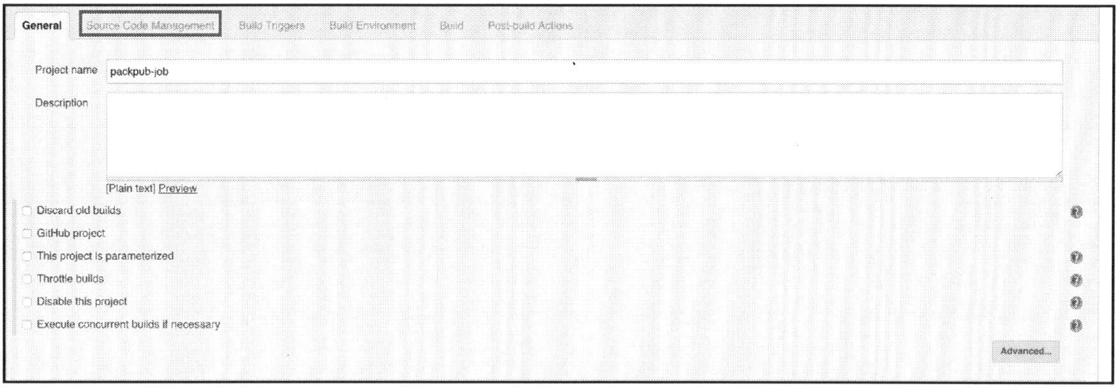

In the preceding page, you can define your job details such as **Project name**, **Description**, **GitHub project**, and so on.

Next, click on the **Source Code Management** tab; you will see the following screen:

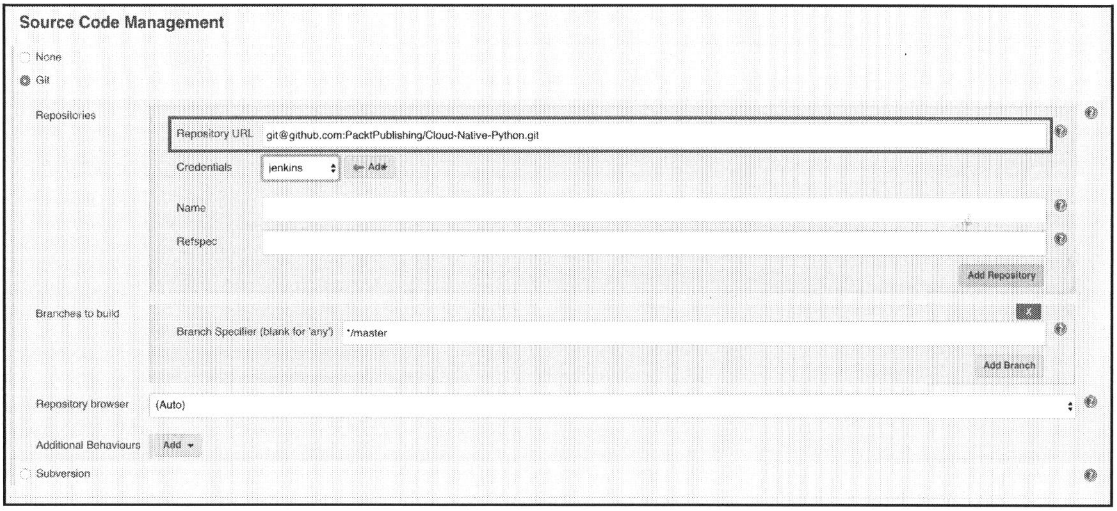

In this preceding section, you will define your source code details. You also need to set up the Jenkins user credentials if you haven't done so previously in the configuration section. Click on the **Add** button near credentials if it is not set up. It will open a popup, which will look something like this:

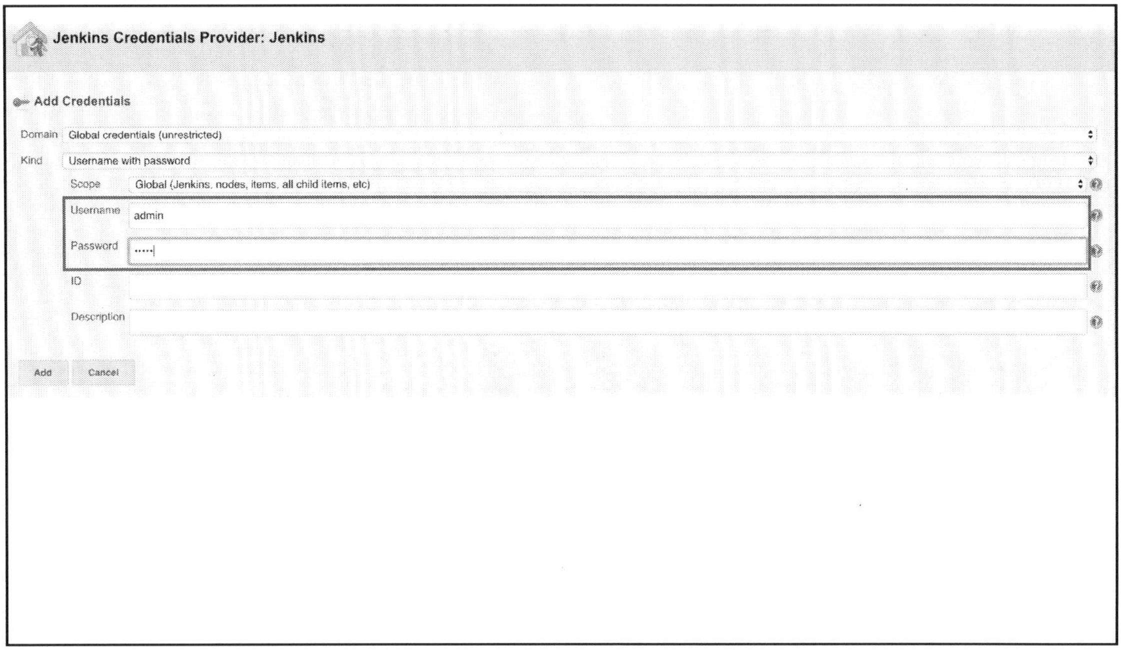

The user you define here (that is, the admin) needs to have permission in the code repository to access it.

There are ways by which you can set up authentication for the mentioned user on the repository, which are defined in **Kind** (the drop-down menu):

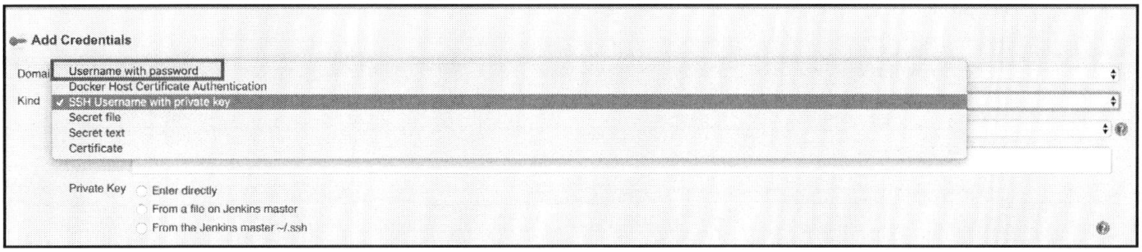

It is important to note that Jenkins will immediately test the credentials against the repository URL mentioned. If it fails, it will show you the error as seen in this screenshot:

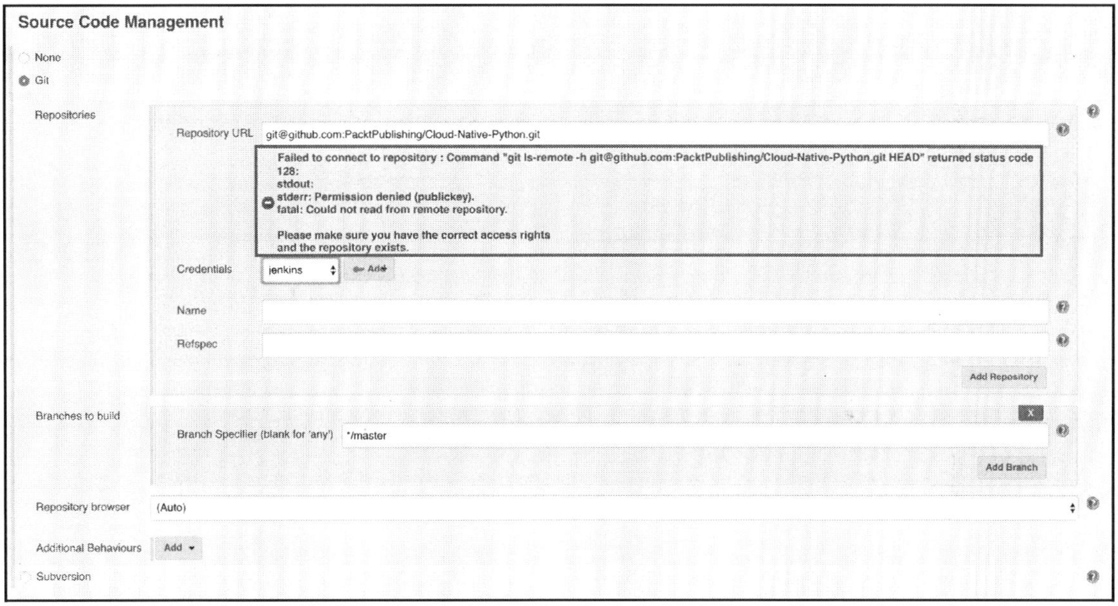

Assuming that the credentials match against the repository URL, let's move on to clicking the **Build Trigger** tab to scroll on it. The following screen shows the **Build Trigger** options which can be imposed on a job for continuous deployment:

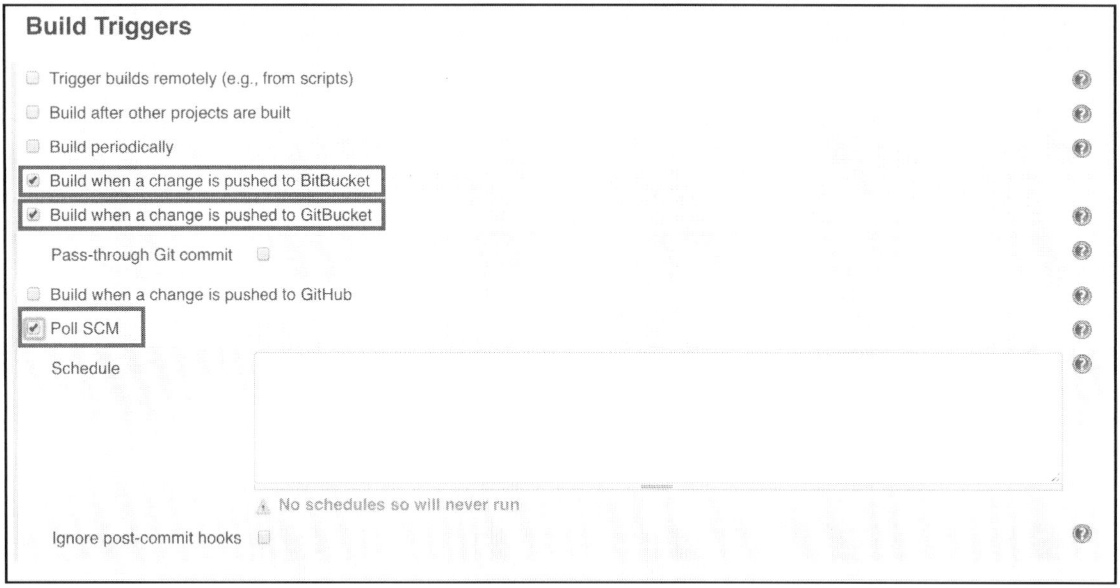

This **Build Trigger** section is very important, as it determines how often your build should run, and also the parameters which trigger your build. For example, if you want to build your application after every Git commit, you can select the option **Build when a change is pushed to GitBucket**.

So, as soon as the developer commits any changes in the repository in a certain branch (generally, master), then this job gets triggered automatically. It's like a hook on top of your repository, and it keeps a track of the activities on it. Alternatively, if you want to build your application or run this job periodically, then you can specify the condition like this-- `H/15 * * * *`--in **Poll SCM** to schedule, which means that this job will run every 15 minutes. It is similar to a cron job, which we, usually, set up in Linux-based systems.

The next two sections, **Build environment** and **Build**, are defined for workspace-related tasks. Since we are dealing with a Python-based application, and we have already built our application, we can skip these sections for now. But if you have an application written in Java or a .NET application, you can go with the ANT and Maven build tools, and branch to build. Alternatively, if you want to build a Python-based application, then go for tools such as pyBuilder (`http://pybuilder.github.io/`). The following screen shows the build option:

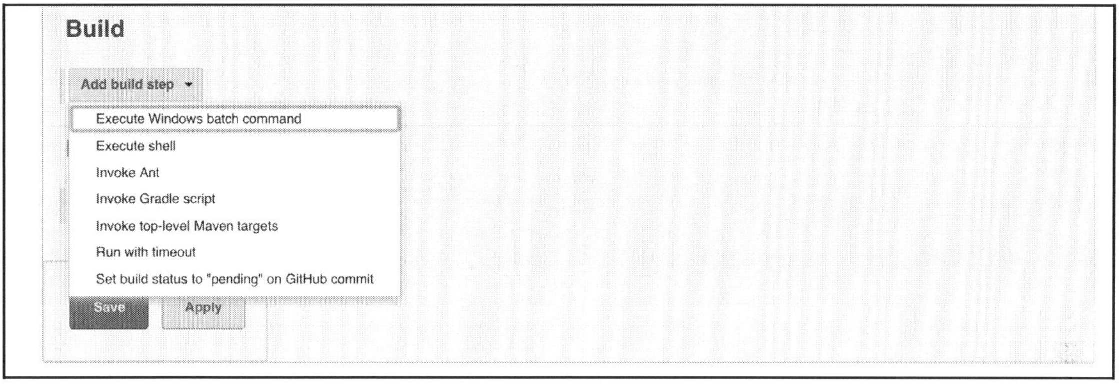

Once you are done, you can click on the next tab, which is **Post-build Actions**. This is used to define what needs to be done once the build is successful. Because of this section, Jenkins can also be used as a continuous deployment tool. So, in this post-build action, you can specify the platform where your application needs to be deployed, such as on an AWS EC2 machine, Code deploy, Azure VM, or others.

In the post-build section, in the context of continuous integration, we can also perform operations such as Git merge after a successful build, publish results on Git, and so on. Also, you can set up email notifications for your stakeholders to give them updates about the build results over email. See the following screenshot for more details:

That's all. Once you have filled the required details, click on **Save** to save the configuration. Now you are ready to build your application--click on the **Build Now** link in the left panel, as seen in the following screenshot:

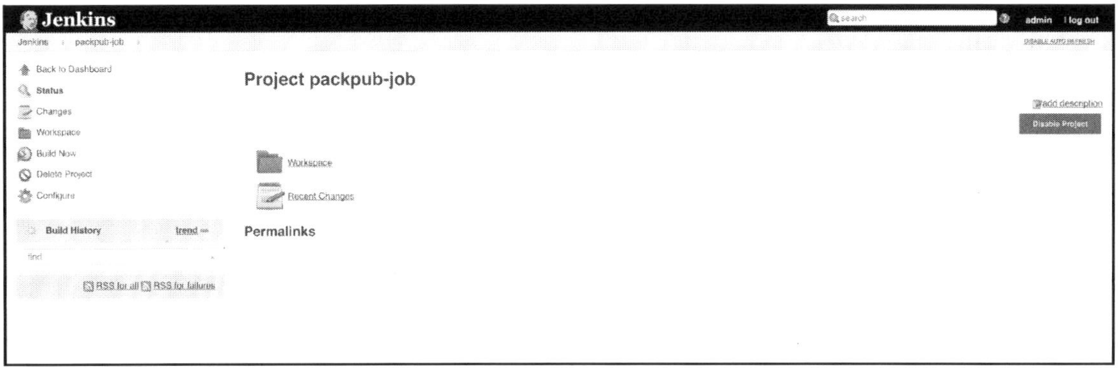

Note: For first time build execution, you need to trigger it manually if you haven't set the poll SCM or the Build Triggers section.

That's all we have from Jenkins at this point of time in terms of job creation. However, we will be using Jenkins as a continuous delivery and continuous integration tool in the upcoming chapters, where we deploy our React application that we created in the previous chapters on different platforms such as AWS, Azure, or Docker. We will also see the integration of the AWS service with Jenkins to automate application delivery to the GitHub repository by a single commit.

Understanding continuous delivery

Continuous delivery is a software engineering practice where production-ready features are produced and deployed to production.

The primary objective of continuous delivery is to perform successful application deployments irrespective of the platform, which could be a large-scale distributed system or a complex production environment.

In multinational companies, we always ensure that the application code is in a stable as well as deployable state even if there are many developers working on the different application components at the same time. In continuous delivery, we also ensure that unit testing and integration testing are successfully performed, making it production ready.

Need for continuous delivery

It has been assumed that if we try to deploy software more frequently, we should expect lower levels of stability and reliability in our systems, but that's not entirely correct. Continuous delivery provides practices which provide incredible competitive advantages for organizations that are willing to release stable and reliable software in a competitive market.

The practices in continuous delivery give us the following important benefits:

- **Risk free releases**: The primary requirement of any application in a software release is to have a minimal or zero downtime. After all, it's always about business, and the user should not be affected because of frequent releases. By using patterns such as BlueGreenDeployment (`https://martinfowler.com/bliki/BlueGreenDeployment.html`), we can achieve zero downtime during deployments.
- **Competitive market**: In continuous delivery, all the teams, such as the build and deployment team, testing team, developers, and others, work together, which makes different activities such as testing, integration, and so on, happen on a daily basis. This makes the feature release process faster (a week or two), and we will have frequent releases to the production environment for customer usage.
- **Quality improvement**: In continuous delivery, developers don't need to worry about the testing process, as it is taken care of by the pipeline, and showcases the result to the QA team as well. This enables the QA team and the developers to take a closer look at exploratory testing, usability testing, and performance and security testing, which can improve the customer experience.
- **Better products**: By using continuous delivery in build, test, deployment, and environment setups, we reduce the cost of making and delivering incremental changes in software, which makes the product much better over the course of time.

Continuous delivery versus continuous deployment

Continuous delivery and continuous deployment are similar in terms of the stages they have to build, tests, and the software release cycles they have to deploy, but they are slightly different in terms of the *process*, which you can understand from the following diagram:

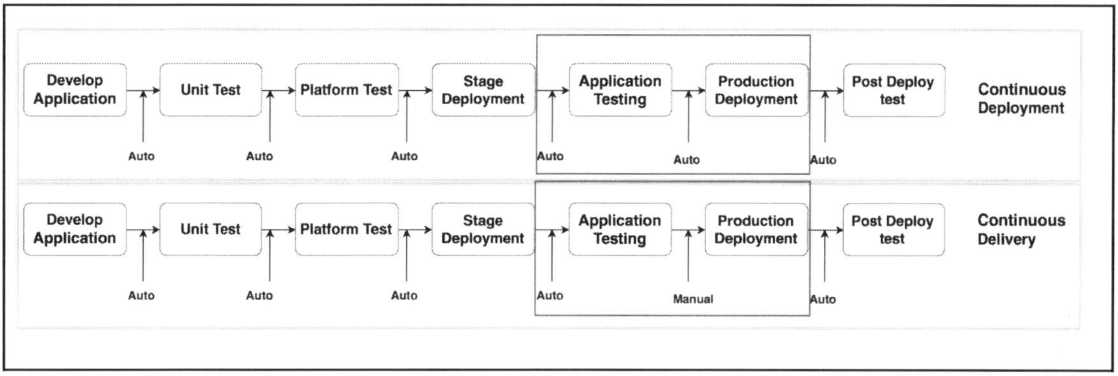

In continuous deployment, production-ready code is directly deployed to the production environment once it passes all the testing checks, which makes the software release frequent. But in the case of continuous delivery, the production-ready application code is not deployed unless manually triggered or approved by the concerned authority.

Summary

Throughout the chapter, we discussed the CI and CD tools such as Jenkins, and also looked at the different functionalities of the same. It is very crucial to understand these tools at this stage, as most companies which deal with cloud platforms use these processes for their software development as well as deployment. So, now that you have understood the deployment pipeline, you are ready to understand the platform where we will deploy our application.

In the next chapter, we will talk about Docker (based on the container technology). I'm sure most of you have heard of Docker before, so stay tuned for a deep exposure to Docker. See you in the next chapter!

10
Dockerizing Your Services

Now that we have an understanding of continuous integration and continuous delivery/deployment from the previous chapter, it is the right time to dive deeply into container-based technologies, such as Docker, where we will deploy our application. In this chapter, we will take a look at Docker and its features, and we will deploy our cloud native application on Docker.

This chapter will cover the following topics:

- Understanding Docker and how it is different from virtualization
- Installing Docker and Docker Swarm on a different OS
- Deploying a cloud native app on Docker
- Using Docker Compose

Understanding Docker

Docker is a **Container Management System** (**CMS**) that enables you to separate your application from your infrastructure, which makes it easier to develop, ship, and run your application. It is useful for managing **Linux Containers** (**LXC**). This let's you create images, and also perform actions on the containers as well as run commands or operations against containers.

In simple words, Docker provides a platform to package and run your application in an isolated environment called a **container**, and then ship it across different of software release environments, such as stage, pre-production, production, and so on.

Docker is lightweight in comparison to any **Traditional VMs**, as depicted in the following image:

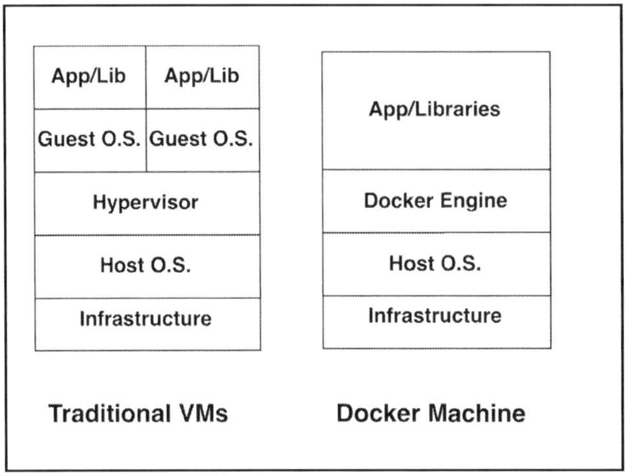

Few facts about Docker versus virtualization

There are a lot of organizations that are still working successfully on traditional VMs. Having said that, there are organizations that have either moved their application to Docker or are ready to do so. Here are a few reasons why Docker has more potential than virtual machines:

- When it comes to comparing Docker and virtual machines, Docker presents a lower system overhead than the virtual machine.
- Secondly, applications in the Docker environment have a generally higher performance than the virtual machines.
- While the VM software technology named **Hypervisor**, which acts as an agent between the VM environment and the underlying hardware, providing the necessary layer of abstraction; in Docker, we have the Docker engine that gives us more control than the Docker machine.

- Also, as you can see in the preceding image, Docker shares the **Host O.S.** across the Docker environment, whereas, the virtual machine needs its own OS for application deployment. This makes Docker lightweight and spin up and destroy them much faster, as compared to the virtual machine. Docker is similar to any other processes running on top of the host OS.
- In the case of a cloud native application, where we need to test our microservices quickly after every stage of development, Docker would be a good platform option to test our application, which is highly recommended.

Docker Engine - The backbone of Docker

Docker Engine is a client-server application that has the following components:

- **Dockerd**: This is a daemon process that keeps running in the background of the host OS to keep a track of the Docker container attributes, such as status (up/running/stopped)
- **Rest API**: This provides the interface to interact with daemon and perform actions on containers
- **Docker command line**: This provides the command-line interface to create and manage Docker objects, such as images, containers, networks, and volumes

Setting up the Docker environment

In this section, we will take a look at the installation procedure for Docker on different operating systems, such as Debian and Windows, among others.

Installing Docker on Ubuntu

Setting up Docker is pretty straightforward. There are mainly two editions of Docker in the marketplace.

Docker Inc., which owns the **containerization** Docker product, renamed the Docker **Commercially Supported** (**CS**) edition to Docker **Enterprises Edition** (**EE**), and also converted the Docker Engine to Docker **Community Edition** (**CE**).

There are a couple of changes from EE and CE; obviously, the commercial support being one of them. However, in the Docker Enterprise Edition, they have built a couple of certifications around the container content, platform plugins, and many more.

In this book, we will use the Docker Community Edition, so we will begin by updating the APT repository:

```
$ apt-get update -y
```

Now, let's add the GPG key from the Docker official system as follows:

```
$ sudo apt-key adv --keyserver hkp://p80.pool.sks-keyservers.net:80 --recv-
keys 58118E89F3A912897C070ADBF76221572C52609D
```

Then let's add the Docker repository to the APT source list of Ubuntu:

```
$ sudo apt-add-repository 'deb https://apt.dockerproject.org/repo ubuntu-
xenial main'
```

Sometimes, in Ubuntu 14.04/16.04, the `apt-add-repository` utility is not found. In order to install the mentioned utility, use the following command to install the `software-properties-common` package: **$ sudo apt-get install software-properties-common -y**.

Next, update your APT package manager to download the latest Docker list as follows:

```
$ apt-get update -y
```

If you want to download and install the Docker Engine from the Docker repository instead of the default 14.04 repository, use the following command to do so:
$ apt-cache policy docker-engine.

You will see the following output on the terminal:

```
root@packtpub:~# apt-cache policy docker-engine
docker-engine:
  Installed: (none)
  Candidate: 17.05.0~ce-0~ubuntu-xenial
  Version table:
     17.05.0~ce-0~ubuntu-xenial 0
        500 https://apt.dockerproject.org/repo/ ubuntu-xenial/main amd64 Packages
     17.04.0~ce-0~ubuntu-xenial 0
        500 https://apt.dockerproject.org/repo/ ubuntu-xenial/main amd64 Packages
     17.03.1~ce-0~ubuntu-xenial 0
        500 https://apt.dockerproject.org/repo/ ubuntu-xenial/main amd64 Packages
     17.03.0~ce-0~ubuntu-xenial 0
        500 https://apt.dockerproject.org/repo/ ubuntu-xenial/main amd64 Packages
     1.13.1-0~ubuntu-xenial 0
        500 https://apt.dockerproject.org/repo/ ubuntu-xenial/main amd64 Packages
     1.13.0-0~ubuntu-xenial 0
        500 https://apt.dockerproject.org/repo/ ubuntu-xenial/main amd64 Packages
     1.12.6-0~ubuntu-xenial 0
        500 https://apt.dockerproject.org/repo/ ubuntu-xenial/main amd64 Packages
     1.12.5-0~ubuntu-xenial 0
        500 https://apt.dockerproject.org/repo/ ubuntu-xenial/main amd64 Packages
     1.12.4-0~ubuntu-xenial 0
        500 https://apt.dockerproject.org/repo/ ubuntu-xenial/main amd64 Packages
     1.12.3-0~xenial 0
        500 https://apt.dockerproject.org/repo/ ubuntu-xenial/main amd64 Packages
     1.12.2-0~xenial 0
        500 https://apt.dockerproject.org/repo/ ubuntu-xenial/main amd64 Packages
     1.12.1-0~xenial 0
        500 https://apt.dockerproject.org/repo/ ubuntu-xenial/main amd64 Packages
     1.12.0-0~xenial 0
        500 https://apt.dockerproject.org/repo/ ubuntu-xenial/main amd64 Packages
     1.11.2-0~xenial 0
        500 https://apt.dockerproject.org/repo/ ubuntu-xenial/main amd64 Packages
     1.11.1-0~xenial 0
        500 https://apt.dockerproject.org/repo/ ubuntu-xenial/main amd64 Packages
     1.11.0-0~xenial 0
        500 https://apt.dockerproject.org/repo/ ubuntu-xenial/main amd64 Packages
```

Now, we are ready to install our Docker Engine, so let's fire the following command to install it:

```
$ sudo apt-get install -y docker-engine -y
```

Since Docker depends on a couple of system libraries, it might face an error similar to the one shown in the following screenshot:

```
root@packtpub:~# sudo apt-get install -y docker-engine
Reading package lists... Done
Building dependency tree
Reading state information... Done
Some packages could not be installed. This may mean that you have
requested an impossible situation or if you are using the unstable
distribution that some required packages have not yet been created
or been moved out of Incoming.
The following information may help to resolve the situation:

The following packages have unmet dependencies:
 docker-engine : Depends: init-system-helpers (>= 1.18~) but 1.14 is to be installed
                 Depends: lsb-base (>= 4.1+Debian11ubuntu7) but 4.1+Debian11ubuntu6 is to be installed
                 Depends: libdevmapper1.02.1 (>= 2:1.02.97) but 2:1.02.77-6ubuntu2 is to be installed
                 Depends: libltdl7 (>= 2.4.6) but it is not going to be installed
                 Depends: libsystemd0 but it is not installable
E: Unable to correct problems, you have held broken packages.
```

If you catch this kind of error, then make sure that you have these libraries installed with the defined version as well.

After the Docker Engine installation is successful, it's time to validate it by executing the following command:

```
$ docker -v
Docker version 17.05.0-ce, build 89658be
```

If you see a version similar to the one shown in the preceding terminal, then we are good to go.

To get help on Docker, you can execute the following command:

```
$ docker help
```

TIP

If you really want to go with the Docker Enterprise Edition, you can go ahead with the installation steps shown on the official Docker website (`https://docs.docker.com/engine/installation/linux/ubuntu/`).

Installation on Windows

Ideally, Windows is not suitable for Docker, and that's why you don't see the container technology around on the Windows system. Having said that, we have a couple of workarounds for it. One of them is using Chocolatey.

In order to install Docker on the Windows system using Chocolatey, follow these steps:

1. Install Chocolatey from their official website (`https://chocolatey.org/install`).

   There are couple of ways shown in the preceding link to install Chocolatey.

2. Once Chocolatey is installed, you simply have to execute the following command in cmd or PowerShell:

   ```
   $ choco install docker
   ```

   This will install Docker on Windows 7 and 8 operating systems.

Similarly, if you want to go with the Docker Enterprise edition, you can follow the steps shown in this link:

`https://docs.docker.com/docker-ee-for-windows/install/#install-docker-ee.`

Setting up Docker Swarm

Docker Swarm is a popular term for a pool of Docker machines. Docker Swarm is very useful for hosting your website as it can be used to scale your infrastructure up or down very quickly.

In the Docker Swarm, we can club together a couple of Docker machines that work as one unit and share their resources, such as CPU, memory, and so on, where one machine becomes the master that we call leader, and the remaining nodes work as a worker.

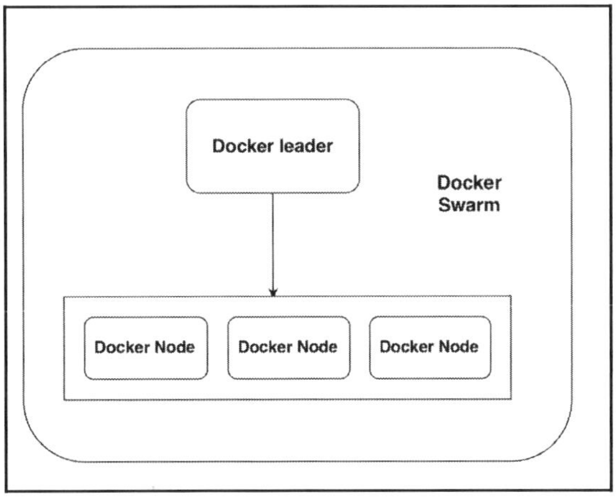

Setting up the Docker environment

In this section, we will be setting up the Docker Swarm by selecting the leader from the Docker machine and connecting the remaining machines with the leader.

Assumption

The following are a few assumptions for the Docker environment:

- We are taking two machines, which could be VM's or instances from the cloud platform, for the demo purpose named master and node1. Also, we have installed Docker on both the machines by following the procedure described in the Docker installation section.
- Port `2377` must be opened for communication between the master and node1.
- Make sure the required port for application access should be opened; we will need port `80` for nginx, just like in our example.
- The master Docker machine could be based on any kind of OS, such as Ubuntu, Windows, and so on.

Now, let's begin with our Docker Swarm setup.

Initializing the Docker manager

At this point, we need to decide which node should be the leader. Let's select the master node as our Docker manager. So, login into the master machine and execute the following command to initialize this machine to be a leader for the Docker Swarm:

```
$ docker swarm init --advertise-addr master_ip_address
```

This command will set the provided host to be the master (leader) and generate a token for the node to connect to. See the following output for your reference:

```
root@ip-10-0-0-217:~# docker swarm init --advertise-addr 54.158.3.255
Swarm initialized: current node (zc0r8kzmjf7wa18h0m2i33u4b) is now a manager.

To add a worker to this swarm, run the following command:

    docker swarm join \
    --token SWMTKN-1-1le69e43paf0vxyvjdslxaluk1a1mvi5lb6ftvxdoldul6k3dl-1dr9qdmbmni5hnn9y3oh1nfxp \
    54.158.3.255:2377

To add a manager to this swarm, run 'docker swarm join-token manager' and follow the instructions.
```

A few important points to keep in mind:

- Don't share your token and IP address with anyone
- Secondly, it is possible to have multiple masters in case of failovers

Add node1 to master

Now that we selected the leader, we will need to add a new node to the cluster to complete the setup. Log in to node1 and execute the following command, which is specified in the previous command output:

```
$ docker swarm join    --token SWMTKN-1-
1le69e43paf0vxyvjdslxaluk1a1mvi5lb6ftvxdoldul6k3dl-
1dr9qdmbmni5hnn9y3oh1nfxp    master-ip-address:2377
```

You can refer to the following screenshot for an output:

```
root@ip-10-0-0-64:~# docker swarm join \
>     --token SWMTKN-1-1le69e43paf0vxyvjdslxaluk1a1mvi5lb6ftvxdoldul6k3dl-1dr9qdmbmni5hnn9y3oh1nfxp \
>     54.158.3.255:2377
This node joined a swarm as a worker.
root@ip-10-0-0-64:~#
```

This means our setup is successful. Let's check if it is added in the master Docker machine or not.

Execute the following command to verify it:

```
$ docker node ls
```

```
root@ip-10-0-0-217:~# docker node ls
ID                            HOSTNAME          STATUS     AVAILABILITY     MANAGER STATUS
cycsh0kdfnyucfo1pr7ari8qw     ip-10-0-0-64      Ready      Active
zc0r8kzmjf7wa18h0m2i33u4b *   ip-10-0-0-217     Ready      Active           Leader
```

Testing the Docker Swarm

Now that we have set up the Docker Swarm, it's time to run some services on top of it, say, the nginx service. Execute the following command on the master Docker machine to start your nginx service on port `80`:

```
$ docker service create  --detach=false -p 80:80 --name webserver
nginx
```

The output of the preceding command should be similar to the following screenshot:

```
root@ip-10-0-0-217:~# docker service create  --detach=false -p 80:80 --name webserver nginx
vawxbicnq616gblt5cfo875mh
overall progress: 1 out of 1 tasks
1/1: running   [==================================================>]
verify: Waiting 1 seconds to verify that tasks are stable...
root@ip-10-0-0-217:~#
```

Let's use the following Docker command to see if our service is running or not:

```
$ docker service ps webserver
```

The output of preceding command should be similar to the following screenshot:

```
root@ip-10-0-0-217:~# docker service ps webserver
ID                  NAME                IMAGE               NODE                DESIRED STATE       CURRENT STATE               ERROR
   PORTS
u7oj15hcifpm        webserver.1         nginx:latest        ip-10-0-0-217       Running             Running about a minute ago
```

A few other commands to validate are as follows:

To validate which services are running and on which port, use the following command:

```
$ docker service ls
```

If you are seeing output similar to the following screenshot, then we are good:

```
root@ip-10-0-0-217:~# docker service ls
ID                  NAME                MODE                REPLICAS            IMAGE               PORTS
vawxbicnq616        webserver           replicated          1/1                 nginx:latest        *:80->80/tcp
```

To scale up the Docker instances for the service, use the following command:

```
$ docker service scale webserver=3
```

```
root@ip-10-0-0-217:~# docker service scale webserver=3
webserver scaled to 3
root@ip-10-0-0-217:~# docker service ps webserver
ID                  NAME                IMAGE               NODE                DESIRED STATE       CURRENT STATE            ERROR
ORTS
u7oj15hcifpm        webserver.1         nginx:latest        ip-10-0-0-217       Running             Running 6 minutes ago
loqmks4894gx        webserver.2         nginx:latest        ip-10-0-0-64        Running             Running 34 seconds ago
5qw9xz92agl4        webserver.3         nginx:latest        ip-10-0-0-217       Running             Running 10 seconds ago
```

Let's check if our nginx is up or not by accessing its default page. Try to hit `http://master-ip-address:80/` on your browser. If you see the following output, then your service is deployed successfully:

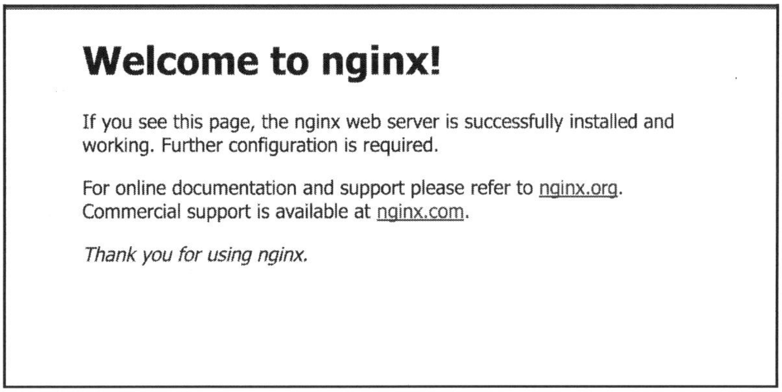

Welcome to nginx!
If you see this page, the nginx web server is successfully installed and working. Further configuration is required.
For online documentation and support please refer to nginx.org.
Commercial support is available at nginx.com.
Thank you for using nginx.

Awesome! In the upcoming section, we will deploy our cloud native application on Docker machines.

Deploying an application on Docker

In this section, we will deploy our cloud native application, which we developed in the previous chapters. However, before we begin with the creation of our application architecture, there are a few concepts of Docker one should be aware of, some of which are as follows:

- **Docker images**: These are basically a combination of library and the applications deployed on top of it. These images can be downloaded from the Docker Hub public repository, or you can create your customized images as well.
- **Dockerfile**: This is a configuration file to build your images that can be used to run your Docker machine later on.
- **Docker Hub**: This is a centralized repository where you can keep your images, which can be shared across the team.

We will use all these concepts during our application deployment. Also, we will keep using our Docker Swarm setup to deploy our application as we don't want to run out of resources.

We will follow this architecture to deploy our application, where we are deploying our application and MongoDB (basically, application data) in separate Docker instances as it is recommended to always keep your application and data separate:

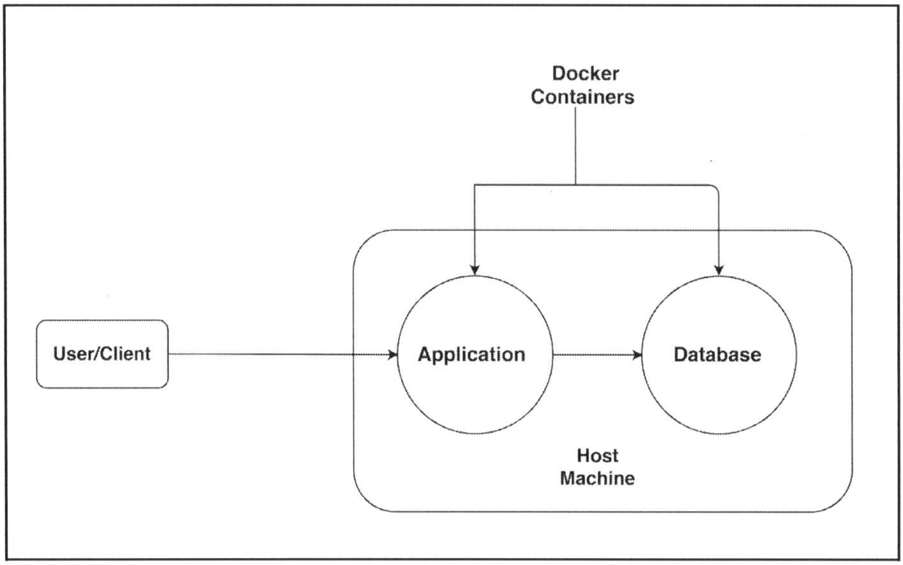

Building and running our MongoDB Docker service

In this section, we will be creating the Dockerfile to build `MongoDB`, which will have all the information, such as base image, port to be exposed, how to install the `MongoDB` service, and so on.

Now, let's log in to your Docker master (leader) account and create a Dockerfile with the name `Dockerfile` using the following contents:

```
# MongoDB Dockerfile
# Pull base image.
FROM ubuntu
MAINTAINER Manish Sethi<manish@sethis.in>
# Install MongoDB.
RUN \
apt-key adv --keyserver hkp://keyserver.ubuntu.com:80 --recv
7F0CEB10 && \
echo 'deb http://downloads-distro.mongodb.org/repo/ubuntu-upstart
```

```
dist 10gen' > /etc/apt/sources.list.d/mongodb.list && \
apt-get update && \
apt-get install -y mongodb-org && \
rm -rf /var/lib/apt/lists/*
# Define mountable directories.
VOLUME ["/data/db"]
# Define working directory.
WORKDIR /data
# Define default command.
CMD ["mongod"]
# Expose ports.
EXPOSE 27017
EXPOSE 28017
```

Save it, and, before we move ahead, let's understand its different sections as follows:

```
# Pull base image.
FROM ubuntu
```

The preceding code will tell you to pull the Ubuntu public image from the Docker Hub and make it the base image on which the following command needs to be run:

```
# Install MongoDB
RUN \
apt-key adv --keyserver hkp://keyserver.ubuntu.com:80 --recv
7F0CEB10 && \
echo 'deb http://downloads-distro.mongodb.org/repo/ubuntu-upstart
dist 10gen' > /etc/apt/sources.list.d/mongodb.list && \
apt-get update && \
apt-get install -y mongodb-org && \
rm -rf /var/lib/apt/lists/*
```

The preceding section of code is similar to the one where we execute these commands manually for `MongoDB`; however, in this case, it is automatically taken care of by Docker.

Next is the volume section, which is kind of optional. It is creating mountable directories where we can store the data to keep it safe in an external volume.

```
# Define mountable directories.
VOLUME ["/data/db"]
```

The next section is to expose the ports by which users/clients will be able to communicate with the MongoDB server:

```
EXPOSE 27017
EXPOSE 28017
```

Once you have saved the file, execute the following command to build the image:

```
$ docker build --tag mongodb:ms-packtpub-mongodb
```

Building an image can take around 4-5 minutes, depending on the internet bandwidth and system performance.

The following screen shows the output of the Docker build command:

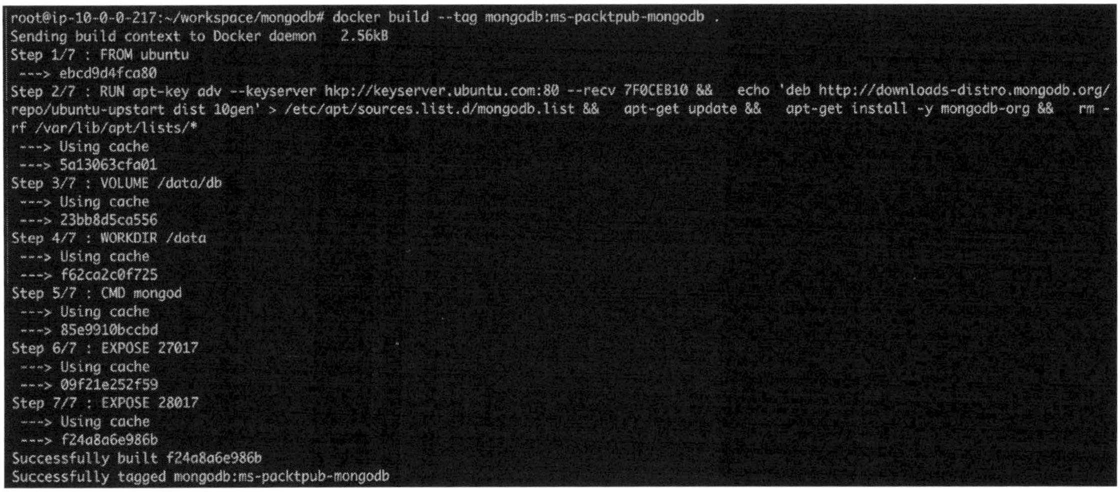

```
root@ip-10-0-0-217:~/workspace/mongodb# docker build --tag mongodb:ms-packtpub-mongodb .
Sending build context to Docker daemon   2.56kB
Step 1/7 : FROM ubuntu
 ---> ebcd9d4fca80
Step 2/7 : RUN apt-key adv --keyserver hkp://keyserver.ubuntu.com:80 --recv 7F0CEB10 &&   echo 'deb http://downloads-distro.mongodb.org/
repo/ubuntu-upstart dist 10gen' > /etc/apt/sources.list.d/mongodb.list &&   apt-get update &&   apt-get install -y mongodb-org &&   rm -
rf /var/lib/apt/lists/*
 ---> Using cache
 ---> 5a13063cfa01
Step 3/7 : VOLUME /data/db
 ---> Using cache
 ---> 23bb8d5ca556
Step 4/7 : WORKDIR /data
 ---> Using cache
 ---> f62ca2c0f725
Step 5/7 : CMD mongod
 ---> Using cache
 ---> 85e9910bccbd
Step 6/7 : EXPOSE 27017
 ---> Using cache
 ---> 09f21e252f59
Step 7/7 : EXPOSE 28017
 ---> Using cache
 ---> f24a8a6e986b
Successfully built f24a8a6e986b
Successfully tagged mongodb:ms-packtpub-mongodb
```

In the preceding screenshot, as it's showing a successful build, you can now see the images list to validate, whether the image with the mentioned tag name (**ms-packtpub-mongodb**) is present or not.

Use the following command to list the images:

```
$ docker images
```

The following screen lists the Docker images available:

```
root@ip-10-0-0-217:~/workspace/mongodb# docker images
REPOSITORY          TAG                   IMAGE ID            CREATED              SIZE
mongodb             ms-packtpub-mongodb   f24a8a6e986b        About a minute ago   411MB
ubuntu              latest                ebcd9d4fca80        12 days ago          118MB
httpd               <none>                e0645af13ada        2 weeks ago          177MB
nginx               <none>                3448f27c273f        2 weeks ago          109MB
```

Awesome! Our image is present. Now let's run the `mongodb` service on the master Docker machine using the following command:

```
$ docker run -d -p 27017:27017 -p 28017:28017 --name mongodb mongodb:ms-
packtpub-mongodb mongod --rest --httpinterface
```

In the output, you will get a random Docker ID, as shown in the following screenshot:

```
root@ip-10-0-0-217:~/workspace/mongodb# docker run -d -p 27017:27017 -p 28017:28017 --name mongodb mongodb:ms-packtpub-mongodb mongod --
rest --httpinterface
0e849fb79a486b22f882460cf4032f0182e8b503b29b653d0eeb3664fc364c5b
```

Let's check the state of the Docker container by executing the `docker ps` command. It should have an output similar to the following screenshot:

```
root@ip-10-0-0-217:~/workspace/mongodb# docker ps
CONTAINER ID        IMAGE                          COMMAND                  CREATED             STATUS              PORTS
                         NAMES
0e849fb79a48        mongodb:ms-packtpub-mongodb    "mongod --rest --h..."   6 minutes ago       Up 6 minutes        0.0.0.0:27017->27017/
tcp, 0.0.0.0:28017->28017/tcp   mongodb
bb240462626a        nginx:latest                   "nginx -g 'daemon ..."   3 hours ago         Up 3 hours          80/tcp
                         webserver.3.5qw9xz92agl4fzthw1j7lh7xr
1c6ed0dd5bd6        nginx:latest                   "nginx -g 'daemon ..."   3 hours ago         Up 3 hours          80/tcp
                         webserver.1.u7oj15hcifpmu9frvfuxdx968
```

A very few developers as well as sysadmins know that there is an HTTP interface for the `mongoDB` service, which we exposed using port `28017`.

So, if we try to access `http://your-master-ip-address:28017/` in the browser, we will see a screen similar to the following screenshot:

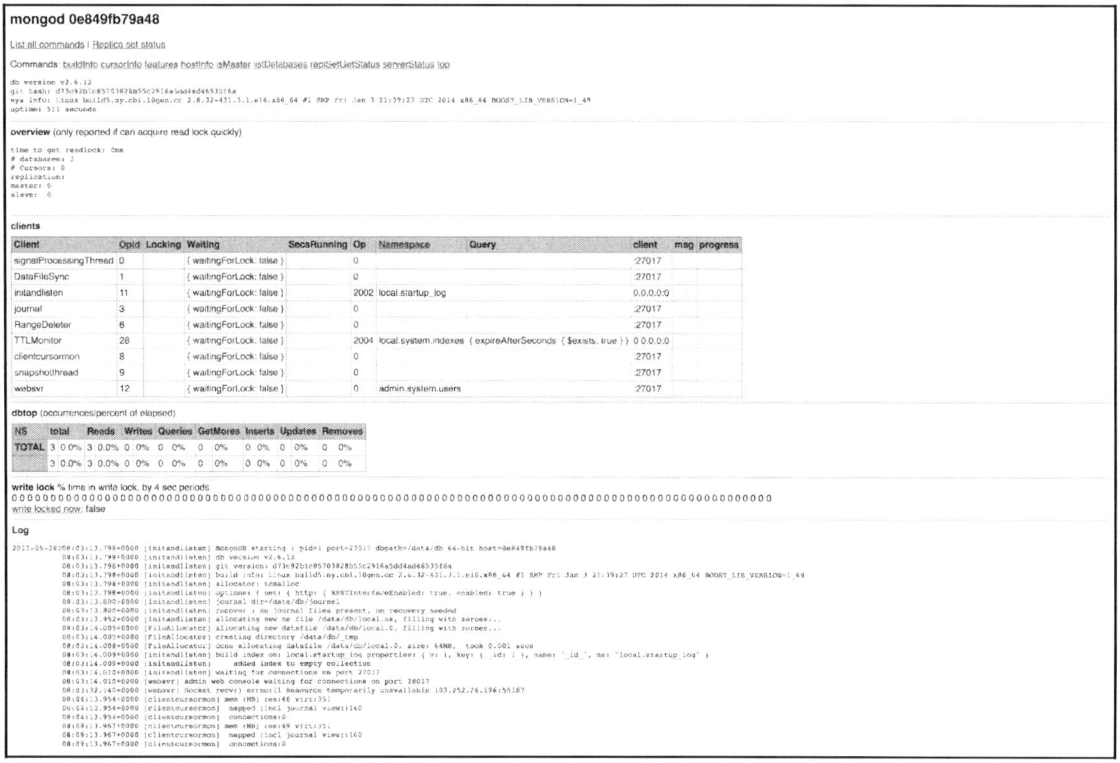

Awesome! Our MongoDB is up and running now!!

Before we move ahead with launching containers for the application, let's understand how the Docker Hub is useful for us.

Docker Hub - what is it all about?

As per the Docker Hub official documentation, Docker Hub is a cloud-based registry service that allows you to link to code repositories, build your images and test them, and store manually pushed images, and links to Docker Cloud so you can deploy images to your hosts.

In simpler words, Docker Hub is a centralized store for images which anyone around the globe can access, provided they have the required privileges and can perform operations around images to deploy and run their application on their hosts.

Advantages of Docker Hub are as follows:

- Docker Hub provides the functionality for automated create builds if any change in the source code repository is reported
- It provides WebHook to trigger for application deployment after a successful push to the repository
- It provides functionality to create a private work space to store images and is accessible only within your organization or team
- Docker Hub has an integration with your version control system, such as GitHub, BitBucket, and so on, which is useful with continuous integration and delivery

Now, let's see how we can push our custom `MongoDB` images to a private repository that we created recently.

First, you need to create an account at `https://hub.docker.com` and activate it. Once you are logged in, you need to create a private/public repository based on your preference, as shown in the following screenshot:

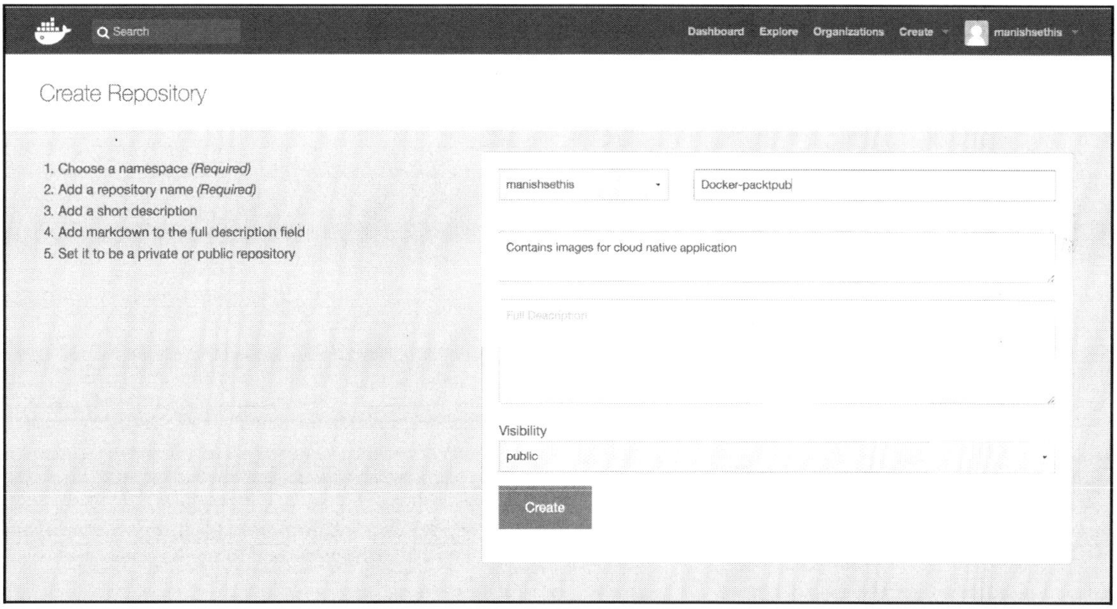

Click on the **Create** button to set up the repository and you will be redirected to the following screen:

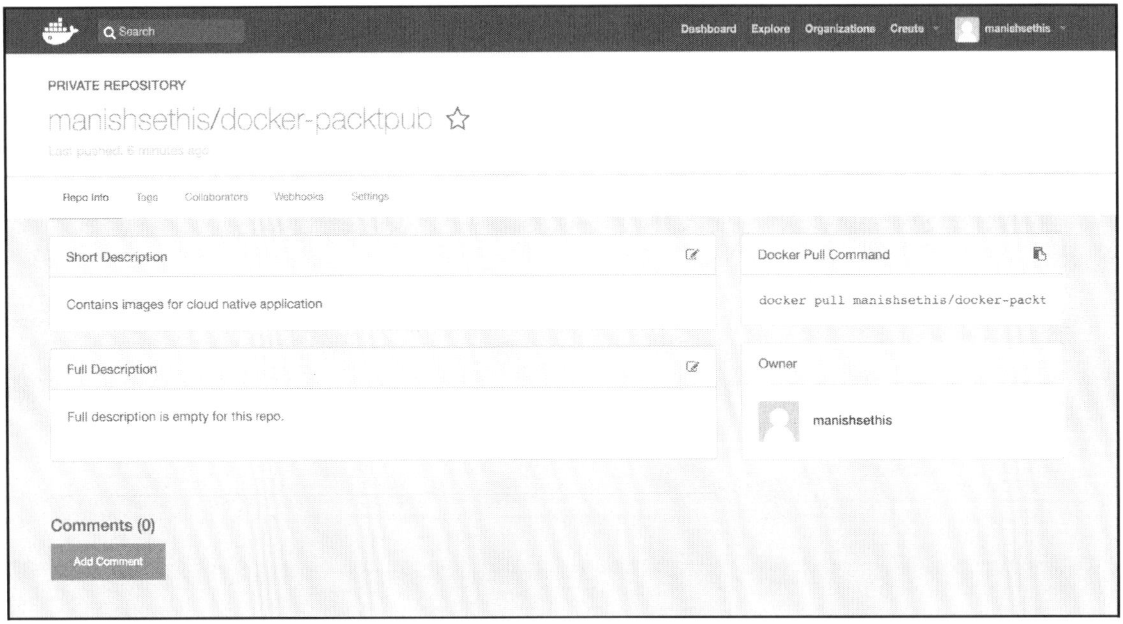

Docker Hub provides only one private repository on a free account.

Now that we have created the repository, let's come back to our master Docker machine and execute the following command:

```
$ docker login
```

This will ask for your credentials for the Docker Hub account, as shown in the following screenshot:

root@ip-10-0-0-217:~/workspace/mongodb# docker login
Login with your Docker ID to push and pull images from Docker Hub. If you don't have a Docker ID, head over to https://hub.docker.com to create one.
Username: manishsethis
Password:
Login Succeeded

Once the login is successful, it's time to tag the image you want to push to the repository using the following command:

```
$ docker tag mongodb:ms-packtpub-mongodb manishsethis/docker-packtpub
```

TIP: If we don't specify the tag, then it will take the latest tag by default.

Once the tag is created, it's time to push the tag to the repository. Use the following command to do so:

```
$ docker push manishsethis/docker-packtpub
```

The Following screen shows the Docker `push` command output:

```
root@ip-10-0-0-217:~/workspace/mongodb# docker push manishsethis/docker-packtpub
The push refers to a repository [docker.io/manishsethis/docker-packtpub]
a4c9b6de5784: Pushed
532078e28fc7: Pushed
33f1a94ed7fc: Mounted from library/ubuntu
b27287a6dbce: Mounted from library/ubuntu
47c2386f248c: Mounted from library/ubuntu
2be95f0d8a0c: Mounted from library/ubuntu
2df9b8def18a: Mounted from library/ubuntu
latest: digest: sha256:f99835f0d7c7178bc69afc5f5aebc067dbfee08b4409a988365a3f20ffee0589 size: 1776
```

Once the push is completed, you will see the image in Docker Hub in the **Tags** tab, as shown here:

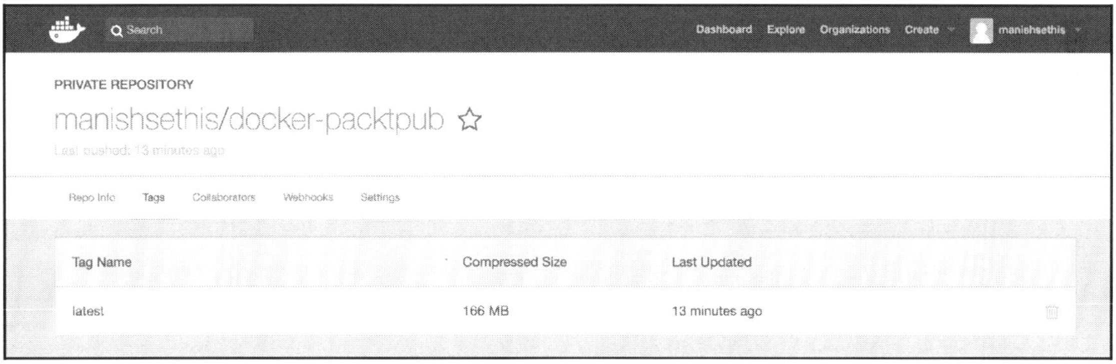

This means that your image is pushed successfully.

In order to pull this image, you will simply have to use the following command:

```
$ docker pull manishsethis/docker-packtpub
```

Oh, wow! It's too simple and you can access it from anywhere, provided you have credentials.

There are other Docker registry providers such as AWS (EC2 container registry), Azure (Azure container registry), and so on.

For now, this is all we have from the Docker Hub side. We will keep on using Docker Hub during this chapter to push the images.

Moving ahead now, we are ready to deploy our cloud native application to another container, but, before that, we need to build an image for it using the Dockerfile. So, let's create a directory called `app` and also create an empty Dockerfile with the following contents:

```
FROM ubuntu:14.04
MAINTAINER Manish Sethi<manish@sethis.in>
# no tty
ENV DEBIAN_FRONTEND noninteractive
# get up to date
RUN apt-get -qq update --fix-missing
# Bootstrap the image so that it includes all of our dependencies
RUN apt-get -qq install python3  python-dev python-virtualenv
python3-pip --assume-yes
RUN sudo apt-get install build-essential autoconf libtool libssl-
dev libffi-dev --assume-yes
# Setup locale
RUN export LC_ALL=en_US.UTF-8
RUN export LANG=en_US.UTF-8
RUN export LANGUAGE=en_US.UTF-8
# copy the contents of the cloud-native-app(i.e. complete
application) folder into the container at build time
COPY cloud-native-app/ /app/
# Create Virtual environment
RUN mkdir -p /venv/
RUN virtualenv /venv/ --python=python3
# Python dependencies inside the virtualenv
RUN /venv/bin/pip3 install -r /app/requirements.txt
# expose a port for the flask development server
EXPOSE 5000
# Running our flask application
CMD cd /app/ && /venv/bin/python app.py
```

I believe I have explained most of the section inside the Dockerfile earlier, although, there are a few sections that still need to be explained.

```
COPY cloud-native-app/ /app/
```

In the preceding section of the Dockerfile, we copied the contents of the application, that is, the code, from a local machine to the Docker container. Alternatively, we can also use ADD to do the same.

The `CMD` is short for the command that we want to execute inside the Docker container, which is defined as follows in the Dockerfile:

```
# Running our flask application
CMD cd /app/ && /venv/bin/python app.py
```

Now, save the file and run the following command to build the image:

```
$ docker build --tag cloud-native-app:latest .
```

This might take a while as there are lot of libraries that need to be installed and compiled as well. It is good practice to build an image after every change to make sure images are updated with the current config. The output will be similar to one shown here:

```
root@ip-10-0-0-217:~/workspace/mongodb# docker build --tag cloud-native-app:latest .
Sending build context to Docker daemon   2.56kB
Step 1/7 : FROM ubuntu
 ---> ebcd9d4fca80
Step 2/7 : RUN apt-key adv --keyserver hkp://keyserver.ubuntu.com:80 --recv 7F0CEB10 &&   echo 'deb http://downloads-distro.mongodb.org/
repo/ubuntu-upstart dist 10gen' > /etc/apt/sources.list.d/mongodb.list &&   apt-get update &&   apt-get install -y mongodb-org &&   rm -
rf /var/lib/apt/lists/*
 ---> Using cache
 ---> 5a13063cfa01
Step 3/7 : VOLUME /data/db
 ---> Using cache
 ---> 23bb8d5ca556
Step 4/7 : WORKDIR /data
 ---> Using cache
 ---> f62ca2c0f725
Step 5/7 : CMD mongod
 ---> Using cache
 ---> 85e9910bccbd
Step 6/7 : EXPOSE 27017
 ---> Using cache
 ---> 09f21e252f59
Step 7/7 : EXPOSE 28017
 ---> Using cache
 ---> f24a8a6e986b
Successfully built f24a8a6e986b
Successfully tagged cloud-native-app:latest
```

Make sure every section of the build process is successful.

Now that we are ready with our image, it's time to spin our container with the latest image.

Execute the following command to spin the container, and always remember to expose port `5000` to access our application:

```
$ docker run -d -p 5000:5000  --name=myapp  cloud-native-app:latest
```

Now, run the `docker ps` command to check the container status:

```
root@ip-10-0-0-217:~/workspace/mongodb# docker ps
CONTAINER ID        IMAGE                          COMMAND                  CREATED             STATUS              PORTS
                    NAMES
99aeb9ef94e8        177f23e53413                   "/bin/sh -c 'cd /a..."   35 minutes ago      Up 35 minutes       0.0.0.0:5000->5000/tc
p                   myapp
69a23999fefa        mongodb:ms-packtpub-mongodb    "mongod --rest --h..."   About an hour ago   Up About an hour    0.0.0.0:27017->27017/
tcp, 0.0.0.0:28017->28017/tcp   mongodb
```

As you can see, there are two containers running in the `myapp` container: we will have our application running and on the `mongodb` container, you will have your `mongodb` service running.

Next, check the application URL (`http://your-master-ip-address:5000/`). If you see the following screen, it means that our application is deployed successfully and we are live on Docker:

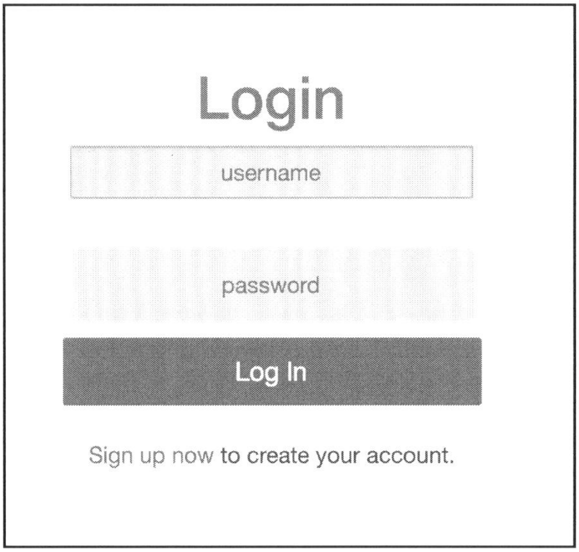

Now we can test out our application by creating new users and logging in, and then posting tweets. I will not do it again as we have already done it at the time of application creation.

From experience, I know there may be some challenges to the communication between your application and database, that is, MongoDB, as both, the app and the database are on separate containers and might be in a separate network. In order to deal with this kind of problem, you can create a network and connect both the containers to that network.

For instance, if we have to do so for our container (`myapp` and `mongodb`), we will follow these steps:

1. Use the following command to create a separate network:

```
$ docker network create -d bridge --subnet 172.25.0.0/16
mynetwork
```

2. Now that our network is created, we can add both containers to this network using the following commands:

```
$ docker network connect mynetwork  myapp
$ docker network connect mynetwork  mongodb
```

3. In order to find the IP that is assigned to these containers, we can use the following commands:

```
$ docker inspect --format '{{ .NetworkSettings.IPAddress }}'
$(docker ps -q)
```

This network creation is an alternative way to set up the communication between application and database.

Alright, we have deployed our application on Docker and learned its different concepts. The only concept that is left is Docker Compose. Let's understand what it is and how different it is from the others.

Docker Compose

As per the official Docker Compose website (`https://docs.docker.com/compose/overview/`), Compose is a tool for defining and running multicontainer Docker applications. With Compose, you use a Compose file to configure your application's services.

In simpler terms, it helps us build and run our application in a much simpler and faster way.

In the previous section, where we were deploying our application and building the images, we first created a Dockerfile and then executed the `Docker build` command to build it. Once it is built, we usually use the `docker run` command to spin up the container, but, instead of that, in Docker Compose, we will define a `.yml` file with config details, such as ports, command to execute, and so on.

Firstly, Docker Compose is a separate utility from Docker Engine and can be installed using the following link, based on the type of OS you are working on:

`https://docs.docker.com/compose/install/`.

Once you have installed it, let's see how we can use Docker Compose to run our containers. Let's assume we have to run the cloud native application container using Docker Compose. We already have the Dockerfile generated for it, and we also have the application at the same location (path).

Next, using the following content, we will need to create a `Docker-compose.yml` file in the same location where the Dockerfile is present:

```
#Compose.yml
version: '2'
services:
web:
 build: .
  ports:
  - "5000:5000"
  volumes:
   - /app/
 flask:
  image: "cloud-native-app:latest"
```

Once you have added the config in `docker-compose.yml`, save it and execute the `docker-compose up` command. After building the image, we will see the following output:

```
root@ip-10-0-0-217:~/workspace/app# docker-compose up
WARNING: The Docker Engine you're using is running in swarm mode.

Compose does not use swarm mode to deploy services to multiple nodes in a swarm. All containers will be scheduled on the current node.

To deploy your application across the swarm, use `docker stack deploy`.

Starting app_flask_1 ...
Starting app_web_1 ...
Starting app_flask_1
Starting app_web_1 ... done
Attaching to app_flask_1, app_web_1
web_1    | * Running on http://0.0.0.0:5000/ (Press CTRL+C to quit)
flask_1  | * Running on http://0.0.0.0:5000/ (Press CTRL+C to quit)
web_1    | * Restarting with stat
flask_1  | * Restarting with stat
web_1    | * Debugger is active!
web_1    | * Debugger PIN: 190-114-053
flask_1  | * Debugger is active!
flask_1  | * Debugger PIN: 994-542-714
web_1    | 103.252.26.196 - - [28/May/2017 17:47:29] "GET / HTTP/1.1" 200 -
```

Also, if you see the container's state, you will find multiple containers (in our case, `app_web-1` and `app_flask_1`) spin by compose, which is why it is useful for mutlicontainer applications that need large-scale infrastructure, as it creates a cluster of Docker machines similar to the Docker Swarm. The following screen shows the status of the Docker machine:

```
CONTAINER ID        IMAGE                          COMMAND                  CREATED             STATUS              PORTS
                          NAMES
7f8649ad3863        app_web                        "/bin/sh -c 'cd /a..."   3 minutes ago       Up About a minute   0.0.0.0:5000->5000/tc
p                         app_web_1
4d7d59ae4978        cloud-native-app:latest        "/bin/sh -c 'cd /a..."   6 minutes ago       Up About a minute   5000/tcp
                          app_flask_1
69a23999fefa        mongodb:ms-packtpub-mongodb    "mongod --rest --h..."   3 hours ago         Up 13 minutes       0.0.0.0:27017->27017/
tcp, 0.0.0.0:28017->28017/tcp   mongodb
```

Awesome! We have deployed our application through Docker-compose as well. Now you can try to access the public URL for the application (`http://your-ip-address:5000`) to confirm the successful application deployment.

Finally, make sure you push your images to the Docker Hub to keep it in a centralized repository. Since we have already pushed the MongoDB images, use the following command to push the `cloud-native-app` image as well:

```
$ docker tag cloud-native-app:latest manishsethis/docker-packtpub:cloud-
native-app
$ docker push manishsethis/docker-packtpub:cloud-native-app
```

We should see similar output for, Docker `push` command as shown:

```
root@ip-10-0-0-217:~/workspace/mongodb# docker tag cloud-native-app:latest manishsethis/docker-packtpub:cloud-native-app
(reverse-i-search)`': ^C
root@ip-10-0-0-217:~/workspace/mongodb# docker push manishsethis/docker-packtpub:cloud-native-app
The push refers to a repository [docker.io/manishsethis/docker-packtpub]
1e756c41967f: Pushed
03551bc2634a: Pushed
6feb34ef35c6: Pushed
21761af77f90: Pushed
50931687bd6d: Pushed
f160490bd2ed: Pushed
ec3db9fc1b33: Pushed
776d5289b76e: Mounted from library/ubuntu
0fb55a72eab2: Mounted from library/ubuntu
a30ab2bcda94: Mounted from library/ubuntu
99840408c5ea: Mounted from library/ubuntu
a8e78858b03b: Mounted from library/ubuntu
cloud-native-app: digest: sha256:99f80e75dd377db5a45b806a6ed8ef6a5f201f14d399b4888f112170757c4d2f size: 2833
```

Summary

In this chapter, we first looked at one of the most interesting technologies--Docker--, which is based on containers. We looked at the different concepts around Docker, and we already deployed our application and looked at the way we can manage it over Docker. We also explored multiple ways to deploy our application using Docker Compose and Dockerfile.

In the upcoming chapter, things will be a lot more interesting as we will finally reach a stage where we will be exposed to the cloud platform, build our infrastructure over the platform based on our application, and also try to deploy it as well. So, stay tuned for the next chapter! See you there.

11
Deploying on the AWS Platform

In the previous chapter, we saw one of the platforms for our application, which is called Docker. It can isolate your application, and can be used to respond to your application request from the customer. During the course of this chapter, we will introduce you to the cloud platform, especially AWS (Amazon Cloud Services), which mainly deals with the IaaS (Infrastructure) and **PaaS** (**Platform as a Service**) Services. We will also look at how we can build up infrastructure, and deploy our application.

This chapter includes the following topics:

- Introducing AWS and its services
- Building application infrastructure using Terraform/CloudFormation
- **Continuous Deployment** using Jenkins

Getting started with Amazon Web Services (AWS)

Amazon Web Services (**AWS**) is a secure cloud platform. It has various offerings in IaaS as well as PaaS, including computing power, database storage, and content delivery, which help in scaling applications, and also grows our business across the globe. AWS is a public cloud, and as per the cloud computing concepts, it provides all its resources in an on-demand delivery with a pay-as-you-go plan.

You can read more about AWS and its services at `https://aws.amazon.com/`.

As specified previously in `Chapter 1`, *Introducing Cloud Native Architecture and Microservices*, you need to create an AWS account to start using the services. You can use the following link to create an account:

`https://medium.com/appliedcode/setup-aws-account-1727ce89353e`

Once you are logged in, you will see the following screen, which showcases the AWS and its categories. A few of the services are in the beta stage. We will be using some of the services related to **compute** and **networking** to build an infrastructure for our application:

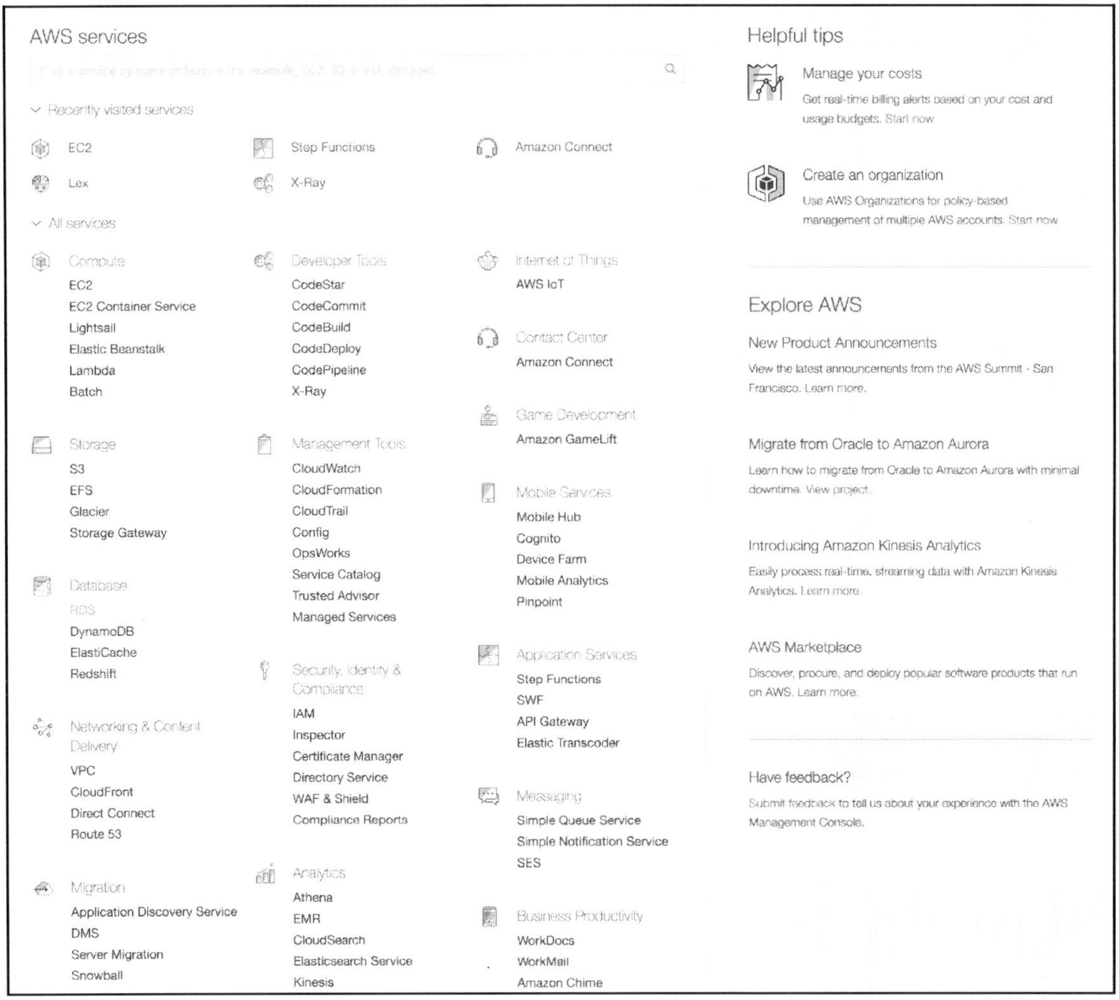

Some of the commonly used AWS services for applications are as follows:

- **EC2 (Elastic compute cloud)**: This is a compute offering from AWS, which, in simply put, offers a server.
- **ECS (Elastic Container Services)**: This is similar to the Docker services on top of a public cloud, that is, Amazon. It manages Docker on top of an EC2 machine only. Instead of creating a Docker cluster on-premises, you can easily set it up in the Amazon cloud within a few minutes, and with less overhead.
- **EBS (Elasticbeanstalk)**: This is a PaaS offering where you just need to upload your code, and specify how much infrastructure (basically, app server (EC2)) is required. EBS will take care of creating the machines, and deploy the code on it as well.
- **S3 (Simple storage service)**: This is a storage service offered by AWS where we usually keep our application data or static content, which could be used for static website hosting. We will be using it for Continuous Deployment.
- **Glacièr**: This is another storage service, which is mainly used for backup, as it is less costly, and hence, has a slow data storing and retrieving capability as compared to S3.
- **VPC (Virtual Private Network)**: This is a networking service which gives you control over your resources' accessibility. We will be using this service to keep our infrastructure. This service is very useful for securing our application service and database services, and exposes only selective resources, which are required, to the outside world.
- **CloudFront**: This is a content delivery service which distributes your content in S3 across the globe, and makes sure it is quickly retrievable irrespective of the location of the request source.
- **CloudFormation**: This gives developers and system administrators an easy way to create and manage a collection of related AWS resources, such as provisioning, and updating them in the form of code. We will be using this service to build our infrastructure.
- **CloudWatch**: This service keeps track of the activity of your resources. It also keeps track of any activity on your AWS account in the form of logs, which is useful for identifying any suspicious activity or account compromise.
- **IAM (Identity and Access Management)**: This service, as the name suggests, is very useful for managing users on the AWS account, and to provide them roles/privileges as per their usage and requirement.
- **Route 53**: This is a highly available and scalable cloud DNS Cloud service. We can either migrate our Domain from any other Registrar such as GoDaddy, and others to Route 53, or purchase the Domain AWS.

There are many more services offered by AWS that can't be covered in this chapter. If you are interested and would like to explore other services, you can go through the AWS product list (`https://aws.amazon.com/products/`).

We will be using most of the aforementioned AWS services. Let's begin by building our infrastructure on AWS as per our application.

Building application infrastructure on AWS

At this stage of our application, the system architect or a DevOps guy comes into the picture, and suggests different infrastructure plans which are secure and efficient enough to handle application requests, and are cost effective as well.

As far as our application is concerned, we will build its infrastructure the same as shown in the following image:

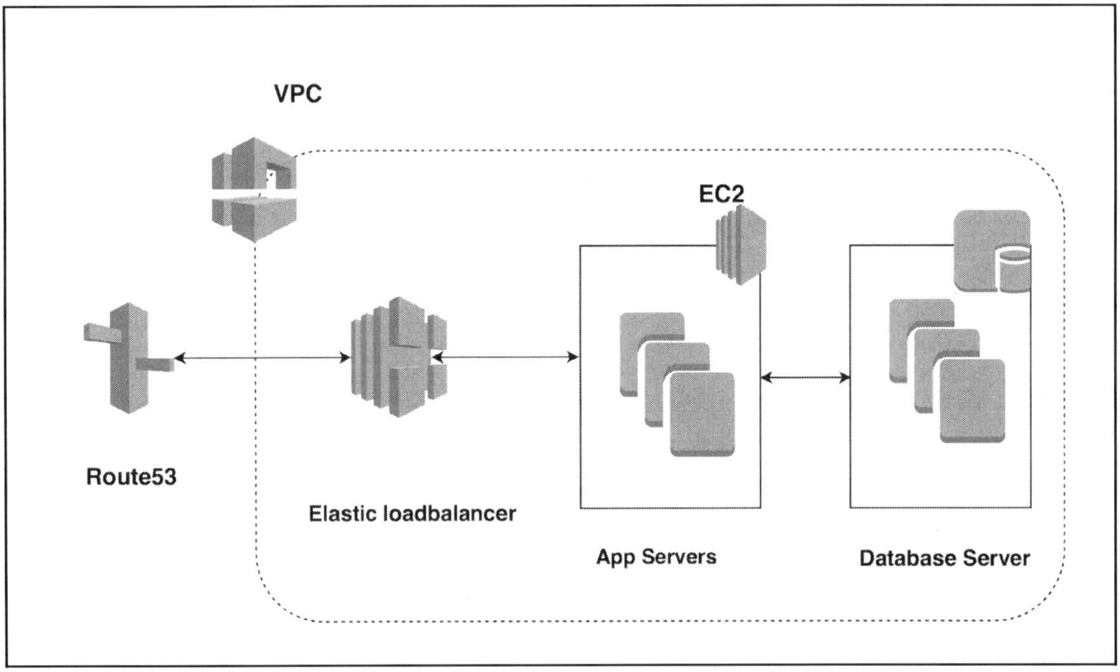

We will follow the preceding architecture diagram for our application, which includes a few of AWS services such as EC2, VPC, Route 53, and so on.

There are three different ways by which you can provision your resources on the AWS cloud, which are as follows:

- **Management console**: This is the user interface which we have already logged into, and can be used to launch resources on the cloud. (Check this link for your reference: `https://console.aws.amazon.com/console/`)
- **Programmatically**: We may use a couple of programming languages such as Python, Ruby, and the like to create resources, for which different development tools have been created by AWS, like Codecom. Also, you can use SDK to create your resources based on your preferred choice of language. You can check `https://aws.amazon.com/tools/` for more information.
- **AWS CLI (Command-line interface)**: It is an open source tool built on top of SDK for Python which offers commands to interact with the AWS resources. You can check the link at: `http://docs.aws.amazon.com/cli/latest/userguide/cli-chap-welcome.html` to understand its working, and the steps to set this up on your system.

Creating resources is pretty easy and straightforward, so we won't be covering that, but you can check the AWS documentation (`https://aws.amazon.com/documentation/`) to do so.

I will show you how to build your infrastructure using Terraform and an AWS-based service called CloudFormation.

Generating authentication keys

Authentication is an important feature for any product or platform to check the authenticity of a user who is trying to access and perform operations on the product, and also to keep the system secure. Since here we are going to access the AWS account using APIs, we need authorization keys to validate our request. Now, an important AWS service enters the picture called **IAM** (**Identity and Access Management**).

In IAM, we define the users and generate access/secret keys, and also assign roles based on the resources which we want to access using it.

TIP: It is highly recommended NEVER to generate access/secrets keys as the root user, because it will have, by default, full access over your account.

The following are the steps to create a user, and to generate access/secret keys:

1. Go to `https://console.aws.amazon.com/iam/home?region=us-east-1#/home`; you should see the following screen:

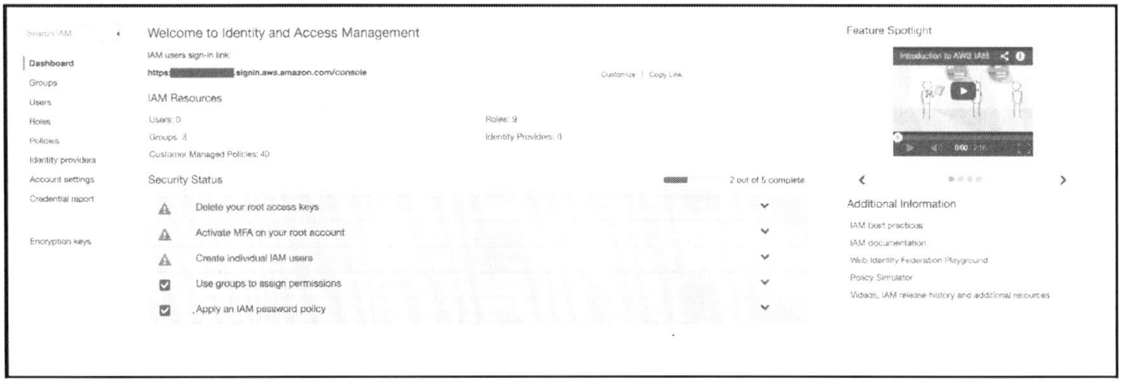

2. Now, click on the third option, named **Users**, in the left pane. If your account is new, you will see no users. Now, let's create a new user--for that, click on the **Add user** button in the right pane:

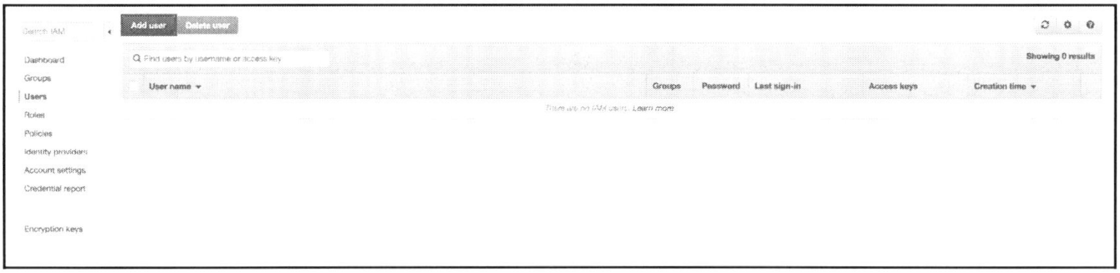

3. Once you click on the **Add user** button, a new page will load and ask for the username and the way you want your user to access the account. If you are going to use this user, for example, `manish`, only for programmatic purposes, in that case, I recommend that you uncheck the **AWS Management Console access** box so that the user doesn't need to log in using the AWS management console. Check the following screenshot for reference:

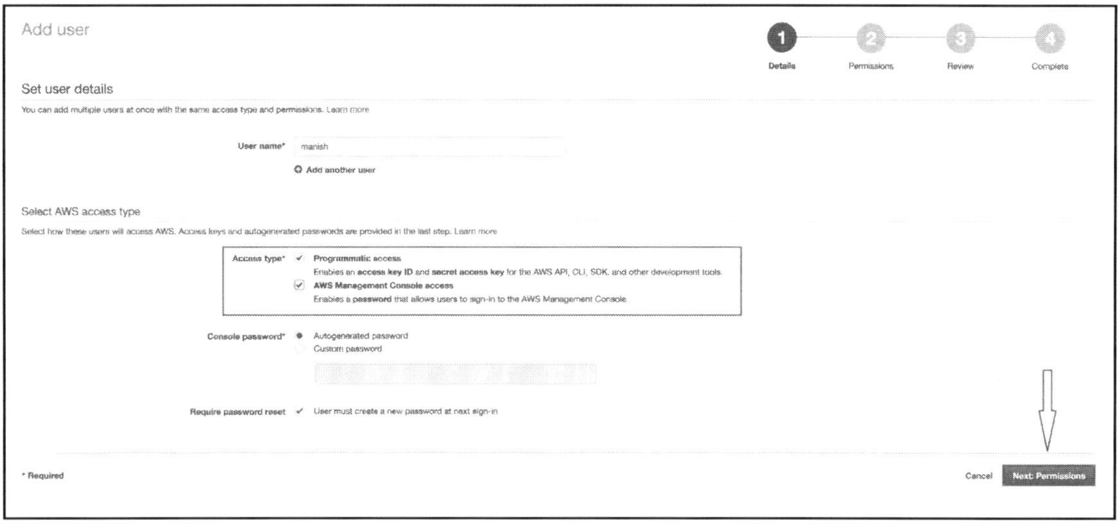

4. Once you are done, click on the **Next: Permissions** button on the bottom-right side of the screen. Next, you need to select the permission you want to give to this user, which we call the IAM Policies. That means now, the user should be able to access the resources as per the policy defined, and also the kind of operations allowed for the user on the resources. For now, we add the **Power User Access** policy to this user.
5. Internally, **Power User Access** will have a policy in the JSON format, something like this:

```
{
  "Version": "2012-10-17",
  "Statement": [
       {
         "Effect": "Allow",
         "NotAction": [
           "iam:*",
           "organizations:*"
         ],
         "Resource": "*"
       },
       {
         "Effect": "Allow",
           "Action": "organizations:DescribeOrganization",
           "Resource": "*"
       }
     ]
 }
```

For more information about the IAM policy, read the documentation at the following link:
`http://docs.aws.amazon.com/IAM/latest/UserGuide/access_policies.html`

> Readers who have been using Microsoft Active Directory can integrate AD with IAM easily using the AD connector. For more info, read the article given at this link:
> `https://aws.amazon.com/blogs/security/how-to-connect-your-on-premises-active-directory-to-aws-using-ad-connector/`

Consider the following screenshot:

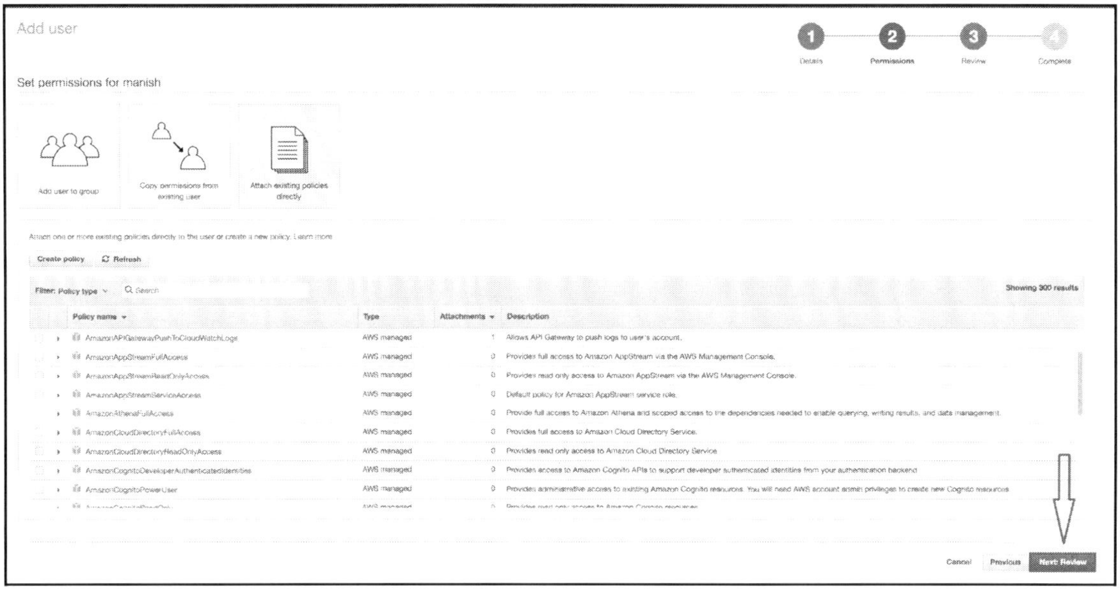

1. Once you have added the policies to the user, click on the **Next: Review** button on the bottom-right side of the screen to move forward.
2. The next screen will ask you to review it, and once you are sure, you can click on the **Create user** button to create the user:

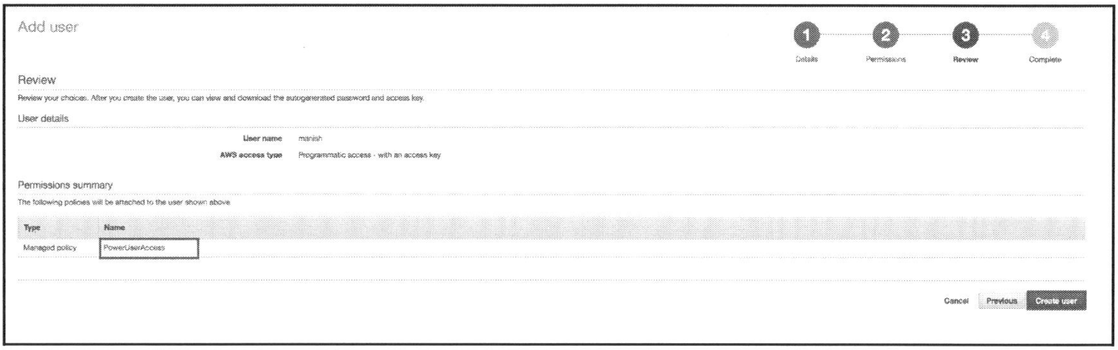

3. Once you click on the **Create user** button, the user will be created, and the policy will be attached to it. You will now see the following screen which has auto-generated the access key as well as the secret key, which you need to keep safe and NEVER ever share with anyone:

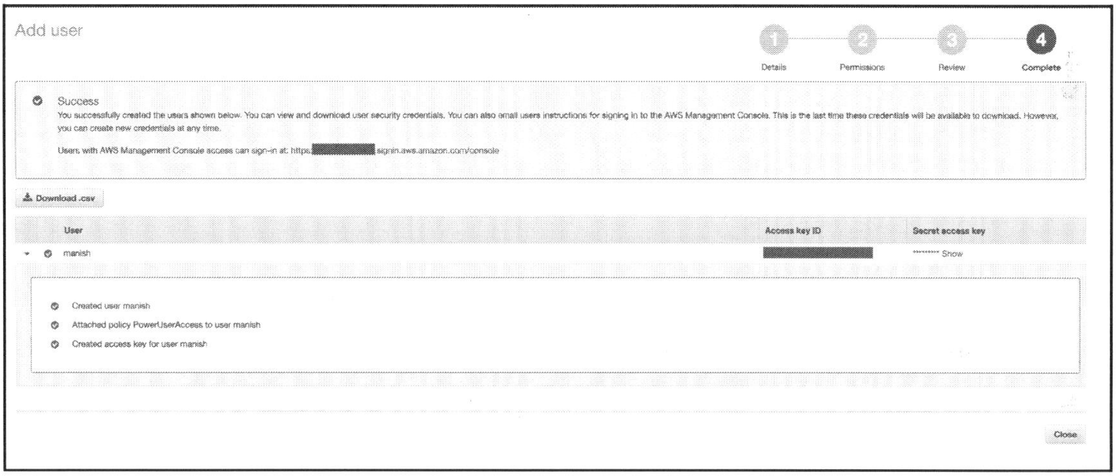

4. Now that our access/secret key has been generated, it's time to build our application infrastructure on AWS. We will use the following tools to do so:

- **Terraform**: This is an open-source tool for building infrastructure on different cloud platforms
- **CloudFormation**: These are AWS services to build application infrastructure using the AWS resources

Terraform - a tool to build infrastructure as code

Terraform is a tool for building, managing, and versioning infrastructure over different cloud platforms such as AWS, Azure, and so on. It can manage the low-level components of the infrastructure such as compute, storage, networking, and others.

In Terraform, we specify the configuration files which describe the resources specification for the infrastructure of the application. Terraform describes the execution plan, and the desired state to be achieved. Then it starts building the resources as per specification, and keeps track of the current state of infrastructure after build up, always performing incremental execution if the configuration changes.

The following are a few features of Terraform:

- Terraform describes your data center onto a blueprint, which can be versioned and can be managed into code.
- Terraform provides you the execution plan before actual implementation, which helps you to match the execution plan with the desired result.
- Terraform helps you architect all your resources and parallelize your resources creation. It gives you an insight into the dependencies on the resources, and also makes sure that the dependencies are fulfilled before resources creation.
- With its insight capability, it gives more control to the developer over the revisions to be performed over the infrastructure with less human errors.

In Terraform, we consider every service in AWS in terms of the resources which need to be created, so we need to provide its mandatory attributes for its creation. Now, let's begin by creating the resources:

1. Firstly, we need to create **VPC** (**Virtual Private Cloud**) in which we will launch all the other resources.

   Note: We will need to create all the files with the `.tf` file extension as per convention.

2. So, let's create an empty `main.tf` file. Add the following code, which will set the access and secret key of the service provider for authentication:

```
# Specify the provider and access details
    provider "aws" {
      region = "${var.aws_region}"
      access_key = "${var.aws_access_key}"
```

```
    secret_key = "${var.aws_secret_key}"
}
```

3. As you can see in the preceding code, there is a value like `${var.aws_region}`. Actually, it is a convention to keep all your values in a separate file called `variables.tf`, so we do this here. Let's change the `variables.tf` file with the following content:

```
variable "aws_access_key" {
    description = "AWS access key"
    default = ""                        # Access key
 }
variable "aws_secret_key" {
   description = "AWS secret access key"
   default = ""                             # Secret key
 }
 variable "aws_region" {
    description = "AWS region to launch servers."
    default = "us-east-1"
 }
```

4. Next, we need to create the VPC resource, so let's add this code to `main.tf`:

```
 # Create a VPC to launch our instances into
   resource "aws_vpc" "default" {
     cidr_block = "${var.vpc_cidr}"
     enable_dns_hostnames = true
     tags {
       Name = "ms-cloud-native-app"
     }
 }
```

5. We have used one variable, which needs to be defined in `variables.tf` as follows:

```
 variable "vpc_cidr"{
    default = "10.127.0.0/16"             # user defined
 }
```

6. Once the VPC resource is defined, we need to create a subnet which will be associated with the EC2 machine, Elastic Load Balancer, or other resources. So, add the following code to `main.tf`:

```
  # Create a subnet to launch our instances into
  resource "aws_subnet" "default" {
    vpc_id                  = "${aws_vpc.default.id}"
    cidr_block              = "${var.subnet_cidr}"
```

```
    map_public_ip_on_launch = true
  }
Now, define the variable we have used in above code in
variables.tf
variable "subnet_cidr"{
 default = "10.127.0.0/24"
}
```

7. Since we want our resources to be accessible from the internet, we need to create an internet gateway, and associate it with our subnet so that the resources created inside it are accessible over the internet.

> Note: We can create multiple subnets to secure the network of our resources.

8. Add this code to `main.tf`:

```
# Create an internet gateway to give our subnet access to the
outside world
resource "aws_internet_gateway" "default" {
vpc_id = "${aws_vpc.default.id}"
 }
# Grant the VPC internet access on its main route table
resource "aws_route" "internet_access" {
route_table_id         = "${aws_vpc.default.main_route_table_id}"
destination_cidr_block = "0.0.0.0/0"
gateway_id             = "${aws_internet_gateway.default.id}"
```

9. Next, we need to make sure that the subnet where you will be launching your EC2 machine provides a public address to the machines. This can be achieved by adding the code given next to your `main.tf`:

```
# Create a subnet to launch our instances into
resource "aws_subnet" "default" {
  vpc_id                  = "${aws_vpc.default.id}"
  cidr_block              = "${var.subnet_cidr}"
  map_public_ip_on_launch = true
}
```

10. Once this is configured, it's time to begin with the creation of the app server and the MongoDB server.
11. Initially, we need to create the dependent resources, such as the security group, without which, EC2 cannot be launched.

12. Add the following code to `main.tf` to create the security group resource:

```
# the instances over SSH and HTTP
resource "aws_security_group" "default" {
name        = "cna-sg-ec2"
description = "Security group of app servers"
vpc_id      = "${aws_vpc.default.id}"
# SSH access from anywhere
ingress {
 from_port   = 22
 to_port     = 22
 protocol    = "tcp"
 cidr_blocks = ["0.0.0.0/0"]
}
# HTTP access from the VPC
ingress {
  from_port   = 5000
  to_port     = 5000
  protocol    = "tcp"
  cidr_blocks = ["${var.vpc_cidr}"]
 }
 # outbound internet access
 egress {
  from_port   = 0
  to_port     = 0
  protocol    = "-1"
  cidr_blocks = ["0.0.0.0/0"]
}
}
```

13. In this security group, we open ports `22` and `5000` only in order to ssh and access our application.
14. Next, we need to add/create ssh key-pairs, which you can generate on your local machine and upload to AWS, or can get it generated from the AWS console as well. In our case, I have generated an ssh key on my local machine using the `ssh-keygen` command. Now to create an ssh-key pairs resource in AWS, add this code to `main.tf`:

```
resource "aws_key_pair" "auth" {
  key_name   = "${var.key_name}"
   public_key = "${file(var.public_key_path)}"
}
```

15. Add the following code snippet to `variables.tf` to provide parameters to the variables:

```
variable "public_key_path" {
  default = "ms-cna.pub"
}
```

16. Now that we have created dependent resources, it's time to create the app server (that is, EC2 machine). So, add the following code snippet to `main.tf`:

```
resource "aws_instance" "web" {
 # The connection block tells our provisioner how to
 # communicate with the resource (instance)
  connection {
   # The default username for our AMI
    user = "ubuntu"
    key_file = "${var.key_file_path}"
    timeout = "5m"
  }
 # Tags for machine
 tags {Name = "cna-web"}
 instance_type = "t2.micro"
 # Number of EC2 to spin up
  count = "1"
  ami = "${lookup(var.aws_amis, var.aws_region)}"
  iam_instance_profile = "CodeDeploy-Instance-Role"
  # The name of our SSH keypair we created above.
  key_name = "${aws_key_pair.auth.id}"
 # Our Security group to allow HTTP and SSH access
 vpc_security_group_ids = ["${aws_security_group.default.id}"]
 subnet_id = "${aws_subnet.default.id}"
}
```

17. We have used a couple of variables in the EC2 configuration as well, so we need to add the variable values in the `variables.tf` file:

```
variable "key_name" {
  description = "Desired name of AWS key pair"
  default = "ms-cna"
}
variable "key_file_path" {
  description = "Private Key Location"
  default = "~/.ssh/ms-cna"
}
 # Ubuntu Precise 12.04 LTS (x64)
  variable "aws_amis" {
   default = {
```

```
        eu-west-1 = "ami-b1cf19c6"
        us-east-1 = "ami-0a92db1d"
        #us-east-1 = "ami-e881c6ff"
        us-west-1 = "ami-3f75767a"
        us-west-2 = "ami-21f78e11"
      }
    }
```

Great! Now our app server resource configuration is ready. Now, we have added the app server configuration, and next, we need to add a similar setting for the MongoDB server, which is needed for keeping our data. Once both are ready, we will create ELB (which will be the user's point of application access), and then attach the app servers to ELB.

Let's move on to add the configuration for the MongoDB server.

Configuring the MongoDB server

Add following code to `main.tf` for the creation of a security group for the MongoDB server:

```
resource "aws_security_group" "mongodb" {
 name        = "cna-sg-mongodb"
 description = "Security group of mongodb server"
 vpc_id      = "${aws_vpc.default.id}"
# SSH access from anywhere
ingress {
  from_port   = 22
  to_port     = 22
  protocol    = "tcp"
  cidr_blocks = ["0.0.0.0/0"]
 }
# HTTP access from the VPC
ingress {
  from_port   = 27017
  to_port     = 27017
  protocol    = "tcp"
  cidr_blocks = ["${var.vpc_cidr}"]
 }
# HTTP access from the VPC
 ingress {
  from_port   = 28017
  to_port     = 28017
  protocol    = "tcp"
  cidr_blocks = ["${var.vpc_cidr}"]
  }
# outbound internet access
```

```
    egress {
      from_port   = 0
      to_port     = 0
      protocol    = "-1"
      cidr_blocks = ["0.0.0.0/0"]
    }
  }
```

Next, we need to add the configuration for the MongoDB server. Also notice that in the following configuration, we provision the server with the MongoDB installation at the time of creation of the EC2 machine:

```
resource "aws_instance" "mongodb" {
# The connection block tells our provisioner how to
# communicate with the resource (instance)
connection {
 # The default username for our AMI
 user = "ubuntu"
 private_key = "${file(var.key_file_path)}"
 timeout = "5m"
 # The connection will use the local SSH agent for authentication.
 }
# Tags for machine
tags {Name = "cna-web-mongodb"}
instance_type = "t2.micro"
# Number of EC2 to spin up
count = "1"
# Lookup the correct AMI based on the region
# we specified
ami = "${lookup(var.aws_amis, var.aws_region)}"
iam_instance_profile = "CodeDeploy-Instance-Role"
# The name of our SSH keypair we created above.
 key_name = "${aws_key_pair.auth.id}"
 # Our Security group to allow HTTP and SSH access
 vpc_security_group_ids = ["${aws_security_group.mongodb.id}"]
 subnet_id = "${aws_subnet.default.id}"
 provisioner "remote-exec" {
  inline = [
    "sudo echo -ne '\n' | apt-key adv --keyserver
     hkp://keyserver.ubuntu.com:80 --recv 7F0CEB10",
   "echo 'deb http://repo.mongodb.org/apt/ubuntu trusty/mongodb-
    org/3.2 multiverse' | sudo tee /etc/apt/sources.list.d/mongodb-
     org-3.2.list",
   "sudo apt-get update -y && sudo apt-get install mongodb-org --
   force-yes -y",
   ]
 }
}
```

One last resource which still needs to be configured is the Elastic Load Balancer, which will balance the customer requests to provide high availability.

Configuring the Elastic Load balancer

Firstly, we need to create a security group resource for our ELB by adding this code to `main.tf`:

```
# A security group for the ELB so it is accessible via the web
 resource "aws_security_group" "elb" {
 name        = "cna_sg_elb"
 description = "Security_group_elb"
 vpc_id      = "${aws_vpc.default.id}"
# HTTP access from anywhere
ingress {
  from_port   = 5000
  to_port     = 5000
  protocol    = "tcp"
  cidr_blocks = ["0.0.0.0/0"]
 }
# outbound internet access
egress {
  from_port   = 0
  to_port     = 0
  protocol    = "-1"
  cidr_blocks = ["0.0.0.0/0"]
 }
```

Now, we need to add the following configuration for creating the ELB resources, and to add the app server into it as well:

```
resource "aws_elb" "web" {
name = "cna-elb"
 subnets            = ["${aws_subnet.default.id}"]
 security_groups    = ["${aws_security_group.elb.id}"]
 instances          = ["${aws_instance.web.*.id}"]
 listener {
   instance_port = 5000
   instance_protocol = "http"
   lb_port = 80
   lb_protocol = "http"
  }
 }
```

Now, we are all set for our first run of the Terraform configuration.

Our infrastructure configuration is ready to be deployed. It is a good practice to use the following command to understand the execution plan:

```
$ terraform plan
```

The output of the last command should be similar to the following screenshot:

```
root@packtpub:/vagrant/github/Cloud-Native-Python/chapter 11/terraform-app# terraform plan
Refreshing Terraform state in-memory prior to plan...
The refreshed state will be used to calculate this plan, but will not be
persisted to local or remote state storage.

The Terraform execution plan has been generated and is shown below.
Resources are shown in alphabetical order for quick scanning. Green resources
will be created (or destroyed and then created if an existing resource
exists), yellow resources are being changed in-place, and red resources
will be destroyed. Cyan entries are data sources to be read.

Note: You didn't specify an "-out" parameter to save this plan, so when
"apply" is called, Terraform can't guarantee this is what will execute.

+ aws_elb.web
    availability_zones.#:                     "<computed>"
    connection_draining:                      "false"
    connection_draining_timeout:              "300"
    cross_zone_load_balancing:                "true"
    dns_name:                                 "<computed>"
    health_check.#:                           "<computed>"
    idle_timeout:                             "60"
    instances.#:                              "<computed>"
    internal:                                 "<computed>"
    listener.#:                               "1"
    listener.996561874.instance_port:         "5000"
    listener.996561874.instance_protocol:     "http"
    listener.996561874.lb_port:               "80"
    listener.996561874.lb_protocol:           "http"
    listener.996561874.ssl_certificate_id:    ""
    name:                                     "cna-elb"
    security_groups.#:                        "<computed>"
    source_security_group:                    "<computed>"
    source_security_group_id:                 "<computed>"
    subnets.#:                                "<computed>"
```

If you don't see any errors, you can execute the following command for actual creation of the resource:

```
$ terraform apply
```

The output should look something like this:

```
root@packtpub:/vagrant/github/Cloud-Native-Python/chapter 11/terraform-app# terraform apply
aws_vpc.default: Creating...
  assign_generated_ipv6_cidr_block: "" => "false"
  cidr_block:                       "" => "10.127.0.0/16"
  default_network_acl_id:           "" => "<computed>"
  default_route_table_id:           "" => "<computed>"
  default_security_group_id:        "" => "<computed>"
  dhcp_options_id:                  "" => "<computed>"
  enable_classiclink:               "" => "<computed>"
  enable_dns_hostnames:             "" => "true"
  enable_dns_support:               "" => "true"
  instance_tenancy:                 "" => "<computed>"
  ipv6_association_id:              "" => "<computed>"
  ipv6_cidr_block:                  "" => "<computed>"
  main_route_table_id:              "" => "<computed>"
  tags.%:                           "" => "1"
  tags.Name:                        "" => "ms-cloud-native-app"
aws_key_pair.auth: Creating...
  fingerprint: "" => "<computed>"
  key_name:    "" => "ms-cna"
  public_key:  "" => "ssh-rsa AAAAB3NzaC1yc2EAAAADAQABAAABAQDUSpeFPkaru+J3l5MXWlVUJp/vFC+IJKCtrj9R+FInUIAE6gxJ5TffUKSHHPODW4Xa9s6V0QOShp/HtzIlyBar
LrDgbDMN+laXlIy3vdBP4ZWxvEDUIuGTAepRDWpun5ANeVnTPpVRb9eWQtkaKSb1cB+BXN3t0qAWY9bwFyTSijqyXmMg16W4ihgRR5trlcdhpTTc6DG310uFmChDjxN+vArRGcduIJYMQgFJaF
JDJDtjjJ5mDq4JHza89I4ziCN6sv6g7ea8stVDXdc47w7Sn4unySWD8kG2nHO2Xjl8YPAHCEwJapgu/tTB/sXReeKEDh8ZKBrXJGpkkAB7/ZtV root@packtpub"
aws_vpc.default: Still creating... (10s elapsed)
aws_key_pair.auth: Still creating... (10s elapsed)
aws_vpc.default: Still creating... (20s elapsed)
aws_key_pair.auth: Still creating... (20s elapsed)
aws_vpc.default: Still creating... (30s elapsed)
aws_key_pair.auth: Still creating... (30s elapsed)
aws_key_pair.auth: Creation complete (ID: ms-cna)
aws_vpc.default: Still creating... (40s elapsed)
aws_vpc.default: Still creating... (50s elapsed)
aws_vpc.default: Still creating... (1m0s elapsed)
aws_vpc.default: Still creating... (1m10s elapsed)
aws_vpc.default: Still creating... (1m20s elapsed)
aws_vpc.default: Still creating... (1m30s elapsed)
aws_vpc.default: Still creating... (1m40s elapsed)
aws_vpc.default: Still creating... (1m50s elapsed)
```

Currently, we don't have the domain registered with us, but if we have the domain name registered and configured in Route 53, we need to create an additional resource in `main.tf` to add an entry for our application. We can do so by using the following code:

```
resource "aws_route53_record" "www" {
  zone_id = "${var.zone_id}"
  name = "www.domain.com"
  type = "A"
  alias {
   name = "${aws_elb.web.dns_name}"
   zone_id = "${aws_elb.web.zone_id}"
   evaluate_target_health = true
  }
}
```

That's all we need to do. Also, another quick, and the most crucial, way of making your infrastructure high available is to create an auto scaling service, based on server metric usage (CPU or memory). We provide conditions which decides whether we need to scale our infrastructure up or down so that our application performance should see less latency.

In order to do so , you can check the Terraform documentation at https://www.terraform.io/docs/providers/aws/r/autoscaling_group.html.

Currently, our application is not deployed, we will be using the Code Deploy service to deploy our application using continuous delivery which we will discuss in a later part of this chapter.

Before that, let's see how we can create the same setup using a Cloud Platform Service called **CloudFormation**, provided by AWS.

CloudFormation - an AWS tool for building infrastructure using code

CloudFormation is an AWS service, which works in a similar fashion to Terraform. However, in CloudFormation, we don't need the access/secret keys. Instead, we need to create an IAM role, which will have the required access to launch all the resources needed to architect our application.

You can write your CloudFormation configuration using the YAML or JSON format.

Let's begin our infrastructure setup using CloudFormation by building the VPC, where we will create a VPC with, a public and a private subnet.

Let's create a new file, `vpc.template`, with the VPC and subnet's (public and private) configurations as follows:

```
"Resources" : {
   "VPC" : {
     "Type" : "AWS::EC2::VPC",
     "Properties" : {
       "CidrBlock" : "172.31.0.0/16",
       "Tags" : [
         {"Key" : "Application", "Value" : { "Ref" : "AWS::StackName"} },
         {"Key" : "Network", "Value" : "Public" }
       ]
     }
   },
"PublicSubnet" : {
     "Type" : "AWS::EC2::Subnet",
     "Properties" : {
       "VpcId" : { "Ref" : "VPC" },
```

```
        "CidrBlock" : "172.31.16.0/20",
        "AvailabilityZone" : { "Fn::Select": [ "0", {"Fn::GetAZs": {"Ref":
"AWS::Region"}} ]},
        "Tags" : [
          {"Key" : "Application", "Value" : { "Ref" : "AWS::StackName"} },
          {"Key" : "Network", "Value" : "Public" }
        ]
      }
    },
    "PrivateSubnet" : {
      "Type" : "AWS::EC2::Subnet",
      "Properties" : {
        "VpcId" : { "Ref" : "VPC" },
        "CidrBlock" : "172.31.0.0/20",
        "AvailabilityZone" : { "Fn::Select": [ "0", {"Fn::GetAZs": {"Ref":
"AWS::Region"}} ]},
        "Tags" : [
          {"Key" : "Application", "Value" : { "Ref" : "AWS::StackName"} },
          {"Key" : "Network", "Value" : "Public" }
        ]
      }
    },
```

The preceding configuration is written in the JSON format to give you an understanding of the JSON configuration. Also, we need to specify the configuration for routing the table and internet gateway as follows:

```
"PublicRouteTable" : {
      "Type" : "AWS::EC2::RouteTable",
      "Properties" : {
        "VpcId" : {"Ref" : "VPC"},
        "Tags" : [
          {"Key" : "Application", "Value" : { "Ref" : "AWS::StackName"} },
          {"Key" : "Network", "Value" : "Public" }
        ]
      }
    },
    "PublicRoute" : {
      "Type" : "AWS::EC2::Route",
      "Properties" : {
        "RouteTableId" : { "Ref" : "PublicRouteTable" },
        "DestinationCidrBlock" : "0.0.0.0/0",
        "GatewayId" : { "Ref" : "InternetGateway" }
      }
    },
    "PublicSubnetRouteTableAssociation" : {
      "Type" : "AWS::EC2::SubnetRouteTableAssociation",
      "Properties" : {
```

```
            "SubnetId" : { "Ref" : "PublicSubnet" },
            "RouteTableId" : { "Ref" : "PublicRouteTable" }
          }
        }
      },
```

Now that we have the configuration available, it's time to create a stack for the VPC from the AWS console.

The VPC stack on AWS

Perform the following steps to create a stack for the VPC from the AWS console:

1. Go to `https://console.aws.amazon.com/cloudformation/home?region=us-east-1#/stacks/new` to create a new stack using CloudFormation. You should see a screen as shown in this screenshot:

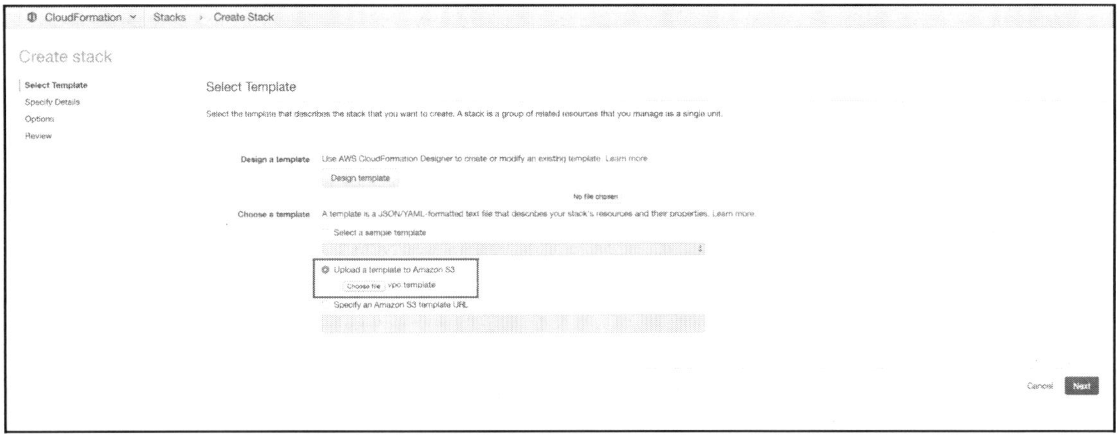

Provide the path for your template file, and click on the **Next** button.

2. In the next window, we need to specify **Stack name**, which is the unique identifier for our stack, as follows:

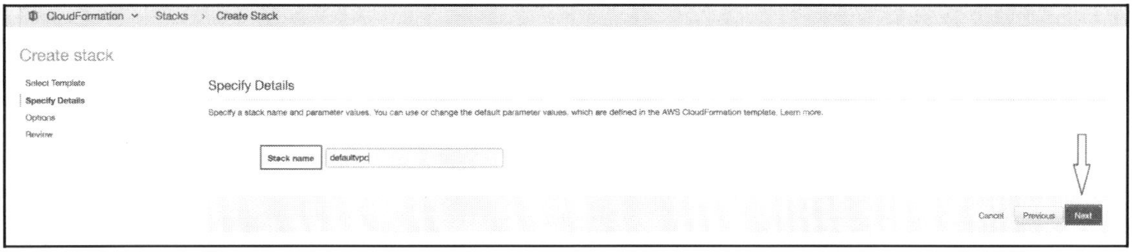

Provide the stack name, and click on **Next.**

3. The next screen is optional; in case we want to set up **SNS** (**Notification service**), or add IAM roles for it, we need to add it here:

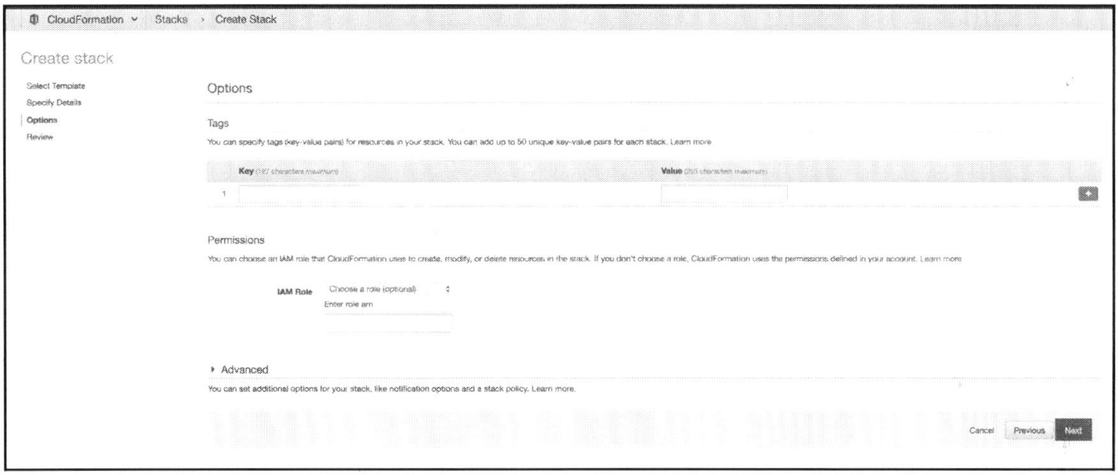

If you want to enable Notifications and the IAM role, add the details, and click on **Next.**

4. The next screen is for reviewing the details, and to make sure they are correct for creating the stack:

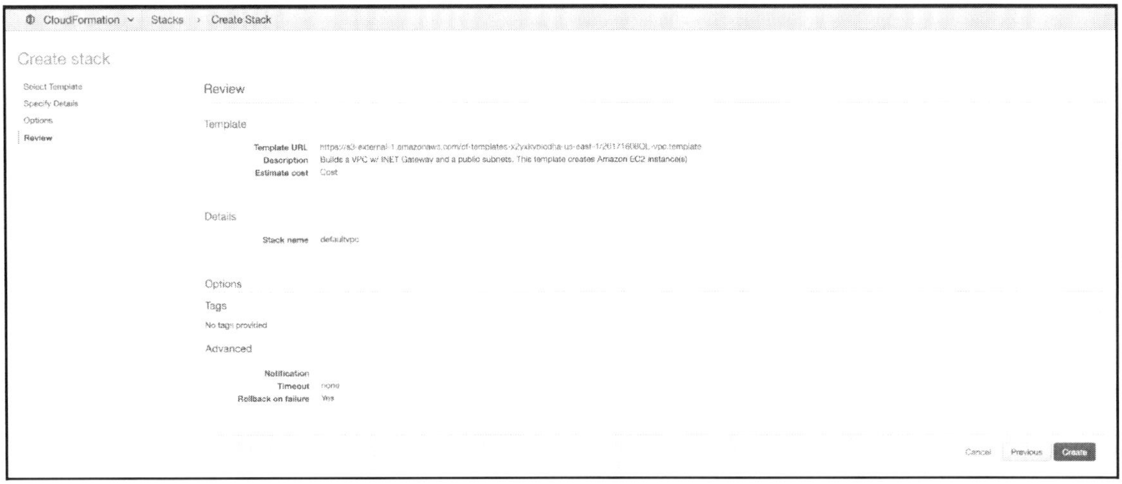

Once ready, click on **Create** to initiate the stack creation. At the time of creation, you can check the events to know the status of your resource's creation.

You should see a screen similar to this one:

In the preceding screen, you will be able to see the progress of the stack, and in case some errors occur, you can identify them using these events.

Once our VPC stack is ready, we need to create the EC2, ELB, and autoscaling resources in our VPC. We will use the YAML format to give you an overview of how to write the configuration in the YAML format.

You can find the complete code at `<path of repository>`. We will use the `main.yml` file, which has the details about the VPC and the subnet where you need to launch the instance.

5. In order to launch the stack, go to the following link: `https://console.aws.amazon.com/cloudformation/home?region=us-east-1#/stacks/new`

There will be one change in the launch configuration--instead of specifying values in the file, we will specify it in the AWS console at the time of providing the details as shown:

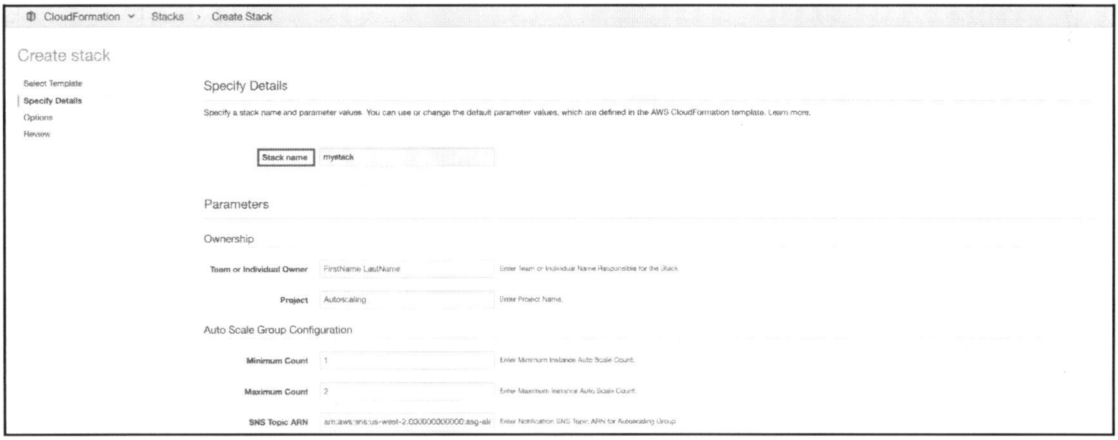

6. Refer to the following screenshot to provide the instance details in which you want to deploy your application:

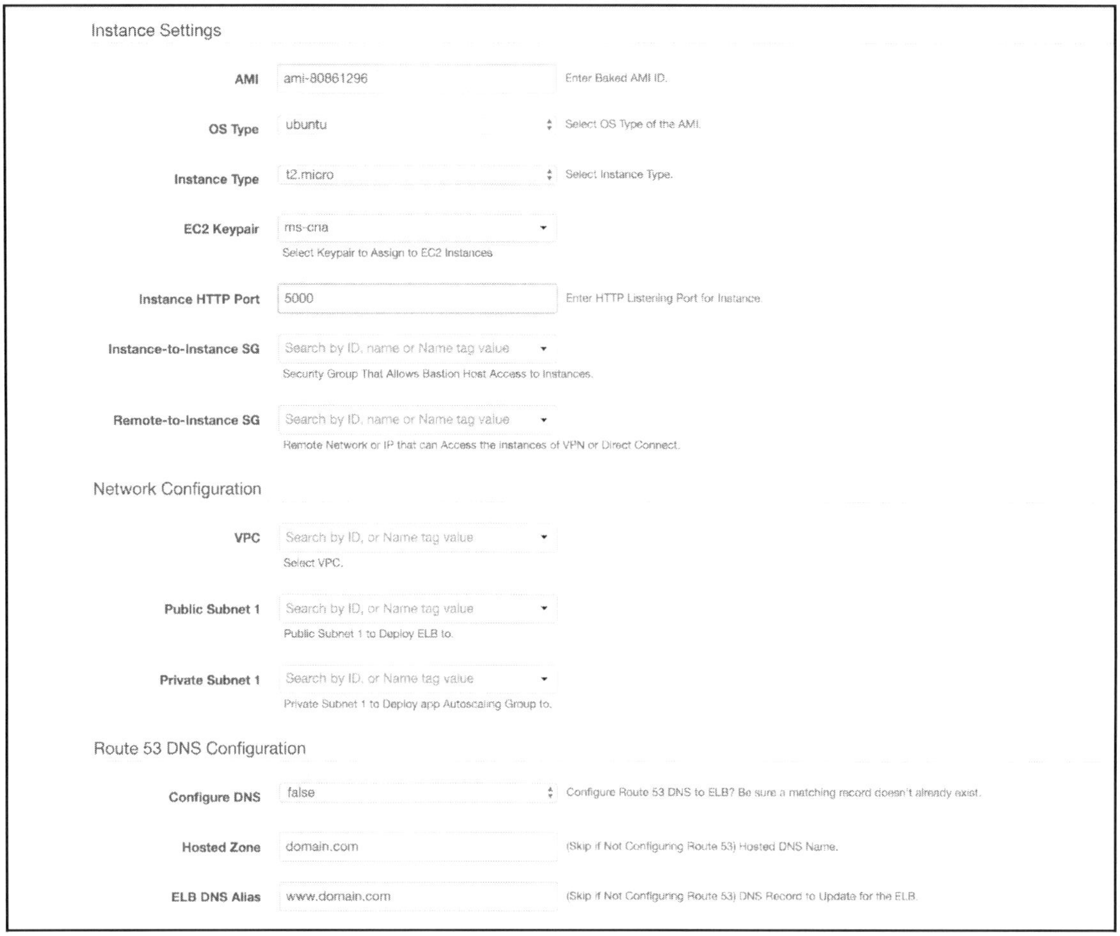

7. Once you have provided all the details in the preceding screen, scroll down to the next section, where it will ask for the ELB details, as shown in the next screenshot:

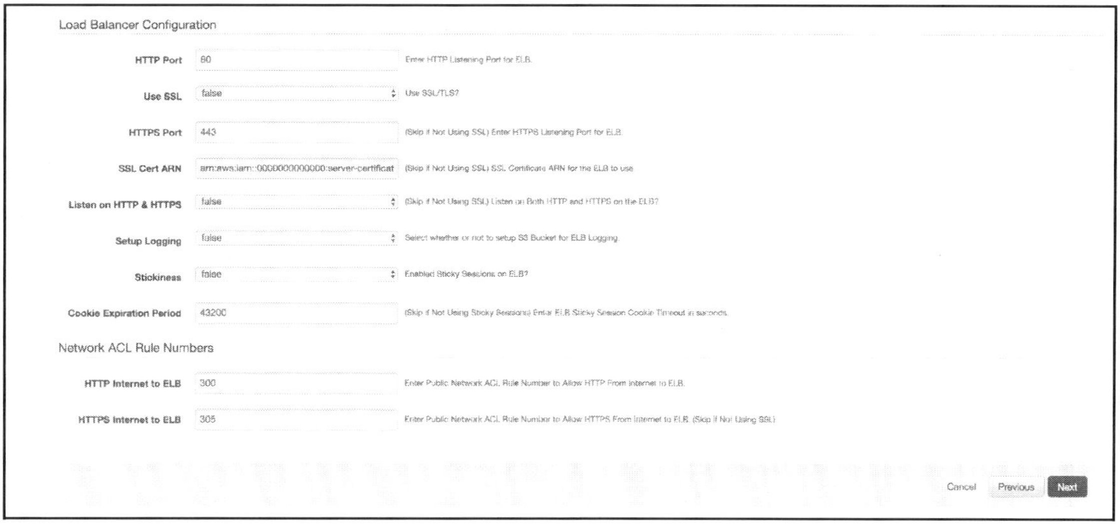

The remaining steps remain the same for creating the AWS CloudFormation stack. In order to add the MongoDB server, we need to add the configuration for the EC2 machine in `main.yml`.

> Creating the configuration in AWS CloudFormation is straightforward, as AWS provides a couple of templates which we use as a reference to create our template. The following is the link for the templates: `https://aws.amazon.com/cloudformation/aws-cloudformation-templates/`

That's all we have for building the infrastructure; it's time for our application to be deployed on the app servers.

Continuous Deployment for a cloud native application

In the previous section, we successfully set up the infrastructure, but we are yet to deploy the application. Also, we need to make sure that further deployment should be taken care of using Continuous Deployment. Since we have our development environment in our local machine, we don't need to set up the continuous integration cycle. However, for large-scale companies where many developers work collaboratively, we need to set up a separate pipeline for Continuous Integration using Jenkins. In our case, we only need Continuous Deployment. Our Continuous Deployment pipeline would be something like this:

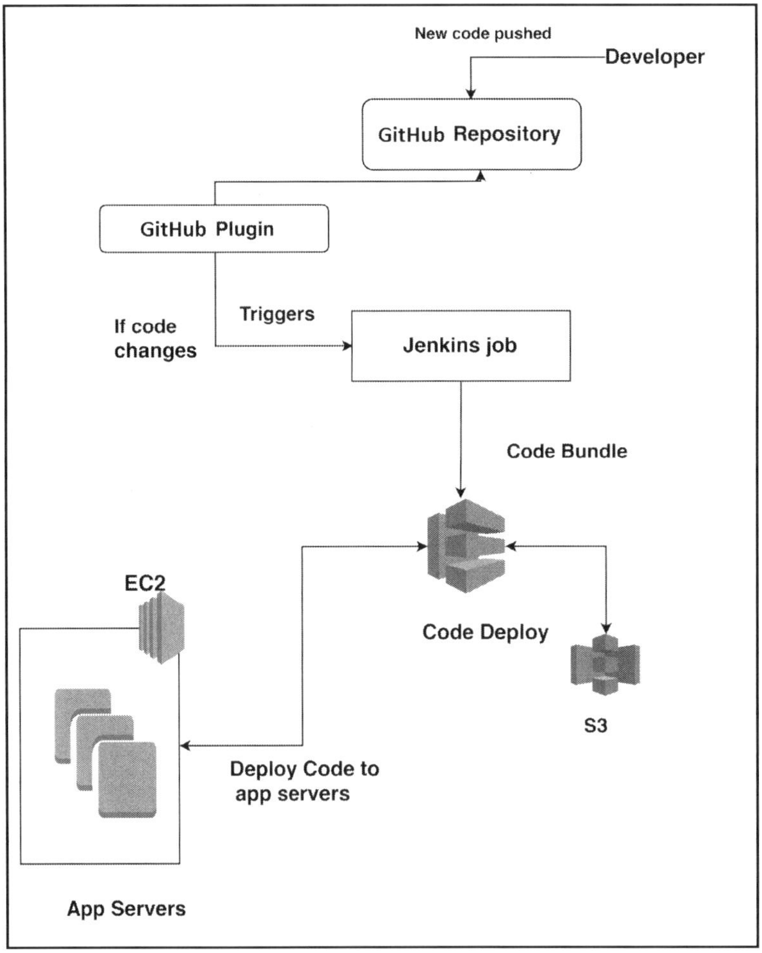

How it works

It starts with the developer pushing new code to the main branch of its version control system (in our case, it's GitHub). As soon as the new code is pushed, the Jenkins **GitHub plugin** detects the change as per its defined job, and triggers the **Jenkins job** to deploy the new code to its infrastructure. Jenkins then communicates with **Code Deploy** to trigger the code to the Amazon EC2 machine. Since we need to make sure that our deployment is successful, we can set up a notification section, which will notify us of the status of deployment so that it can reverted back if needed.

Implementation of the Continuous Deployment pipeline

Let's first configure our AWS service beginning with Code Deploy, which will help us to deploy the application on the available app servers.

1. Initially, when you switch to the code deploy service (`https://us-west-1.console.aws.amazon.com/codedeploy/`), you should see the following screen:

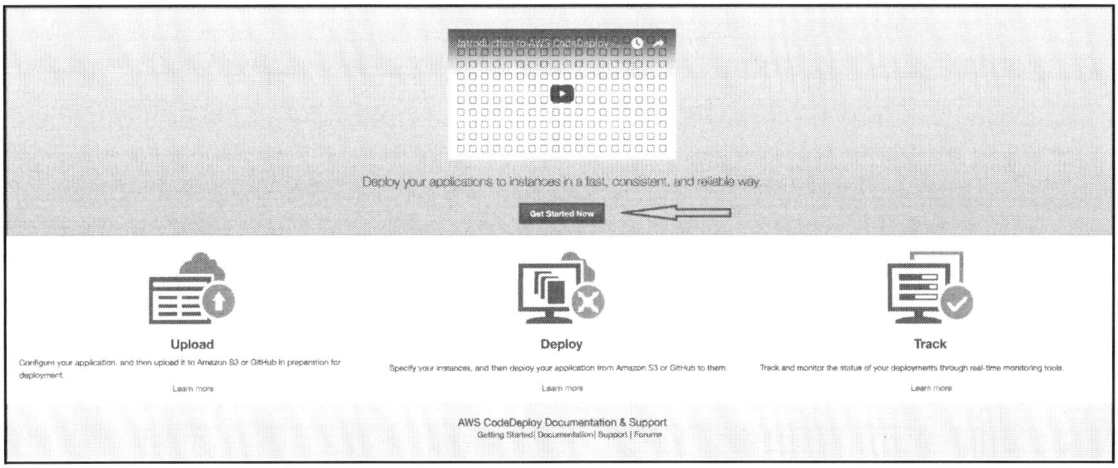

The preceding screenshot is the introduction page for Code Deploy, which showcases its capabilities.

2. Click on the **Get Started Now** button in the middle of the page to move forward.

3. Next, you should see the following screen, which will recommend you to deploy a sample application, which is fine for the initial stage. But since we have already built up our infrastructure, in that case, we need to select **Custom Deployment**--this will skip the walkthrough. So, select the option, and click on **Next.**

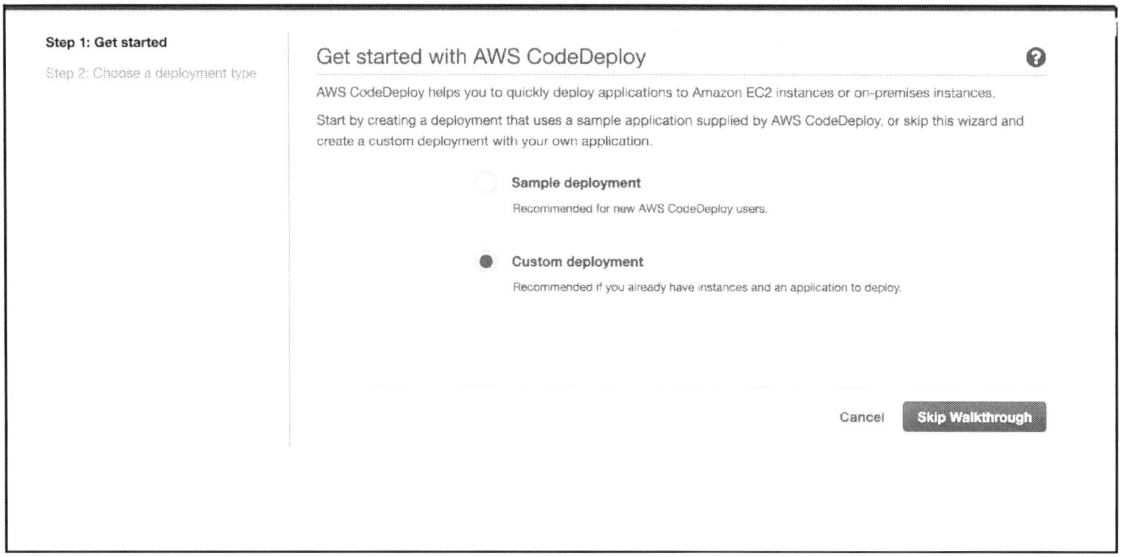

4. Click on **Skip Walkthrough** to move forward.
5. In the next wizard screen, there are a couple of sections which need to be reviewed.

   The first section will ask you to **Create application--**you need to provide a user-defined **Application name** and **Deployment group name**, which is mandatory, as it becomes the identifier for your application:

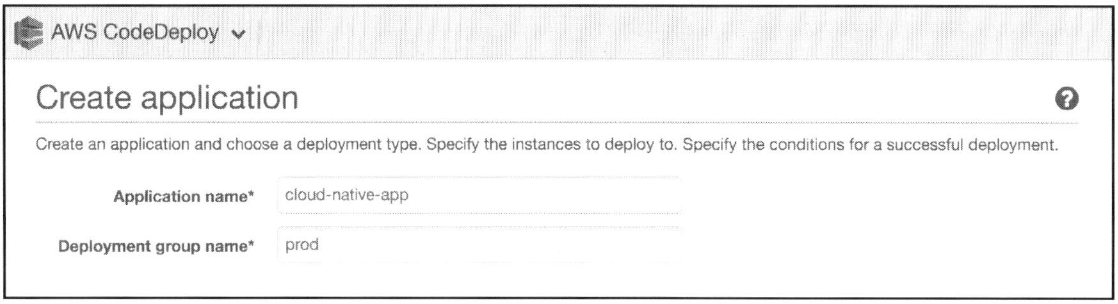

6. Scroll down to the next section, which talks about the type of deployment you want for your application. There are two methods, which are defined as follows:

- **Blue/green deployment**: In this type, during deployment, new instances are launched and new code is deployed to it, and if its health check is fine, it is replaced with the old one, and old instances are then terminated. This is recommended for the production environment, where customers can't afford downtime.
- **In-place deployment**: In this deployment type, new code is deployed directly into the existing instances. In this deployment, each instance is taken offline for updates.

We will go with **In-place deployment**, but the choice changes with the use case and product owner's decision. Say, for example, applications like Uber or Facebook, which can't afford a downtime at the time of deployment, will go for the Blue/green deployment, which will give them high availability.

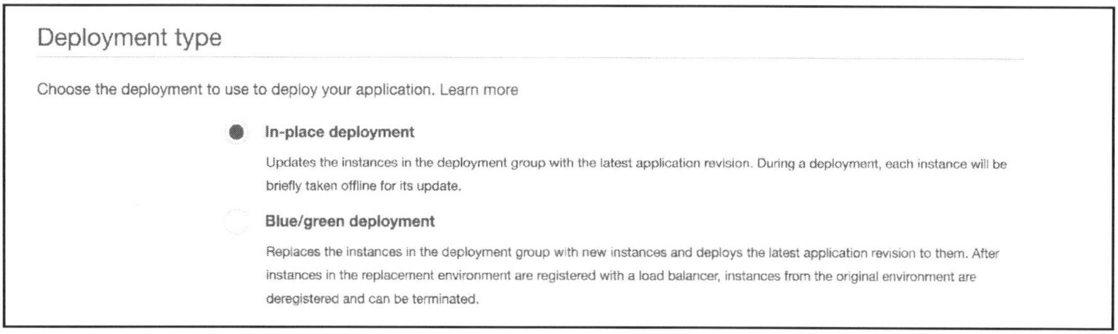

Deployment type
Choose the deployment to use to deploy your application. Learn more
In-place deployment
Updates the instances in the deployment group with the latest application revision. During a deployment, each instance will be briefly taken offline for its update.
Blue/green deployment
Replaces the instances in the deployment group with new instances and deploys the latest application revision to them. After instances in the replacement environment are registered with a load balancer, instances from the original environment are deregistered and can be terminated.

7. Let's move on to the next section, which talks about the infrastructure where the application is going to be deployed. We will specify the instances and ELB details as shown in this screenshot:

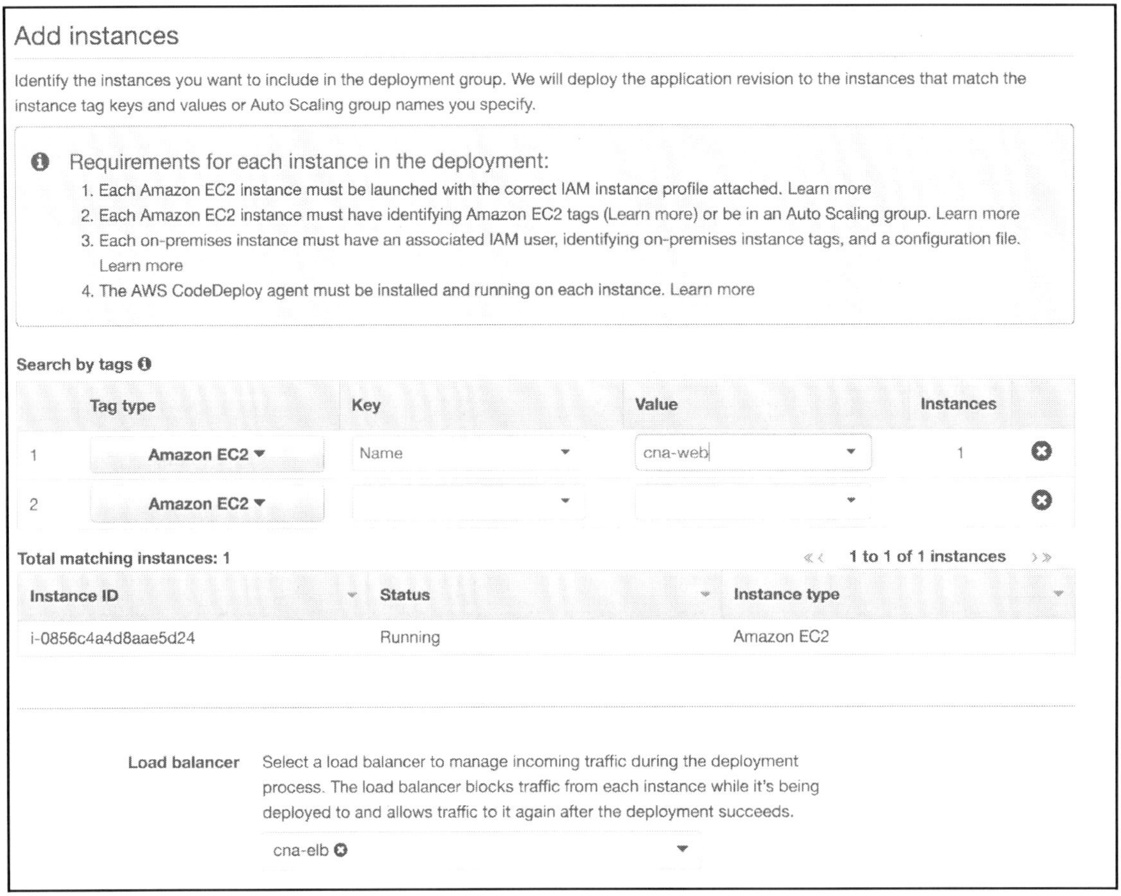

8. In the next segment, we will define the way to deploy the application. For example, suppose you have 10 instances. You may want to deploy the application on all these instances at one time, or one at a time, or half at a time. We will go with the default option, that is, `CodeDeployDefault.OneAtATime`:

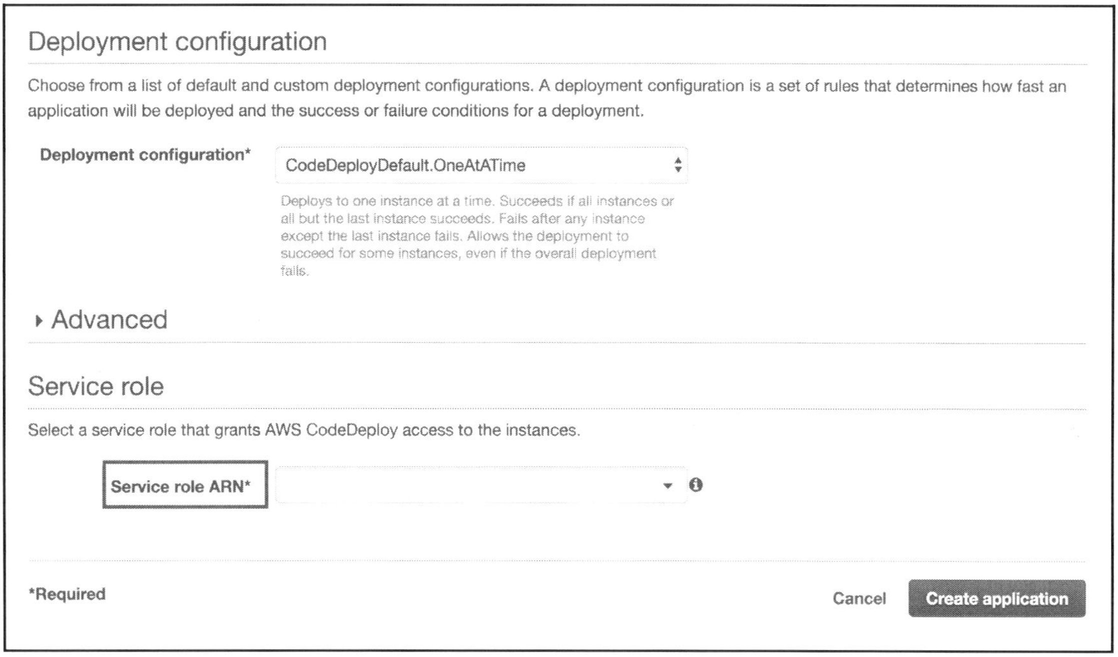

In this section, we also need to specify a **Service role**, which is needed by Code Deploy to perform operations on your AWS resources, more specifically, on EC2 and ELB.

In order to understand more about service role creation, go to the AWS documentation at this link:
`http://docs.aws.amazon.com/IAM/latest/UserGuide/id_roles_create.html`

9. Once you have provided the required information, click on **Create Application.**

   You will see the following screen once your application is ready:

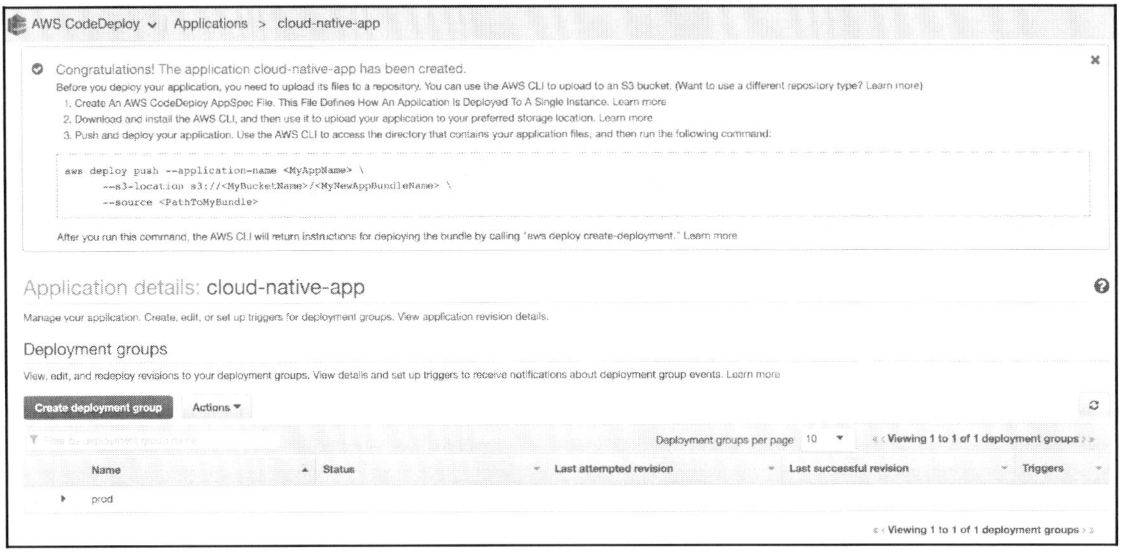

Now we are all set for deployment. All we need to create is a job in Jenkins, and add a post-built section with the CodeDeploy details.

The creation of a job is similar to what we explained in the previous chapter. The following few changes are needed though:

1. Firstly, we need to make sure we have installed a few Jenkins plugins, namely, **AWS CodeDeploy Plugin for Jenkins**, **Git plugin**, **GitHub plugin,** and so on.
2. Once you have installed the plugins, you should see new actions in the post-build actions list, as shown in the following screenshot:

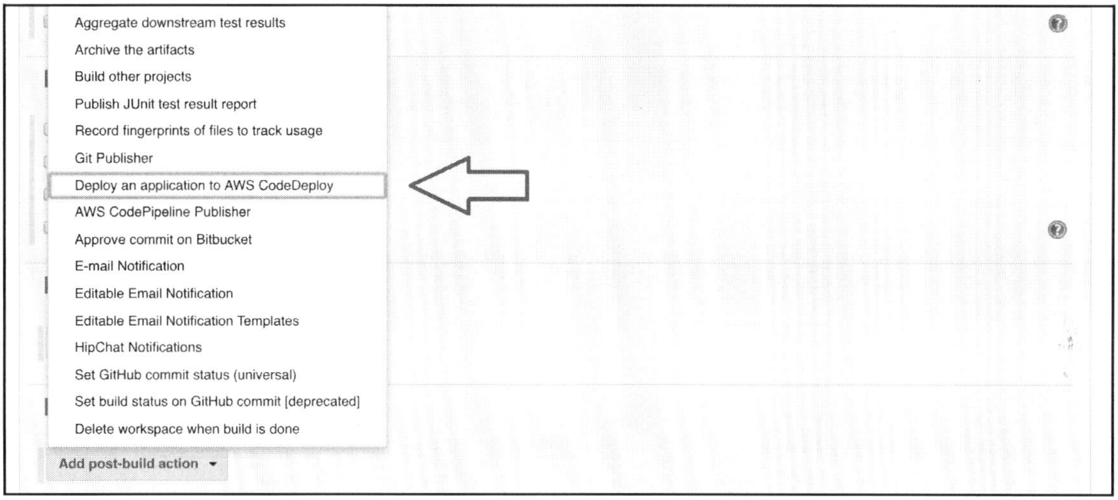

3. Next, you need to select the **Deploy an application to AWS CodeDeploy** action. A new section will be added, and we need to provide the details of the CodeDeploy application we created in the AWS console, as shown in this screenshot:

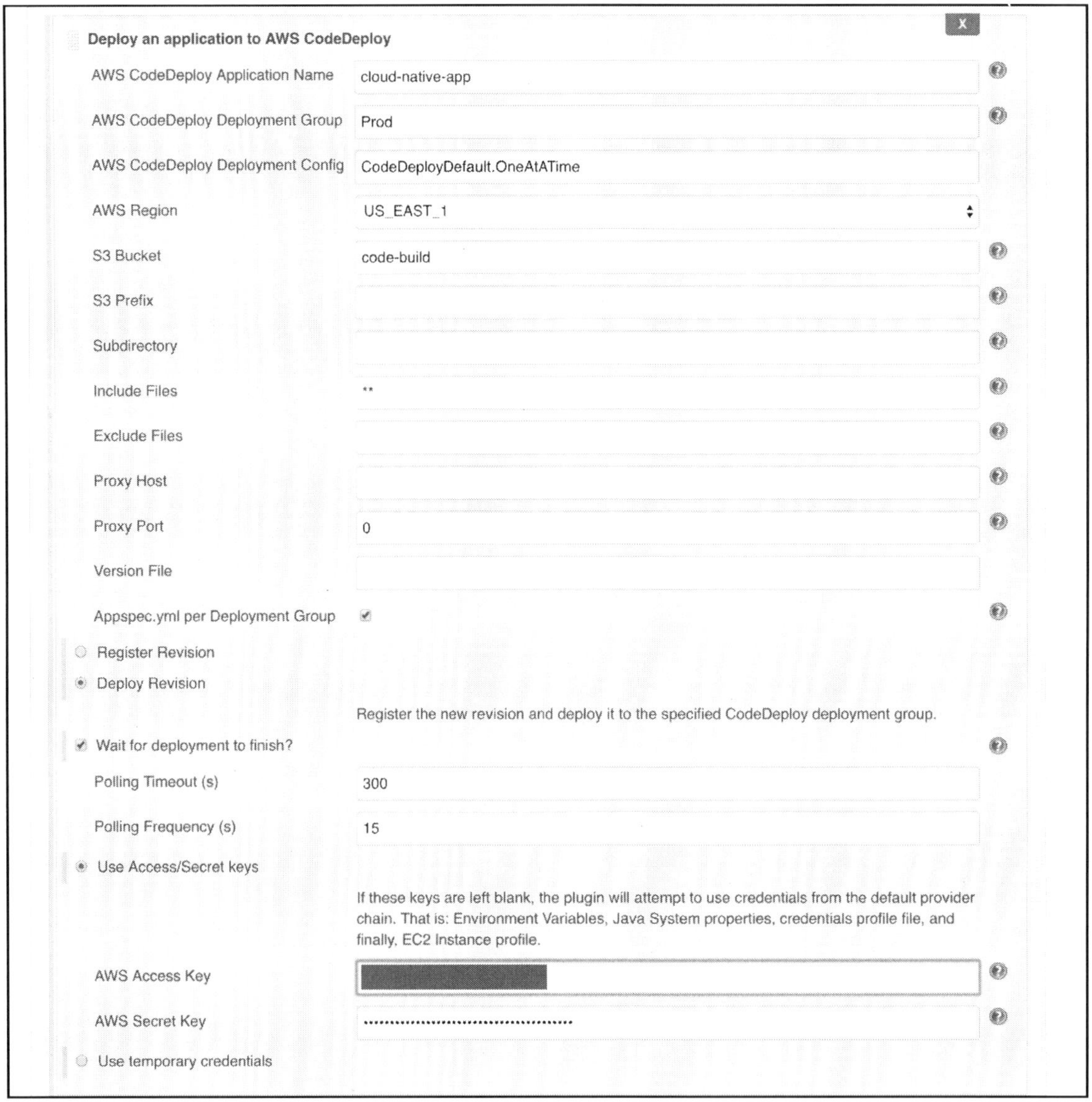

4. We also need to provide access/secret keys which we created at the beginning of this chapter in the section, *Generating authentication keys*. This is needed, as Jenkins, after packaging the application, needs to upload it to S3 and instruct CodeDeploy to deploy the latest build from the specified bucket.

That's all we need to do. Now our Jenkins job is ready to deploy the application. Try it out, and it should work as smooth as butter.

Summary

This chapter is very interesting in various ways. Firstly, you got the basic understanding about AWS services, and how to make the most out of them. Next, we explored the architecture of our application on the AWS cloud, which will shape your views on architecture designing for different application/products that you might plan to create in the future. We also made use of Terraform, which is a third-party tool used to build infrastructure on AWS as code. Finally, we deployed our application, and created a continuous pipeline for deployment using Jenkins. In the next chapter, we will explore another cloud platform owned by Microsoft--Microsoft Azure. Stay alive, and get ready to explore Azure in the coming chapter. See you there!

12
Implementing on the Azure Platform

In the previous chapter, we saw one of the cloud computing platforms for hosting our application--AWS--which contains all the features to make an application with high availability, and with no downtime. In this chapter, we will have a discussion about another cloud platform called **Microsoft Azure**.

This chapter includes the following topics:

- Introducing Microsoft Azure
- Building application infrastructure Azure services
- CI/CD using Jenkins with Azure

Getting started with Microsoft Azure

As the name suggests, Microsoft Azure is a public cloud platform owned by Microsoft, which provides different PaaS and IaaS services for their customers. Some of the popular services are virtual machine, app service, SQL database, Resource Manager, and so on.

The Azure services fall mainly into these two categories:

- **Platform services**: These are the services where customers are provided with an environment to build, manage, and execute their applications while taking care of the infrastructure themselves. The following are some of the Azure services by its various categories:
    - **Management services**: These provide a management portal and marketplace services, which provide galleries and tools for automation in Azure.
    - **Compute**: These are services such as fabric, functions, and so on, which help the developer to develop and deploy highly scalable applications.
    - **CDN and media**: These provides secure and reliable content delivery around the globe and real-time streaming respectively.
    - **Web + Mobile**: These are services related to apps such as web apps and API apps, mostly for web and mobile applications.
    - **Analytics**: These are big-data-related services, which can help a machine learning developer to perform real-time data processing, and give you insights into data such as HDInsight, Machine learning, Stream Analytics, Bot service, and so on.
    - **Development tools**: These services are used for version control, collaboration, and others. It includes SDKs as well.
    - **AI and Cognitive Service**: These are artificial-intelligence-based services, such as for speech, vision, and so on. A few of the services which do so are Text Analytics API, Cognitive, and others.
- **Infrastructure Services**: These are services where the service provider is responsible for the hardware failures. Customization of the servers is the customer's responsibility. Also, the customer manages its specifications as well:
    - **Server compute and containers**: These are services such as virtual machine and containers, which provide computing power to the customer application with variants.
    - **Storage**: These are of two types--BLOB and file storage. It has varying storage capabilities available based on latency and speed.
    - **Networking**: These provide a couple of network-related services such as load balancer and virtual network, which help you to secure your network, and make it efficient for customer response.

The following diagram will give more understanding about the Azure platform:

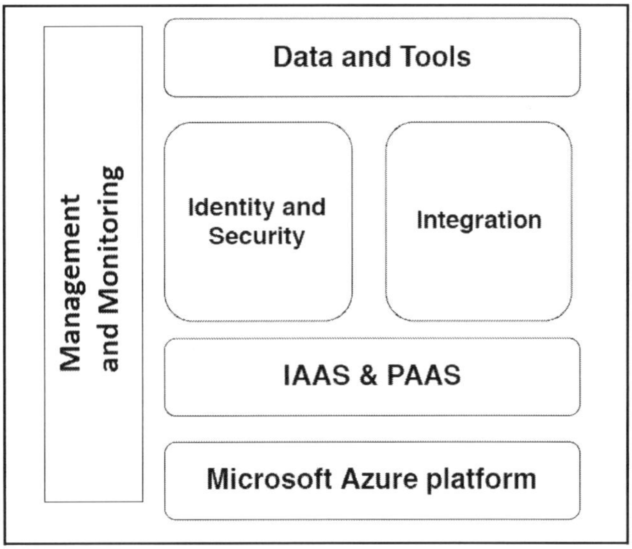

You can review all the Microsoft Azure product offerings in detail at the following link:

`https://azure.microsoft.com/en-in/services/`

To get started with Microsoft Azure, you are required to have an account. Since this chapter is concerned with implementing our application on Azure, we won't get into how to create an account. If you do need help, you could read the article given at the following link, which will definitely help you out:

`https://medium.com/appliedcode/setup-microsoft-azure-account-cbd635ebf14b`

Azure provides some SaaS-based services, which you can review at `https://azuremarketplace.microsoft.com/en-us`.

A few points on Microsoft Azure basics

Once you are ready and logged into your Azure account, you will be redirected to the Azure portal (`https://portal.azure.com`), which will showcase the Azure service. Initially, Azure provides a free account, and gives you a credit value of $200 for your usage for 30 days. Microsoft Azure also believes in the pay-as-you-go model, and when you have finished all your free credit, you can switch to a paid account.

The following are some of the basic concepts of Azure that you should know before moving forward:

- **Azure Resource Manager**: Initially, Azure was based on a deployment model called **ASM** (**Azure Service Manager**). In the latest version of Azure, **ARM** (**Azure Resource Manager**) is adopted, which provides high availability and more flexibility.
- **Azure Regions**: There are around 34 regions distributed around the globe.
- The list of Azure regions is available at `https://azure.microsoft.com/en-us/regions/`.
- A list of all the services in specific regions is available at `https://azure.microsoft.com/en-us/regions/services/`.
- **Azure automation**: Azure provides a number of templates in the different Windows-based tools, such as Azure-PowerShell, Azure-CLI, and so on. You can find these templates at `https://github.com/Azure`.

Since Azure is owned by Microsoft, we will mostly work on the Azure console (UI), and create resources through it. The Azure environment is very friendly for the developers or DevOps professionals who love to deploy their applications on the Windows system, and their applications are written in .NET or VB. It also supports the latest programming languages such as Python, ROR, and so on.

Microsoft Azure is the ideal choice for people who love to work on Microsoft-based products such as Visual Studio.

Architecturing our application infrastructure using Azure

Once you are on the Azure portal, you should see the following default dashboard on your screen:

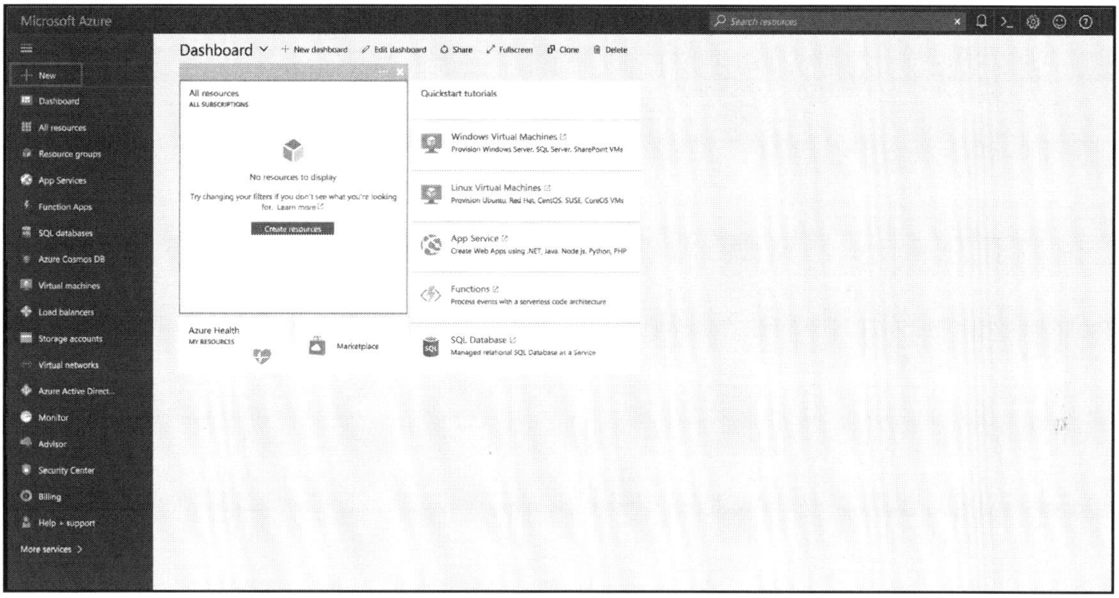

It's time to architect our application infrastructure on MS Azure. We will follow the architecture diagram given next to create our production environment on Azure:

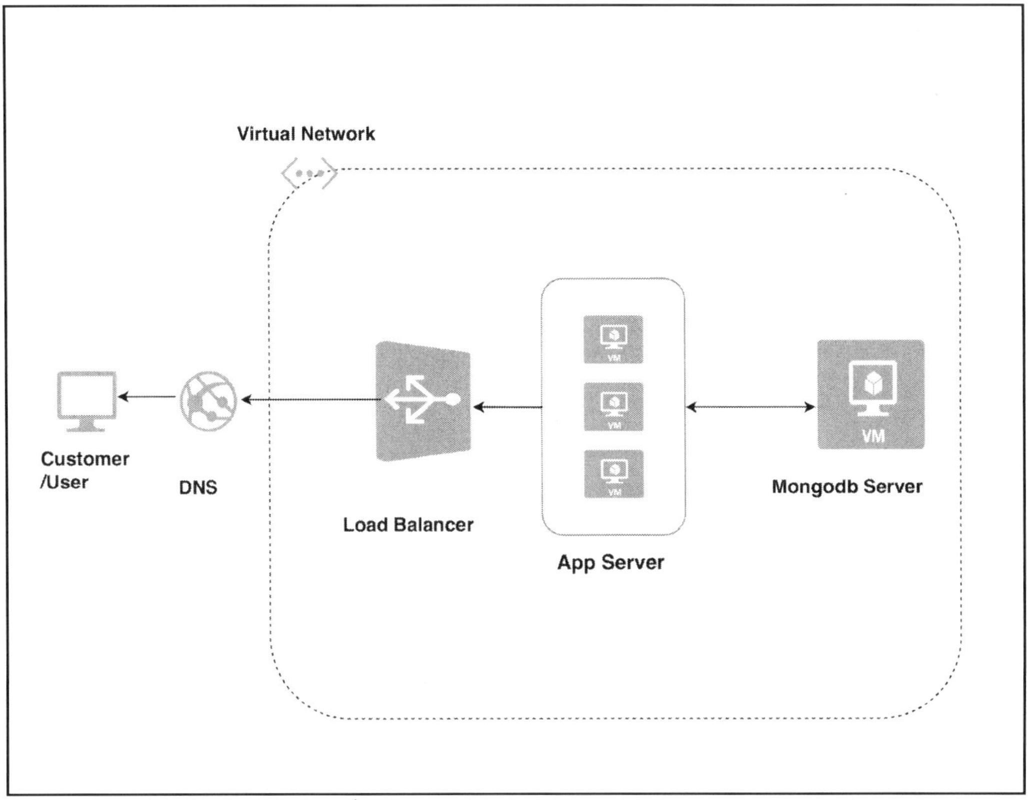

In this architecture, we will use a couple of Azure services, which are as follows:

- **Virtual Machine**: This is similar to our EC2 machine in AWS. We will deploy our application and the MongoDB server in a Virtual Machine.
- **Virtual Network**: Virtual Network is synonymous with the VPC in AWS, and needs to be created in order to keep our communication network secure.
- **Storage**: Each VM is backed by a storage account that we don't create explicitly, as it is created along with the VM to store your data.
- **Load Balancer**: This Load Balancer has the same usage as the Load Balancer in AWS, but they have a slight variation in the algorithm, as Azure mainly follows either hash-based balancing or source IP algorithm, whereas, AWS follows the Round-Robin Algorithm or the sticky session algorithm.

- **DNS**: DNS is useful when we have a domain register, and we need to manage our DNS from Azure. In the cloud platform, we call it the **Zone**.
- **Subnet**: We will create a Subnet inside the Virtual Network to distinguish our resources, which need to be internet facing or not.
- **Auto scaling**: We haven't mentioned this in the diagram, as it depends on your application need and customer response.

So, let's begin by creating our app server (that is, the virtual machine) where our application resides.

As I mentioned earlier, Azure has a very user friendly UI, which creates a programmatic code in the background as per your defined resources, and gives it to you using the Resource Manager, which makes the DevOps guy's job easier.

Creating a virtual machine in Azure

Follow the steps listed next to create a VM in Microsoft Azure:

1. Go to the Azure dashboard, and select **New** in the left panel to launch the VM Wizard, as shown in the following screenshot:

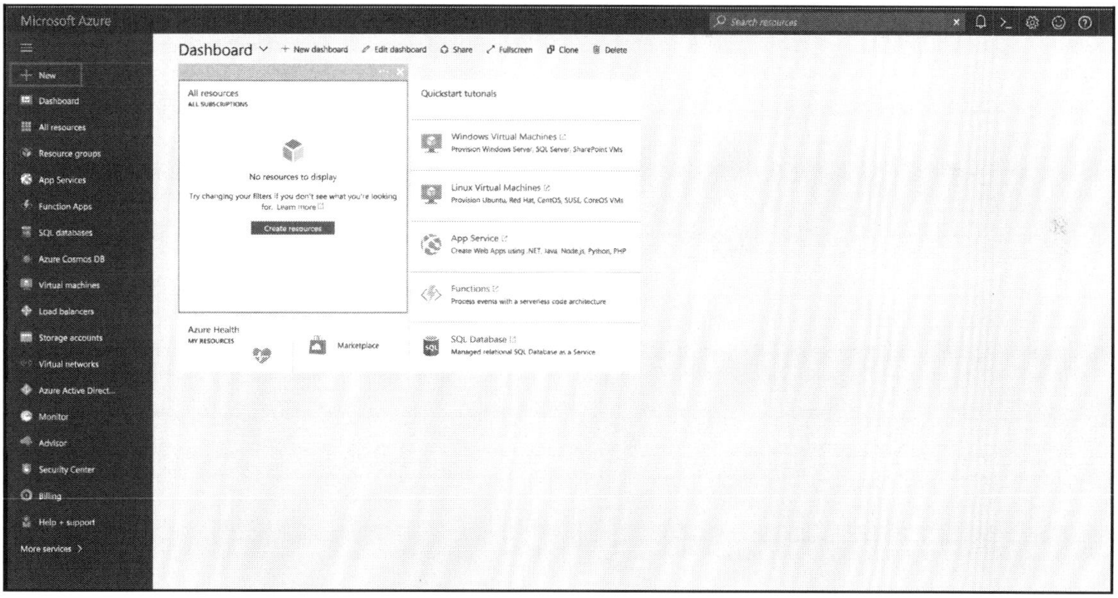

2. Now we need to select the OS that needs to be launched. We will select the **Ubuntu Server 16.04 LTS** server option (we select this option, since our application is developed on the Ubuntu OS) in the list.

In the following screen, we need to select the deployment model. There are two deployment models available. They are classic (it is a standard VM) and Resource Manager (high availability VM). Select **Resource manager model**, as shown in the next screenshot, and click on the **Create** button to proceed further:

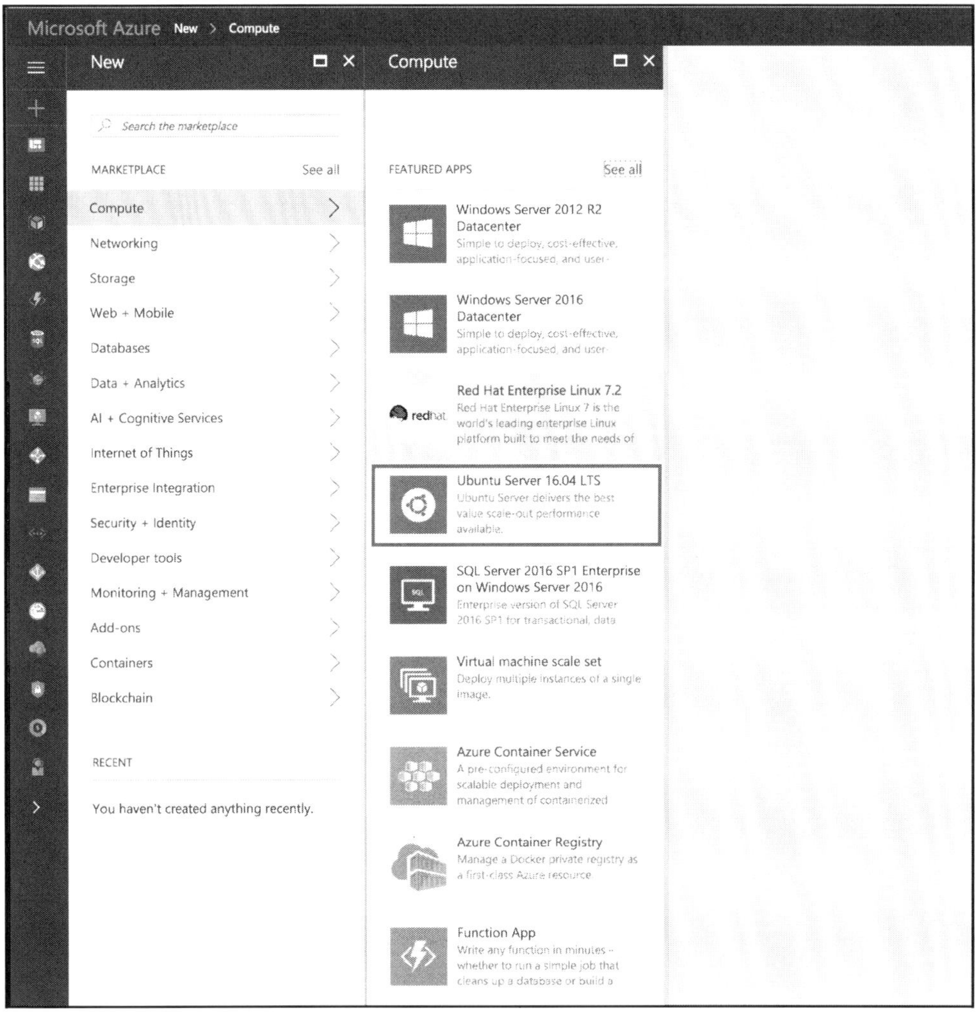

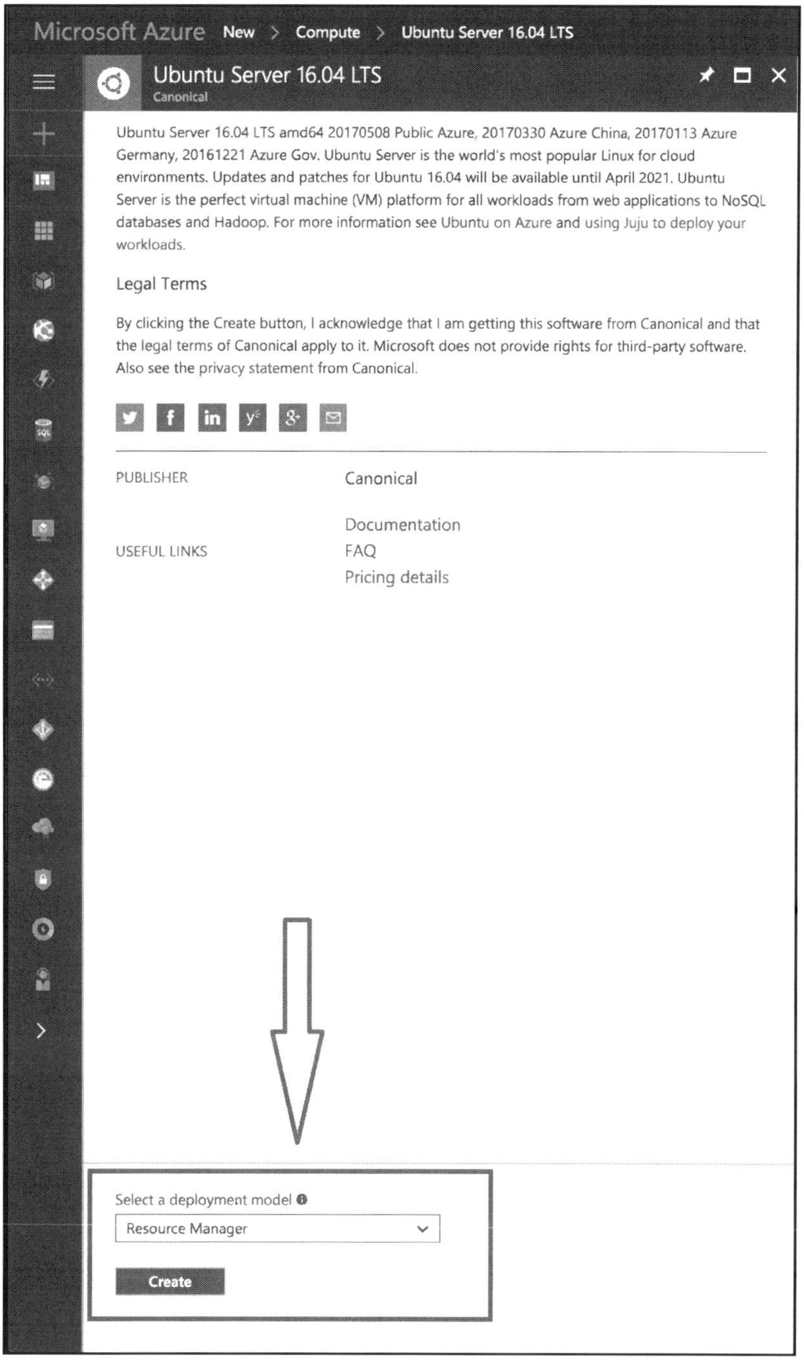
Microsoft Azure New > Compute > Ubuntu Server 16.04 LTS
Ubuntu Server 16.04 LTS
Canonical
Ubuntu Server 16.04 LTS amd64 20170508 Public Azure, 20170330 Azure China, 20170113 Azure Germany, 20161221 Azure Gov. Ubuntu Server is the world's most popular Linux for cloud environments. Updates and patches for Ubuntu 16.04 will be available until April 2021. Ubuntu Server is the perfect virtual machine (VM) platform for all workloads from web applications to NoSQL databases and Hadoop. For more information see Ubuntu on Azure and using Juju to deploy your workloads.
Legal Terms
By clicking the Create button, I acknowledge that I am getting this software from Canonical and that the legal terms of Canonical apply to it. Microsoft does not provide rights for third-party software. Also see the privacy statement from Canonical.
PUBLISHER
Canonical
USEFUL LINKS
Documentation
FAQ
Pricing details
Select a deployment model
Resource Manager
Create

3. On the next screen, we need to provide the **User name** and method of authentication for the VM, as shown in the following screenshot; click on **OK** to proceed further:

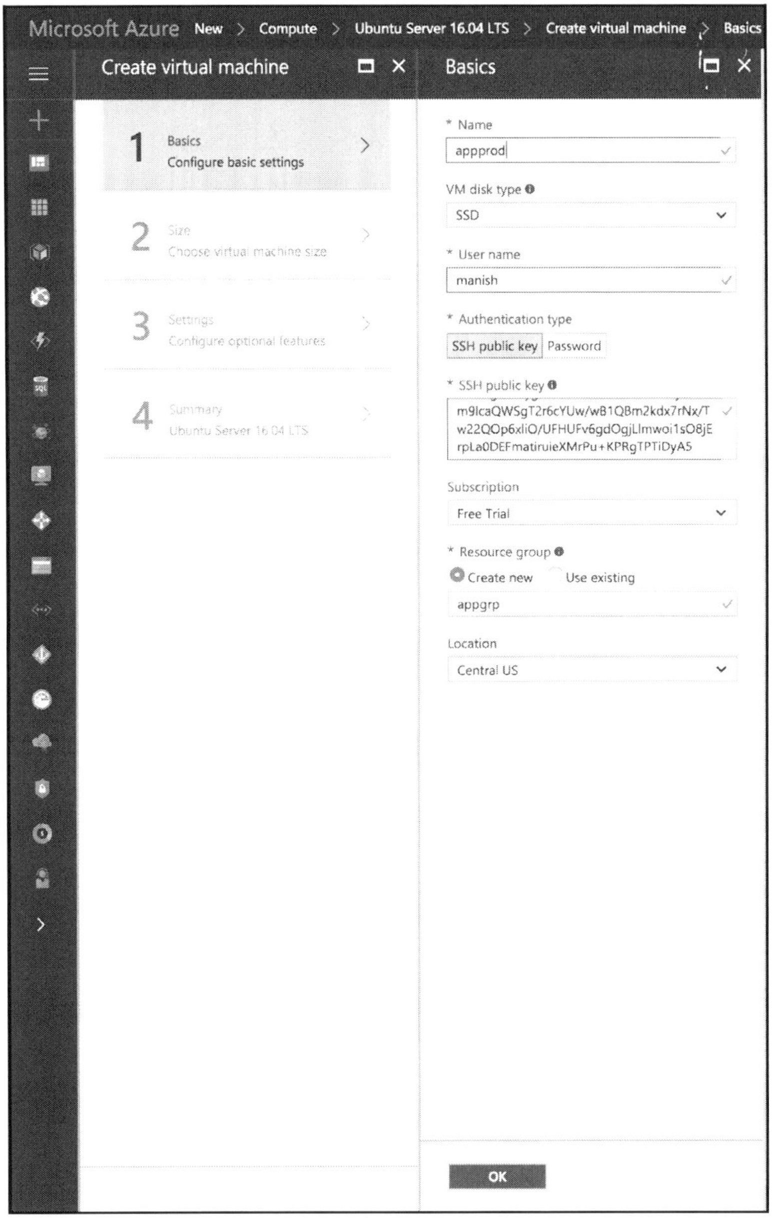

4. Next, we need to select the VM size based on our requirement. We will go with the **DS1_V2 Standard** type. Select it, and click on the **Select** button at the bottom of the page as follows:

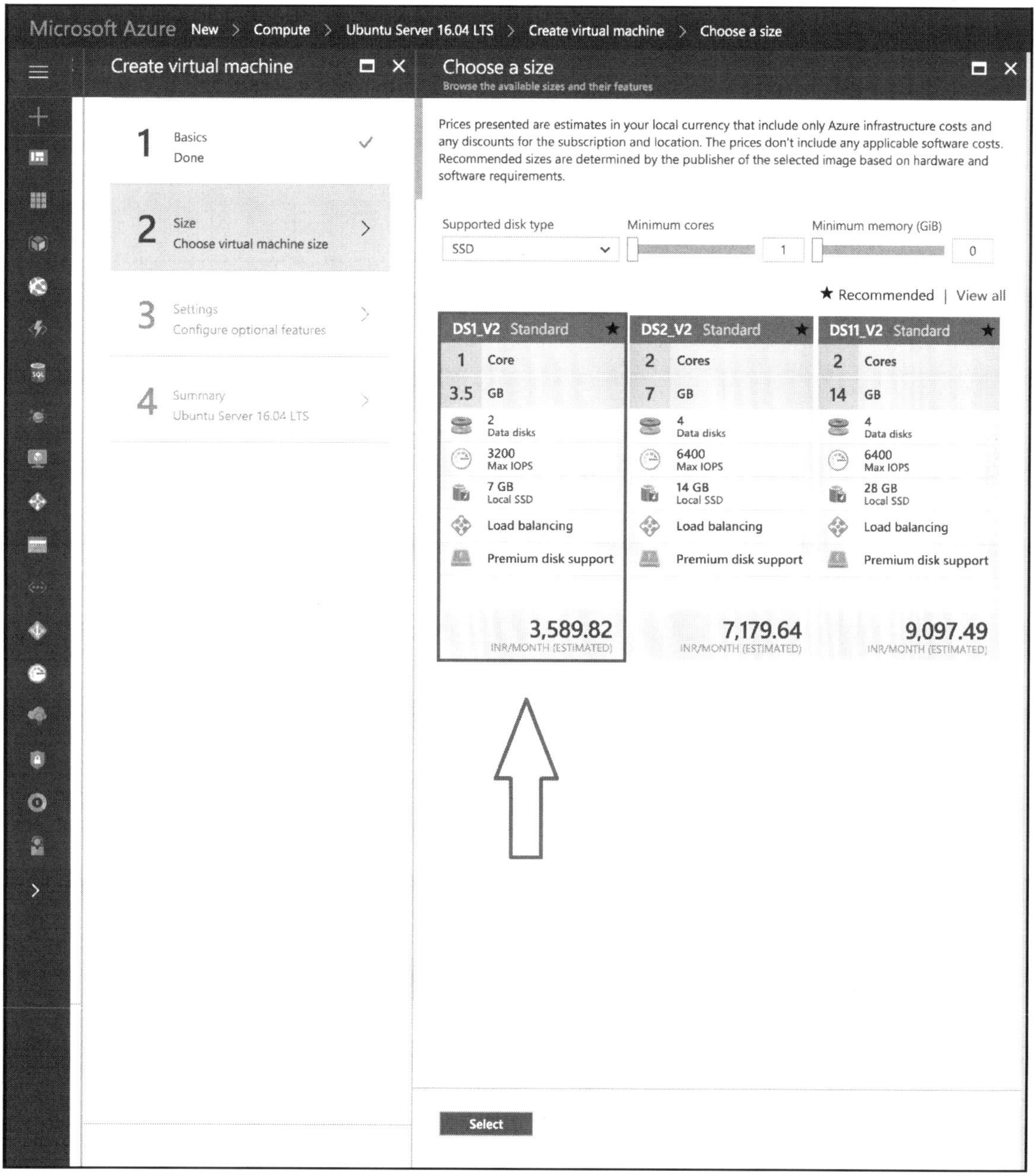

5. In the next screen, we will define a couple of the optional details such as **Network**, **Subnet**, **Public IP address**, security group, **Monitoring**, and others:

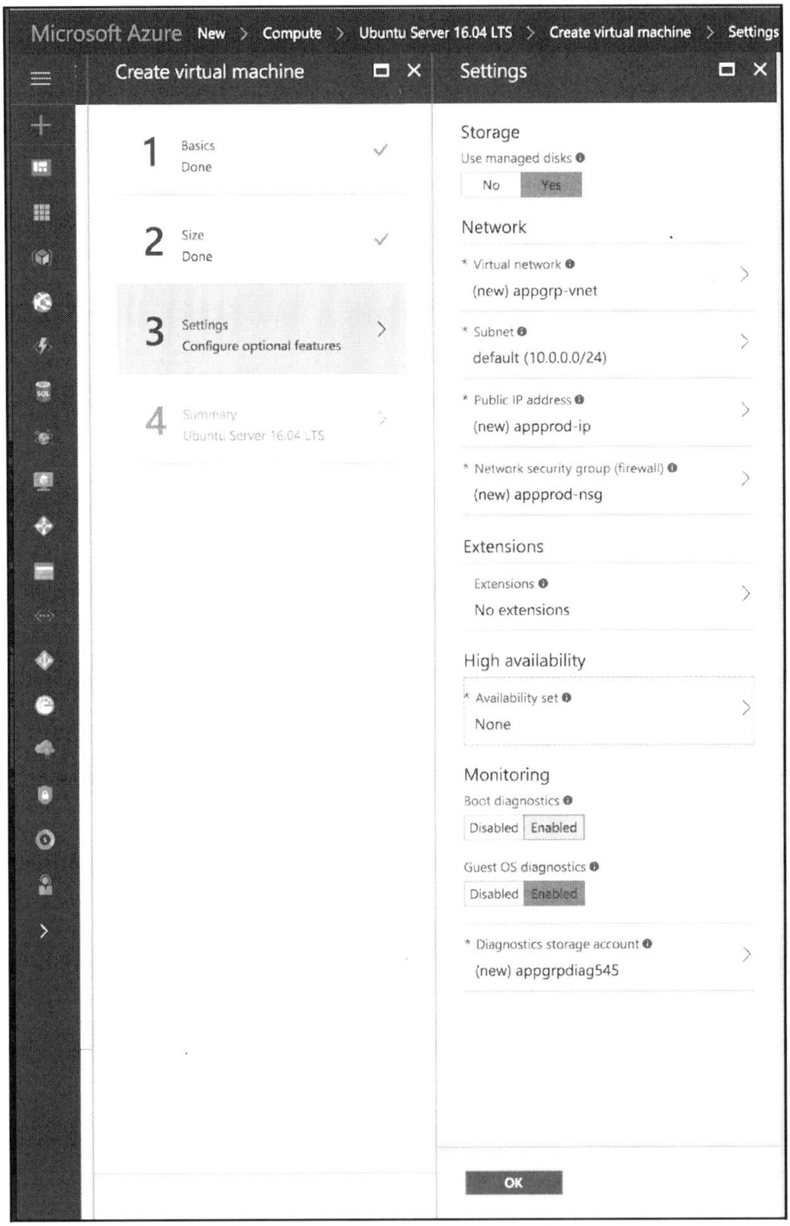

Instead of creating a virtual network everytime, it's recommended to create a virtual network, and choose it by clicking on **virtual network**. When it comes to managed and unmanaged disks, I prefer the managed ones. This is because in unmanaged disks, we choose to create a storage account, and since we are creating it for a multiple app server, each app server will have its separate storage account. It is highly possible that all the storage accounts may fall into a single storage unit, which could cause a single point of failure. On the other hand, in the case of a managed disk, Azure manages our disk by every storage account in a separate storage unit, which makes it highly available.
If you don't provide these details, it will be set automatically.

6. In the next screen, we need to review all the details that we have defined in the wizard, as seen in this screenshot:

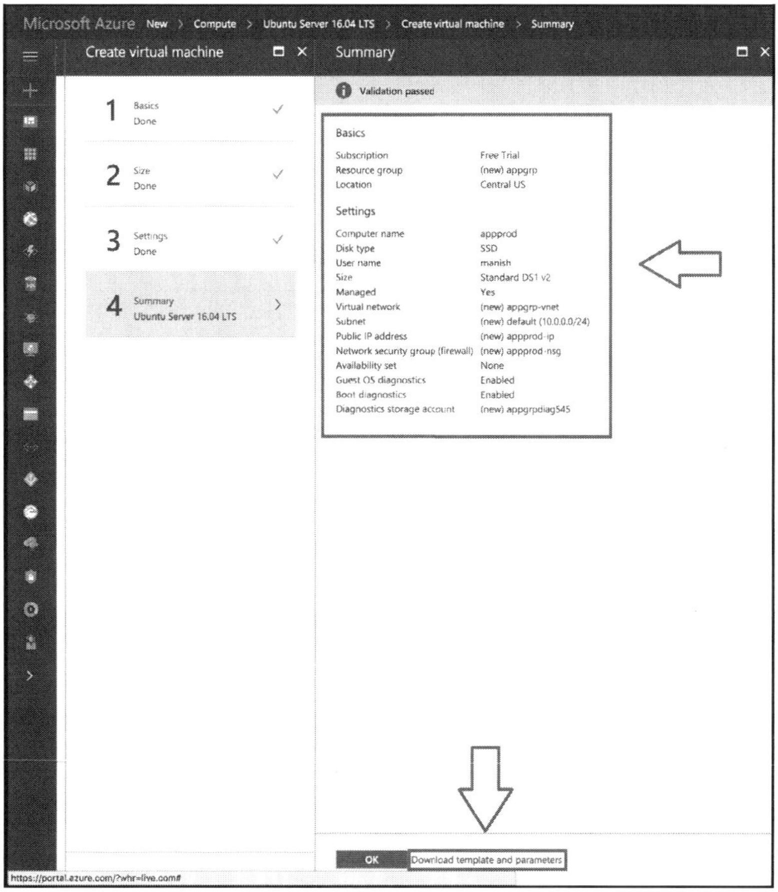

7. At the bottom of the page, you will find a link that will give you the facility to download the complete configuration in the form of a template, or in the form of code in different languages. See the following screenshot that shows the code that got generated as part of the configuration we provided:

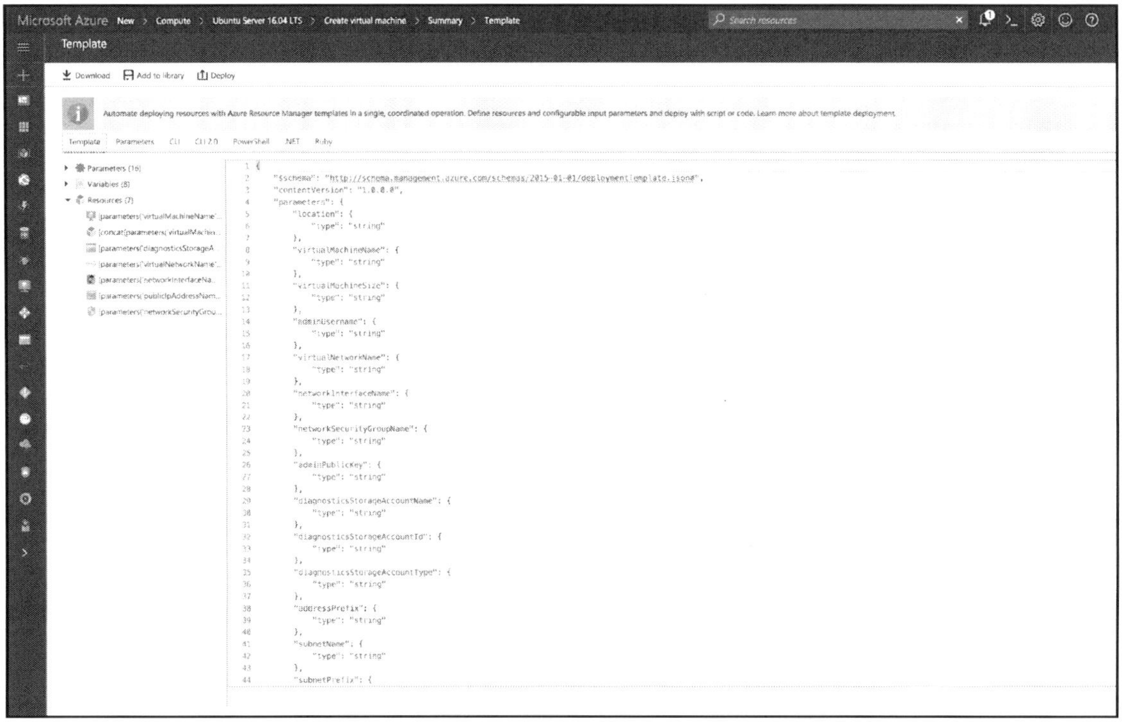

8. Click on **Ok** to begin with the deployment of your virtual machine.

Now our dashboard should have one VM running after some time, as shown in this screenshot:

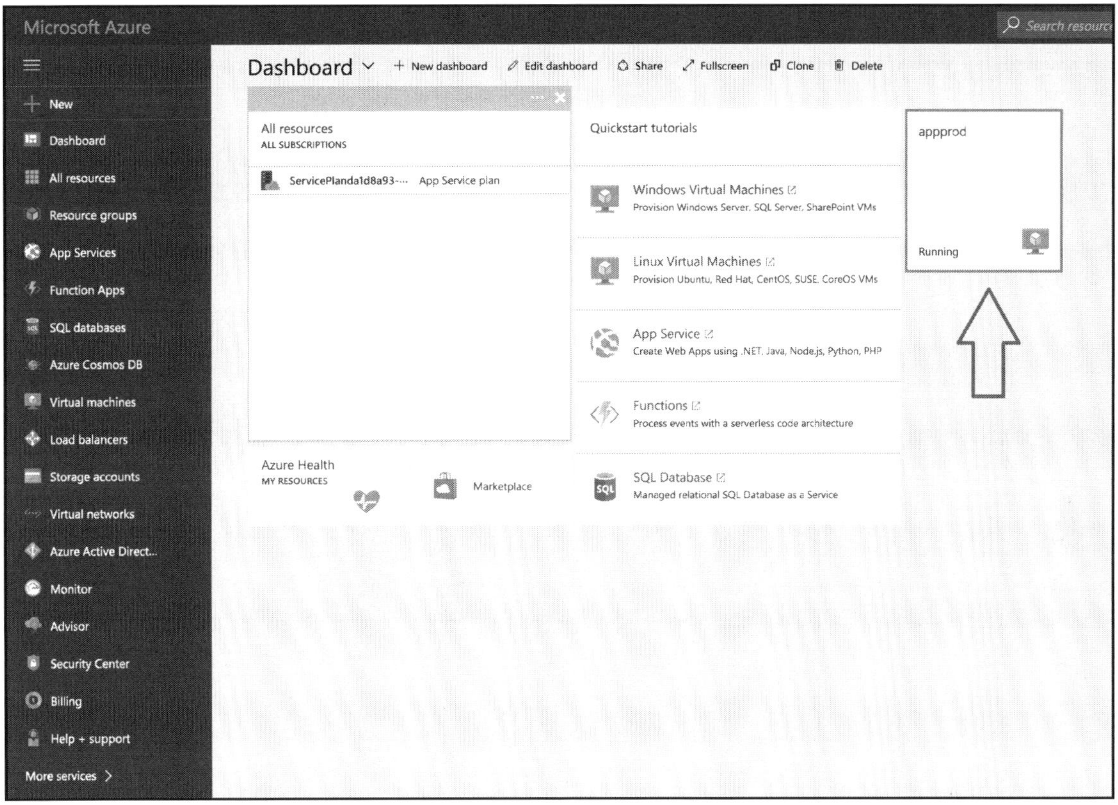

Now that you have access to the VM, you need to download your application and deploy it as you were doing in your local machine.

Similarly, we can create multiple VM instances for your application that act as app servers.

Also, we can create a VM with the MongoDB server installation on top of it. The installation steps you need to follow will be similar to the ones we defined in `Chapter 4`, *Interacting Data Service*.

We can see the performance of the VM by clicking on the VM (that is, **appprod**) icon on the dashboard, which should be as shown in the following screenshot:

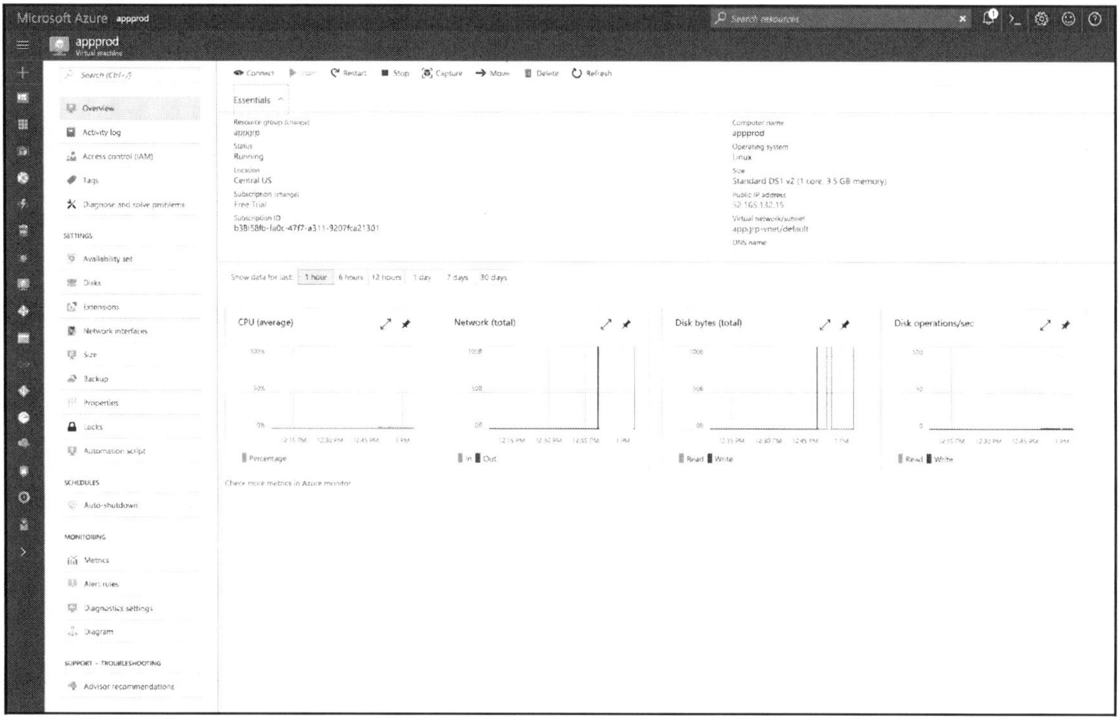

Next, we need to add the app servers created earlier to the load balancer. So, we need to create a load balancer using the following steps:

- Go to `https://portal.azure.com/?whr=live.com#blade/HubsExtension/Resources/resourceType/Microsoft.Network%2FLoadBalancers`, and click on the button **Create Load balancers** in the middle of the screen, as shown in the following screenshot:
- In the next screen, we need to specify the LB Name, and provide the type of LB purpose. We can launch the ELB in the same group as your app server, as seen here:

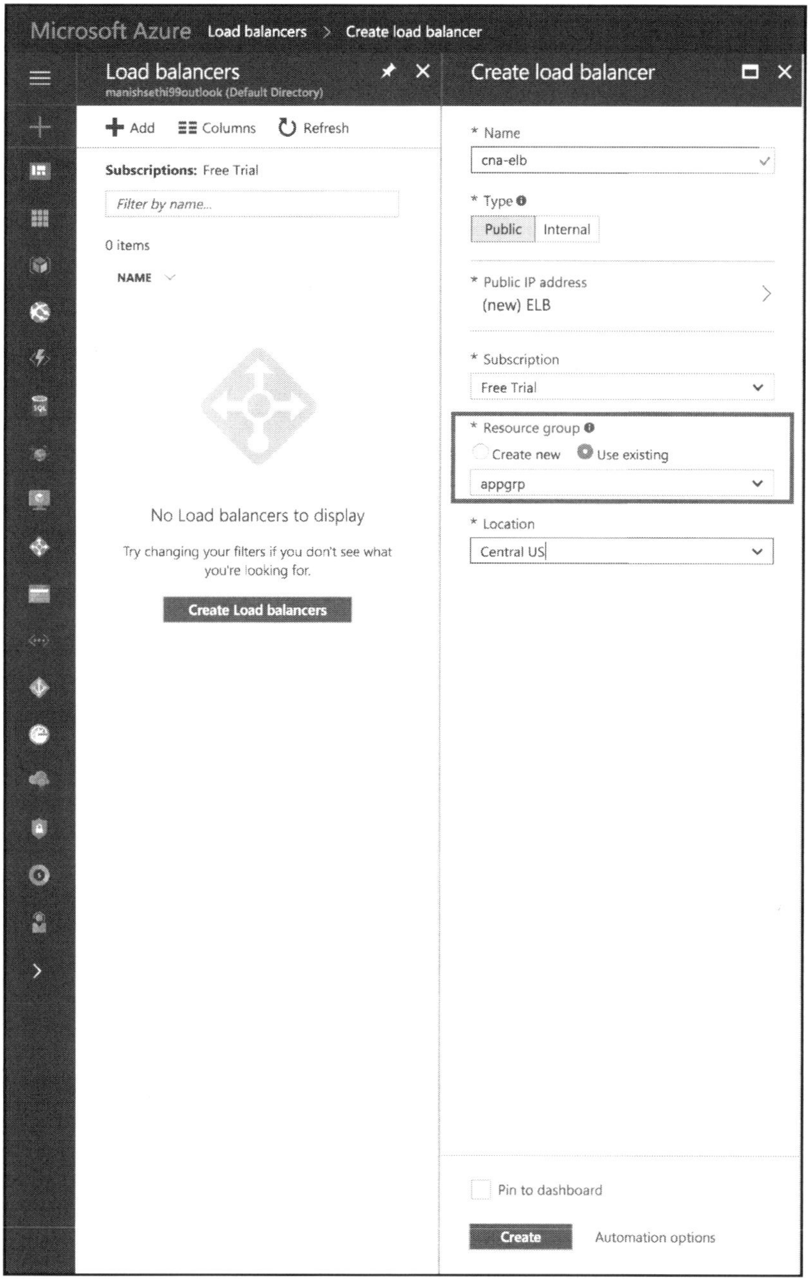

Click on the **Create** button to initiate LB creation.

9. Once the **load balancer** is ready for our usage, we should be able to see the following screen, which shows its details:

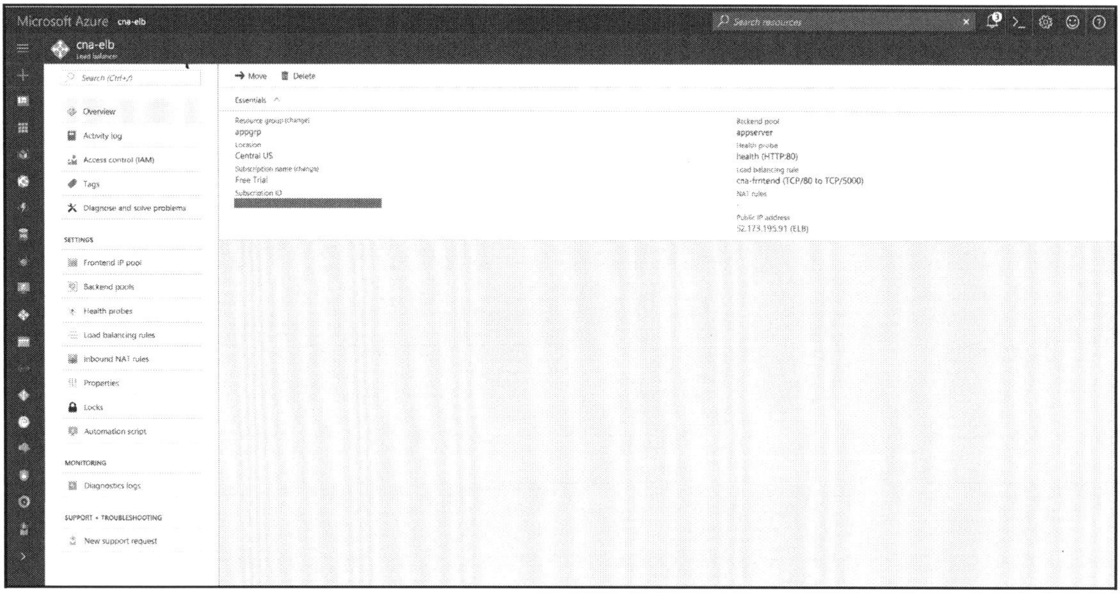

10. Next, we need to add a backend pool, which is our app server, as shown in this screenshot:

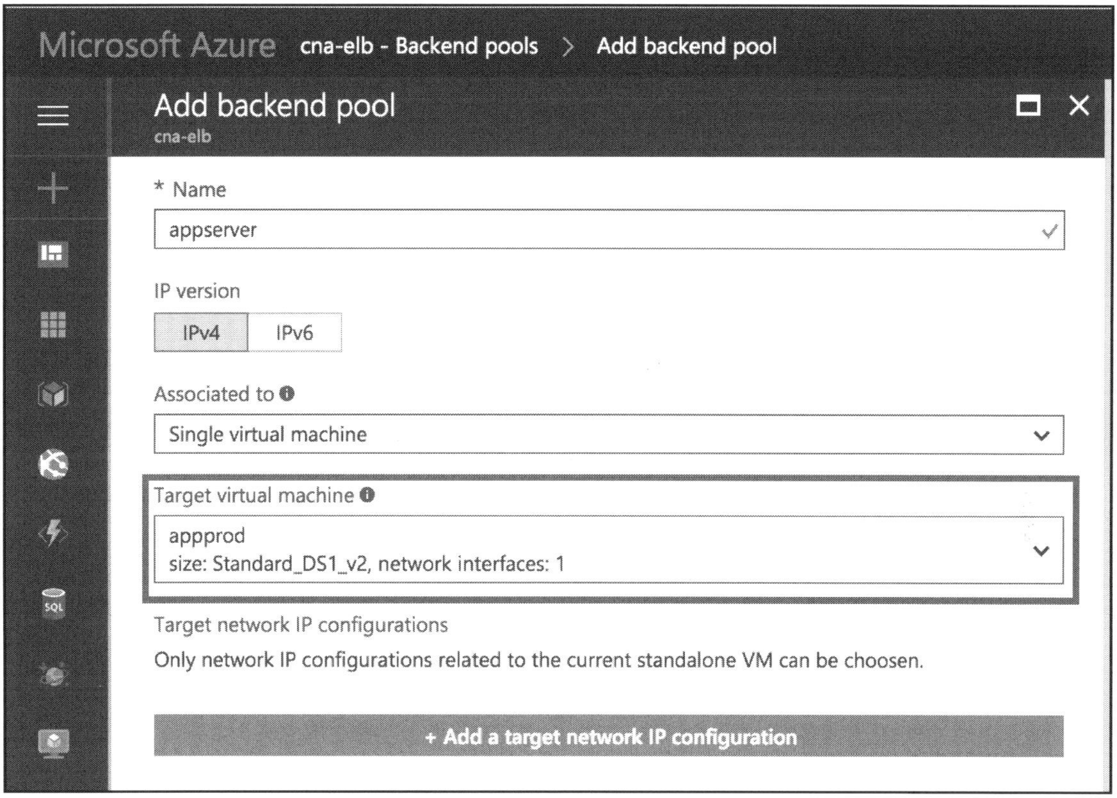

11. Now we need to add **health probe**, which is the health status of your application, as follows:

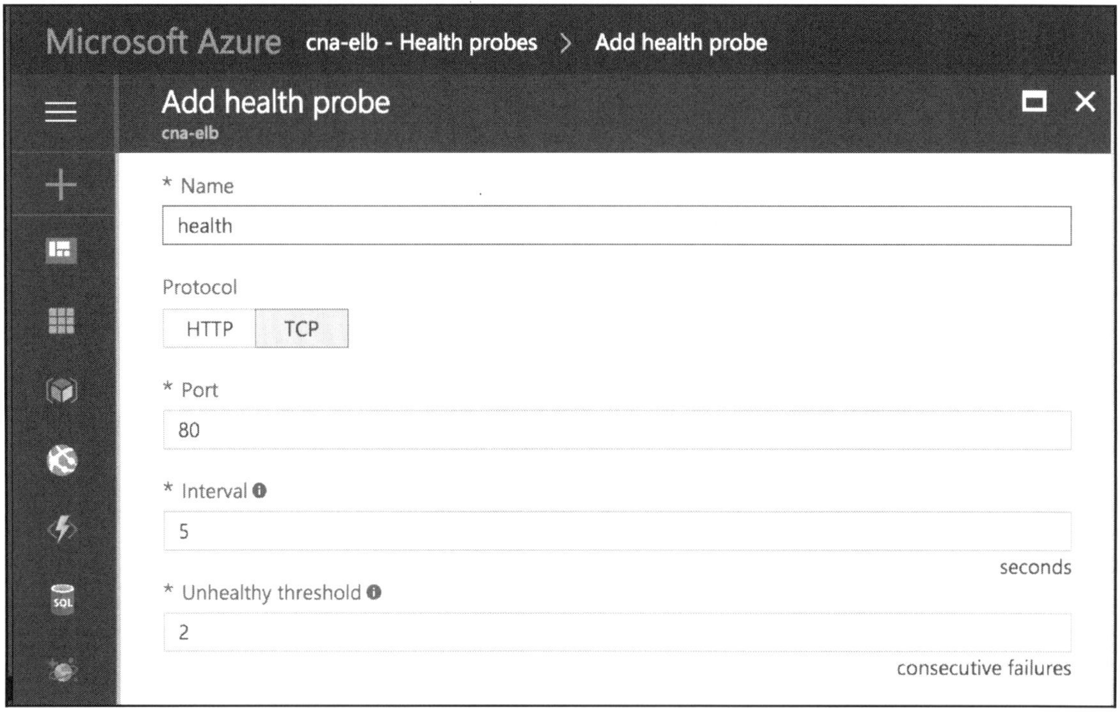

Next we add the frontend pools for our application as shown here:

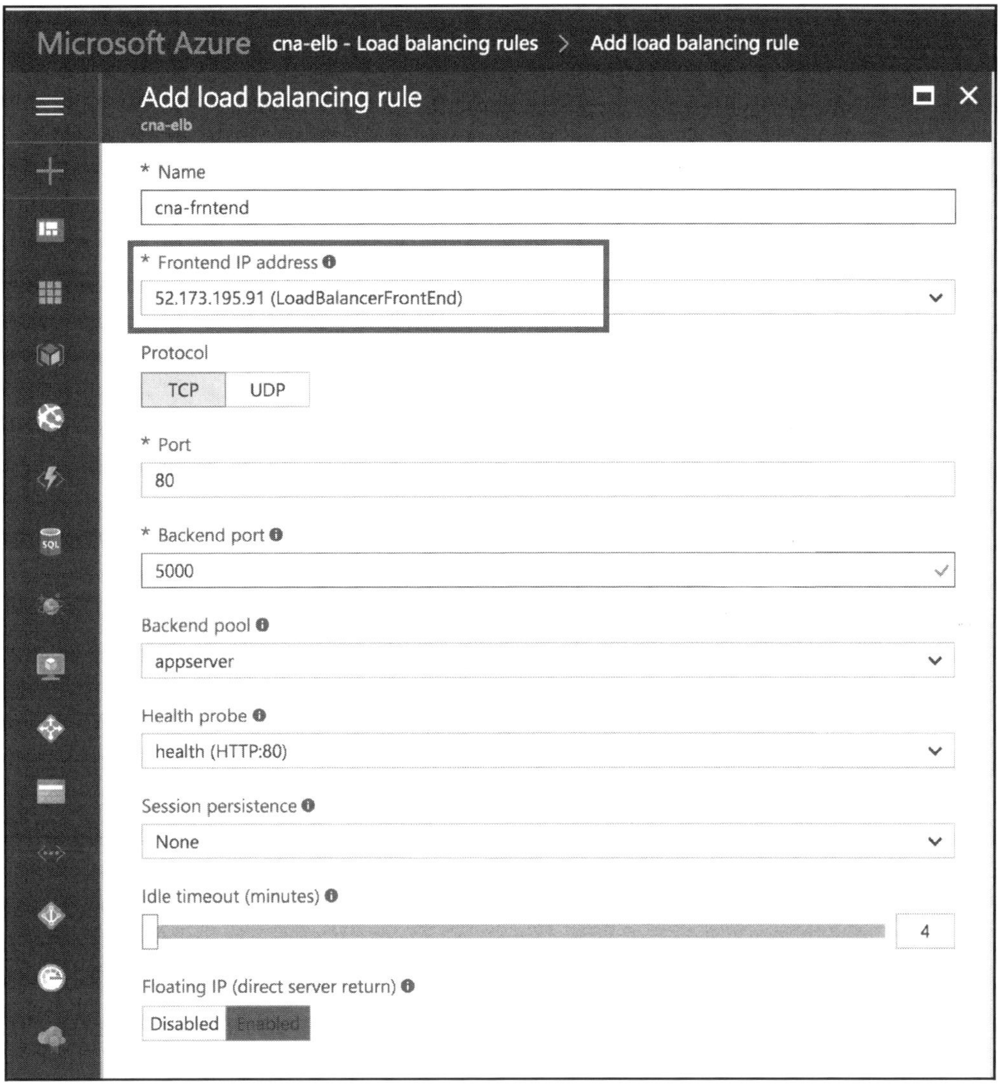

Now we are all set with the **load balancer** for our application.

You can read more about load balancers in the Azure docs at this link: `https://docs.microsoft.com/en-us/azure/load-balancer/load-balancer-overview`

We have now created the infrastructure as per our architecture diagram. It's time to configure Jenkins for our application deployment on our infrastructure in Azure.

CI/CD pipeline using Jenkins with Azure

Firstly, we need to navigate to the active directory service, which you can see in the following screenshot:

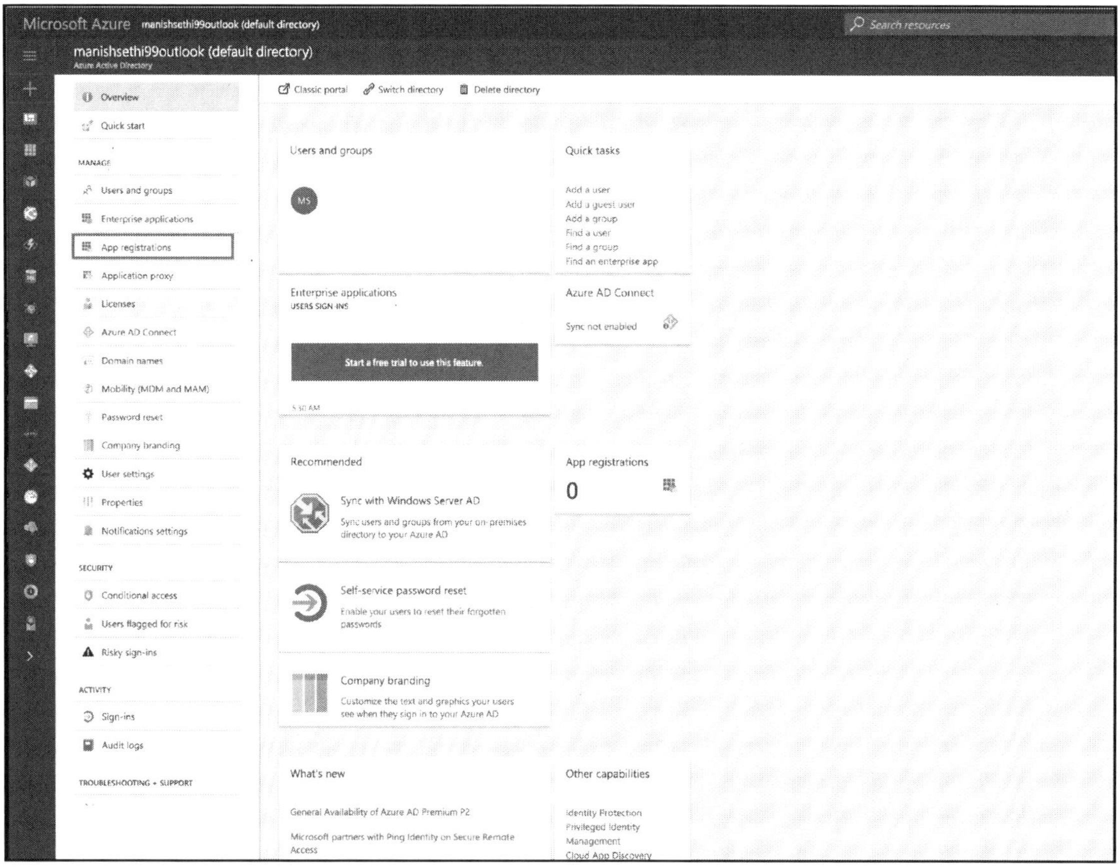

Now we need to register our application, so, select the **App registrations** link in the left pane. You will see a screen similar to the next one, where you need to provide your application details:

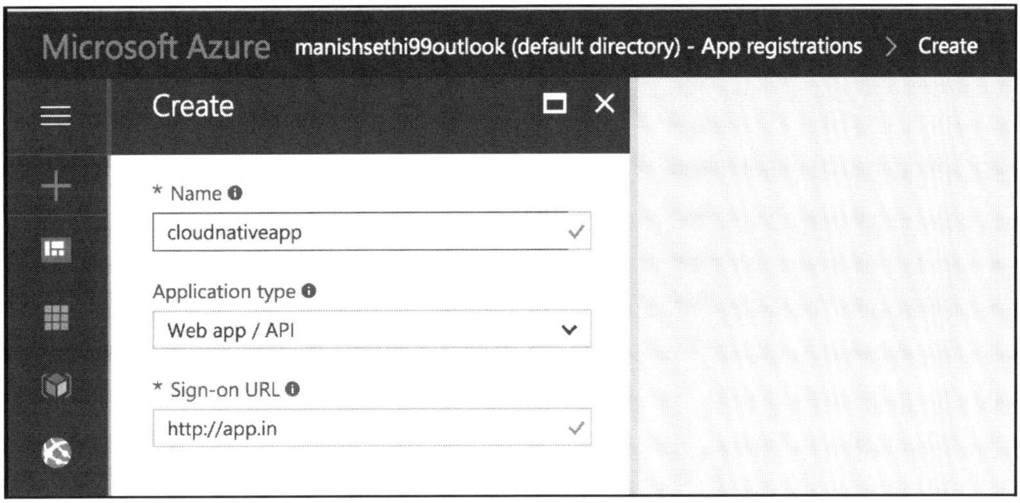

1. After this, you will be able to generate the key which will be needed to access your Jenkins job.
2. You will see the following screen, which has the secret key's details, and you will also find other details such as the **Object ID** and **Application ID** on the same page:

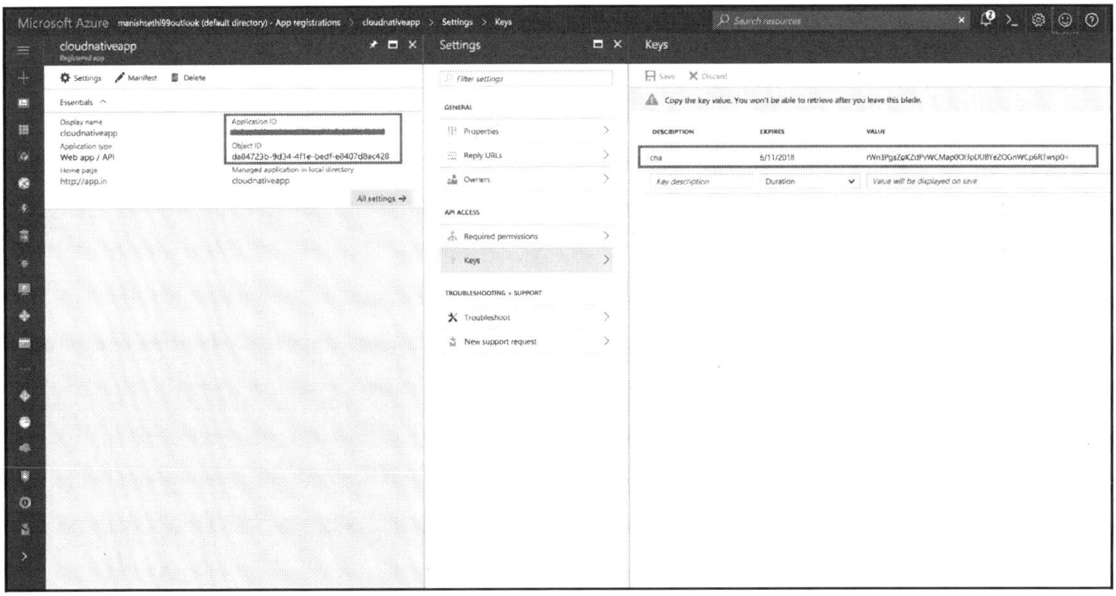

Now we have the required information to configure the job in Jenkins. So, navigate to the Jenkins console, go to **manage plugins** in the **Manage Jenkins** section, and install the plugin, **Azure VM agents**.

Once the plugin is installed, go to Manage Jenkins, and click on **Configure System**, as shown in the next screenshot:

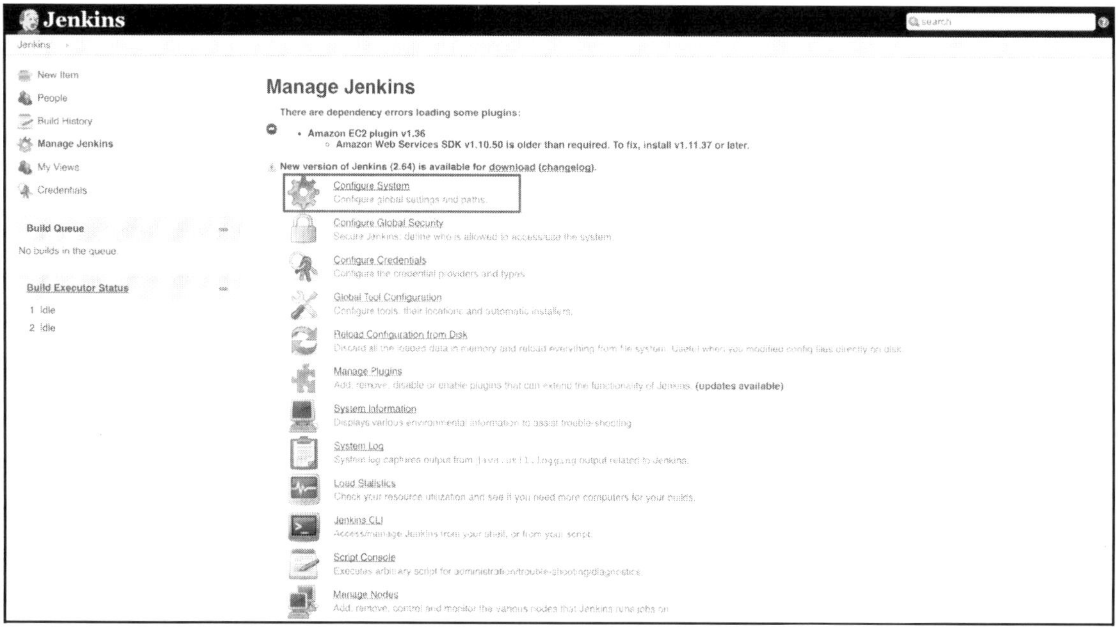

In the next screen, scroll to the bottom section called **Cloud**, click on the button **Add** cloud, and choose the new **Microsoft Azure VM Agents** option. This will generate a section on the same page.

You can read more about the MS Azure VM Agents plugin in its documentation (`https://wiki.jenkins.io/display/JENKINS/Azure+VM+Agents+plugin`).

In the last screen, you need to add your Azure credentials that we had generated previously. If you click on the **Add** button, which you can see in the following screen, you can add values such as **Subscription ID**, and so on:

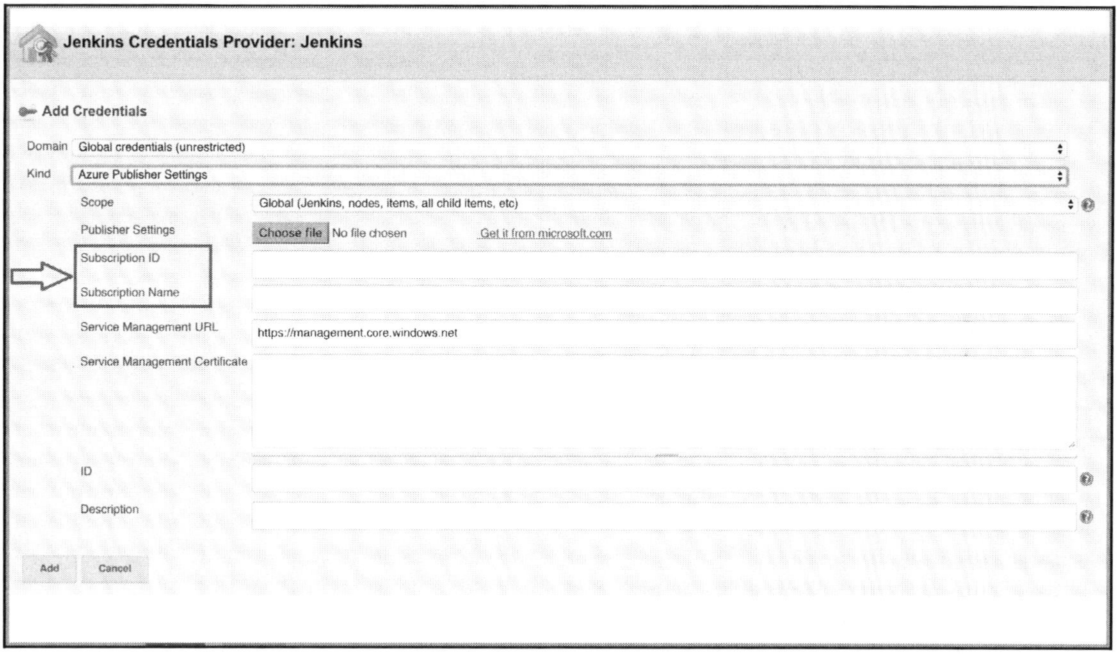

In the next part of the same section, you need to provide the configuration of the VM's details such as the template, VM type, and others:

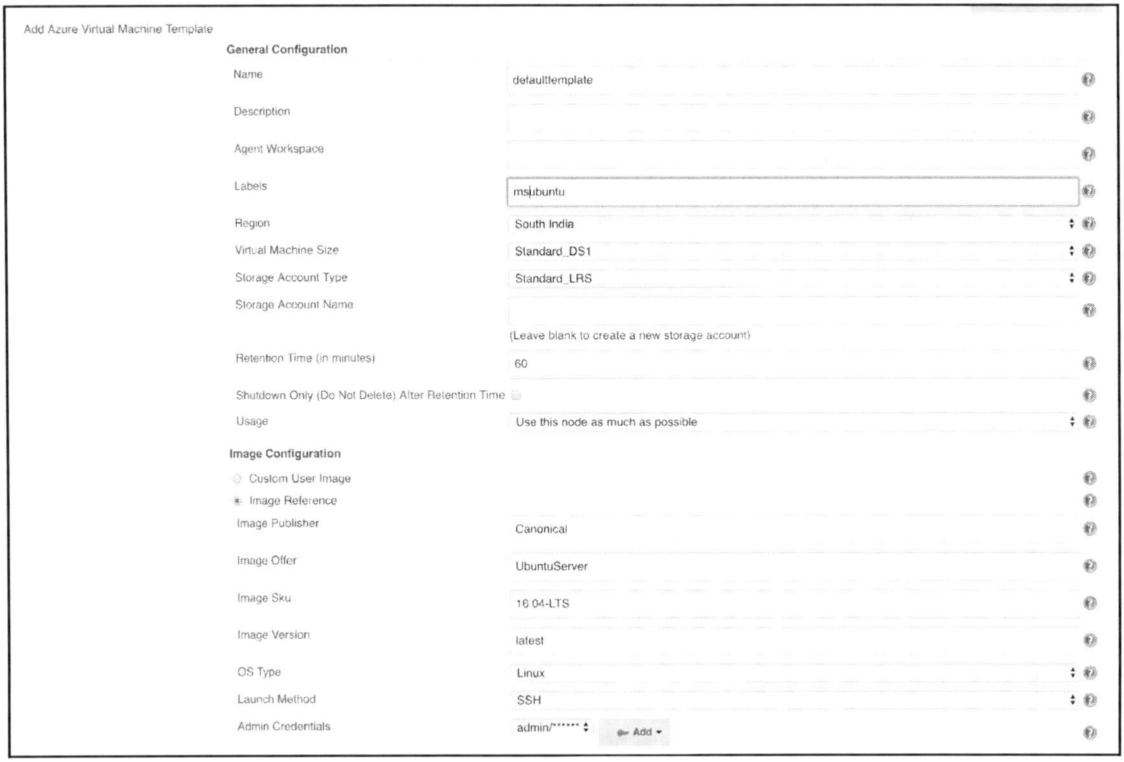

In the preceding screenshot, **Labels** is the most important attribute, which we will be using in Jenkins jobs to identify the group.

Now you need to provide the operation you want to perform, that is, if you want to deploy your application, you can provide the command to download the code and run the application.

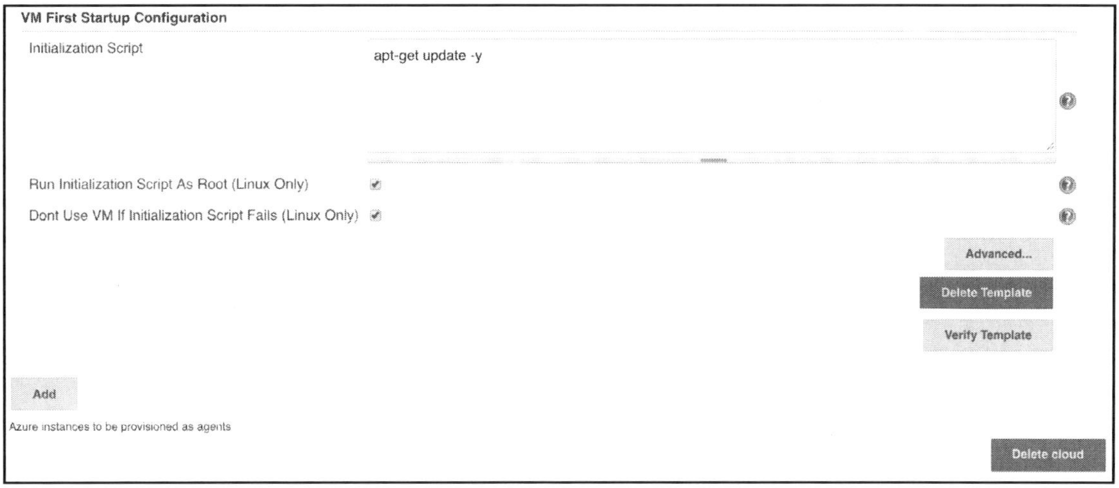

Click on **Save** to apply the settings.

Now, create a new job in Jenkins. Also, in the **GitBucket** section, where you generally provide the repository details, you will find a new checkbox saying **Restrict where this project can be run** and asking you to provide the **Label Expression** name. In our case, it is `msubuntu`. That's it!

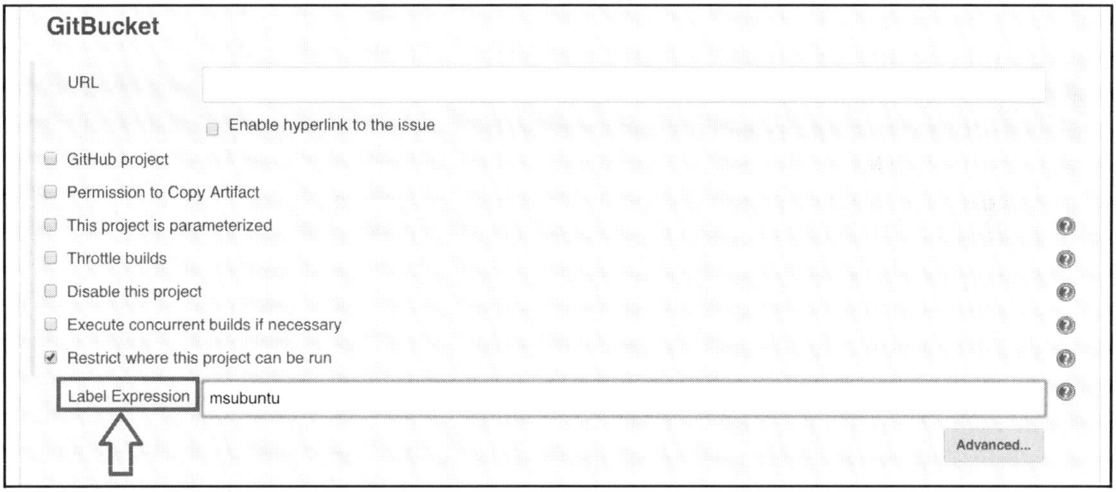

Now we are all set to run our Jenkins job to deploy our application on the VM (that is, the app server).

Finally, we are able to deploy our application on the Azure platform.

Summary

In this chapter, you were introduced to the Azure platform, which is provided by Microsoft, and you deployed your cloud native application on it. We took a look at a different approach to build the same infrastructure on the Azure platform. You also saw the integration of Jenkins with the Azure platform for CI/CD. In the next and final chapter, we will take a look at the different tools that are very helpful to manage and troubleshoot your application-related issues, and address them in a much quicker way so that our application can maintain zero downtime. Stay tuned for the next chapter on Monitoring!

13
Monitoring the Cloud Application

In the previous chapters, we discussed cloud native application development and deploying into a cloud platform for customer usage with higher availability. Our work is not finished yet. Infrastructure and application management is altogether a separate field or stream which monitors the infrastructure, as well as the application's performance, using tools to achieve minimal or zero downtime. In this chapter, we will discuss a few of the tools that could help you do so.

This chapter will cover the following topics:

- AWS services, such as CloudWatch, Config, and more
- Azure services, such as Application Insights, Log Analytics, and more
- Introduction to the ELK stack for Log Analysis
- Open source monitoring tools, such as Prometheus and more

Monitoring on the cloud platform

So far, we have talked about how to develop the application and deploy it across different platforms in order to make it useful for the customer business model. However, even after you have developed the application, you will need personnel with expertize who will make use of tools to manage your application on the platform, which could be a public cloud or on-premise.

In this section, we will mainly focus on discussing tools or services provided by public cloud providers, using those with which we can manage our infrastructure, as well as taking care of Application Insights, that is, performance.

Before we go ahead with discussing tools, here are a few points to consider at the time of infrastructure allocation for any application:

- It is good practice to perform load testing regularly against a certain set of requests. This will help you judge the initial resource requirement for your application. A couple of tools that we can mention are Locust (`http://locust.io/`) and JMeter (`https://jmeter.apache.org/`).
- It is recommended to allocate resources with minimal configuration and use tools related to auto-scaling that manage your resources based on application usage.
- There should be minimal manual interference in terms of resource allocation.

Consider all the preceding points. as it is necessary to make sure a monitoring mechanism is in place to keep track of resource allocation and application performance. Let's discuss the services that are provided by cloud platforms.

AWS-based services

The following are the services provided by **AWS** (**Amazon Web Services**) and their usage in the context of application and infrastructure monitoring.

CloudWatch

This AWS service keeps track of your AWS resource's usage and sends you notifications based on the Alarm configuration defined. Resources such as AWS billing, Route 53, ELB, and so on can be tracked. The following screenshot shows one of the alarms triggered:

Initially, we have to set up the CloudWatch alarm at `https://console.aws.amazon.com/cloudwatch/home?region=us-east-1#alarm:alarmFilter=ANY`.

You should see the following screen, where you need to click on the **Create Alarm** button to create your own alarm based on some metrics:

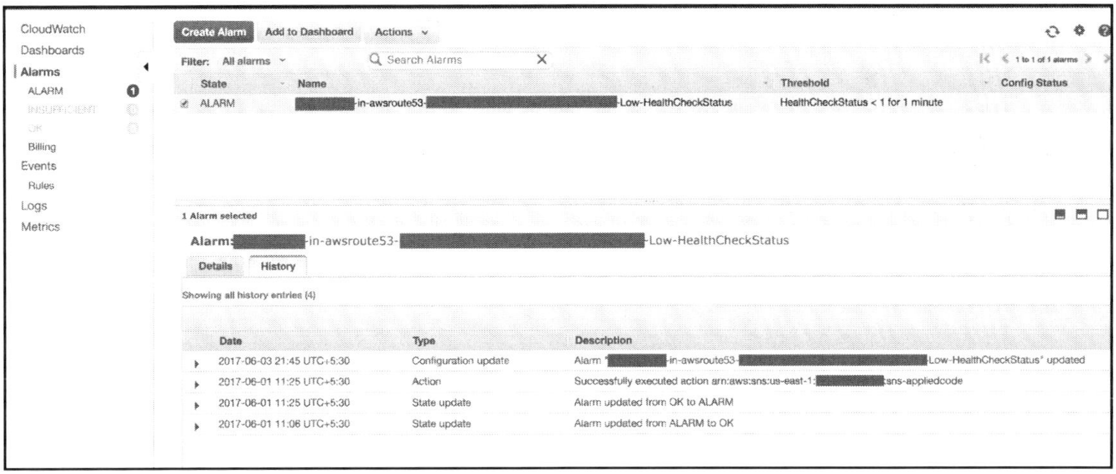

Now, click on the **Create Alarm** button. You will get a pop-up wizard asking about the metrics that need to be monitored:

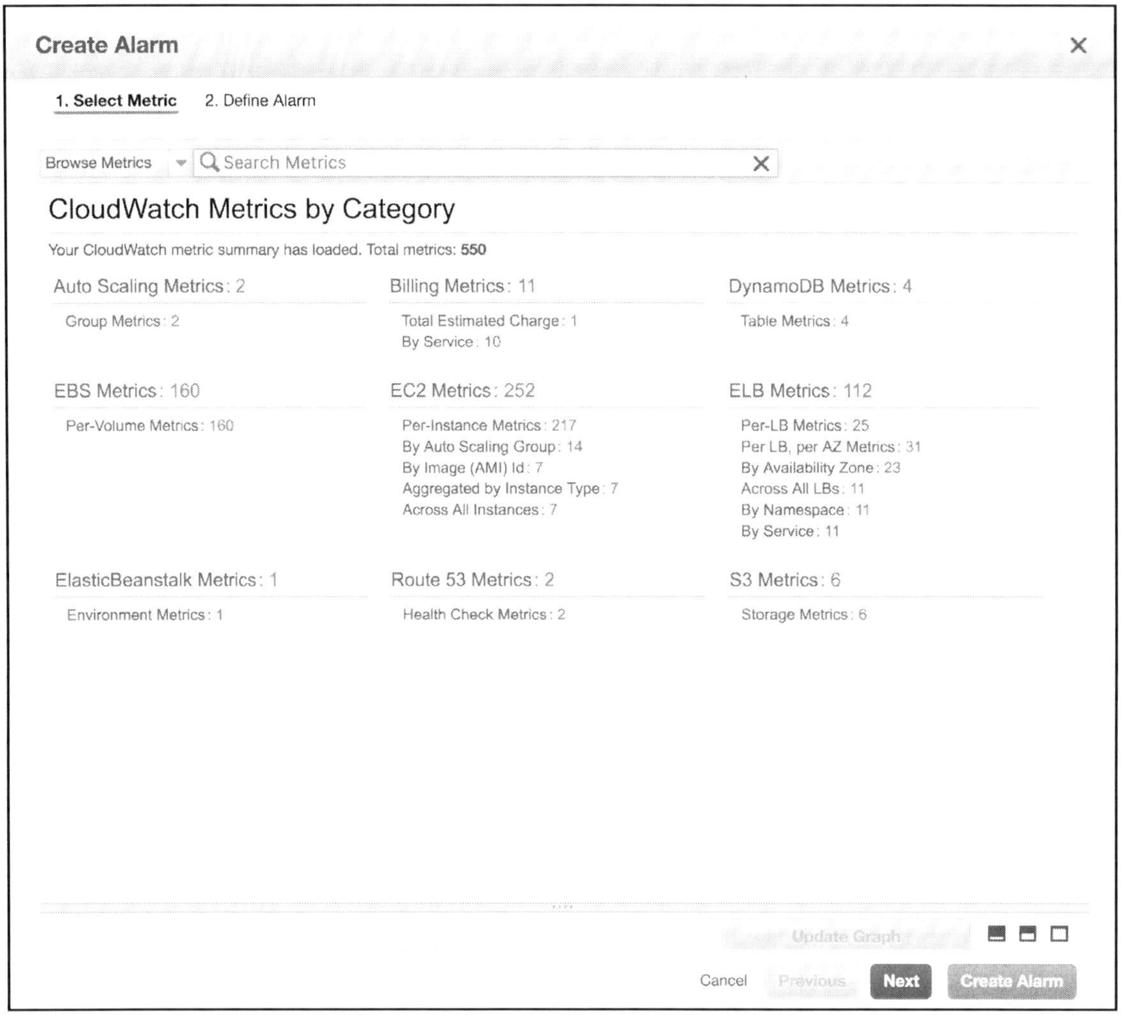

The preceding screenshot lists all the metrics available, which can be monitored, and, for which, an alarm can be set.

In the following screen, we need to check the EC2 metrics. Based on your requirements, you can select any metrics, for instance, we will select the **NetworkIn** metric and click on **Next**:

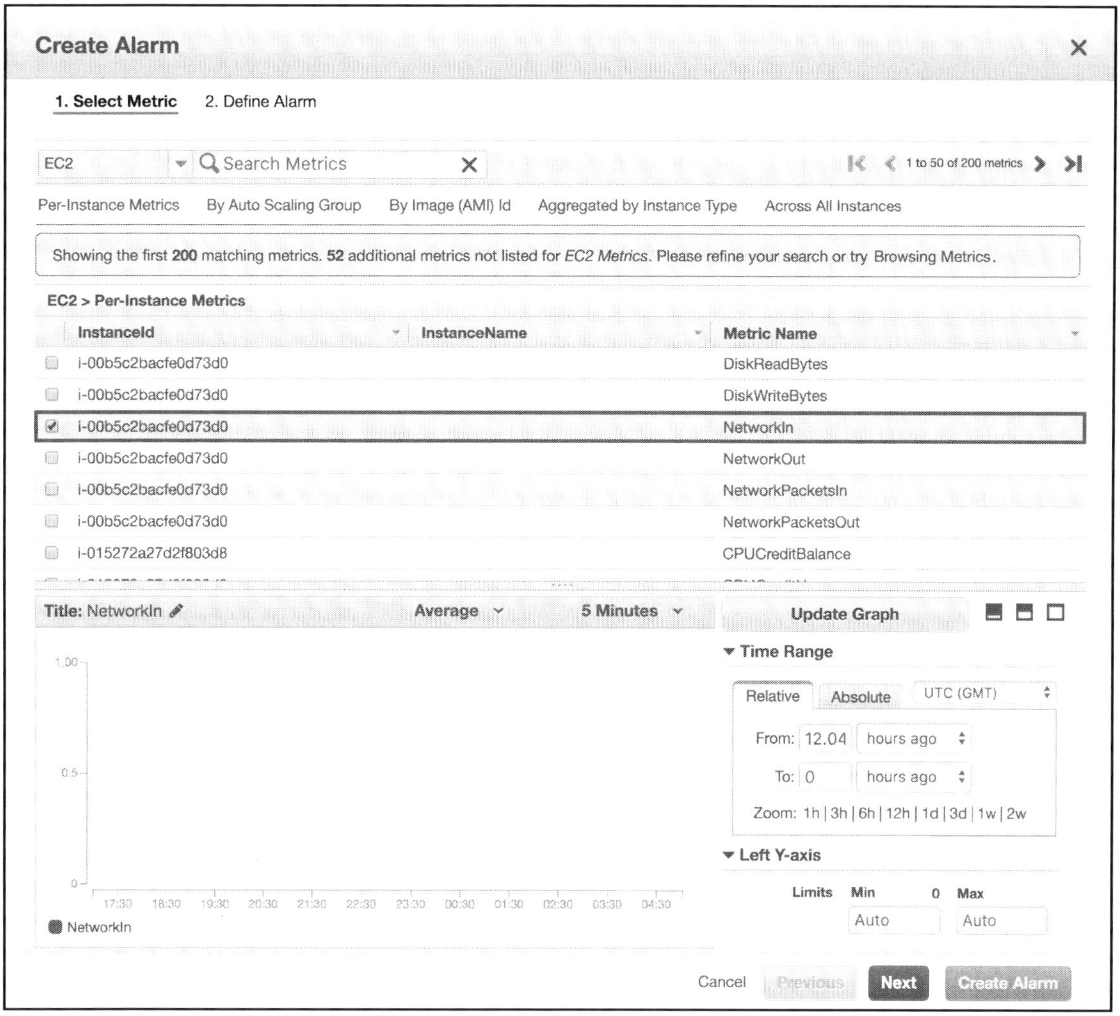

On the next screen, we need to provide the alarm **Name** and **Description**, along with **Alarm Preview**. Also, we need to provide the condition, based on which, the alarm will be triggered.

Also, we need to set up the service notification service where notifications need to be sent as an email:

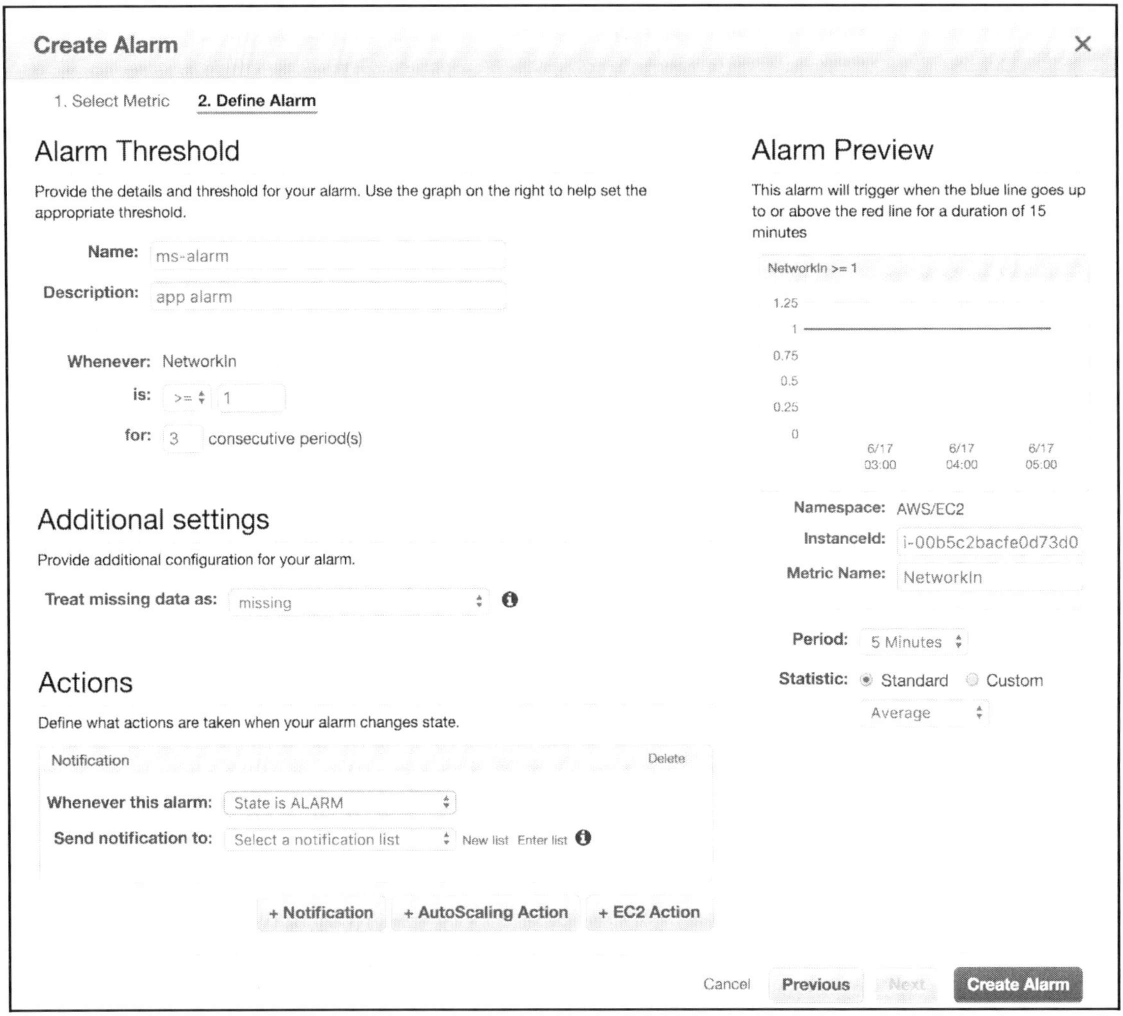

Once you have added the details, click on the **Create Alarm** button to set up the alarm.

Now, whenever the **NetworkIn** metric reaches its threshold, it will send a notification over email.

Similarly, we can set up different metrics to monitor resource utilization.

Another way to create an alarm is by selecting the **Create Alarm** button on the monitoring section of your resource, as shown in the following screenshot:

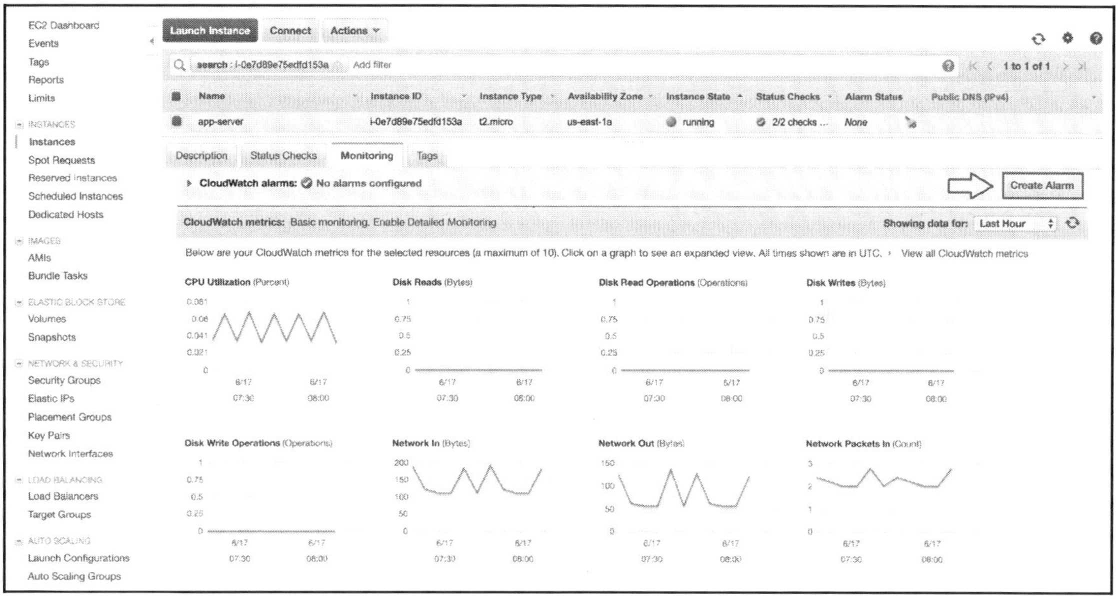

We can go through the AWS documentation (`https://aws.amazon.com/documentation/cloudwatch/`) for more information.

CloudTrail

This is one of the most important AWS cloud services which, by default, keeps track of any activity on your AWS account, whether it is via console or programmatic. We don't need to configure anything in this service. This is needed if your account is compromised, or we need to check the resource operations, and so on.

The following screenshot will show a couple of activities related to the account:

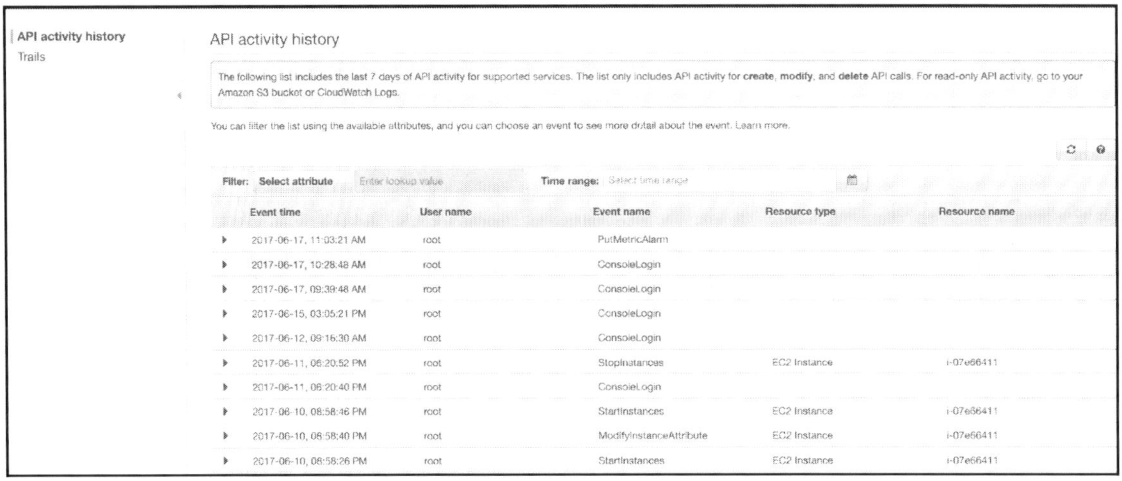

For more information, you can go through the AWS documentation (`https://aws.amazon.com/documentation/cloudtrail/`).

AWS Config service

This is another AWS service in which we can check the configuration of the AWS resources based on the template rules defined.

> Note that this service will need a service role created to access the AWS resources.

In this service, we only need to set up rules based on the template provided. The AWS or customer template is used to create checks on the resources that we have created as part of our application deployment. In order to add a new rule to the service config, go to `https://console.aws.amazon.com/config/home?region=us-east-1#/rules/view`:

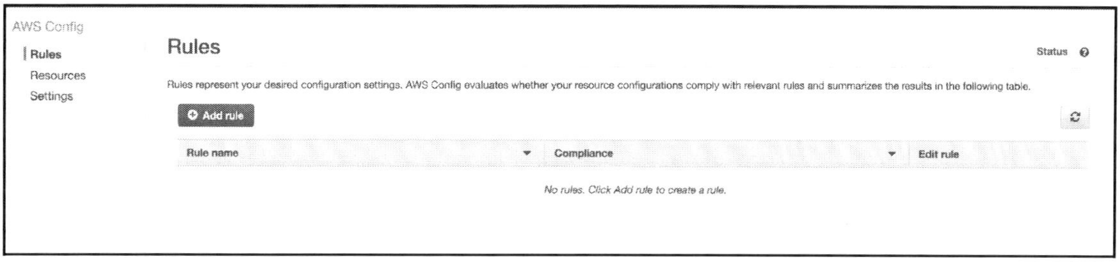

In the preceding screen, we will need to add a new rule, which will evaluate all the resources or your specified resource. Click on **Add rule** to add a new rule, as follows:

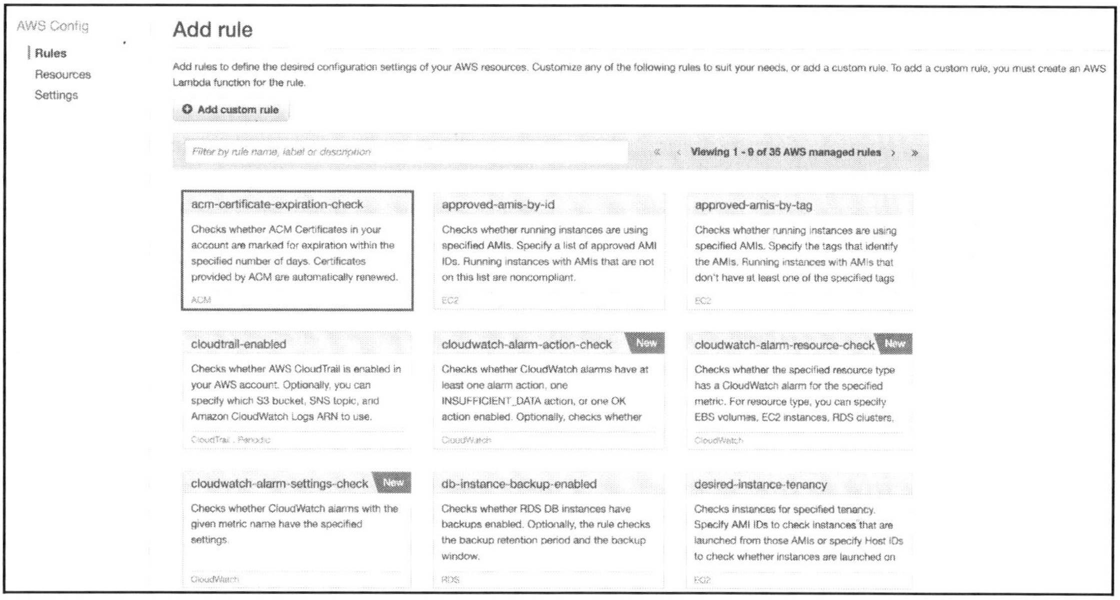

In the preceding screenshot, select the rule to open the configuration for resource monitoring based on resources that need to be tracked.

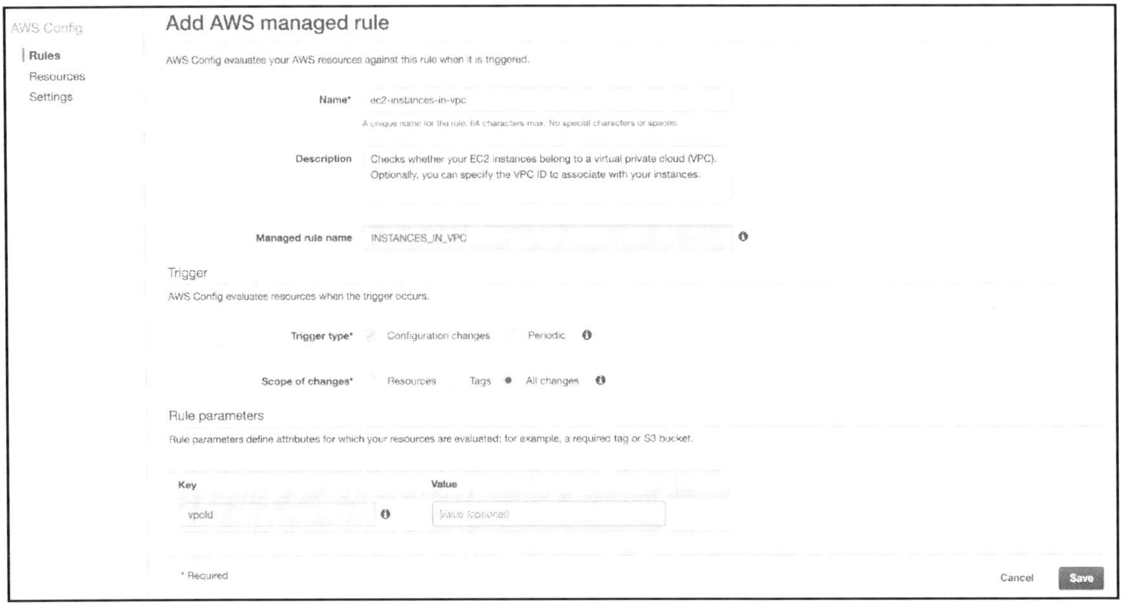

The preceding screenshot is for AWS **ec2-instance-in-vpc** template config, which will help you validate whether or not EC2 is in VPC with the correct config. Here, you can specify which VPC needs to be evaluated.

Click on **Save** to add a new rule. Once it is evaluated, we will see the following screen:

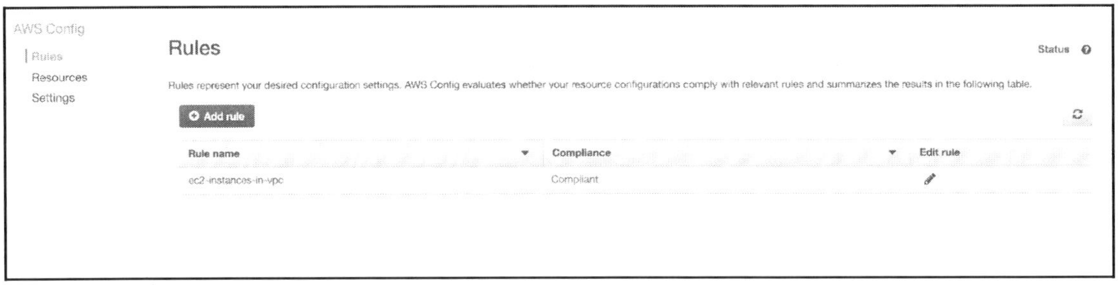

The following resource report is shown like this:

You can go through the AWS documentation (`https://aws.amazon.com/documentation/config/`) for more information.

Microsoft Azure services

The following are the services that are offered by Microsoft Azure, which can help you manage your application performance.

Application Insights

This service, offered by Azure, helps you manage application performance, which is useful for web developers, helping them detect, triage, and diagnose application issues.

In order to set up Application Insights, all you need to know is the application and group name in which your infrastructure lies. Now, if you click on the + Sign on the left pane, you should see a screen similar to the following screenshot:

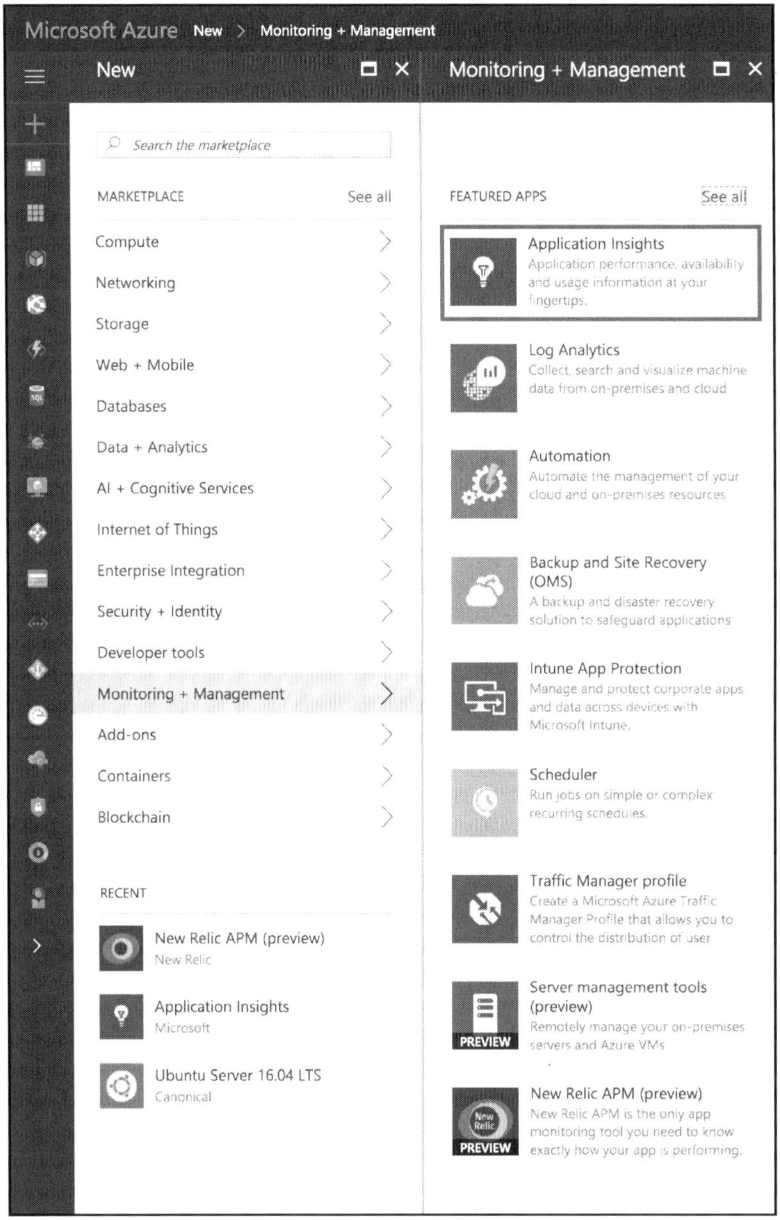

Here, we can select **Application Insights** service, where we need to provide an Application Insight name, a group name that needs to be monitored, and the region where it needs to be launched.

Once it is launched, you will see the following screen, where it will show you how to configure your resources with Application Insights. The following are some of the metrics described:

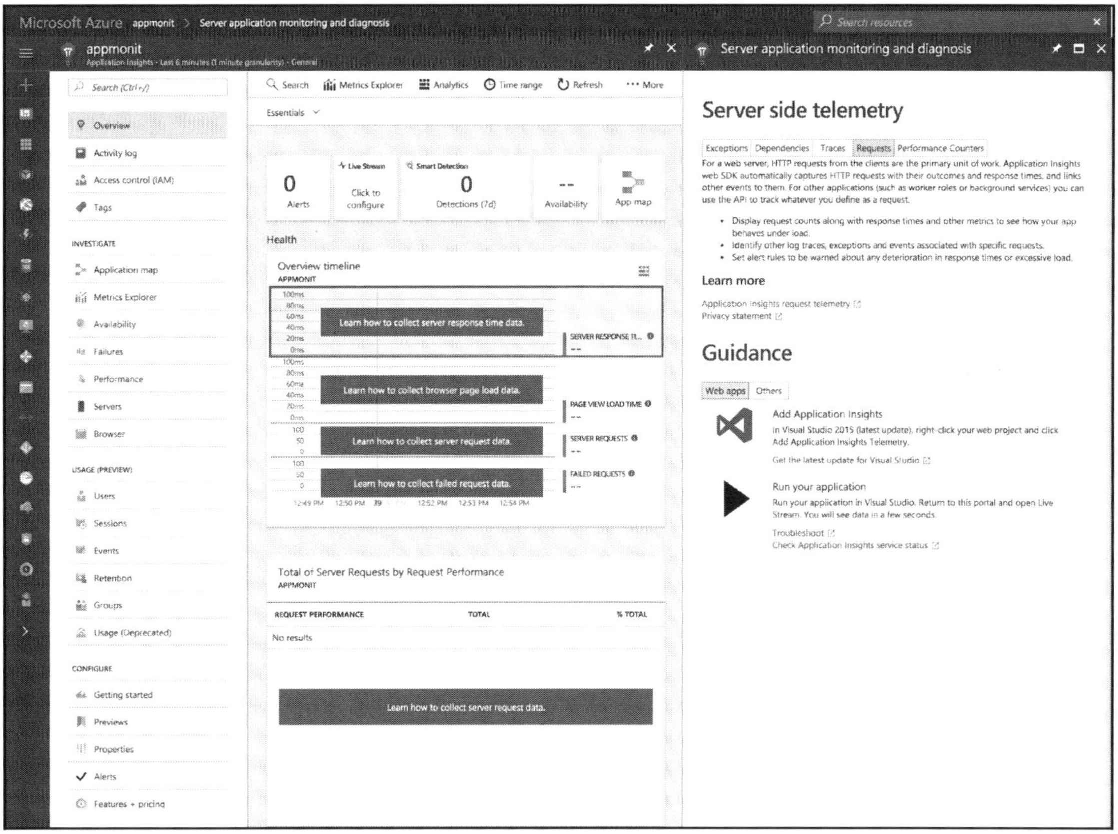

Go through the complete reference documentation at `https://docs.microsoft.com/en-us/azure/application-insights/app-insights-profiler`, which will have complete information on how to configure your Application Insights with resources.

Now, the question that arises is which metrics Application Insights monitors. Below are some of the metrics described:

- **Request rates, response time, and failure rates**: This gives you insights on the type of requests and their response time, which helps with resource management
- **Ajax calls**: This will keep track of rates, response time, and failure rates for web pages.
- *** Users and sessions details**: This tracks user and session information, such as username, login, logout details, and so on
- **Performance management**: This tracks CPU, network, and RAM details
- **Host diagnoses**: This is to compute the resources of Azure
- **Exceptions**: This gives you insights on the server and browser exceptions reported

There are a lot of metrics that you can configure for your system. For more information, check out `https://docs.microsoft.com/en-us/azure/application-insights/app-insights-metrics-explorer`.

You can go through the Azure documentation (`https://docs.microsoft.com/en-us/azure/application-insights/`) for more information-related Application Insights.

So far, we have been validating and monitoring the applications and their infrastructures on cloud platforms. However, a very important question that arises is: What if there is an application issue and we have to troubleshoot it? The next section, which is about the ELK stack, will help you identify the issue, which could be system level or application level.

Introduction to ELK stack

The ELK stack consists of Elasticsearch, Logstash, and Kibana. All these components work together to collect all types of logs that could be system-level logs (that is, Syslog, RSYSLOG, and so on) or application-level logs (that is, access logs, error logs, and so on).

For the set up of the ELK stack, you can follow this article, where, along with the ELK stack, the Filebeat configuration is used to send logs to Elasticsearch:

`https://www.digitalocean.com/community/tutorials/how-to-install-elasticsearch-logstash-and-kibana-elk-stack-on-ubuntu-14-04`.

Logstash

Logstash needs to be installed on the server from where the logs need to be collected and are shipped across to Elasticsearch to create indexes.

Once you have installed Logstash, it is recommended to configure your `logstash.conf` file, which is located at `/etc/logstash`, with details such as Logstash log's file rotation (that is `/var/log/logstash/*.stdout`, `*.err`, or `*.log`) or a suffix format, such as data format. The following code block is a template for your reference:

```
 # see "man logrotate" for details
 # number of backlogs to keep
 rotate 7
 # create new (empty) log files after rotating old ones
 create
 # Define suffix format
 dateformat -%Y%m%d-%s
 # use date as a suffix of the rotated file
 dateext
# uncomment this if you want your log files compressed
compress
# rotate if bigger that size
size 100M
# rotate logstash logs
/var/log/logstash/*.stdout
/var/log/logstash/*.err
/var/log/logstash/*.log {
    rotate 7
    size 100M
    copytruncate
    compress
    delaycompress
    missingok
    notifempty
 }
```

In order to ship your logs to Elasticsearch, you require three sections in the configuration, named INPUT, OUTPUT, and FILTER, which helps them create indexes. These sections can either be in a single file or in separate files.

The Logstash events processing pipeline works as an INPUT-FILTER-OUTPUT section, and, each section has its own advantages and usages, some of which are as follows:

- **Inputs**: This event is needed to get the data from logs files. Some of the common inputs are file, which reads file with `tailf`; Syslog, which reads from the Syslogs service listening on port `514`; beats, which collects events from Filebeat, and so on.
- **Filters**: These middle tier devices in Logstash perform certain actions on the data based on the defined filters and separate data that meets the criteria. Some of them are GROK (structure and parse text based on the defined patter), clone (copycat the events by adding or removing fields), and so on.
- **Outputs**: This is the final phase where we pass on the filtered data to defined output. There could be multiple output locations where we can pass the data for further indexing. Some of the commonly used outputs are Elasticsearch, which is very reliable; an easier, convenient platform to save your data, and it is much easier to query on it; and graphite, which is an open source tool for storing and shows data in the form of graphs.

The following are the examples of logs configuration for Syslog:

- Input section for Syslog is written as follows:

```
input {
  file {
  type => "syslog"
 path => [ "/var/log/messages" ]
 }
}
```

- Filter section for Syslog is written like this:

```
filter {
  grok {
   match => { "message" => "%{COMBINEDAPACHELOG}" }
  }
 date {
  match => [ "timestamp" , "dd/MMM/yyyy:HH:mm:ss Z" ]
 }
}
```

- Output section for Syslog is written as follows:

```
output {
  elasticsearch {
    protocol => "http"
    host => "es.appliedcode.in"
    port => "443"
    ssl => "true"
    ssl_certificate_verification => "false"
    index => "syslog-%{+YYYY.MM.dd}"
    flush_size => 100
   }
}
```

Configuration files to ship logs are usually stored in `/etc/logstash/confd/`.

If you are making separate files for each section, then there is a convention for naming files that needs to be followed; for example, an input file should be named `10-syslog-input.conf` and a filter file should be named `20-syslog-filter.conf`. Similarly, for output, it will be `30-syslog-output.conf`.

In case you want to validate whether your configurations are correct or not, you can do so by executing the following command:

```
$ sudo service logstash configtest
```

For more information on the Logstash configuration, refer to the documentation examples at `https://www.elastic.co/guide/en/logstash/current/config-examples.html`.

Elasticsearch

Elasticsearch (`https://www.elastic.co/products/elasticsearch`) is a Log Analytics tool that helps store and create index out of the bulk of data streams based on the configuration with timestamp, which solves the problem of developers trying to identify the log related to their issue. Elasticsearch is a NoSQL database that is based on the Lucene search engine.

Once you have installed Elasticsearch, you can validate the version and cluster details by clicking on the following URL:
`http://ip-address:9200/`.

The output will look like this:


```
{
  "name" : "Klaw",
  "cluster_name" : "elasticsearch",
  "cluster_uuid" : "k3uzUoIgStm4Bl5heJ0Bag",
  "version" : {
    "number" : "2.4.5",
    "build_hash" : "c849dd13904f53e63e88efc33b2ceeda0b6a1276",
    "build_timestamp" : "2017-04-24T16:18:17Z",
    "build_snapshot" : false,
    "lucene_version" : "5.5.4"
  },
  "tagline" : "You Know, for Search"
}
```


This proves that Elasticsearch is up and running. Now, if you want to see whether logs are being created or not, you can query Elasticsearch using the following URL: `http://ip-address:9200/_search?pretty`.

The output will look like the following screenshot:


```
{
  "took" : 2,
  "timed_out" : false,
  "_shards" : {
    "total" : 6,
    "successful" : 6,
    "failed" : 0
  },
  "hits" : {
    "total" : 2151,
    "max_score" : 1.0,
    "hits" : [ {
      "_index" : ".kibana",
      "_type" : "search",
      "_id" : "Cache-transactions",
      "_score" : 1.0,
      "_source" : {
        "sort" : [ "@timestamp", "desc" ],
        "hits" : 0,
        "description" : "",
        "title" : "Cache transactions",
        "version" : 1,
        "kibanaSavedObjectMeta" : {
          "searchSourceJSON" : "{\"index\":\"packetbeat-*\",\"highlight\":{\"pre_tags\":[\"@kibana-highlighted-
field@\"],\"post_tags\":[\"@/kibana-highlighted-field@\"],\"fields\":{\"*\":{}}},\"filter\":[],\"query\":
{\"query_string\":{\"query\":\"type: redis\",\"analyze_wildcard\":true}}}"
        },
        "columns" : [ "type", "method", "path", "responsetime", "status" ]
      }
    }, {
```

In order to see the indexes already created, you can click on the following URL: `http://ip-address:9200/_cat/indices?v`.

The output will be similar to the following screenshot:

```
health status index               pri rep docs.count docs.deleted store.size pri.store.size
yellow open   .kibana               1   1        103            1     92.8kb         92.8kb
yellow open   filebeat-2017.06.17   5   1       2048            0    576.9kb        576.9kb
```

If you want to know more about the Elasticsearch queries, index operations, and more, read this article:
`https://www.elastic.co/guide/en/elasticsearch/reference/current/indices.html`.

Kibana

Kibana works on the top layer of Elasticsearch, which visualizes the data that provides insights on the data received from the environment and helps them make required decisions. In short, Kibana is a GUI that is used to search for logs from Elasticsearch.

Once you have installed Kibana, the following should appear at `http://ip-address:5601/`, which will ask you to create an index and configure your Kibana dashboard:

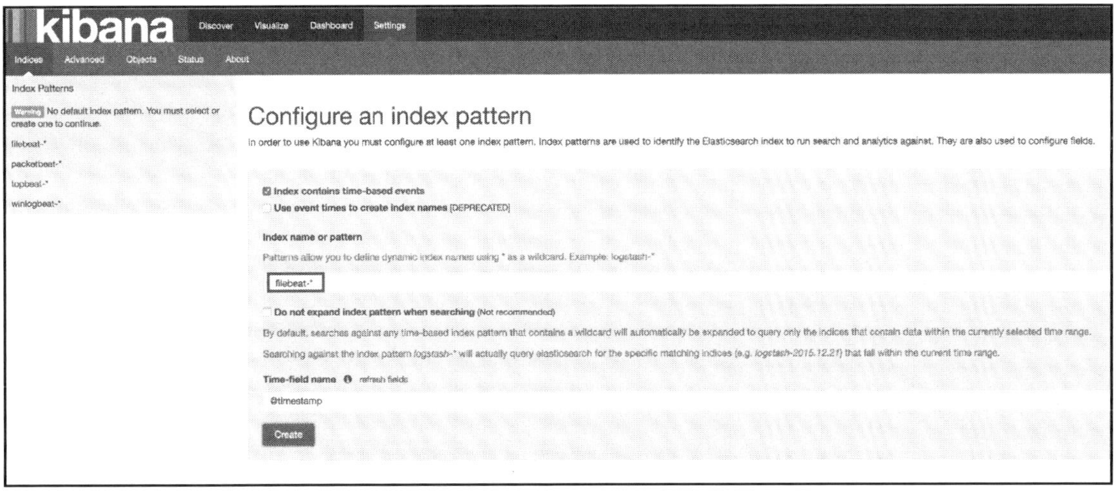

Once you have configured it, the following screen, which shows the logs in a format with the timestamp, should appear:

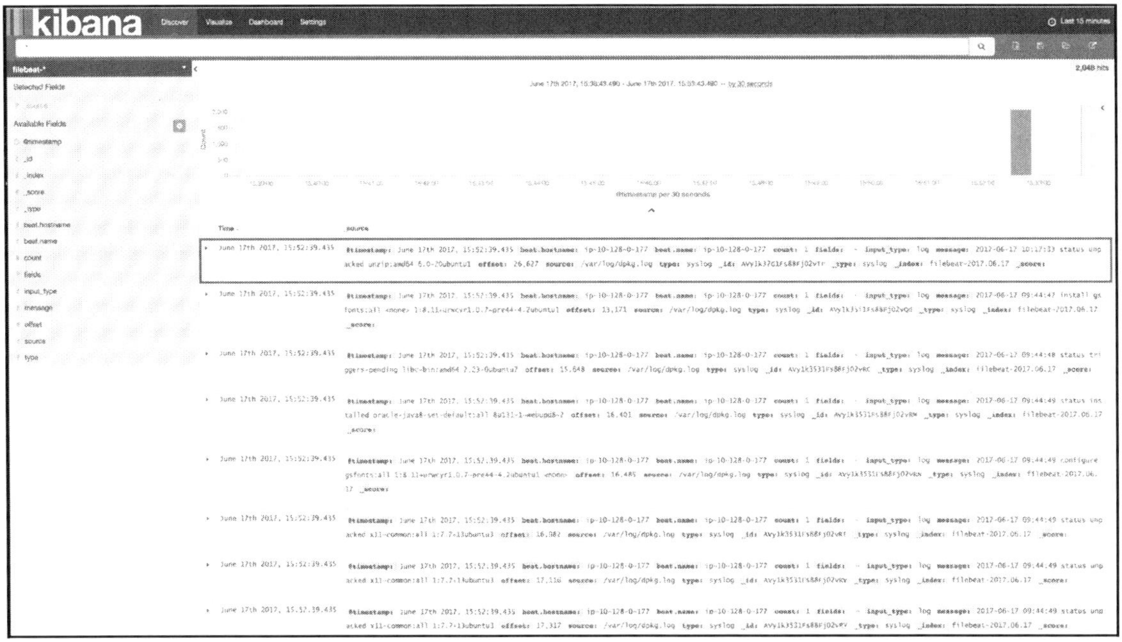

Now, out of these, we need to create dashboards that will give us the view of logs to visualize, which will be in the form of a graph, a pie chart, and so on.

For more information related to the creation of the Kibana dashboard, you can go through the Kibana documentation (`https://www.elastic.co/guide/en/kibana/current/dashboard-getting-started.html`).

As an alternative to Kibana, some of you might be interested in Grafana (`https://grafana.com/`), which is also an analytics and monitoring tool.

Now, the question arises: how is Grafana different from Kibana? Here is the answer to that:

Grafana	**Kibana**
The Grafana dashboard focuses on time-series charts based on system metrics CPU or RAM.	Kibana is specific to Log Analytics.
Grafana's built-in RBA (role-based access) decides the access of dashboard for the users.	Kibana doesn't have control over dashboard access.
Grafana supports different data sources other than Elasticsearch, such as Graphite, InfluxDB, and so on.	Kibana has an integration with the ELK stack, which makes it user-friendly.

This is about the ELK stack, which gives us insights on the application and helps us troubleshoot the application and server issues. In the next section, we will discuss an on-premise open source tool called **Prometheus**, which is useful for monitoring the activity of different servers.

Open source monitoring tool

In this section, we will mainly discuss the tools that are owned by a third party and collect the metrics of the server to troubleshoot application issues.

Prometheus

Prometheus (`https://prometheus.io`) is an open source monitoring solution that keeps track of your system activity metrics and alerts you instantly if there are any actions required from your side. This tool is written in **Golang**.

This tool is gaining popularity similar to tools such as Nagios. It collects the metrics of the server, but it also provides you with template metrics, such as `http_request_duration_microseconds`, based on your requirement, so that you can generate a graph out of it using UI to understand it much better and monitor it with efficiency.

Note that, by default, Prometheus runs on the `9090` port.

To install Prometheus, follow the instructions provided on the official website (`https://prometheus.io/docs/introduction/getting_started/`). Once it is installed and the service is up, try opening `http://ip-address:9090/status` to know the status. The following screen shows the build information, that is, **Version**, **Revision**, and so on, for Prometheus:

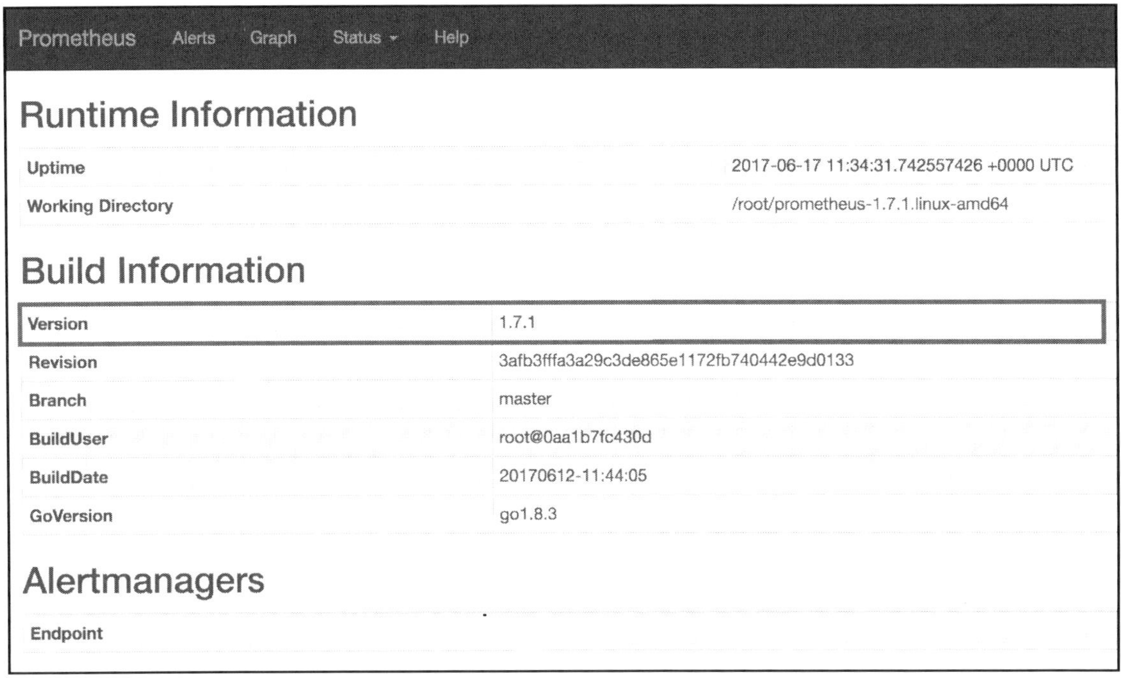

To know the targets configured with it, use the `http://ip-address:9090/targets`. The output will be something like this:

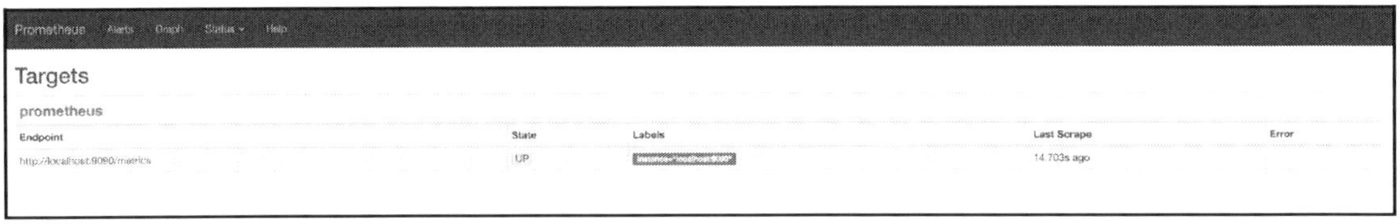

In order to generate the graphs, use `http://ip-address:9090/graph` and select the metric for which the graph needs to be implemented. The output should be similar to the following screenshot:

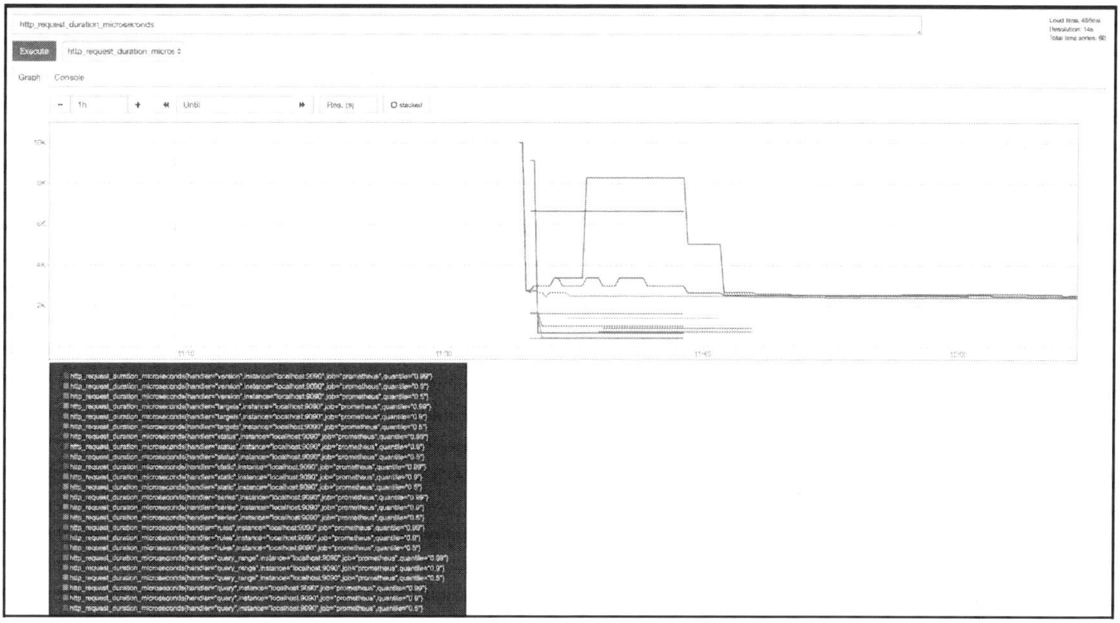

Similarly, we can request a couple of other metrics that are identified by Prometheus, such as a host-up state. The following screenshot shows the host status over a certain period of time:

There are a few components of Prometheus that have a different usage, which are as follows:

- **AlertManager**: This component will help you set up the alerting for your server based on the metrics and define its threshold values. We will need to add configuration in the server to set up an alert. Check the documents for AlertManager on `https://prometheus.io/docs/alerting/alertmanager/`.
- **Node exporter**: This exporter is useful for the hardware and OS metrics. Read more about the different types of exporters at `https://prometheus.io/docs/instrumenting/exporters/`.
- **Pushgateway**: This Pushgateway allows you to run batch jobs to expose your metrics.
- **Grafana**: Prometheus has integration with Grafana, which helps dashboards to query metrics on Prometheus.

Summary

This chapter has been very interesting in different ways. Starting with tools, such as Cloudwatch and Application Insights, which are based on a cloud platforms and help you manage your application on cloud platform. Then, it moved toward open source tools, which have always been a first choice for developers, as they can customize it as per their requirements. We looked at the ELK stack, which has always been popular and is frequently used in many organizations in one way or another.

Now, we have come to the end of this edition of our book, but hopefully, there will be another edition, where we will talk about advanced application development and have more testing cases that could be useful for the QA audience as well. Enjoy coding!

Index

A

B

C

D

E

F

G

N

O

P

Printed in Poland
by Amazon Fulfillment
Poland Sp. z o.o., Wrocław

78881868R00210